THE

HISTORY OF CHRISTIANITY

VOLUME II

AMS PRESS
NEW YORK

THE

HISTORY OF CHRISTIANITY,

FROM THE BIRTH OF CHRIST TO THE ABOLITION OF PAGANISM IN THE ROMAN EMPIRE.

By HENRY HART MILMAN, D.D.,

DEAN OF ST. PAUL'S.

IN THREE VOLUMES.—VOL. II.

A NEW AND REVISED EDITION.

LONDON:

JOHN MURRAY, ALBEMARLE STREET.

1863.

Library of Congress Cataloging in Publication Data

Milman, Henry Hart, 1791-1868.
    The history of Christianity.

    Reprint of the 1863 ed. published by J. Murray,
London.
    Includes index.
    1. Church history—Primitive and early church,
ca. 30-600. I. Title.
BR162.M6   1978   209'.01   78-173733
ISBN 0-404-04350-X

Reprinted from the edition of 1863, London
First AMS edition published in 1978

International Standard Book Number:
Complete Set: 0-404-04350-X
Volume II: 0-404-04352-6

Manufactured in the United States of America

AMS PRESS INC.
NEW YORK, N.Y.

CONTENTS OF VOL. II.

BOOK II.—*continued*.

BOOK III.

HISTORY OF CHRISTIANITY.

BOOK II.—*continued.*

CHAPTER IV.

Christianity to the Close of the First Century. — Constitution of
Christian Churches.

THE changes in the moral are usually wrought as imperceptibly as those in the physical world. Had Great revolutions slow and gradual. any wise man, either convinced of the divine origin of Christianity, or even contemplating with philosophical sagacity the essential nature of the new religion and the existing state of the human mind, ventured to predict that from the ashes of these obscure men would arise a moral sovereignty more extensive and lasting than that of the Cæsars ; that buildings more splendid than any which adorned the new marble city, now rising from the ruins of the conflagration, would be dedicated to their names, and maintain their reverence for an incalculably longer period ; such vaticinations would have met the fate inseparable from the wisdom which outstrips its age, would have been scorned by contemporary pride, and only admired, after their accomplishment, by late posterity. The slight and contemptuous notice excited by Christianity during the first century of its promulgation is in strict accordance with this ordinary development of the great and lasting revo-

lutions in human affairs. The moral world has sometimes, indeed, its volcanic explosions, which suddenly
and violently convulse and reform the order of things;
but its more enduring changes are in general produced
by the slow and silent workings of opinions, remotely
prepared and gradually expanding to their mature and
irresistible influence. In default, therefore, of real information as to the secret but simultaneous progress of
Christianity in so many quarters, and among all ranks,
we are left to speculate on the influence of the passing
events of the time, and of the changes in the public
mind, whether favourable or prejudicial to the cause of
Christianity, catching only faint and uncertain gleams
of its peculiar history through the confused and rapidly
changing course of public affairs.

The Imperial history from the first promulgation of
Christianity down to the accession of Constantine, divides itself into four distinct, but
unequal periods. More than thirty years are
occupied by the line of the first Cæsars, rather less by
the conflicts which followed the death of Nero, and the
government of the Flavian dynasty. The first years of
Trajan, who ascended the Imperial throne A.D. 98,
nearly synchronize with the opening of the second
century of Christianity; and that splendid period of
internal peace and advancing civilisation, of wealth,
and of prosperity, which has been described as the hap-
piest in the annals of mankind, extends over the first
eighty years of that century.[a] Down to the accession of
Constantine, nearly at the commencement of the fourth

Imperial history divided into four periods.

---

[a] Among the writers who have
discussed this question may be consulted Hegewisch, whose work has
been translated by M. Solvet, under
the title of Essai sur l'Epoque de
l'Histoire Romaine la plus heureuse
pour le Genre Humain. Paris, 1834.

century, the Empire became, like the great monarchies of the East, the prize of successful ambition and enterprise : almost every change of ruler is a change of dynasty ; and already the borders of the Empire have ceased to be respected by the menacing, the conquering Barbarians.

It is remarkable how singularly the political cha-racter of each period was calculated to advance the growth of Christianity.

First period, to the death of Nero.

During the first of these periods, the Government, though it still held in respect the old republican institu-tions, was, if not in form, in its administration purely despotic.   The state centered in the person of the Em-peror.   This kind of hereditary autocracy is essentially selfish ; it is content with averting or punishing plots against the person, or detecting and crushing conspi-racies against the power, of the existing monarch.   To those more remote or secret changes which are working in the depths of society, eventually perhaps threatening the existence of the monarchy, or the stability of all the social relations, it is blind or indifferent.[b]   It has neither sagacity to discern, intelligence to comprehend, nor even the disinterested zeal for the perpetuation of its own despotism, to counteract such distant and contin-gent dangers.   Of all innovations it is, in general, sen-sitively jealous ; but they must be palpable and manifest, and directly clashing with the passions or exciting the fears of the sovereign.   Even these are met by tempo-rary measures.   When an outcry was raised against the Egyptian religion as dangerous to public morality, an edict commanded the expulsion of its votaries from the city.   When the superstition of the Emperor shuddered

---

[b] "Sævi proximis ingruunt." In this one pregnant sentence of Tacitus is explained the political secret, that the mass of the people have sometimes been comparatively unoppressed under the most sanguinary tyranny.

B 2

at the predictions of the Mathematicians, the whole fraternity fell under the same interdict. When the public peace was disturbed by the dissensions among the Jewish population of Rome, the summary sentence of Claudius visited both Jews and Christians with the same indifferent severity. So the Neronian persecution was an accident arising out of the fire at Rome, no part of a systematic political plan for the suppression of foreign religions. It might have fallen on any other sect or body of men who might have been designated as victims to appease the popular resentment. The provincial administrations would be actuated by the same principles as the central government, and be alike indifferent to the quiet progress of opinions, however dangerous to the existing order of things. Unless some breach of the public peace demanded their interference, they would rarely put forth their power; and, content with the maintenance of order, the regular collection of the revenue, the more rapacious with the punctual payment of their own exactions, the more enlightened with the improvement and embellishment of the cities under their charge, they would look on the rise and propagation of a new religion with no more concern than that of a new philosophic sect, particularly in the eastern part of the empire, where the religions were in general more foreign to the character of the Greek or Roman Polytheism. The popular feeling during this first period would only under peculiar circumstances outstrip the activity of the Government. Accustomed to the separate worship of the Jews, to the many Christianity appeared at first only as a modification of that belief. Local jealousies or personal animosities might in different places excite a more active hostility. In Rome it is evident that the people were only worked up to find inhuman delight in the sufferings of the Christians, by the misrepresentations of the Government, by superstitious solicitude to find some victims to appease the angry Gods, and that strange consolation of human misery, the delight of wreaking vengeance on whomsoever it can possibly implicate as the cause of the calamity.

During the whole, then, of this first period, to the death of Nero, both the primitive obscurity of Christianity, and the transient importance it assumed, as a dangerous enemy of the people of Rome, and subsequently as the guiltless victim of popular vengeance, would tend to its eventual progress. Its own innate activity, with all the force which it carried with it, both in its internal and external impulse, would propagate it extensively in the inferior and middle classes of society ; while, though the great mass of the higher orders would still remain unacquainted with its real nature, and with its relation to its parent Judaism, it was quite enough before the public attention to awaken the curiosity of the more inquiring, and to excite the interest of those who were seriously concerned in the moral advancement of mankind. In many quarters, it is far from impossible that the strong revulsion of the public mind against Nero, after his death, may have extended some commiseration towards his innocent victims :[c] that the Christians were acquitted by the popular feeling of any real connexion with the fire at Rome, appears evident from Tacitus, who retreats into vague expressions of general scorn and animosity.[d] At all events, the persecution must have had the effect of raising the im-

---

[c] This was the case even in Rome. " Unde quanquam adversus sontes et novissima exempla meritos, miseratio oriebatur, tanquam non utilitate publicâ, sed in sævitiam unius absumerentur." Tac. An. xv. 44.

[d] Odio humani generis convicti.

portance of Christianity, so as to force it upon the notice
of many who might otherwise have been ignorant of its
existence. The new and peculiar fortitude with which
the sufferers endured their unprecedented trials, would
strongly recommend it to those who were dissatisfied
with the moral power of their old religion; while on the
other hand it was yet too feeble and obscure to provoke
a systematic plan for its suppression.

During the second period of the first century, from A.D.
68 to 98, the date of the accession of Trajan,
the larger portion was occupied by the reign of
Domitian, a tyrant in whom the successors of
Augustus might appear to revive, both in the monstrous
vices of his personal character, and of his government.
Of the Flavian dynasty, the father alone, Vespasian,
from the comprehensive vigour of his mind, perhaps
from his knowledge of the Jewish character and religion, obtained during his residence in the East, was
likely to estimate the bearings and future prospects of
Christianity. But the total subjugation of Judæa, and
the destruction of the Temple of Jerusalem, having
reduced the religious parents of the Christians to so low
a state, their nation, and consequently their religion,
being, according to the ordinary course of events, likely
to mingle up with and become absorbed in the general
population of the Roman empire, Christianity, it might
reasonably be supposed, would scarcely survive its
original stock, and might be safely left to burn out by
the same gradual process of extinction. Besides this,
the strong mind of Vespasian was fully occupied by the
restoration of order in the capital and in the provinces,
and in fixing on a firm basis the yet unsettled authority
of the Flavian dynasty. A more formidable, because
more immediate, danger threatened the existing order

of things.   The awful genius of Roman liberty had
entered into an alliance with the higher philosophy of
the time.   Republican stoicism, brooding in   Stoic philo-
the noblest minds of Rome, looked back, with   sophers.
vain though passionate regret, to the free institutions of
their ancestors, and demanded the old liberty of action.
It was this dangerous movement—not the new and
humble religion, which calmly acquiesced in all political
changes, and contented itself with liberty of thought
and opinion—that put to the test the prudence and
moderation of the Emperor Vespasian.   It was the
spirit of Cato, not of Christ, which he found it necessary to control.   The enemy before whom he trembled
was the patriot Thrasea, not the Apostle St. John, who
was silently winning over Ephesus to the new faith.
The edict of expulsion from Rome fell not on the worshippers of foreign religions, but on the philosophers, a
comprehensive term, but which was probably limited to
those whose opinions were considered dangerous to the
Imperial authority.[e]

It was only with the new fiscal regulations of the
rapacious and parsimonious Vespasian that the Christians were accidentally implicated.   The Emperor continued to levy the capitation tax, which had been
willingly and proudly paid by the Jews throughout the
empire for the maintenance of their own Temple at
Jerusalem, for the restoration of the idolatrous fane of
the Capitoline Jupiter, which had been destroyed in the
civil contests.   The Jew submitted with sullen
reluctance to this insulting exaction; but   Temple tax.
even the hope of escaping it would not incline him to

---

[e] Tacit. Hist. iv. 4-9. Dion Cas- | Tillemont, Hist. des Empereurs : Ves-
sius, lxvi. 13. Suetonius, Vespas. 15. | pasian. Art. 15.

disguise or dissemble his faith. But the Judaizing
Christian, and even the Christian of Jewish descent, who
had entirely thrown off his religion, yet was marked by
the indelible sign of his race, was placed in a singularly
perplexing position.[f] The rapacious publican, who
farmed the tax, was not likely to draw any true distinction among those whose features, connexions, names, and
notorious descent, still designated them as liable to the
tax: his coarser mind would consider the profession of
Christianity as a subterfuge to escape a vexatious impost. But to the Jewish Christian of St. Paul's opinions,
the unresisted payment of the burthen, however insignificant, and to which he was not bound, either by the
letter or the spirit of the edict, was an acknowledgment
of his unconverted Judaism, of his being still under the
Law, as well as an indirect contribution to the maintenance of heathenism. It is difficult to suppose that
those who were brought before the public tribunal,
as claiming an exemption from the tax, and exposed to
the most indecent examination of their Jewish descent, were any other than this class of Judaizing
Christians.

In other respects, the connexion of the Christians
with the Jews could not but affect their place in that indiscriminating public estimation which still, in general,
notwithstanding the Neronian persecution, confounded
Change in the them together. The Jewish war appears to
condition and
estimation of have made a great alteration both in the con-
the Jews
after the war dition of the race of Israel, and in the popular
sentiment towards them. From aversion as a sullen

---

[f] Dion Cassius, edit. Reimar, with
his notes, lib. lxvi. p. 1082. Suetonius in Dom. v. 12. Martial, vii. 14.

Basnage, Histoire des Juifs, vol. vii.
ch. xi. p. 304.

and unsocial, they were now looked upon with hatred
and contempt, as a fierce, a desperate, and an enslaved
race. Some of the higher orders, Agrippa and Josephus
the historian, maintained a respectable, and even an
eminent rank at Rome; but the provinces were overrun
by swarms of Jewish slaves, or miserable fugitives, reduced by necessity to the meanest occupations, and
lowering their minds to their sordid and beggarly condition.[g] As then to some of the Romans the Christian
assertion of religious freedom would seem closely allied
with the Jewish attempt to obtain civil independence,
they might appear, especially to those in authority, to
have inherited the intractable and insubordinate spirit
of their religious forefathers; so, on the other hand, in
some places, the Christian might be dragged down, in
the popular apprehension, to the level of the fallen and
outcast Jew. Thus, while Christianity in fact was becoming more and more alienated from Judaism, and
even assuming the most hostile position, the Roman
rulers would be the last to discern the widening breach,
or to discriminate between that religious confederacy
which was destined to absorb within it all the subjects
of the Roman empire, and that race which was to remain
in its social isolation, neither blended into the general
mass of mankind, nor admitting any other within its insuperable pale. If the singular story related *The descendants of the*
by Hegesippus[h] concerning the family of our *brethren of
our Lord*
Lord deserves credit, even the descendants of *brought before the*
His house were endangered by their yet un- *tribunal.*
broken connexion with the Jewish race. Domitian is
said to have issued an edict for the extermination of the
whole house of David, in order to annihilate for ever the

---

[g] Compare Hist. of the Jews, ii. 454.   [h] Eusebius, iii. 20.

hope of the Messiah, which still brooded with dangerous
excitement in the Jewish mind. The grandsons of
St. Jude, "the brother of the Lord," were denounced
by certain heretics as belonging to the proscribed
family, and brought before the tribunal of the Emperor, or, more probably, that of the Procurator of
Judæa.[i] They acknowledged their descent from the
royal race, and their relationship to the Messiah; but
in Christian language they asserted that the kingdom
which they expected was purely spiritual and angelic,
and only to commence at the end of the world, after the
return to judgement. Their poverty, rather than their
renunciation of all temporal views, was their security.
They were peasants, whose hands were hardened with
toil, and whose whole property was a farm of about
twenty-four English acres, and of the value of 9000
drachms, or about three hundred pounds sterling. This
they cultivated by their own labour, and regularly paid
the appointed tribute. They were released as too humble and too harmless to be dangerous to the Roman
authority, and Domitian, according to the singularly
inconsistent account, proceeded to annul his edict of
persecution against the Christians.

Like all the stories which rest on the sole authority of
Hegesippus, this has a very fabulous air. At no period
were the hopes of the Messiah entertained by the Jews
so little likely to awaken the jealousy of the Emperor
as in the reign of Domitian. The Jewish mind was still
stunned, as it were, by the recent blow: the whole land
was in a state of iron subjection. Nor was it till the
latter part of the reign of Trajan, and that of Hadrian,
that they rallied for their last desperate and conclusive

---

[i] Gibbon thus modifies the story, to which he appears to give some credit.

struggle for independence.   Nor, however indistinct the
line of demarcation between the Jews and the Christians, is it easy to trace the connexion between the
stern precaution for the preservation of the peace of the
Eastern world and the stability of the Empire against
any enthusiastic aspirant after an universal sovereignty,
with what is sometimes called the second great persecution of Christianity; for the exterminating edict was
aimed at a single family, and at the extinction of a
purely Jewish tenet, though it may be admitted that,
even yet, the immediate return of the Messiah to reign
on earth was dominant among most of the Jewish
Christians of Palestine.   Even if true, this edict was
rather the hasty and violent expedient of an arbitrary
sovereign, trembling for his personal security, and
watchful to avert danger from his throne, than a profound and vigorous policy, which aimed at the suppression of a new religion, declaredly hostile, and threatening the existence of the established Polytheism.

Christianity, however, appears to have forced itself
upon the knowledge and the fears of Domitian in a more
unexpected quarter—the bosom of his own family.[k]   Of
his two cousins-german, the sons of Flavius Sabinus,
the one fell an early victim to his jealous ap- Flavius
prehensions.   The other, Flavius Clemens, is Clemens.
described by the epigrammatic biographer of the Cæsars
as a man of the most contemptible indolence of character.   His peaceful kinsman, instead of exciting the
fears, enjoyed, for some time, the favour, of Domitian.
He received in marriage Domitilla, the niece of the
Emperor; his children were adopted as heirs to the

---

[k] Suetonius, in Domit. c. 15.   Dion Cassius, lxvii. 14.   Eusebius, iii. 18.

throne; Clemens himself obtained the consulship. On a sudden these harmless kinsmen became dangerous conspirators; they were arraigned on the unprecedented charge of Atheism and Jewish manners; the husband, Clemens, was put to death; the wife, Domitilla, banished to the desert island, either of Pontia, or Pandataria. The crime of Atheism was afterwards the common popular charge against the Christians; the charge to which, in all ages, those are exposed who are superior to the vulgar notion of the Deity. But it was a charge never advanced against Judaism: coupled, therefore, with that of Jewish manners, it is unintelligible, unless it refers to Christianity. Nor is it improbable that the contemptible want of energy, ascribed by Suetonius to Flavius Clemens, might be that unambitious superiority to the world which characterised the early Christians. Clemens had seen his brother cut off by the sudden and capricious fears of the tyrant; and his repugnance to enter on the same dangerous public career, in pursuit of honours which he despised, if it had assumed the lofty language of philosophy, might have commanded the admiration of his contemporaries, but, connected with a new religion, of which the sublimer notions and principles were altogether incomprehensible, only exposed him to their more contemptuous scorn. Neither in his case was it the peril apprehended from the progress of the religion, but the dangerous position of the individuals professing the religion, so near to the throne, which was fatal to Clemens and Domitilla. It was the pretext, not the cause, of their punishment; and the first act of the reign of Nerva was the reversal of these sentences by the authority of the senate. The exiles were recalled, and an act, prohibiting all accusations of Jewish manners,[m] seems to have been intended as a peace offering for the execution of Clemens, and for the especial protection of the Christians.

But Christian history cannot pass over another incident assigned to the reign of Domitian, since it relates to the death of St. John the Apostle. Christian gratitude and reverence soon began to be discontented with the silence of the authentic writings as to the fate of the twelve chosen companions of Christ. It began first with some modest respect for truth, but soon with bold defiance of probability, to brighten their obscure course, till each might be traced by the blaze of miracle into remote regions of the world, where it is clear that, if they had penetrated, no record of their existence was likely to survive.[n] These religious invaders, according to the later Christian romance, made a regular partition of the world, and assigned to each the conquest of his particular province. Thrace, Scythia, Spain, Britain, Ethiopia, the extreme parts of Africa, India, the name of which mysterious region was sometimes assigned to the southern coast of Arabia, had each its Apostle, whose spiritual triumphs and cruel martyrdom were vividly pourtrayed and gradually amplified by the fertile invention of the Greek and Syrian historians of the early Church. Even the history of St. John, whose later days were chiefly passed in the populous and commercial city of Ephesus, has not escaped. Yet legend has delighted in harmonising its tone with the character of the beloved disciple drawn in the Gospel,

Legends of the missions of the Apostles into different countries.

Death of St. John.

---

m Dion Cassius, lxviii. 1.
n Euseb. Ecc. Hist. iii. 1. The tradition is here in its simpler and clearly more genuine form.

and illustrated in his own writings. Even if purely imaginary, these stories show that another spirit was working in the mind of man. While, then, we would reject, as the offspring of a more angry and controversial age, the story of his flying in fear and indignation from a bath polluted by the presence of the heretic Cerinthus, we might admit the pleasing tradition that when he grew so feeble from age as to be unable to utter any long discourse, his last, if we may borrow the expression, his cycnean voice, dwelt on a brief exhortation to mutual charity.[o] His whole sermon consisted in these words: " Little children, love one another ; " and when his audience remonstrated at the wearisome iteration of the same words, he declared that in these words was contained the whole substance of Christianity. The deportation of the Apostle to the wild island of Patmos, where general tradition places his writing the Book of Revelations, is by no means improbable, if we suppose it to have taken place under the authority of the pro-consul of Asia, on account of some local disturbance in Ephesus, and, notwithstanding the authority of Tertullian, reject the trial before Domitian at Rome,. and the plunging him into a cauldron of boiling oil, from which he came forth unhurt.[p] Such are the few vestiges of the progress of Christianity which we dimly trace in the obscurity of the latter part of the first century. During this period, however, took place the regular formation of the young Christian republics, in all the more considerable cities of the Empire. The primitive constitution of these churches

Constitution of Christian Churches.

---

[o] Euseb. Ecc. Hist. iii. 22.

[p] " Ubi (in Româ) Apostolus Johannes, postea quam in oleum igneum demersus, nihil passus est." Mosheim suspects that in this passage of Tertullian a metaphor has been converted into a fact. De Reb. Christ. ante Constant. p. 111.

is a subject which it is impossible to decline; though
few points in Christian history rest on more dubious
and imperfect, in general or inferential evidence, yet
few have been contested with greater pertinacity.

The whole of Christendom, when it emerges out of
the obscurity of the first century, appears uniformly
governed by certain superiors of each community, called
bishops.   But the origin and extent of this superiority,
and the manner in which the bishop assumed a distinct
authority from the inferior presbyters, is one of those
difficult questions of Christian history which, since the
Reformation, has been more and more darkened by
those fatal enemies to candid and dispassionate inquiry,
Prejudice and Interest.   The earliest Christian communities appear to have been ruled and represented, in
the absence of the Apostle who was their first founder,
by their elders, who are likewise called bishops, or
overseers of the churches.   These presbyter bishops
and the deacons are the only two orders which we
discover at first in the Church of Ephesus, at Philippi,
and perhaps in Crete.[q]   On the other hand, at a very
early period, one religious functionary, superior to the
rest, appears to have been almost universally recognised;
at least, it is difficult to understand how, in so short a
time, among communities, though not entirely disconnected, yet scattered over the whole Roman world, a
scheme of government popular, or rather aristocratical,
should become, even in form, monarchical.   Neither
the times nor the circumstances of the infant Church,
nor the primitive spirit of the religion, appear to favour
a general, a systematic, and an unauthorised usurpation
of power on the part of the supreme religious func-

---

q Acts xx. 17, compared with 28.   Philip. i. 1.   Titus i. 5-7.

tionary.[r] Yet the change has already taken place within the Apostolic times. The Church of Ephesus, which in the Acts is represented by its elders, in the Revelations[s] is represented by its angel or bishop. We may, perhaps, arrive at a more clear and intelligible view of this subject, by endeavouring to trace the origin and development of the Christian communities.

The Christian Church was almost universally formed by a secession from a Jewish synagogue. Some synagogues may have become altogether Christian; but, in

---

[r] The most plausible way of accounting for this total revolution is by supposing that the affairs of each community or church were governed by a college of presbyters, one of whom necessarily presided at their meetings, and gradually assumed and was recognised as possessing a superior function and authority. In expressing my dissatisfaction with a theory adopted by Mosheim, by Gibbon, by Neander, and by most of the learned foreign writers, I have scrutinised my own motives with the utmost suspicion, and can only declare that I believe myself actuated only by the calm and candid desire of truth. But the universal and almost simultaneous elevation of the bishop, under such circumstances, in every part of the world (though it must be admitted that he was for a long time assisted by the presbyters in the discharge of his office), appears to me an insuperable objection to this hypothesis. The later the date which is assumed for the general establishment of the episcopal authority, the less likely was it to be general. It was only during the first period of undivided unity that such an usurpation (for such it must have been according to this theory) could have been universally acquiesced in without resistance. All presbyters, according to this view, with one consent, gave up or allowed themselves to be deprived of their co-ordinate and coequal dignity. The further we advance in Christian history, the more we discover the common motives of human nature at work. In this case alone are we to suppose them without influence? Yet we discover no struggle, no resistance, no controversy. The uninterrupted line of bishops is traced by the ecclesiastical historian up to the Apostles; but no murmur of remonstrance against this usurpation has transpired: no schism, no breach of Christian unity, followed upon this momentous innovation. Nor does any such change appear to have taken place in the office of elder in the Jewish communities: the Rabbinical teachers took the form of a regular hierarchy; their patriarch grew up into a kind of pope, but *episcopal* authority never took root in the synagogue.

[s] Chap ii. 1.

general, a certain part of an existing community of Jews and Gentile proselytes incorporated them- Christian churches formed from, and on the model of, the synagogue. selves into a new society, and met for the purpose of divine worship in some private chamber —sometimes, perhaps, in a public place, as rather later, during the times of persecution, in a cemetery. The first of these may have answered to a synagogue, the latter to an unwalled proseucha. The model of the ancient community would naturally, as far as circumstances might admit, become that of the new. But in their primary constitution there was an essential point of difference. The Jews were a civil as well as a religious, the Christians exclusively a religious, community. Everywhere that the Jews were settled, they were the colony of a nation, they were held together by a kindred, as well as by a religious, bond of union. The governors, therefore, of the community, the Zakinim or Elders, the Parnasim or Pastors (if this be an early appellation), were by no means necessarily religious functionaries.[t]   Another kind of influence besides that of piety—age, worldly experience, wealth— would obtain the chief and ruling power in the society. The government of these Elders neither rested on, nor required, spiritual authority.   Their grave example would enforce the general observance, their censure repress any flagrant departure from the Law : they might be consulted on any difficult or unusual point of practice ; but it was not till the new Rabbinical priesthood was established, and the Mischna and the Talmud uni-

---

[t] In some places, the Jews seem to have been ruled by an Ethnarch, recognised by the Roman civil authorities. Strabo, quoted by Josephus, Antiq. xiv. 12, speaks of the Ethnarch in Alexandria. Josephus mentions their Archon or chief, in Antioch. The more common constitution seems to have been the γεραιοὶ and δυνατοὶ —the elders or authorities.

versally received as the national code, that the foreign
Jews fell under what may be considered sacerdotal
dominion.   At this time, the synagogue itself was only
supplementary to the great national religious ceremonial
Essential
difference
between the
church and
the syna-
gogue. of the Temple.   The Levitical race claimed
no peculiar sanctity, at least it discharged no
priestly office, beyond the bounds of the Holy
Land, or the precincts of the Temple ; nor was
an authorised instructor of the people necessary to the
service of the synagogue.   It was an assembly for the
purpose of worship, not of teaching.   The instructor of
the people, the copy of the Law, lay in the ark at the
east end of the building ; it was brought forth with
solemn reverence, and an appointed portion read during
the service.   But oral instruction, though it might
sometimes be, and no doubt frequently was, delivered, was
no *necessary* part of the ceremonial.   Any one, it should
seem, who considered himself qualified, and obtained
permission from the archisynagogi, the governors of the
community, who exercised a sort of presidence in the
synagogue, might address the assembly.   It was in this
character that the Christian Apostle usually began to
announce his religion.   But neither the chazan, or
angel [u] of the synagogue (which was a purely ministerial, comparatively a servile, office), nor the heads of
the assembly, possessed any peculiar privilege, or were
endowed with any official function as teachers [x] of the
people.   Many of the more remote synagogues can

---

[u] The angel here seems to bear
its lower meaning—a messenger or
minister.

[x] Vitringa labours to prove the
point, that the chief of the synagogue
exercised an office of this kind, but in
my opinion without success. It appears to have been a regular part of
the Essenian service, a distinction
which Vitringa has neglected to observe. De Syn. Vet. lib. iii. c. 6, 7.

rarely have been honoured by the presence of the
" Wise Men," as they were afterwards called—the
lawyers of this period.   The Jewish religion was, at this
time, entirely ceremonial ; it did not necessarily demand
exposition ; its form was moulded into the habits of the
people ; and till disturbed by the invasion of Christianity, or among very flourishing communities, where it
assumed a more intellectual tone, and extended itself
by the proselytism of the Gentiles, it was content to
rest in that form.[y]   In the great days of Jewish intellectual activity, the adjacent Law-school, usually
inseparable from the synagogue, might rather be considered the place of religious instruction.   This was a
kind of chapter-house or court of ecclesiastical, with the
Jews identical with their national, law.   Here knotty
points were publicly debated ; and " the Wise," or the
more distinguished of the lawyers or interpreters of the
Law, as the Rabbinical hierarchy of a later period, established their character for sagacious discernment of the
meaning and intimate acquaintance with the whole
body of the Law.

Thus, then, the model upon which the Church might
be expected to form itself, may be called purely aristocratical.   The process by which it passed into the
monarchical form, however limited the supreme power
of the individual, may be traced to the existence of a
monarchical principle anterior to their religious oli-
garchy, and which distinguished the Christian Church
in its first origin from the Jewish synagogue.   The

---

[y] The reading of the Law, prayers, and psalms, were the ceremonial of the synagogue. Probably the greater part of their proselytism took place in private, though, as we know from Horace, the Jewish synagogue was even in Rome a place of resort to the curious, the speculative, and the idle.

Christians from the first were a purely religious community; this was their primary bond of union; they had no national law which held them together as a separate people. Their civil union was a subordinate effect,·arising out of their incorporation as a spiritual body. The submission of their temporal concerns to the adjudication of their own community was a consequence of their respect for the superior justice and wisdom which sprung from their religious principles, and an aversion from the litigious spirit engendered by the complicated system of Roman jurisprudence.[z] In their origin they were almost universally a community, formed, as it were, round an individual.

Christian Church formed round an individual.

The Apostle, or primitive teacher, was installed at once in the office of chief religious functionary; and the chief religious functionary is the natural head of a purely religious community. Oral instruction, as it was the first, so it must have continued to be the living, conservative, and expansive principle of the community.[a] It was, anterior to the existence of any book, the inspired record and supreme authority of the faith. As long as this teacher remained in the city, or as often as he returned, he would be recognised as the

---

[z] The Apostle enjoined this secession from the ordinary courts of justice. 1 Cor. vi. 1-8.

[a] For some time, indeed, as in the Jewish synagogue, what was called the gift of prophecy seems to have been more general; any individual who professed to speak under the direct impulse of the Holy Spirit was heard with attentive reverence. But it may be questioned whether this, and the display of the other χαρίσματα recounted by the Apostle, 1 Cor. xii. 4-10, were more than subsidiary to the regular and systematic teaching of the apostolic founder of the community. The question is not whether each member was not at liberty to contribute, by any faculty which had been bestowed on him by God, to the general edification; but whether, above and anterior to all this, there was not some recognised parent of each church, who was treated with paternal deference, and exercised, when present, paternal authority.

legitimate head of the society. But not only the Apostle, in general the primitive teacher likewise, was a missionary, travelling incessantly into distant regions for the general dissemination of Christianity, rather than residing in one spot to organise a local community.[b] In his absence, the government, and even the instruction of the community devolved upon the senate of Elders, who were likewise overseers, ἐπίσκοποι (no doubt the name was used interchangeably for some time); [c] yet there was still a recognised supremacy in the founder of the church.[d] The wider, however, the dissemination of Christianity, the more rare, and at longer intervals, the presence of the Apostle. An appeal to his authority, by letter, became more precarious and interrupted; while, at the same time, in many communities, the necessity for his interposition became more frequent and manifest; [e] and in the common order

---

[b] Yet we have an account of a residence even of St. Paul of eighteen months at Corinth, of two years at Ephesus, and he was two years during his first imprisonment at Rome. Acts xviii. 11; xix. 10; xxviii. 30.

[c] I have now read with care the best and fairest book on this subject, Rothe, Anfänge der Christlicher Kirche. Though my view of the original monarchical principle is stronger than Rothe's, I see no reason to retract or modify my statement.—(1863.)

Rothe's argument, pp. 227-238, against what are called Lay Elders seems to me conclusive.

[d] St. Paul considered himself invested with the superintendence of all the churches which he had planted. 2 Cor. xi. 28.

[e] St. Jerome, quoted by Hooker (Eccles. Polity, b. vii. vol. iii. p. 130), assigns the origin of episcopacy to the dissensions in the Church, which required a stronger coercive authority. "Till through instinct of the devil, there grew in the church factions, and among the people it began to be professed, I am of Paul, I of Apollos, and I of Cephas, churches were governed by the common advice of presbyters: but when every one began to reckon those whom he had baptized his own, and not Christ's, it was decreed in the whole world that one chosen out of the presbyters should be placed above the rest, to whom all care of the church should belong, and so all seeds of schism be removed."

The government of the church

of nature, even independent of the danger of persecution, the primitive founder, the legitimate head of the
community, would vacate his place by death. That
the Apostle should appoint some distinguished individual as the delegate, the representative, the successor,
to his authority, as primary instructor of the community; invest him in an episcopacy or overseership,
superior to that of the co-ordinate body of Elders, is, in
itself, by no means improbable; it harmonises with the
period in which we discover, in the Sacred Writings,
this change in the form of the permanent government
of the different bodies; accounts most easily for the
general submission to the authority of one religious
chief magistrate, so unsatisfactorily explained by the
accidental pre-eminence of the president of a college of
coequal presbyters; and is confirmed by general tradition, which has ever, in strict unison with every other
part of Christian history, preserved the names of many
successors of the Apostles, the first bishops in most of
the larger cities in which Christianity was first established.

But the authority of the bishop was that of influence,
Authority of   rather than of power. After the first nomina-
the bishop.   tion by the Apostle (if such nomination, as we
suppose, generally took place), his successor was elective
by that kind of acclamation which raised at once the
individual most eminent for his piety and virtue to the
post, which was that of danger, as well as of distinction.
For a long period, the suffrages of the community
ratified the appointment. Episcopal government was

---

seems to have been considered a subordinate function. " And God hath
set some in the church, first apostles,
secondly prophets, thirdly teachers:

after that, miracles, the gifts of heal-
ing, helps, *governments*, diversities of
tongues." 1 Cor. xii. 28.

thus, as long as Christianity remained unleavened by
worldly passions and interests, essentially popular.
The principle of subordination was inseparable from the
humility of the first converts. Rights are never clearly
defined till they are contested ; nor is authority limited
so long as it rests upon general reverence. When, on
the one side, aggression, on the other, jealousy and
mistrust, begin, then it must be fenced by usage and
defined by law. Thus while I am inclined to consider
the succession of bishops from the Apostolic times to be
undeniable, the nature and extent of the authority which
they derived from the Apostles are altogether uncertain.
The ordination or consecration, whatever it might be, to
that office, of itself conveyed neither inspiration nor the
power of working miracles, which, with the direct commission from the Lord himself, distinguished and set
apart the primary Apostles from the rest of mankind.
It was only in a very limited and imperfect sense that
they could, even in the sees founded by the Apostles,
be called the successors of the Apostles.

The presbyters were, in their origin, the *ruling* powers
of the young communities ; but in a society founded
solely on a religious basis, religious qualifications would
be almost exclusively considered. In the absence, therefore, of the primary teacher, they would assume that
office likewise. In this they would differ from The presby-
the Jewish elders. As the most eminent in ters.
piety and Christian attainments, they would be advanced
by, or at least with, the general consent, to their dignified station. The same piety and attainments would
designate them as best qualified to keep up and to
extend the general system of instruction. They would
be the regular and perpetual expositors of the Christian

law [f]—the reciters of the life, the doctrines, the death, the resurrection of Christ; till the Gospels were written, and generally received, they would be the living Evangelists, the oral Scriptures, the spoken Gospel. They would not merely regulate and lead the devotions, administer the rites of baptism and the Lord's Supper, but repeat again and again, for the further confirmation of the believers and the conversion of Jews and Heathens, the facts and the tenets of the new religion. The government, in fact, in communities bound together by Christian brotherhood (such as we may suppose to have been the first Christian churches, which were happily undistracted by the disputes arising out of the Judaical controversy), would be an easy office, and entirely subordinate to that of instruction and edification. The communities would be almost self-governed by the principle of Christian love which first drew them together. The deacons were from the first an inferior order, and exercised a purely ministerial office—distributing the common fund to the poorer members, though the administration of the pecuniary concerns of the Church soon became of such importance as to require the superintendence of the higher rulers. The other functions of the deacons were altogether of a subordinate character.

Such would be the ordinary development of a Chris-

---

[f] Here, likewise, the possessors of the χαρίσματα would be the casual and subsidiary instructors, or rather the gifted promoters of Christian piety, each in his separate sphere, according to his distinctive grace. But besides these, even if they were found in all churches, which is by no means clear, regular and systematic teachers would be necessary to a religion which probably could only subsist, certainly could not propagate itself with activity or to any great extent, except by this constant exposition of its principles in the public assembly, as well as in the more private communications of individuals.

tian community, in the first case, monarchical, as founded
by an individual Apostle or recognised teacher of Christianity; subsequently, in the absence of that teacher,
aristocratical, under a senate formed according to Jewish
usage, though not precisely on Jewish principles; until,
the place of the Apostle being supplied by a bishop, in
a certain sense his representative or successor, it would
revert to a monarchical form, limited rather by the
religion itself than by any appointed controlling power.
As long as the same holy spirit of love and charity
actuated the whole body, the result would be an harmony,
not from the counteracting powers of opposing forces,
but from the consentient will of the general body; and
the will of the government would be the expression of
the universal popular sentiment.[g]   Where, however,
from the first, the Christian community was formed of
conflicting parties, or where conflicting principles began
to operate immediately upon the foundation of the
society, no single person would be generally recognised as
the authoritative teacher, and the assumption and recognition of the episcopate would be more slow; or, indeed,
would not take place at all till the final triumph of one of
the conflicting parties.   These communities retained, of
necessity, the republican form.   Such was the Church of
state of the Corinthian Church, which was from Corinth an
exception.
its origin, or almost immediately after, divided into

---

[g] Such is the theory of episcopal
government in a pleasing passage
in the Epistles of Ignatius: Ὅθεν
πρέπει ὑμῖν συντρέχειν τῇ τοῦ ἐπι-
σκόπου γνώμῃ. ὅπερ καὶ ποιεῖτε. Τὸ
γὰρ ἀξιονόμαστον ὑμῶν πρεσβυτέριον,
τοῦ θεοῦ ἄξιον οὕτως συνήρμοσται τῷ
ἐπισκόπῳ ὡς χορδαὶ κιθάρᾳ· διὰ τοῦτο
ἐν τῇ ὁμονοίᾳ ὑμῶν, καὶ συμφώνῳ
ἀγάπῃ Ἰησοῦς Χρίστος ᾄδεται καὶ
οἱ κατ᾽ ἄνδρα δὲ χορὸς γίνεσθε, ἵνα
σύμφωνοι ὄντες ἐν ὁμονοίᾳ, χρῶμα
θεοῦ λαβόντες ἐν ἑνότητι, ᾄδετε ἐν
φωνῇ μιᾷ διὰ Ἰησοῦ Χριστοῦ τᾀ
πατρὶ, κ.τ.λ.   Ad Ephes. p. 12, edit.
Cotel.   I speak of these epistles in a
subsequent note.

three separate parties, with a leading teacher or teachers at the head of each.[h]   The Petrine, or the ultra-Judaic, the Apolline, or more moderate Jewish party, contested the supremacy with the followers of St. Paul.   Different individuals possessed, exercised, and even abused different gifts.   The authority of Paul himself appears clearly, by his elaborate vindication of his Apostolic office, by no means to have been generally recognised. No Apostolic head, therefore, would assume an uncontested supremacy, nor would the parties coalesce in the choice of a superior.   Corinth, probably, was the last community which settled down under the general episcopal constitution.

The manner and the period of the separation of a distinct class, a hierarchy, from the general body of the community, and the progress of the great division between the clergy and the laity,[i] are equally obscure with the primitive constitution of the Church.   Like the Judaism of the provinces, Christianity had no sacerdotal order.   But as the more eminent members of the community were admitted to take the lead, on account of their acknowledged religious superiority, from their zeal, their talents, their gifts, their sanctity, the general

---

[h] I was led to conjecture that the distracted state of the Church of Corinth might induce the Apostles to establish elsewhere a more firm and vigorous authority, before I remembered the passage of St. Jerome quoted above, which coincides with this view. Corinth has been generally taken as the model of the early Christian constitution ; I suspect that it was rather an anomaly.

[i] Already the λαίκοι are a distinct class in the Epistle of Clemens to the Corinthians (c. xl. p. 170, edit. Coteler). This epistle is confidently appealed to by both parties in the controversy about church-government, and altogether satisfies neither. It is clear, however, from the tone of the whole epistle, that the Church at Corinth was anything rather than a model of church-government: it had been rent with schisms ever since the days of the Apostle.

reverence would, of itself, speedily set them apart as of
a higher order; they would form the purest aristocracy,
and soon be divided by a distinct line of demarcation
from the rest of the community. Whatever the ordination might be which designated them for their peculiar
function, whatever power or authority might be communicated by the " imposition of hands," it would add little
to the reverence with which they were invested. It was
at first the Christian who sanctified the function, afterwards the function sanctified the man. But the civil
and religious concerns of the Church were so moulded
up together, or rather, the temporal were so absorbed
by the spiritual, that not merely the teacher, but the
governor—not merely the bishop, properly so called,
but the presbyter, in his character of ruler as well as
of teacher—shared in the same peculiar veneration. The
bishop would be necessarily mingled up in the few
secular affairs of the community, the governors bear
their part in the religious ceremonial. In this respect,
again, they differed from their prototypes, or elders of
the synagogue. Their office was, of necessity, more
religious. The admission of members into the Jewish
synagogue, except in the case of proselytes of righteousness, was a matter of hereditary right : circumcision was
a domestic, not a public ceremony. But baptism, or the
initiation into the Christian community, was a solemn
ceremonial, requiring previous examination and proba-
tion. The governing power would possess and exercise
the authority to admit into the community. They would
perform, or at all events superintend, the initiatory rite
of baptism. The other distinctive rite of Christianity,
the celebration of the Lord's Supper, would require a
more active interference and co-operation on the part

of those who presided over the community. To this
there was nothing analogous in the office of the Jewish
elder. Order would require that this ceremony should
be administered by certain functionaries. If the bishop
presided, after his appointment, both at the Lord's
Supper itself and in the agape or feast which followed
it, the elders would assist, not merely in maintaining
order, but would officiate throughout the ceremony. In
proportion to the reverence for the consecrated elements
would be the respect towards those under whose especial
prayers, and in whose hands, probably from the earliest
period, they were sanctified for the use of the assembly.
The presbyters would likewise possess the chief voice, a
practical initiative, in the nomination of the bishop.
From all these different functions the presbyters, and
at length the deacons, became, as well as the bishop, a
sacred order. But the exclusive or sacerdotal principle
once admitted in a religious community, its own corporate spirit, and the public reverence, would cause it to
recede further and further, and draw the line of demarcation with greater rigour and depth. They would
more and more insulate themselves from the common-
alty of the Christian republic; they would become a
senate, a patrician, or a privileged order; and this secession into their peculiar sphere would be greatly
facilitated by the regular gradations of the faithful and
the catechumen, the perfect and the imperfect, the
initiate and half-initiate, Christians. The greater the
variety, the more strict the subordination of ranks.

Thus the bishop gradually assumed the title of pontiff;
the presbyters became a sacerdotal order. From the
Old Testament, and even from paganism, the Christians,
at first as ennobling metaphors, adopted their sacred

appellations. Insensibly the meaning of these significant titles worked into the Christian system. They assumed, as it were, a privilege of nearer approach to the Deity ; and a priestly caste grew rapidly up in a religion which, in its primary institution, acknowledged only one mediator between earth and heaven. I shall subsequently trace the growth of the sacerdotal principle, and the universal establishment of the hierarchy.

CHAPTER V.

Christianity and Orientalism.

CHRISTIANITY had not only to contend with the Judaism
Oriental of its native region, and the Paganism of the
religions. Western world, but likewise with the Asiatic
religions, which, in the Eastern provinces of the Roman
empire, maintained their ground, or mingled themselves
with the Grecian Polytheism, and had even penetrated
into Palestine. In the silence of its authentic records,
the direct progress of Christianity in the East can neither
be accurately traced nor clearly estimated; its conflict
with Orientalism is chiefly visible in the influence of
the latter upon the general system of Christianity, and
in the tenets of the different sects which, from Simon
Magus to Manes, attempted to reconcile the doctrines
of the Gospel with the theogonical system of Asia. In
the West Christianity advanced with gradual, but un-
obstructed and unreceding, progress, till, first the Roman
Empire, and successively the barbarous nations who
occupied or subdued the rest of Europe, were brought
within its pale. No new religion arose to dispute its
supremacy; and the feeble attempt of Julian to raise
up a Platonic Paganism in opposition to the religion of
Christ must have failed, even if it had not been cut
short in its first growth by the death of its imperial
patron. In Asia, the progress of Christianity was suddenly arrested by the revival of Zoroastrianism, after
the restoration of the Persian kingdom upon the ruins

of the Parthian monarchy; and, at a later period, the vestiges of its former success were almost entirely obliterated by the desolating and all-absorbing conquests of Mohammedanism. The Armenian was the only national church which resisted alike the persecuting edicts of the Sassanian fire-worshippers, and, submitting to the yoke of the Mohammedan conqueror, rejected the worship of the Prophet. The other scattered communities of Christians, disseminated through various parts of Asia, on the coast of Malabar, perhaps in China, have no satisfactory evidence of Apostolic or even of very early date: they are so deeply impregnated with the Nestorian system of Christianity, which, during the interval between the decline of the reformed Zoroastrianism and the first outburst of Islamism, spread to a great extent throughout every part of the Eastern continent,[a] that there is every reason to suppose them Nestorian in their origin.[b] The contest, then, of Christianity with the Eastern religions must be traced in their reaction upon the new religion of the West. By their treacherous alliance, they probably operated more extensively to the detriment of the Evangelic religion than Paganism by its open opposition. Asiatic influences have worked more completely into the body and essence of Christianity than any other foreign elements; and it is by no means improbable that tenets, which had their origin in India, have for many centuries predominated in, or materially affected the Christianity of the whole Western world.

Palestine was admirably situated to become the centre

---

[a] There is an extremely good view of the origin and history of the Christian communities in India, in Bohlen, Das alte Indien.

[b] Compare the new edition of Gibbon and the editor's note on the Nestorian Christians with the famous inscription of Siganfu, viii. 347.

and point of emanation for an universal religion. On the *Situation of Palestine favourable for a new religion.* confines of Asia and Europe, yet sufficiently secluded from both to be out of the way of the constant flux and reflux of a foreign population, it commanded Egypt, and, through Egypt, associated Africa with the general moral kingdom. But it was not merely calculated for the birthplace of an universal faith by its local position. *Judaism.* Judaism, as it were, in its character (putting out of sight, for an instant, its divine origin) stood between the religions of the East and the West. It was the connecting link between the European and the Asiatic mind. In speculative sublimity, the doctrine of the Divine Unity soared to an equal height with the vast and imaginative cosmogonies of the East, while in its practical tendencies it approximated to the active and rational genius of the West.

The religions of Asia appear, if not of regularly affiliated descent, yet to possess a common and generic character, modified, indeed, by the genius of the different people, and, perhaps; by the prevailing tone of mind in the authors and founders of new doctrines. From the banks of the Ganges, probably from the shores of the Yellow Sea and the coasts of further India, to the Phœnician borders of the Mediterranean and the undefined limits of Phrygia in Asia Minor, there was that connexion and similitude, that community of certain elementary principles, that tendency to certain combinations of physical and moral ideas, which may be expressed by the term Orientalism.[c] The speculative

---

[c] Compare Windischman, Philosophie in fortgang der Welt Geschichte. Windischman was a friend, I believe I may venture to say, a disciple, of F. Schlegel, and belongs to the high Roman Catholic school in Germany.

theology of the higher, the sacerdotal, order, which in some countries left the superstitions of General character of Orientalism. the vulgar undisturbed, or allowed their own more sublime conceptions to be lowered to their rude and limited material notions, aspired to the primal Source of Being. The Emanation system of India, according to which the whole worlds flowed from the Godhead and were finally to be reabsorbed into it; the Pantheism into which this degenerated, and which made the collective Universe itself the Deity; the Dualism of Persia, according to which the antagonist powers were created by, or proceeded from, the One Supreme and Uncreated; the Chaldean doctrine of divine Energies or Intelligences, the prototypes of the Cabalistic Sephiroth, and of the later Gnostic Æons, the same, no doubt, under different names, with the Æon and Protogenes, the Genos and Genea, with their regularly-coupled descendants in the Phœnician cosmogony of Sanchoniathon; and finally, the primitive and simpler worship of Egypt; all these are either branches of one common stock, or expressions of the same state of the human mind, working with kindred activity on the same visible phenomena of nature, and with the same object.

The Asiatic mind impersonated, though it did not, with the Greek, humanise everything. Light and Darkness, Good and Evil, the Creative and Destructive energy of nature, the active and passive Powers of generation, moral Perfection and Wisdom, Reason and Speech, even Agriculture and the Pastoral life, each was a distinct and intelligent being; they wedded each

---

His book, which is full of abstruse thought and learning, developes the theory of a primitive tradition diffused through the East.

other according to their apparent correspondences; they begat progeny according to the natural affiliation or consequence of ideas.

One great elementary principle pervaded the whole religious systems of the East, the connexion of *moral* with *physical ideas*, the inherent *purity, the divinity, of mind or spirit*, the inalienable *evil of its antagonist, matter*. Whether Matter coexisted with the First Great Cause; whether it was created by his power, but from its innate malignity became insubordinate to his will; whether it was extraneous to his existence, necessarily subsisting, though without form, till its inert and shapeless mass was worked upon by the Deity himself, or by his primal Power or Emanation, the Demiurge or Creator of the existing worlds: on these points the different national creeds were endlessly diversified. But in its various forms, the principle itself was the universal doctrine of the Eastern world; it was developed in their loftiest philosophy (in fact, their higher philosophy and their speculative religion were the same thing); it gave a kind of colouring even to their vulgar superstition, and operated, in many cases almost to an incredible extent, on their social and political system.

This great primal tenet is alike the elementary principle of the higher Brahminism and the more moral Buddhism of India and the remoter East. The theory of the division of castes supposes that a larger portion of the pure mind of the Deity is infused into the sacerdotal and superior orders; they are nearer the Deity, and with more immediate hope of being reabsorbed into the divine essence; while the lower classes are more inextricably immersed in the grosser matter of the world, their feeble portion of the essential

[marginal notes:] Purity of Mind. Malignity of Matter. The universal primary principle.

spirit of the Divinity contracted and lost in the predominant mass of corruption and malignity.[d]   The
Buddhist, substituting a moral for a hereditary approximation to the pure and elementary mind, rests,
nevertheless, on the same primal theory, and carries the
notion of the abstraction of the spiritual part from the
foul and corporeal being to an equal, if not a greater,
height of contemplative mysticism.[e]   Hence the sanctity
of fire among the Persians;[f] that element which is most
subtle and defæcated from all material corruption; it is
therefore the representative of pure elementary mind,
of Deity itself.[g]   It exists independent of the material
forms in which it abides, the sun and the heavenly
bodies.   To infect this holy element with any excretion
or emanation from the material form of man; to con-
taminate it with the putrescent effluvia of the dead and
soulless corpse, was the height of guilt and impiety.

This one simple principle is the parent of that Asceticism which maintained its authority among   Source of
all the older religions of the remoter East,   Asceticism.
forced its way at a very early period into Christianity,
where, for some centuries, it exercised a predominant
influence, and subdued even the active and warlike

---

[d] The self-existing power declared
the purest part of him to be the
mouth. Since the Brahmen sprung
from the most excellent part; since
he was the first-born, and since he
possesses the Veda, he is by right the
chief of the whole creation.   Jones's
Menu, i. 92, 93.

[e] See the tracts of Mahony, Join-
ville, Hodgson, and Wilson, in the
Asiatic Researches; Schmidt, Ges-

chichte der Ost Mongolen; Bergman,
Nomadische Streifereyen, &c.

[f] Hyde, De Relig. Persarum, p. 13,
et alibi.   Kleuker, Anhang zum
Zendavesta, vol. i. p. 116, 117.
De Guigniaut, Religions de l'Antiquité, l. ii. c. 3, p. 333.

[g] Kleuker, Anhang zum Zendavesta,
vol. i. pt. 2, p. 147. De Guigniaut,
ubi supra.

genius of Mohammedanism to its dreamy and ecstatic
influence.   On the cold table-lands of Thibet, in the
forests of India, among the busy population of China,
on the burning shores of Siam, in Egypt and in Palestine, in Christianised Europe, in Mohammedanised Asia,
the worshipper of the Lama, the Faquir, the Bonze, the
Talapoin, the Essene, the Therapeutist, the Monk, and
the Dervish, have withdrawn from the society of man,
in order to abstract the pure mind from the dominion of
foul and corrupting matter.   Under each system, the
perfection of human nature was estrangement from the
influence of the senses,—those senses which were enslaved to the material elements of the world ; an
approximation to the essence of the Deity, by a total
secession from the affairs, the interests, the passions,
the thoughts, the common being and nature of man.
The practical operation of this elementary principle of
Eastern religion has deeply influenced the whole history
of man.   But it had made no progress in Europe till
after the introduction of Christianity.   The manner in
which it allied itself with, or rather incorporated itself
into, a system, to the original nature and design of
which it appears altogether foreign, will form a most
important and perhaps not uninteresting chapter in the
History of Christianity.

Celibacy was the offspring of Asceticism, but it does
not appear absolutely essential to it ; whether
insulted nature reasserts its rights, and recon-
ciles to the practice that which is in apparent opposition
to the theory, or whether it revenges, as it were, this
rebellion of nature on one point, by its more violent
and successful invasions upon its unconquerable propensities on others.   The Muni in India is accompanied

Celibacy.

by his wife, who shares his solitude, and seems to offer no impediment to his sanctity,[h] though in some cases it may be that all connubial intercourse is sternly renounced. In Palestine, the Essene, in his higher state of perfection, stood in direct opposition to the spirit of the books of Moses, on which he still looked with the profoundest reverence, by altogether refraining from marriage. It was perhaps in this form that Eastern Asceticism first crept into Christianity. It assumed the elevating and attractive character of higher personal purity; it drew the line of demarcation more rigidly against the loose morality of the Heathen; it afforded the advantage of detaching the first itinerant preachers of Christianity more entirely from worldly interests; enabled them to devote their whole undistracted attention to the propagation of the Faith, and left them, as it were, more loose from the world, ready to break the few and slender ties which connected them with it at the first summons to a glorious martyrdom.[i] But it was not, as we shall presently observe, till Gnosticism began to exercise its influence on Christianity [k] that,

---

[h] Abandoning all food eaten in towns, and all his household utensils, let him repair to the lonely wood, committing the care of his wife to his sons, or accompanied by her, if she choose to attend him. Sir W. Jones's Menu, vi. 3. I venture to refer to the pathetic tale of the hermit with his wife and son, from the Mahá Bhárata, in my translations from the Sanskrit. Compare Vishnu Purana, p. 295.

In the very curious account of the Buddhist monks (the Σαμάναιοι—the Schamans) in Porphyrius de Abstinentiâ, lib. iv. 17, the Buddhist ascetic abandons his wife; and this in general agrees with the Buddhist theory. Female contact is unlawful to the Buddha ascetic. See a curious instance in Mr. Wilson's Hindu Theatre —*The Toyoart,* Act viii., in fine.

[i] Clement of Alexandria, however, asserts that St. Paul was really married, but left his wife behind him, lest she should interfere with his ministry. This is his interpretation of 1 Cor. ix. 5.

[k] Tertullian adv. Marc. i. 29. Non tingitur apud illum caro, nisi virgo, nisi vidua, nisi cælebs, nisi divortio baptismum mereatur . . . nec præscri-

emulous of its dangerous rival, or infected with its
foreign opinions, the Church, in its general sentiment,
espoused and magnified the pre-eminent virtue of
celibacy.[m]

The European mind of the older world, as repre-
Unknown in sented by the Greeks and Romans, repelled
Greece and
Rome. for a long time, in the busy turmoil of political
development and the absorbing career of war and conquest, this principle of inactivity and secession from the
ordinary affairs of life. No sacerdotal caste established
this principle of superiority over the active warrior, or
even over the laborious husbandman. With the citizen
of the stirring and factious republics of Greece, the
highest virtue was of a purely political and practical
character. The whole man was public : his indivi-
duality, the sense of which was continually suggested
and fostered under the other system, was lost in the
member of the commonwealth. That which contributed
nothing to the service of the state was held in no
respect. The mind, in its abstracted flights, obtained
little honour ; it was only as it worked upon the welfare,
the amusement, or the glory of the republic, that its
dignity was estimated. The philosopher might discuss
the comparative superiority of the practical or the contemplative life, but his loftiest contemplations were
occupied with realities, or what may be considered

---

bimus sed suademus sanctitatem . . .
tunc denique conjugium exertè de-
fendentes cum inimicè accusatur spur-
citiæ nomine in destructionem creatoris
qui proinde conjugium pro rei hones-
tate benedixit, incrementum generis
humani . . .

[m] Compare the whole argument of
the third book of the Stromata of

Clement of Alexandria. In one passage he condemns celibacy, as leading
to misanthropy. Συνορῶ δὲ ὅπως τῇ
προφάσει τοῦ γάμου οἱ μὲν ἀπεσχη-
μένοι τούτου, μὴ κατὰ τὴν ἁγίαν
γνῶσιν, εἰς μισανθρωπίαν ὑπερρύησαν,
καὶ τὸ τῆς ἀγάπης οἴχεται παρ'
αὐτοῖς. Strom. iii. 9.

idealising those realities to a higher degree of perfection : to make good citizens was the utmost ambition of
his wisdom ; an Utopia was his heaven. The Cynic, who
in the East, or in Europe after it became impregnated
with Eastern doctrines, would have retired into the
desert to his solitary hermitage, in order to withdraw
himself entirely from the common interests, sentiments,
and connexions of mankind ; in Greece, took up his
station in the crowded forum, or, pitching his tub in the
midst of the concourse at the public games, inveighed
against the vices and follies of mankind. Plato, if he
had followed the natural bent of his genius,
might have introduced, and indeed did introduce, as much as the Grecian mind was capable of
imbibing of this theory of the opposition of mind and
matter, with its ordinary consequences. The communities of his older master Pythagoras, who had probably visited the East, and drank deep of the Oriental
mysticism, approached in some respects nearer to the
contemplative character of monastic institutions. But
the active mind of the Greek predominated ; and the
followers of Pythagoras, instead of founding cœnobitic
institutions, or secluding themselves in meditative solitude, settled some of the flourishing republics of Magna
Græcia. The great master, in whose steps Plato professed to tread more closely, was so essentially practical and unimaginative, as to bind his followers down
to a less Oriental system of philosophy. While, therefore, in his Timæus, Plato attempted to harmonise parts
of the cosmogonical theories of Asia with the more
humanised mythology of Greece, the work which was
more accordant to the genius of his country, was his
Republic, in which all his idealism was, as it were, confined to the earth. Even his religion, though of much

sublimer cast than the popular superstition, was yet
considered chiefly in its practical operation on the
welfare of the state.   It was his design to elevate
humanity to a higher state of moral dignity; to cultivate the material body as well as the immaterial soul,
to the height of perfection; not to sever, as far as
possible, the connexion between these ill-assorted companions, or to withdraw the purer mind from its social
and political sphere, into solitary and inactive communion with the Deity.

In Rome, the general tendency of the national mind
was still more essentially public and political.
Rome.   In the Republic, except in a few less distinguished men, the Lælii and the Attici, even their philosophy was an intellectual recreation between the more
pressing avocations of their higher duties: it was either
to brace and mature the mind for future service to the
state, or as a solace in hours of disappointed ambition
or the haughty satiety of glory.   Civil science was the
end and aim of all their philosophic meditation.   Like
their ancient king, if they retired for communion with
the Egeria of philosophy, it was in order to bring forth,
on their return, more ample stores of political and legis-
lative wisdom.   Under the imperial government, they
took refuge in the lofty reveries of the porch, as they
did in inordinate luxury, from the degradation and
enforced inactivity of servitude.   They fled to the philosophic retirement, from the barrenness, in all high or
stirring emotions, which had smitten the Senate and the
Comitia; still looking back with a vain but lingering
hope that the State might summon them again from
retirement without dignity, from a contemplative life,
which by no means implied an approximation to the
divine, but rather a debasement of the human nature.

Some, indeed, degraded their high tone of philosophy
by still mingling in the servile politics of the day:
Seneca lived and died the votary and the victim of
court intrigue. The Thraseas stood aloof, not in ecstatic meditation on the primal Author of Being, but on
the departed liberties of Rome; their soul aspired no
higher than to unite itself with the ancient genius of the
Republic.

Orientalism had made considerable progress towards
the West before the appearance of Christianity. Orientalism
While the popular Pharisaism of the Jews had in Western
embodied some of the more practical tenets of Zoroastrianism, the doctrines of the remoter East had found a
welcome reception with the Essene. Yet even with
him, regular and unintermitting labour, not inert and
meditative abstraction, was the principle of the ascetic
community. It might almost seem that there subsisted
some secret and indelible congeniality, some latent con-
sanguinity, whether from kindred, common descent, or
from conquest, between the caste-divided population on
the shores of the Ganges, and the same artificial state
of society in the valley of the Nile, so as to assimilate in
so remarkable a manner their religion.[n] It is certain,
that the genuine Indian mysticism first established a
permanent western settlement in the deserts of Egypt.
Its first combination seems to have been with the
Egyptian Judaism of Alexandria, and to have arisen
from the dreaming Platonism, which in the schools of
that city had been engrafted on the Mosaic Institutes.

---

[n] Bohlen's work, Das alte Indien, of which the excellence in all other respects, as a condensed abstract of all that our own countrymen and the scholars of Germany and France have collected concerning India, will be universally acknowledged, is written to maintain the theory of the early connexion of India and Egypt.

The Egyptian Monks were the lineal descendants of the Jewish Therapeutæ, described by Philo.[o] Though the Therapeutæ, like the Essenes, were in some respects a productive community, yet they approached much nearer to the contemplative and indolent fraternities of the farther East. The arid and rocky desert around them was too stubborn to make much return to their less regular and less systematic cultivation; visionary indolence would grow upon them by degrees. The communities either broke up into the lairs of solitary hermits, or were constantly throwing off their more enthusiastic votaries deeper into the desert: the severer mortifications of the flesh required a more complete isolation from the occupations, as well as the amusements or enjoyments of life. To change the wilderness into a garden by patient industry, was to enthral the spirit in some degree to the service of the body; and in process of time, the principle was carried to its height. The more dreary the wilderness, the more unquestioned the sanctity of its inhabitant; the more complete and painful the privation, the more holy the worshipper; the more the man put off his own nature, and sank below the animal to vegetative existence, the more consummate his spiritual perfection. The full growth of this system was of a much later period; it did not come to maturity till after Christianity had passed through its conflict with Gnosticism; but its elements were, no doubt, floating about in the different western regions of Asia, and either directly through Gnosticism, or from the emulation of the two sects, which outbid each other, as it were, in austerity, it worked, at length, into the very intimate being of the Gospel religion.

---

[o] Philonis Opera. Mangey, vol. ii. p. 471.

The singular felicity, the skill and dexterity, if I may so speak, with which Christianity at first wound its way through these conflicting elements, combining what was pure and lofty in each, in some instances unavoidably speaking their language, and simplifying, harmonising, and modifying each to its own peculiar system, increases our admiration of its unrivalled wisdom, its deep insight into the universal nature of man, and its pre-acquaintance, as it were, with the countless diversities of human character prevailing at the time of its propagation. But, unless the same profound wisdom had watched over its inviolable preservation, which presided over its origin; unless it had been constantly administered with the same superiority to the common passions and interests and speculative curiosity of man, a reaction of the several systems over which it prevailed was inevitable. On a wide and comprehensive survey of the whole history of Christianity, and considering it as left altogether to its own native force and impulse, it is difficult to estimate how far the admission, even the predominance, of these foreign elements, by which it was enabled to maintain its hold on different ages and races, may not have contributed both to its original success and its final permanence. The Eastern asceticism outbid Christianity in that austerity, that imposing self-sacrifice, that intensity of devotion, which acts with the greatest rapidity, and secures the most lasting authority over rude and unenlightened minds. By coalescing to a certain point with its antagonist, it embraced within its expanding pale those who would otherwise, according to the spirit of their age, have been carried beyond its sphere by some enthusiasm more popular and better suited to the genius of the time, or the temperament of

Combination of Orientalism with Christianity.

the individual. If it lost in purity, it gained in power, perhaps in permanence. No doubt, in its first contest with Orientalism were sown those seeds which grew up at a later period into Monasticism; it rejected the tenets, but admitted the more insidious principle of Gnosticism; yet there can be little doubt that in the dark ages, the monastic spirit was among the great conservative and influential elements of Christianity.

The form in which Christianity first encountered this wide-spread Orientalism, was either Gnosticism,[p] or, if that philosophy had not then become consolidated into a system, those opinions which subsequently grew up into that prevalent doctrine of Western Asia. The first

---

[p] In this view of Gnosticism, besides constant reference to the original authorities, I must acknowledge my obligations to Brucker, Hist. Phil. vol. ii. p. 1, c. 3; to Mosheim, De Reb. Christ. ante Const. Mag.; to Beausobre, Hist. du Manichéisme; but above all, to the excellent Histoire du Gnosticisme, by M. Matter of Strasburg, 2 vols. 8vo. Paris, 1828. Since the first publication of this work new light has been thrown on Gnosticism and the Gnostic Teaching by the discovery of the (imperfect) Philosophumena, first erroneously attributed to Origen by the editor E. Miller, first and conclusively proved by the learning and sagacity of Bunsen to be the work of Hippolytus, Bishop of Porto near Rome, in the early part of the third century. On this point almost all are agreed—even Bunsen's most learned antagonists on other questions raised by this book, Dr. Wordsworth and Döllinger. On this controversy I have expressed my judgement fully in a note to Latin Christianity, vol. i. p. 35. I think Bunsen triumphant in most points. In the Epistles to Archdeacon Hare, and in the Analecta published by Bunsen, in his great work Christianity and Mankind, will be found selected and illustrated the chief texts of the Philosophumena which bear on the rise and development of Gnosticism. Perhaps, as usual, Bunsen's bold and imaginative divination sees much which eyes not less keen, but endowed with less magnifying powers, will fail to discern.

Besides this work, the Christliche Gnosis of Baur, and the mature opinions of Neander in the second edition of his History, will satisfy readers who care to plunge into that dim labyrinth of Gnosticism, and to investigate its mysteries at greater length than the extent and proportions of my work, and my judgement as to the importance of such researches, permit me to expand into.—(1863.)

Orientalist was Simon Magus. In the conflict with St.
Peter, related in the Acts, nothing transpires
as to the personal history of this remarkable Simon Magus.
man, excepting the extensive success with which he had
practised his magical arts in Samaria, and the Oriental
title which he assumed—" the Power of God." His
first overtures to the Apostle appear as though he were
desirous of conciliating the friendship and favour of the
new teacher, and would not have been unwilling to
have acted a subordinate part in the formation of his
increasing sect. But from his first rejection, Simon
Magus was an opponent, if there be any truth in the
wild legends, which are still extant, the rival, of Christianity.[q] On the arrival of the Christian teachers in
Samaria, where, up to that period, his influence had predominated, Simon paid homage to the reality of his
miracles, by acknowledging their superiority to his own.
Still, it should seem that he only considered them as
more adroit wonder-workers, or, as is more probable,
possessed of some peculiar secrets beyond his own knowledge of the laws of nature, or, possibly (for imposture
and superstition are ever closely allied), he may have
supposed that they had intercourse with more powerful
Spirits or Intelligences than his own. Jesus was to him
either some extraordinary proficient in magic, who had
imparted his prevailing gifts to his followers, the Apostles;
or some superior genius, who lent himself to their bid-

---

[q] It is among the most hopeless
difficulties in early Christian history
to decide, to one's own satisfaction,
what groundwork of truth there may
be in those works which bear the
name of St. Clement, and relate the
contests of St. Peter and Simon Magus.
That in their present form they are a
kind of religious romance, few will
doubt; but they are certainly of great
antiquity, and it is difficult to suppose them either pure invention or
mere embellishments of the simple
history in the Acts.

ding; or what Simon asserted himself to be, some power emanating more directly from the primal Deity. The "gift of the Holy Ghost" seemed to communicate a great portion, at least, of this magic influence, and to place the initiated in possession of some mighty secrets, or to endow him with the control of some potent spirits. Simon's offer of pecuniary remuneration betrays at once either that his own object was sordid, as he suspected theirs to be; or, at the highest, he sought to increase, by a combination with them, his own reputation and influence. Nor, on the indignant refusal of St. Peter, does his entreaty for their prayers, lest he should incur the wrath of their offended Deity, by any means imply a more accurate and Christian conception of their religion; it is exactly the tone of a man, half impostor and half enthusiast, who trembles before the offended anger of some mightier superhuman being, whom his ineffectual magic has no power to control or to appease. We collect no more than this from the narrative in the Acts.[r]

Yet, unless Simon was in fact a personage of considerable importance during the early history of Christianity, it is difficult to account for his becoming, as he is called by Beausobre, the hero of the Romance of Heresy. If Simon was the same with that magician, a Cypriot by birth, who was employed by Felix as agent in his intrigue to detach Drusilla from her husband,[s] this part of his character accords with the charge of licentiousness advanced both against his life and his doctrines by his Christian opponents. This is by no means improbable; and indeed, even if he was not a person thus

---

[r] Acts viii. 9, 24.
[s] Joseph. Ant. xx. 5, 2. Compare Krebs and Kuinoel, in loco Act Apost.

politically prominent and influential, the early writers
of Christianity would scarcely have concurred in representing him as a formidable and dangerous antagonist
of the Faith, as a kind of personal rival of St. Peter,
without some other groundwork for the fiction besides
the collision recorded in the Acts. The doctrines which
are ascribed to him and to his followers, who continued
to exist for two or three centuries,[t] harmonise with the
glimpse of his character and tenets in the writings of
St. Luke.

Simon probably was one of that class of adventurers
which abounded at this period, or like Apollo- His real cha-
nius of Tyana and others at a later time, with racter and tenets.
whom the opponents of Christianity attempted to con-
found Jesus and his Apostles. His doctrine was Oriental in its language and in its pretensions.[u] He was
the first Æon or Emanation, or rather perhaps the first
manifestation of the primal Deity. He assumed not
merely the title of the Great Power or Virtue of God,
but all the other appellations—the Word, the Perfection, the Paraclete, the Almighty, the whole combined
attributes of the Deity.[x] He had a companion, His Helena.
Helena, according to the statement of his
enemies, a beautiful prostitute,[y] whom he found at Tyre,

---

[t] Origen denies the existence of
living Simonians in his day (Contra
Cels. lib. i.); which implies that they
had subsisted nearly up to that time.

[u] Irenæus, lib. i. c. 20; the fullest
of the early authorities on Simon.
Compare Grabe's notes. The personal
conflict with St. Peter in Rome, and the
famous inscription "Semoni Sanco,"
must, I think, be abandoned to legend.
That Simon was a heresiarch, and a

heresiarch of great power and wide
influence, not a mythical personage
created out of the passage in the Acts
of the Apostles, is further and still
more conclusively shown in the Sixth
Book of the Philosophumena.

[x] Ego sum Sermo Dei, ego sum
Speciosus, ego Paracletus, ego Om-
nipotens, ego omnia Dei. Hieronym.
in Matth. Op. iv. 114.

[y] Irenæus, as above.

who became in like manner the first conception (the
Ennœa) of the Deity; but who, by her conjunction with
matter, had been enslaved to its malignant influence,
and having fallen under the power of evil angels, had
been in a constant state of transmigration, and among
other mortal bodies, had occupied that of the famous
Helen of Troy. Beausobre,[z] who elevates Simon into a
Platonic philosopher, explains the Helena as a sublime
allegory. She was the Psyche of his philosophic romance. The soul, by evil influences, had become imprisoned in matter. By her the Deity had created the
angels: the angels, enamoured of her, had inextricably
entangled her in that polluting bondage, in order to
prevent her return to heaven. To fly from their embraces, she had passed from body to body. Connecting
this fiction with the Grecian mythology, she was Minerva, or impersonated Wisdom;[a] perhaps, also, Helena,
or embodied Beauty.[b]

It is by no means inconsistent with the character of
Orientalism, or with the spirit of the times, to reconcile
much of these different theories. According to the
Eastern system of teaching by symbolic action, Simon
may have carried about a living and real illustration of
his allegory: his Helena may have been to his disciples the mystic image of an Emanation from the
divine Mind; her native purity, indeed, originally

---

[z] Beausobre, Hist. du Manichéisme,
i. 35.

[a] His disciples worshipped two
statues : of Simon as Zeus, of Helen as
Athene. Εἰκόνα τε τοῦ Σίμωνος
ἔχουσιν εἰς Διὸς μορφήν, καὶ τῆς
Ἑλένης ἐν μορφῇ Αθηνᾶς, καὶ ταύτας
προσκυνοῦσι, τὸν μὲν καλοῦντες κύ-
ριον, τὴν δὲ κυρίαν. Philosophu-

mena, vi. p. 176.

[b] ἥτις ἀεὶ καταγινομένη ἐν γυναιξὶν
ἐτάρασσε τὰς ἐν κόσμῳ δυνάμεις
διὰ τὸ ἀνυπέρβλητον αὐτῆς κάλλος,
p. 174. The Trojan war seems to
have been held as a type of this strife
among the world-ruling angels, caused
by Helen.

defiled by the contagious malignity of matter, but under the guidance of the Hierophant, or rather by her sanctifying association with the "Power of God," either soaring again to her primal sanctity, or even while the grosser body was still abandoned to its inalienable corruption, emancipating the uninfected and unparticipant soul from all the depravation, almost from the consciousness, of corporeal indulgence. Be this as it *Probability* may; whether the opinions of Simon were *of the history* *of Simon.* derived from Platonism, or, as it is much more likely, immediately from Eastern sources, his history is singularly characteristic of the state of the public mind at this period of the world. A man assuming the lofty appellation of the Power of God, and, with his female associate, personating the male and female Energies or Intelligences of the Deity, appears to our colder European reason a fiction too monstrous even for the proverbial credulity of human kind. But this Magianism of Simon must be considered in reference to the whole theory of theurgy or magic, and the prevalent theosophy or notions of the divine nature. In the East, superstition had in general repudiated the grossly material forms in which the Western anthropomorphism had embodied its gods; it remained more spiritual, but it made up for this by the fantastic manner in which it multiplied the gradations of spiritual beings more or less remotely connected with the first great Supreme. The more subtile the spirits, in general they were the more beneficent; the more intimately associated with matter, the more malignant. The avowed object of Simon was to destroy the authority of the evil spirits, and to emancipate mankind from their control. This peopling of the universe with a regularly descending succession of beings was common to the whole East,

perhaps, in great part, to the West. The later Jewish
doctrine of angels and devils approached nearly to it; it
lurked in Platonism, and assumed a higher form in the
Eastern cosmogonies. In these it not merely assigned
guardian or hostile beings to individuals or to nations,
but its peculiar creator to the material universe, from
which it aspired altogether to keep aloof the origin and
author of the spiritual world; though the latter superior
and benignant Being was ordinarily introduced as interfering in some manner to correct, to sanctify, and to
spiritualise the world of man; and it was in accordance
with this part of the theory that Simon proclaimed
himself the representative of Deity. That such was the
Simonian doctrine, I think there can be no doubt; a
very small part, however, only its elementary notions,
can with any probability be traced to Simon himself.
He was but the remote parent of a numerous, wide-
spread, and inventive line of successors.[c]

---

[c] According to the Philosophumena,
Simon of Gettim in Samaria called
himself a god, in imitation of a certain
Apsethus, who in Libya trained some
parrots to say "Apsethus is a god,"
and then let them loose. They flew
abroad, all over Libya and as far as
Greece. He obtained divine worship.
But a clever Greek found out the trick,
caught some of the parrots, and taught
them to say, "Apsethus shut us up,
and taught us to say, 'Apsethus is a
god.'" He let them fly to Libya. Upon
which the Libyans burned Apsethus
as an impostor. This is an old story
told of Hanno the Carthaginian, Ælian,
Var. Hist., xiv. 30. Its introduction,
and the stress laid upon it by Hippolytus, do not give a very high notion
either of the learning or the fairness
of the "Refuter of Heresies." But
what is really curious and valuable in
the work is the citations from the
ἀπόφασις μεγάλη (the Great Announcement, the Scriptures, it may be
called, of the Simonian sect). Of the
existence of this book there can be no
doubt. That it was written by the
Simon Magus of the Acts, it were
utter absurdity to suppose. It may
have been the work of Dositheus or
Menander, or of both of them, the
true founders and inventors of Si-
monianism. Yet there can be no doubt
that it was accepted by Hippolytus as
the authentic work of Simon. The
chaos of opinions which it discloses
is almost inconceivable. Simon must
have been well read in Plato and
Aristotle, if not in Pythagoras (Hip-

But Simon, himself, was at no time a Christian; neither was the heir and successor of his doctrines, Me-

polytus everywhere discerns the influence, almost the exclusive influence, of Greek philosophy). He quotes the poet Empedocles. His Helena (he also allegorised the wooden horse) is derived from Homer and Stesichorus. He is equally familiar with the Old Testament (among other points he holds Fire to be the Primal Godhead; this he borrowed, according to Hippolytus, from the saying of Moses, "Our God is a consuming fire") and with the New; his Helena is the "lost sheep" of the Gospels. And we read the following strange parody, to our ears profane, on the great truths of Christianity: "As he had redeemed his Helena, so by his own wisdom (ἐπιγνώσεως, his Gnosis), he had brought salvation to the world. For the angels, through their ambition, having administered the world badly, He had come for the restoration of all things, metamorphosed and made equal to the Principalities and Powers, and to the Angels, so as to appear as a man, not being man, and to suffer seemingly in Judæa, though he did not suffer [with Bunsen, I erase the καὶ], and appeared to the Jews as the Son, in Samaria as the Father, among the Gentiles as the Holy Ghost. But he permitted himself to be called by any name by which men chose to call him. The Prophets, he avers, altered their prophecies inspired by the angels who created the world [the evil Demiurge], whom therefore the believers in Simon and Helena do not regard, but assert their own perfect freedom. For they say that they are saved by his grace [the grace of Simon]." (Bunsen,

by one of his arbitrary decisions, to my judgement in contradiction to the whole text, supposes all this to be the Simonian description of our Saviour, Jesus, not that of Simon.)

Indeed, the most remarkable part of this doctrine is its strong opposition to that of the Clementine Homilies. Here throughout Simon is the Saviour; he is the Christ, he that hath stood, that stands, that will stand (Hippolytus would show that he is not the Saviour) ὅτι χριστὸς οὐκ ἦν Σίμων, ὁ ἐστὼς, στὰς, στησόμενος, p. 162.

In the Acts we read that Simon's followers said "this man is the great Power of God" (δυνάμις τοῦ Θεοῦ ἡ μεγάλη), and according to all this system the great Power was the efflux of the Ineffable, Unapproachable, Unknown Godhead, the Redeemer of the materialised souls of men. In the Clementines he is the Antagonist of St. Peter. Even in his end there is a singular peculiarity in the fable. Here, too, in Rome he is opposed to St. Peter. But instead of attempting to fly, as in the vulgar tradition (Apost. Const. vi. 9), and falling and breaking his neck, Simon offered to be buried alive, and declared that he would rise again on the third day. His disciples buried him in a deep trench, "but to this day," says Hippolytus, "they await his resurrection."

Neander dismisses Simon and the Simonians almost with contempt. The Philosophumena, I think, show that I am right in attaching more importance to these doctrines, as an early source and manifestation of Gnostic opinions.

E 2

nander;[d] and it was not till it had made some progress
in the Syrian and Asiatic cities, that Christianity came
into closer contact with those Gnostic, or pre-Gnostic,
systems, which, instead of opposing it with direct hostility, received it with more insidious veneration, and
warped it into an unnatural accordance with their own
principles. As the Jew watched the appearance of
Jesus, and listened to his announcement as the Messiah,
in anxious suspense, expecting that even yet He would
assume those attributes of temporal grandeur and
visible majesty which, according to his conceptions,
were inseparable from the true Messiah; as, even after
the death of Jesus, the Jewish Christians still eagerly
anticipated his immediate return to Judgement, his millennial reign, and his universal dominion: so many of

Gnosticism the Oriental speculatists, as soon as Chris-
connects
itself with tianity began to be developed, hailed it as the
Christianity. completion of their own wild theories, and
forced it into accordance with their universal tenet of
distinct intelligences emanating from the primal Being.
Thus Christ, who to the vulgar Jew was to be a temporal king, to the Cabalist or the Chaldean, or to
men of kindred opinions, became a Sephiroth, an
Æon, an emanation from the One Supreme. While
the author of the religion remained on earth, and while
the religion itself was still in its infancy, Jesus was in
danger of being degraded into a King of the Jews, his
Gospel of becoming the code of a new religious republic.[e] Directly it got beyond the borders of Pales-

---

[d] Menander baptized in his own
name, being *sent* by the *Supreme
Power of God.* His baptism conferred
a resurrection not only to eternal life,
but to eternal youth. An opinion, as

M. Matter justly observ s, not easily
reconcileable to those who considered
the body the unworthy prison of the
soul. Irenæus, i. 21. Matter, i. 219.
   [e] The Ebionites of Neander. Nean-

tine, and the name of Christ had acquired sanctity and
veneration in the Eastern cities, he became a kind of
metaphysical impersonation, while the religion lost its
purely moral cast, and assumed the character of a speculative theogony.

Ephesus is the scene of the first collision between
Christianity and Orientalism of which we can
trace any authentic record. Ephesus, I have   Ephesus.
before described as the great emporium of magic arts,
and the place where the unwieldy allegory of the East
lingered in the bosom of the more elegant Grecian
Humanism.[f] Here the Greek, the Oriental, the Jew,
the philosopher, the magician, the follower of John the
Baptist, the teacher of Christianity, were no doubt
encouraged to settle by the peaceful opulence of the
inhabitants, and the constant influx of strangers, under
the proudly indifferent protection of the municipal authorities and of the Roman Government.   In Ephesus, according to universal tradition, survived the last of the
Apostles ; and here the last of the Gospels—
some have supposed, I think rightly, the latest   St. John.
of the writings of the New Testament—appeared in the
midst of this struggle with the foreign elements of con-

---

der's chapter on the Ebionites and Na-
zarenes is excellent.   I acquiesce in his
explanation of Ebion (from the Hebrew
word אֶבְיוֹן, the poor) ; but instead
of taking the word, as Origen did, in
his allegoric vein, as a contemptuous
appellation from their poverty of doctrine, I would suppose that these re-
fugees, who fled during the war of
Titus and the war of Hadrian, and
stole back to Jerusalem, were poor as
compared with the Gentile Christians,

and the earlier Christians of Palestine
addressed by St. James in his Epistle,
" Go, to now, ye rich men."

[f] The Temple of Diana was the
triumph of pure Grecian architecture :
but her statue was not that of the
divine Huntress like that twin sister
of the Belvidere Apollo in the gallery
at Paris ; she was the Diana multi-
mamma, the emblematic impersonation of All-productive, All-nutritive
Nature.

flicting systems. This Gospel was written, I conceive,
not against any peculiar sect or individual, but
to arrest the spirit of Orientalism, which was
working into the essence of Christianity, destroying its
beautiful simplicity, and threatening altogether to
change both its design and its effects upon mankind.
In some points, it necessarily spoke the language, which
was common alike, though not precisely with the same
meaning, to the Platonism of the West and the Theo-
gonism of the East. But how different and peculiar its
sense! It kept the moral and religious, if not altogether distinct from the physical notions, yet clearly
and invariably predominant. While it appropriated
the well-known and almost universal term, the Logos,
or Word of God, to the divine author of Christianity,[g]
and even adopted some of the imagery from the hypothesis of conflicting light and darkness ; yet it altogether
rejected all the wild cosmogonical speculations on the
formation of the world ; it was silent on that elementary
distinction of the Eastern creed, the separation of matter
from the ethereal mind. The union of the soul with the
Deity, though in the writings of John it takes something of a mystic tone, is not the Pantheistic absorption
into the parent Deity ; it is an union by the aspiration
of the pious heart, the conjunction by pure and holy
love with the Deity, who, to the ecstatic moral affection
of the adorer, is himself pure love. It insists not on
abstraction from matter, but from sin, from hatred,
from all fierce and corrupting passions ; its new life is
active as well as meditative ; a social principle, which
incorporates together all pure and holy men, and con-
joins them with their federal head, Christ, the image

His Gospel.

---

[g] Compare Burton (Bampton Lectures), who fully admits this.

and representative of the God of Love; it is no principle of isolation in solitary and rapturous meditation;
it is a moral, not an imaginative purity.

Among the opponents to the holy and sublime Christianity of St. John, during his residence at Ephesus, the
names of the Nicolaitans and of Cerinthus
alone have survived.[h] Of the tenets of the *Nicolaitans.*
former, and the author of the doctrine, nothing precise
is known; but the indignant language with which they
are alluded to in the Sacred Writings implies that they
were not merely hostile to the abstract doctrines, but
also to the moral effects of the Gospel. Nor does
it appear quite clear that the Nicolaitans were a distinct
and organised sect.

Cerinthus was the first of whose tenets we have any
distinct statement, who, admitting the truth of
Christianity, attempted to incorporate with it *Cerinthus.*
foreign and Oriental tenets.[i] Cerinthus was of Jewish
descent, and educated in the Judæo-Platonic school of
Alexandria.[k] His system was a singular and, appa-

---

[h] General tradition derived the Nicolaitans from Nicolas, one of the
seven deacons. Acts vi. 5. Eusebius
(Eccl. Hist. l. iii. c. 29) relates a story
that Nicolas, accused of being jealous
of his beautiful wife, offered her in
matrimony to whoever chose to take
her. His followers, on this example,
founded the tenet of promiscuous concubinage. Wetstein, with whom Michaelis and Rosenmüller are inclined
to agree, supposed that Nicolas was a
translation of the Hebrew word Bi-
leam, both signifying, in their respective languages, the subduer or the
destroyer of the people. Michaelis,

Eichhorn, and Storr, suppose, therefore, that it was the name rather of a
sect than an individual, and the same
with those mentioned in 2 Pet. ii. 10,
13, 18; iii. 3; Jud. 8, 16. See Rosenmüller on Rev. ii. 6. The Philosophumena takes the popular view of the
Nicolaitans from Nicolas the deacon;
it is precisely the same view and in
the same words with Irenæus.

[i] See Mosheim, De Rebus ante C. M.,
p. 199. Matter, i. 221.

[k] Theodoret, ii. c. 3. This is expressed by the Philosophumena. It confirms also Neander's ingenious connexion
of the tenets with those of Philo.

rently, incongruous fusion of Jewish, Christian, and
Oriental notions. He did not, like Simon or Menander,
invest himself in a sacred and mysterious character,
though he pretended to angelic revelations.[m] Like all
the Orientals, his imagination was haunted with the
notion of the malignity of matter; and his object seems
to have been to keep both the primal Being and the
Christ uninfected with its contagion. The Creator of
the material world, therefore, was a secondary being—
an angel or angels; as Cerinthus seems to have adhered
to the Jewish, and did not adopt the Oriental language.[n]
But his national and hereditary reverence for the Law
withheld him from that bold and hostile step which was
taken by most of the other Gnostic sects, to which, no
doubt, the general animosity to the Jews in Syria and
Egypt concurred—the identification of the God of the
Jewish covenant with the inferior and malignant author
of the material creation. He retained, according to one
account, his reverence for the rites, the ceremonies, the
Law, and the Prophets,[o] of Judaism, to which he was
probably reconciled by the allegoric interpretations of
Philo. The Christ, in his theory, was of a higher order
than those secondary and subordinate beings who had
presided over the older world. But, with the jealousy
of all the Gnostic sects, lest the pure Emanation from
the Father should be unnecessarily contaminated by too
intimate a conjunction with a material and mortal form,
he relieved him from the degradation of a human birth,

---

[m] Eusebius, E. H. iii. 28, from
Caius the presbyter, τερατολογίας
ἡμῖν ὡς δι' ἀγγέλων αὐτῷ δεδειγμέ-
νας ψευδομενος.

[n] Epiphanii Hær. viii. 28. According to Irenæus, "a virtute quadam

valdè separatâ, et distante ab eâ prin-
cipalitate quæ est super universa et
ignorante eum qui est super omnia
Deum." Iren. i. 25.

[o] Inferior angels to those of the
Law inspired the Prophets.

by supposing that the Christ above descended on the
man Jesus at his baptism ; and from the ignominy of a
mortal death, by making him reascend before that
crisis, having accomplished his mission of making
known "the Unknown Father," the pure and primal
Being, of whom the worshippers of the Creator of the
material universe, and of the Jehovah of the Jews, were
alike ignorant. But the most inconsequential part of
the doctrine of Cerinthus was his retention of the Jewish
doctrine of the millennium. It must, indeed, have been
purified from some of its grosser and more sensual
images ; for the Christos, the immaterial Emanation
from the Father, was to preside during its long period of
harmony and peace.[P]

The later Gnostics were bolder but more consistent
innovators on the simple scheme of Chris- Later
tianity. It was not till the second century Gnostics.
that the combination of Orientalism with Christianity
was matured into the more perfect Gnosticism. This
was, perhaps, at its height from about the year 120 to
140. In all the great cities of the East, in which
Christianity had established its most flourishing communities, sprang up this rival, which aspired to a still
higher degree of knowledge than was revealed in the
Gospel, and boasted that it soared almost as much above
the vulgar Christianity as above the vulgar Paganism.
Antioch, where the first church of the Christians had
been opened, beheld the followers of Saturninus withdrawing, in a proud assurance of their superiority, from
the common brotherhood of believers, and insulating

[P] Cerinthus was considered by some
early writers the author of the Apocalypse, because that work appeared
to contain his grosser doctrine of the
millennial reign of Christ. Dionysius
apud Euseb. iii. 282 ; vii. 25.

themselves as the gifted possessors of still higher spiritual secrets.   Edessa, whose king very early Christian
fable had exalted into a personal correspondent with
the Saviour, rang with the mystic hymns of Bardesanes; to the countless religious and philosophical
factions of Alexandria were added those of Basilides
and Valentinus; until a still more unscrupulous and
ardent enthusiast, Marcion of Pontus, threw aside in
disdain the whole existing religion of the Gospel, remodelled the sacred books, and established himself as
the genuine hierophant of the real Christian mysteries.

Gnosticism, though very different from Christianity,
The primal was of a sublime and imposing character as
Deity of
Gnosticism. an imaginative creed, and not more unreason-
able than the other attempts of human reason to solve
the inexplicable secret, the origin of evil.   Though
variously modified, the systems of the different teachers
were essentially the same.   The primal Deity remained
aloof in his unapproachable majesty; the Unspeakable,
the Ineffable, the Nameless, the Self-existing.[q]   The
              Pleroma, the fulness of the Godhead, expanded
The Pleroma.
              itself in still outspreading circles, and ap-
proached, till it comprehended, the universe.   From
the Pleroma emanated all spiritual being, and to the
Pleroma all such being was to return and mingle again
in indissoluble unity.   By their entanglement in malign
and hostile matter—the source of moral as well as physical evil—all outwardly existing beings had degenerated

---

[q] The author of the Apostolic Constitutions asserts, as the first principle
of all the early heresies, τὸν μὲν
παντοκράτορα Θεὸν βλασφημεῖν,
ἄγνωστον δοξάζειν, καὶ μὴ εἶναι
Πατέρα τοῦ Χριστοῦ, μηδὲ τοῦ
κόσμου δημιουργὸν. ἀλλ' ἄλεκτον,
ἄῤῥητον, ἀκατονόμαστον, αὐτογένεθ-
λον. Lib. vi. c. 10.

from their high origin ; their redemption from this
foreign bondage, their restoration to purity and peace
in the bosom of Divinity, the universal harmony of all
immaterial existence, thus resolved again into the Pleroma, was the merciful design of the Æon The Æon
Christ, who had for this purpose invaded and Christ.
subdued the foreign and hostile provinces of the presiding Energy, or Deity, of matter.

In all the Oriental sects this primary principle, the
malignity of matter, haunted the imagination; Malignity of
and to this principle every tenet must be ac- matter.
commodated. The sublimest doctrines of the Old Testament—the creative omnipotence, the sovereignty, the
providence of God, as well as the grosser and anthropo-
morphic images, in which the acts and passions, and
even the form of man, are assigned to the Deity—fell
under the same remorseless proscription. It was pollu-
tion, it was degradation to the pure and elementary
spirit, to mingle with, to approximate, to exercise even
the remotest influence over, the material world. The
creation of the visible universe was made over, according
to all, to a secondary, with most, to a hostile Demiurge.
The hereditary reverence which had modified the opinions
of Cerinthus, with regard to the Jehovah of his fathers,
had no hold on the Syrian and Egyptian speculatists.
They fearlessly pursued their system to its consequences,
and the whole of the Old Testament was abandoned to
the inspiration of an inferior and evil dæmon ; the Jews
were left in exclusive possession of their national Deity,
whom the Gnostic Christians disdained to ac- Rejection of
knowledge as bearing any resemblance to the tament.
abstract, remote, and impassive Spirit. To them, the
mission of Christ revealed a Deity altogether unknown
in the dark ages of a world which was the creation and

the domain of an inferior being. They would not, like
the philosophising Jews, take refuge in allegory to
explain the too material images of the works of the
Deity in the act of creation, and his subsequent rest;
the intercourse with man in the garden of Eden; the
trees of knowledge and of life; the Serpent, and the
Fall. They rejected the whole as altogether extraneous
to Christianity, belonging to another world, with which
the God revealed by Christ had no concern or relation.
If they condescended to discuss the later Jewish history,
it was merely to confirm their preconceived notions.
The apparent investiture of the Jehovah with the state
and attributes of a temporal sovereign, the imperfection
of the Law; the barbarity of the people, the bloody wars
in which they were engaged; in short, whatever in
Judaism was irreconcileable with a purely intellectual
and morally perfect system, argued its origin from an
imperfect and secondary author.

But some tenets of primitive Christianity came no less
Of some   into direct collision with the leading principles
parts of the
New.   of Orientalism. The human nature of Jesus
was too deeply impressed upon all the Gospel history,
and perplexed the whole school, as well the precursors
of Gnosticism as the more perfect Gnostics. His birth
and death bore equal evidence to the unspiritualised
materialism of his mortal body. The Gnostics seized
with avidity the distinction between the divine and
human nature; but the Christ, the Æon, which emanated from the pure and primal Deity, as yet unknown
in the world of the inferior creator, must be relieved as
far as possible from the degrading and contaminating
association with the mortal Jesus. The simpler hypothesis of the union of the two natures, mingled too
closely, according to their views, the ill-assorted com-

panions. The human birth of Jesus, though guarded by the virginity of his mother, was still offensive to their subtler and more fastidious purity. The Christ, therefore, the Emanation from the Pleroma, descended upon the man Jesus at his baptism. The death of Jesus was a still more serious cause of embarrassment. They seem never to have entertained the notion of an expiatory sacrifice; and the connexion of the ethereal mind with the pains and sufferings of a carnal body, was altogether repulsive to their strongest prejudices. Before the death, therefore, of Jesus, the Christ had broken off his temporary association with the perishable body of Jesus, and surrendered it to the impotent resentment of Pilate and of the Jews; or, according to the theory of the Docetæ, adopted by almost all the Gnostic sects, the whole union with the material human form was an illusion upon the senses of men; it was but an apparent human being, an impassive phantom, which *seemed* to undergo all the insults and the agony of the cross.

Such were the general tenets of the Gnostic sects, emanating from one simple principle. But the details of their cosmogony, their philosophy, and their religion, were infinitely modified by local circumstances, by the more or less fanciful genius of their founders, and by the stronger infusion of the different elements of Platonism, Cabalism, or that which, in its stricter sense, may be called Orientalism. The number of circles, or emanations, or procreations, which intervened between the spiritual and the material world; the nature and the rank of the Creator of that material world; his more or less close identification with the Jehovah of Judaism; the degree of malignity which they attributed to the latter; the office and the nature of the Christos,—these were open points, upon which they admitted, or, at least, assumed, the utmost latitude.

The earliest of the more distinguished Gnostics is Saturninus, who is represented as a pupil of Menander, the successor of Simon Magus.[r] But this Samaritan sect was always in direct hostility with Christianity, while Saturninus departed less from the Christian system than most of the wilder and more imaginative teachers of Gnosticism. The strength of the Christian party in Antioch may in some degree have overawed and restrained the aberrations of his fancy. Saturninus did not altogether exclude the primal spiritual Being from all concern or interest in the material world. For the Creator of the visible universe, he assumed the seven great angels (which the later Jews had probably borrowed, though with different powers, from the seven Amschaspands of Zoroastrianism) or rather the Chief of these seven, who was the God of the Jews. Neither were these angels essentially evil, nor was the domain on which they exercised their creative power altogether surrendered to the malignity of matter; it was a kind of debateable ground between the powers of evil and of good. The historian of Gnosticism has remarked the singular beauty of the fiction regarding the creation of man. " The angels tried their utmost efforts to form man; but there arose under their creative influence only 'a worm creeping upon the earth.' God, condescending to interpose, sent down his Spirit, which breathed into the reptile the living soul of man." It is

---

[r] On Saturninus, see Irenæus, i. 22; Euseb. iv. 7; Epiphan. Hær. 23; Theodoret, Hær. Fab. lib. iii.; Tertullian, De Animâ, 23; De Præscrip. cont. Hær. c. 46. Of the moderns, Mosheim, p. 336; Matter, i. 276. He lived under Hadrian.

not quite easy to connect with this view of the origin
of man the tenets of Saturninus, that human kind
was divided into two distinct races, the good and the
bad. Whether the latter became so from receiving a
feebler and less influential portion of the divine Spirit,
or whether they were a subsequent creation of Satan,
who assumes the station of the Ahriman of the Persian
system, does not clearly appear.[s] But the descent of
Christ was to separate finally these two conflicting races.
He was to rescue the good from the predominant power
of the wicked; to destroy the kingdom of the spirits of
evil, who, emanating in countless numbers from Satan
their chief, waged a fatal war against the good; and to
elevate them far above the power of the chief of the
angels, the God of the Jews, for whose imperfect laws
were to be substituted the purifying principles of Asceticism, by which the children of light were reunited to
the source and origin of light. The Christ himself was
the Supreme Power of God, immaterial, incorporeal,
formless, but assuming the *semblance* of man; and his
followers were, as far as possible, to detach themselves
from their corporeal bondage, and assimilate themselves
to his spiritual being. Marriage was the invention of
Satan and his evil spirits, or at best, of the great Angel,
the God of the Jews, in order to continue the impure
generation. The elect were to abstain from propagating
a race of darkness and imperfection. Whether Saturninus, with the Essenes, maintained this total abstinence
as the especial privilege of the higher class of his followers, and permitted to the less perfect the continuation

---

[s] The latter opinion is that of
Mosheim. M. Matter, on the contrary,
says,—"Satan n'a pas pourtant créé
ces hommes, il les a trouvé tout faits,
il s'en est emparé; c'est là sa sphère
d'activité et la limite de sa puissance."
t. i. p. 285.

of their kind, or whether he abandoned altogether this
perilous and degrading office to the wicked, his system
appears incomplete, as it seems to yield up as desperate
the greater part of the human race; to perpetuate the
dominion of evil; and to want the general and final
absorption of all existence into the purity and happiness
of the primal Being.

Alexandria, the centre, as it were, of the speculative
and intellectual activity of the Roman world,
to which ancient Egypt, Asia, Palestine, and
Greece, furnished the mingled population of her streets,
and the conflicting opinions of her schools, gave birth
to the two succeeding and most widely disseminated
sects of Gnosticism, those of Basilides and Valentinus.

Basilides was a Syrian by birth, and by some is supposed to have been a scholar of Menander, at
the same time with Saturninus. He claimed,
however, Glaucias, a disciple of St. Peter, as his original
teacher; and his doctrines assumed the boastful title of
the Secret Traditions of the great Apostle.[t] He also had
some ancient prophecies, those of Cham and Barkaph,[u]
peculiar to his sect. According to another authority,
he was a Persian; but this may have originated from
the Zoroastrian cast of his primary tenets.[x] From the
Zendavesta, Basilides drew the eternal hostility of mind
and matter, of light and darkness; but the Zoroastrian
doctrine seems to have accommodated itself to the

---

[t] According to the Philosophumena,
the Basilidians professed to derive their
doctrines from the Apostle Matthias.

[u] Irenæus differs, in his view of the
Basilidian theory, from the remains of
the Basilidian books appealed to by
Clement of Alexandria, Strom. vi.

p. 375, 795; Theodoret, Hæret. Fabul.
1, 2; Euseb. E. H. iv. 7. Basilides
published twenty-four volumes of
Exegetica, or interpretations of his
doctrines.

[x] Clemens Alex., Stromata, vi. 642.
Euseb., H. E. iv. 7.

kindred systems of Egypt. In fact, the Gnosticism of
Basilides appears to have been a fusion of·the ancient
sacerdotal religion of Egypt with the angelic and dæmo-
niac theory of Zoroaster.[y] Basilides did not, it seems,
maintain his one abstract unapproachable Deity far
above the rest of the universe, but connected him, by a
long and insensible gradation of intellectual develop-
ments or manifestations, with the visible and material
world. From the Father proceeded seven beings, who
together with him made up an ogdoad; constituted the
first scale of intellectual beings, and inhabited the highest
heaven, the purest intellectual sphere. According to
their names—Mind, Reason, Intelligence (Φρόνησις),
Wisdom, Power, Justice, and Peace—they are merely,
in our language, the attributes of the Deity, impersonated
in this system.

The number of these primary Æons is the same as
the Persian system of the Deity and the seven Amschaspands, and the Sephiroth of the Cabala, and, pro-

---

[y] The Philosophumena enters at
some length into the doctrines of Basilides, and has, seemingly, many citations from his writings. Hippolytus,
as is his wont, traces the origin of
them to the Greek philosopher. According to the Philosophumena, the
primal Deity was so absolutely secluded from all beings as himself to
cease to be a being. Basilides went
on in his negation till he denied the
existence of God. It is a strange
passage, which Bunsen seems to me
to have eluded : Ἐπεὶ οὐδὲν ἦν, οὐχ
ὕλη, οὐκ οὐσία, οὐκ ἀνούσιον, οὐχ
ἁπλοῦν, οὐ σύνθετον, οὐ νοητὸν,
οὐκ ἀναίσθητον, οὐκ ἄνθρωπος, οὐκ

VOL. II.

ἄγγελος, οὐ θεὸς, οὐδὲ ὅλως τι τῶν
ὀνομαζόμενων ἢ δι᾽ αἰσθήσεως λαμ-
βανομένων ἢ νοητῶν πραγμάτων,
ἀλλ᾽ οὕτω λεπτομεροτόρως πάντων
ἁπλῶς περιγεγραμμένων, οὐκ ὤν
θεὸς

(ὃν Ἀριστοτέλης καλεῖ νόησιν νοήσεως,
οὗτοι δὲ οὐκ ὄντα)

ἀνοήτως, ἀναισθήτως, ἀβούλως,
ἀπροαιρέτως, ἀπαθῶς, ἀνεπιθυμήτως
κόσμον ἠθέλησε ποιήσαι (p. 58, in
Bunsen's Analecta. The first seems
to have been a purely intellectual or
metaphysical evolution. But this
Being, or no Being, contained within
itself the seed of the whole universe,
the Cosmos.

F

bably, as far as that abstruse subject is known, of the ancient Egyptian theology.[a]

The seven primary effluxes of the Deity went on producing and multiplying, each forming its own realm or sphere, till they reached the number of 365.[b] The total number formed the mystical Abraxas,[c] the legend

---

[a] See Matter, vol. ii. p. 5-37.

[b] It is difficult to suppose that this number, either as originally borrowed from the Egyptian theology, or as invented by Basilides, had not some astronomical reference. All this, observes Bunsen, is merely the mythological form of psychologic speculation, based upon the simple words of the Prologue and coupled with the imaginary astronomy of the ancient world. Bunsen goes on to describe exceedingly well the next process according to the Philosophumena : " It is stated in our extracts that the words, ' Let there be light,' produced the germ or seed of the world, which, adds Basilides, is the light that came into the world (John i.). The beauty of Divine goodness attracts the element of life in matter ; this Divine element Basilides calls the Sonship. There are three classes of Sonship. The most refined element flies by its own nature up to the Ineffable Father ; the second Sonship uses the Holy Spirit as a wing, but rises by its assistance to the paternal glory, from whence the Holy Spirit, being repulsed by the Ineffable (and attracted by matter), sinks into an intermediate state below the Ineffable (purely intellectual), but still above this earth (the mere psychical or animal). The essence of the life of this earth is concentrated in the Demiurgos, or Spirit of the material world, whose

Son (conscious realization ?) is much more elevated than himself. This material world in its brute resistance, in its blind hostility to the Divine formative and limiting power, is the evil principle." Christianity and Mankind, vol. i. p. 18. In the original of which this is the summary, there is much grace and fancy of imagery ; but how far are we from the simplicity of the Gospel, even from that part of St. John which borders most closely on the mystic ?

[c] Irenæus, i. 23. See in M. Matter, ii. 49, 54, the countless interpretations of this mysterious word. We might add others to those collected by his industry. M. Matter adopts, though with some doubt, the opinion of M. Bellerman and M. Munter. " Le premier de ces écrivains explique le mot d'Abraxas par le kopte, qui est incontestablement à l'ancienne langue d'Egypte ce que la grec moderne est au langage de l'ancienne Gréce. La syllable sadsch, que les Grecs ont dû convertir en σαξ, ou σας, ou σαζ, n'ayant pu exprimer la dernière lettre de cette syllable, que par les lettres X, Σ, ou Z, signifierait parole, et abrak béni, saint, adorable, en sorte que le mot d'Abraxas tout entier offrirait le sens de parole sacrée. M. Munter ne s'éloigne de cette interprétation, que pour les syllables abrak qu'il prend pour le mot kopte ' berra,'

which is found on so many of the ancient gems, the.
greater part of which are of Gnostic origin; though, as
much of this theory was from the doctrines of ancient
Egypt, not only the mode of expressing their tenets by
symbolic inscriptions, but even the inscription itself, may
be originally Egyptian.[d] The lowest of these worlds
bordered on the realm of matter. On this confine the
first confusion and invasion of the hostile elements took
place. At length the chief Angel of this sphere, on the
verge of intellectual being, was seized with a desire of
reducing the confused mass to order. With his assistant
angels, he became the Creator. Though the form was
of a higher origin, it was according to the idea of
Wisdom, who, with the Deity, was part of the first
and highest ogdoad. Basilides professed the most
profound reverence for Divine Providence; and in
Alexandria, the God of the Jews, softened off, as it
were, and harmonised to the philosophic sentiment by
the school of Philo, was looked upon in a less hostile
light than by the Syrian and Asiatic school. The East
lent its system of guardian angels, and the assistant
angels of the Demiurge were the spiritual rulers of the
nations, while the Creator himself was that of the Jews.
Man was formed of a triple nature: his corporeal
form of brute and malignant matter; his animal soul,
the Psychic principle, which he received from the
Demiurge; the higher and purer spirit, with which he
was endowed from a loftier region. This pure and
ethereal spirit was to be emancipated from its impure

---

nouveau, ce qui donne à l'ensemble
le sens de *parole nouveau.*" Matter,
ii. 40.

[d] See, in the supplement to M.
Matter's work, a very curious collec-

tion of these Egyptian and Egypto-
Grecian medals; and a work of Dr.
Walsh on these coins. Compare, likewise, Reuven's Lettres à M. Letronne,
particularly p. 23.

companionship: and Egypt, or rather the whole East, lent the doctrine of the transmigration of souls, in order to carry this stranger upon earth through the gradations of successive purification, till it was readmitted to its parent heaven.

Basilides, in the Christian doctrine which he interwove with this imaginative theory, followed the usual Gnostic course.[e] The Christ, the first Æon of the Deity, descended on the man Jesus at his baptism; but, by a peculiar tenet of their own, the Basilidians rescued even the man Jesus from the degrading sufferings of the cross. Simon the Cyrenian was changed into the form of Jesus; on him the enemies of the Crucified wasted their wrath, while Jesus stood aloof in the form of Simon, and mocked their impotent malice. Their moral perceptions must have been singularly blinded by their passion for their favourite tenet, not to discern how much they lowered their Saviour by making him thus render up an innocent victim as his own substitute.

Valentinus appears to have been considered the most formidable and dangerous of this school of Gnostics.[f] He was twice excommunicated, and twice received again into the bosom of the Church. He did not confine his dangerous opinions to the school of Alexandria; he introduced the wild Oriental speculations into the more peaceful West; taught at Rome; and, a third time being expelled from the Christian society, retired to Cyprus, an island where the Jews

Valentinus.

---

[e] Irenæus, i. 29, compared with the other authors cited above.

[f] Irenæus, Hær. v. Clemens. Alex., Strom. Origen, De Princip. contra Celsum. The author of the Didascalia Orientalis, at the end of the works of Clement of Alexandria. Tertullian adversus Valentin. Theodoret, Fab. Hær. i. 7. Epiphanius, Hær. 31. Philosophumena, p. 177, et seqq. Bunsen's Analecta, vol. i. p. 79-96.

were formerly numerous till the fatal insurrection in the time of Hadrian; and where probably the Oriental philosophy might not find an unwelcome reception, on the border, as it were, of Europe and Asia.[g]

Valentinus annihilated the complexity of pre-existing heavens, which, perhaps, connected the system of Basilides with that of ancient Egypt, and did not interpose the same infinite number of gradations between the primal Deity and the material world. He descended much more rapidly into the sphere of Christian images and Christian language, or rather, he carried up many of the Christian notions and terms, and enshrined them in the Pleroma, the region of spiritual and inaccessible light. The fundamental tenet of Orientalism, the Incomprehensibility of the Great Supreme, was the essential principle of his system, and was represented in terms pregnant with mysterious sublimity. The first Father, the Monad, was called Bythos, the Abyss, the Depth, the Unfathomable, who dwelt alone in inscrutable and ineffable height, with his own first Conception, his Ennoia, who bore the emphatic and awful name of Silence.[h] The first development took place after endless ages, in which the Unfathomable dwelt in his majestic solitude, but he found not delight in his solitude. Love was his motive. Love must have an object—something to love.[i]

---

[g] Tertull. advers. Valentin., c. 4. Epiphan. Massuet. (Diss. in Iren. p. x. 14) doubts this part of the history of Valentinus.

[h] According to Hippolytus (vi. 29-30) the strict Valentinians did not allow that Sigè was to be reckoned as Sizygos, but they maintained that Bythos alone produced the Æons; and this appears to have been the doctrine of Valentinus. Rossel's Picture of the Valentinian System. Bunsen, i. 143.

[i] Φιλέρημος γὰρ οὐκ ἦν. Ἀγάπη γὰρ, φησὶν, ἦν ὅλος, ἡ δὲ ἀγάπη οὐκ ἔστιν ἀγάπη, ἐὰν μὴ ᾖ τὸ ἀγαπώμενον. Philosophumena, p. 184. Hippolytus traces all Valentinianism to Pythagoras and the Timæus of Plato.

This development or self-manifestation was Mind (Nous), whose appropriate consort was Aletheia or Truth. These formed the first great quaternion, the highest scale of being. From Mind and Truth proceeded the Word and Life (Logos and Zöe); their manifestations were Man and the Church, Anthropos and Ecclesia, and so the first ogdoad was complete. From the Word and Life proceeded ten more Æons; but these seem, from their names, rather qualities of the Supreme; at least the five masculine names, for the feminine appear to imply some departure from the pure elementary and unimpassioned nature of the primal Parent. The males are—Buthios, profound, with his consort Mixis, conjunction; Ageratos, that grows not old, with Henosis or union; Autophyes, self-subsistent, with Hedone, pleasure; Akinetos, motionless, with Syncrasis, commixture; the Only Begotten and Blessedness. The offspring of Man and the Church were twelve, and in the females we seem to trace the shadowy prototypes of the Christian graces:—the Paraclete and Faith; the Paternal and Hope; the Maternal and Charity; the Ever-intelligent and Prudence; Ecclesiasticos (a term apparently expressive of church union) and Eternal Happiness; Will and Wisdom (Theletos and Sophia).

These thirty Æons dwelt alone within the sacred and inviolable circle of the Pleroma: they were all, in one sense, manifestations of the Deity, all purely intellectual, an universe apart. But the peace of this metaphysical hierarchy was disturbed; and here we are presented with a noble allegory, which, as it were, brings these abstract conceptions within the reach of human sympathy. The last of the dodecarchy which sprang from Man and the Church was Sophia or

Wisdom. Without intercourse with her consort Will, Wisdom was seized with an irresistible passion for that knowledge and intimate union with the primal Father, the Unfathomable, which was the sole privilege of the first-born, Mind. She would comprehend the Incomprehensible : love was the pretext, but temerity the motive. Pressing onward under this strong impulse, she would have reached the remote sanctuary, and would finally have been absorbed into the primal Essence, had she not encountered Horus (the impersonated boundary between knowledge and the Deity). At the persuasion of this "limitary cherub" (to borrow Milton's words), she acknowledged the incomprehensibility of the Father, returned in humble acquiescence to her lowlier sphere, and allayed the passion begot of Wonder. But the harmony of the intellectual world was destroyed; a redemption, a restoration, was necessary; and (for now Valentinus must incorporate the Christian system into his own) from the first Æon, the divine Mind, proceeded Christ and the Holy Ghost. Christ communicated to the listening Æons the mystery of the imperishable nature of the Father, and their own procession from him; the delighted Æons commemorated the restoration of the holy peace, by each contributing his most splendid gift to form Jesus, encircled with his choir of angels.[k]

Valentinus did not descend immediately from his

---

[k] Each Æon took the best that he possessed, and with these they formed a happy image to the praise of the Heavenly Father, who is also called Saviour (Soter), and Christos and Logos, and the Whole, because he bears within him the flower of everything; and they surrounded him with ministering angels to be his companions. Rossel in Bunsen, p. 149. According to Hippolytus (Bunsen adds in a note), this ideal Christ Jesus is also called Logos, but distinct from the Logos of the inmost Divine sphere, called the heavenly Logos.

domain of metaphysical abstraction; he interposed an
intermediate sphere between that and the material
world. The desire or passion of Sophia, impersonated,
became an inferior Wisdom; she was an outcast from
the Pleroma, and lay floating in the dim and formless
chaos without. The Christos in mercy gave her form
and substance; she preserved, as it were, some fragrance
of immortality. Her passion was still strong for higher
things, for the light which she could not apprehend;
and she incessantly attempted to enter the forbidden
circle of the Pleroma, but was again arrested by Horus,
who uttered the mystic name of Jao. Sadly she returned to the floating elements of inferior being; she
was surrendered to Passion, and with his assistance
produced the material world. The tears which she
shed, at the thought of her outcast condition, formed
the humid element; her smiles, when she thought of
the region of glory, the light; her fears and her sorrows,
the grosser elements. Christ descended no more to her
assistance, but sent Jesus, the Paraclete, the Saviour,
with his angels; and with his aid, all substance was
divided into material, animal, and spiritual. The spiritual, however, altogether emanated from the light of
her divine assistant; the first formation of the animal
(the Psychic) was the Demiurge, the Creator, the
Saviour, the Father, the king of all that was consubstantial with himself, and finally, the material, of which
he was only the Demiurge or Creator. Thus were
formed the seven intermediate spheres, of which the
Demiurge and his assistant angels (the seven again of
the Persian system), with herself, made up a second
Ogdoad—the image and feeble reflection of the former;
Wisdom representing the primal Parent; the Demiurge
the divine Mind, though he was ignorant of his mother,

more ignorant than Satan himself; the other sidereal angels, the rest of the Æons. By the Demiurge the lower world was formed.

Mankind consisted of three classes: the spiritual, who are enlightened with the divine ray from Jesus; the animal or psychic, the offspring and kindred of the Demiurge; the material, the slaves and associates of Satan, the prince of the material world. They were represented, as it were, by Seth, Abel, and Cain. This organisation or distribution of mankind harmonised with tolerable facility with the Christian scheme. But by multiplying his spiritual beings, Valentinus embarrassed himself in the work of redemption or restoration of this lower and still degenerating world. With him, it was the Christos, or rather a faint image and reflection (for all his intelligences multiplied themselves by this reflection of their being), who passed through the material form of the Virgin, like water through a tube. It was Jesus who descended upon the Saviour at his baptism, in the shape of a dove; and Valentinus admitted the common fantastic theory with regard to the death of Jesus. At the final consummation, the latent fire would burst out (here Valentinus admitted the theory common to Zoroastrianism and Christianity) and consume the very scoria of matter; the material men, with their prince, would utterly perish in the conflagration. Those of the animal, the Psychic, purified by the divine ray imparted by the Redeemer, would, with their parent, the Demiurge, occupy the intermediate realm; there were the just men made perfect; while the great mother, Sophia, would at length be admitted into the Pleroma or intellectual sphere.

Gnosticism was pure poetry, and Bardesanes was the

poet of Gnosticism.[m] For above two centuries, the hymns of this remarkable man, and those of his son

Bardesanes.

Harmonius, enchanted the ears of the Syrian Christians, till they were expelled by the more orthodox raptures of Ephraem the Syrian. Among the most remarkable circumstances relating to Bardesanes, who lived at the court of Abgar, king of Edessa, was his inquiry into the doctrines of the ancient Gymnosophists of India, which thus connected, as it were, the remotest East with the great family of religious speculatists; yet the theory of Bardesanes was more nearly allied to the Persian or the Chaldean; and the language of his poetry was in that fervent and amatory strain which borrows the warmest metaphors of human passion to kindle the soul to divine love.[n]

Bardesanes deserved the glory, though he did not suffer the pains, of martyrdom. Pressed by the philosopher Apollonius, in the name of his master, the Emperor Verus, to deny Christianity, he replied, " I fear not death, which I shall not escape by yielding to the wishes of the Emperor." Bardesanes had opposed with vigorous hostility the system of Marcion;[o] he afterwards appears to have seceded, or, outwardly conforming, to have aspired in private to become the head

---

[m] Valentinus, according to Tertullian, wrote psalms (De Carne Christi, c. 20); his disciple Marcus explained his system in verse, and introduced the Æons as speaking. Compare Hahn, p. 26. Bardesanes wrote 150 psalms, the number of those of David.

The reader who is curious to follow out a more complete development of Valentinianism may well consult the disquisition of Rossel (a promising pupil of Neander, who died early) in Bunsen, i. p. 142. It is of course far more full, perhaps occasionally fancifully full, than my outline, which, however, I think shows almost the essential perils of the doctrine.

[n] Theodoret, Hæret. Fab. 209.

[o] According to Eusebius, E. H. v. 38, Bardesanes approached much nearer to orthodoxy, though he still " bore some tokens of the sable streams."

of another Gnostic sect, which, in contradistinction to those of Saturninus and Valentinus, may be called the Mesopotamian or Babylonian. With him, the primal Deity dwelt alone with his consort, his primary thought or conception. Their first offsprings, Æons, or Emanations, were Christ and the Holy Ghost, who, in his system, was feminine, and nearly allied to the Sophia, or Wisdom, of other theories ; the four elements,—the dry earth, and the water, the fire, and the air,—who make up the celestial Ogdoad. The Son and his partner, the Spirit or Wisdom, with the assistance of the elements, made the worlds, which they surrendered to the government of the seven planetary spirits and the sun and moon, the visible types of the primal union. Probably these, as in the other systems, made the second Ogdoad ; and these, with other astral influences, borrowed from the Tsabaism of the region, the twelve signs of the zodiac, and the thirty-six Decani, as he called the rulers of the 360 days, governed the world of man. And here Bardesanes became implicated with the eternal dispute about destiny and freewill, on which he wrote a separate treatise, and which entered into and coloured all his speculations.[p] But the Wisdom which was the consort of the Son was of an inferior nature to that which dwelt with the Father. She was the Sophia Achamoth, and, faithless to her spiritual partner, she had taken delight in assisting the Demiurge in the creation of the visible world ; but in all her wanderings and estrangement, she felt a constant and

---

[p] He seems to have had an esoteric and an exoteric doctrine. Hahn, p. 22, on the authority of St. Ephrem. Compare Hahn, Bardesanes Gnosticus Sy- rorum primus Hymnologus. Much of this bears close analogy to Valentinianism.

impassioned desire for perfect reunion with her first
consort. He assisted her in her course of purification ;
revealed to her his more perfect light, on which she
gazed with reanimating love ; and the second wedding
of these long estranged powers, in the presence of the
parent Deity, and all the Æons and angels, formed the
subject of one of his most ardent and rapturous hymns.
With her, arose into the Pleroma those souls which
partook of her celestial nature, and are rescued, by the
descent of the Christ, according to the usual Gnostic theory, from their imprisonment in the world of matter.

Yet all these theorists preserved some decent show
of respect for the Christian faith, and aimed at an
amicable reconciliation between their own wild theories
and the simpler Gospel. It is not improbable that
most of their leaders were actuated by the ambition of
uniting the higher and more intellectual votaries of the
older Paganism with the Christian community ; the one
by an accommodation with the Egyptian, the others,
with the Syrian or Chaldean, as, in later times, the
Alexandrian school, with the Grecian or Platonic Paganism ; and expected to conciliate all who would not
scruple to engraft the few tenets of Christianity which
they preserved inviolate upon their former belief. They
aspired to retain all that was dazzling, vast, and imaginative in the cosmogonical systems of the East, and
rejected all that was humiliating or offensive to the
common sentiment in Christianity. The Jewish character of the Messiah gave way to a purely immaterial
notion of a celestial Redeemer ; the painful realities of
his life and death were softened off into fantastic appear-
ances ; they yet adopted as much of the Christian language as they could mould to their views, and even
disguised or mitigated their contempt for, or animosity

to, Judaism. But Marcion of Pontus [q] disclaimed all these conciliatory and temporising measures, either with Pagan, Jew, or evangelic Christian.[r] With Marcion, all was hard, cold, implacable antagonism. At once a severe rationalist and a strong enthusiast, Marcion pressed the leading doctrine of the malignity of matter to its extreme speculative and practical consequences. His Creator, his providential Governor, the God of the Jews,—weak, imperfect, enthralled in matter,—was the opposite to the true God. The only virtue of men was the most rigid and painful abstinence. Marcion's doctrine interdicted all animal food but fish; it surpassed the most austere of the other Christian communities in its proscription of the amusements and pleasures of life; it rejected marriage, from hostility to the Demiurge, whose kingdom it would not increase by peopling it with new beings enslaved to matter, to glut death with food.[s] The fundamental principle of Marcion's doctrine was unfolded in his Antitheses, the Contrasts, in which he arrayed against each other the Supreme God and the Demiurge the God of the Jews, the Old and New Testament, the Law and the Gospel.[t] The one was perfect, pure, beneficent,

Marcion of Pontus.

---

[q] Marcion was son of the Bishop of Sinope.

[r] On Marcion, see chiefly the five books of Tertullian adv. Marcion; the Historians of Heresies, Irenæus, i. 27; Epiphanius, 42; Theodoret, i. 24; Origen contra Cels.; Clem. Alex. iii. 425; St. Ephrem, Orat. 14, p. 468.

[s] ᾧ δὴ λογῷ μὴ βουλόμενοι τὸν κοσμὸν τὸν ὑπὸ τοῦ Δημιούργου γενομενὸν συμπληροῦν, ἀπέχεσθαι γάμου βούλονται. — Clem. Alex.

Strom. iii. 3. μηδὲ ἀντεισάγειν τῷ κοσμῷ δυστυχήσοντας ἑτέρους, μηδὲ ἐπιχορηγεῖν τῷ θανατῷ τρόφην. Ch. vi.

[t] Opus ex contrarietatum oppositionibus, *Antitheses*, cognominatum, et ad separationem legis et evangelii coactum; qua duos Deos dividens, proinde diversos, alterum alterius instrumenti vel quod magis est usui dicere, *testamenti* ut exinde evangelio quoque secundum Antitheses cre-

passionless; the other, though not unjust by nature, infected by matter, — subject to all the passions of man,—cruel, changeable; the New Testament, especially, as remodelled by Marcion, was holy, wise, amiable; the Old Testament, the Law, barbarous, inhuman, contradictory, and detestable. On the plundering of the Egyptians, on the massacre of the Canaanites, on every metaphor which ascribed the actions and sentiments of men to the Deity, Marcion enlarged with contemptuous superiority and contrasted it with the tone of the Gospel. It was to rescue mankind from the tyranny of this inferior and hostile deity, that the Supreme manifested himself in Jesus Christ. This manifestation took place by his sudden appearance in the synagogue in Capernaum; for Marcion swept away with remorseless hand all the earlier incidents in the Gospels. But the Messiah which was revealed in Christ was directly the opposite to that announced by the Prophets of the Jews, and of their God. He made no conquests; he was not the Immanuel; he was not the son of David; he came not to restore the temporal kingdom of Israel. His doctrines were equally opposed: he demanded not an eye for an eye, or a tooth for a tooth; but where one smote the right cheek, to turn the other. He demanded no sacrifices but that of the pure heart; he enjoined not the sensual and indecent practice of multiplying the species; he proscribed marriage. The God of the Jews, trembling for his authority, armed himself against the celestial invader of his territory; he succeeded, in the *seeming*

---

dendo patrocinaretur. Tertull. adv. Marc. iv. 1.

Marcion is accused by Rhodon, apud

Euseb. H. E. v. 13, of introducing two principles,—the Zoroastrian theory.

execution of Christ upon the cross, who, by his death, rescued the souls of the true believers from the bondage of the Law; descended to the lower regions, where he rescued, not the pious and holy patriarchs, Abel, Enoch, Noah, Jacob, Moses, David, or Solomon,—these were the adherents of the Demiurge or material creator,—but his implacable enemies, such as Cain and Esau. After the ascension of the Redeemer to heaven, the God of the Jews was to restore his subjects to their native land; and his temporal reign was to commence over his faithful but inferior subjects.[u]

The Gospel of Marcion was that of St. Luke, adapted, by many omissions, and some alterations, to his theory. Every allusion to, every metaphor from, marriage was carefully erased, and every passage amended or rejected which could in any way implicate the pure deity with the material world.[x]

---

[u] I adhere to this somewhat harsher and less charitable summary of Marcionism. The milder view of Neander, in which he had mitigated or softened off its harder tones, has been carried by Bunsen almost to admiration. I cannot think that a mere exaggeration of the Anti-Judaizing Pauline doctrines could have goaded even Tertullian to such a fury of orthodox hatred. I am well aware that contemporary statements, when the writers are full of the passions of their times, are the worst authorities. But Tertullian wrote with the Antitheses, probably with Marcion's Gospel, before him. The fragment of Hippolytus throws no light on the question. Of all the positive paradoxes of my dear friend, I confess that none seems to me so entirely baseless as his ascription of the Epistle to Diognetus, that model of pure, simple, reasonable Christianity, which stands alone in that barren and fantastic age, to the youth of Marcion. I cannot conceive the writer of that Epistle ever having become the author of the Antitheses. But one who has really made such discoveries, as Bunsen has in early Christian literature, may be indulged in some fancies.

[x] This Gospel has been put together, according to the various authorities, especially Tertullian, by M. Hahn. It is reprinted in the Codex Apocryphus Novi Testamenti, by Thilo, of which one volume only has appeared. Among the remarkable alterations of the Gospels which most strongly characterise his system, was that of the text so beautifully descriptive of the providence of God,—which

These were the chief of the Gnostic sects; but they
spread out into almost infinitely diversified
subdivisions, distinguished by some peculiar
tenet or usage. The Carpocratians were avowed Eclec-
tics; they worshipped, as benefactors of the human race,
the images of Zoroaster, Pythagoras, Plato, Aristotle,
and Jesus Christ, as well as that of their own founder.
By this school were received, possibly were invented,
many of the astrologic or theurgic books attributed to
Zoroaster and other ancient sages. The Jewish Scriptures were the works of inferior angels; of the Christian,
they received only the Gospel of St. Matthew. The
supreme, unknown, uncreated Deity, was the Monad;
the visible world was the creation, the domain of inferior
beings. But the Carpocratian system was much simpler, and, in some respects, rejecting generally the
system of Æons or Emanations, approached much nearer
to Christianity than those of most of the other Gnostics.
The contest of Jesus Christ, who was the son of Joseph,
according to their system, was a purely moral one.
Their scheme revived the Oriental notion of the pre-
existence of the soul. The soul of Jesus had a clearer
and more distinct reminiscence of the original knowledge (the Gnosis) and wisdom of their celestial state;
and by communicating these notions to mankind, elevated them to the same superiority over the mundane
deities. This perfection consisted in faith and charity,
perhaps likewise in the ecstatic contemplation of the

" maketh his sun to shine on the evil
and the good, and sendeth rain on the
just and the unjust." Matt. v. 45.
The sun and the rain, those material
elements, were the slaves only of the
God of matter: the Supreme Deity
might not defile himself with the administration of their blessings. Tertull: adv. Marc. iv. 17. The exquisite Parable of the Prodigal Son was
thrown out. The feast at the end
accounts for its proscription.

Monad. Everything except faith and charity,—all good
works, all observances of human laws, which were established by mundane authority,—were exterior, and
more than indifferent. Hence, they were accused of
recommending a community of property, and of women,
—inferences which would be drawn from their avowed
contempt for all human laws. They were accused,
probably without justice, of following out these speculative opinions into practice. Of all heretics, none have
borne a worse name than the followers of Carpocrates
and his son and successor, Epiphanes.[y]

The Ophites[z] are, perhaps, the most perplexing of all
these sects. It is difficult to ascertain whether the
Serpent from which they took or received their name
was a good or an evil spirit—the Agatho-dæmon of the
Egyptian mythology, or the Serpent of the Jewish and
other Oriental schemes. With them, a quaternion seems
to have issued from the primal Being, the Abyss, who
dwelt alone with his Ennoia, or Thought. These were
Christ and Sophia Achamoth, the Spirit and Chaos.
The former of each of these powers was perfect, the
latter imperfect. Sophia Achamoth, departing from
the primal source of purity, formed Ialdabaoth, the

---

[y] I think that we may collect from
Clement of Alexandria, that the community of women, in the Carpocratian
system, was that of Plato. Clement
insinuates that it was carried into
practice. Strom. iii. c. 2. According
to Clement, the different sects, or
sects of sects,· justified their immo-
ralities on different pleas. Some, the
Prodician Gnostics, considered public
prostitution a mystic communion ;
others, that all children of the primary
or good Deity might exercise their
regal privilege of acting as they pleased ;
some, the Antitactæ, thought it right
to break the Seventh Commandment,
because it was uttered by the evil
Demiurge. But these were obscure
sects, and possibly their adversaries
drew these conclusions for them from
their doctrines. Strom. l. iii.

[z] Mosheim, p. 399, who wrote a
particular dissertation on the Ophitæ,
of which he distinguished two sects, a
Jewish and a Christian.

Prince of Darkness, the Demiurge, an inferior, but not directly malignant, being—the Satan, or Samaël, or Michael. The tutelar angel of the Jews was Ophis, the Serpent—a reflection of Ialdabaoth. With others, the Serpent was the symbol of Christ himself; [a] and hence the profound abhorrence with which this obscure sect was beheld by the more orthodox Christians. In other respects, their opinions appear to have approximated more nearly to the common Gnostic form. At the intercession of Sophia, Christ descended on the man Jesus, to rescue the souls of men from the fury of the Demiurge, who had imprisoned them in matter: they ascended through the realm of the seven planetary angels.[b]

---

[a] M. Matter conjectured that they had derived the notion of the beneficent serpent, the emblem or symbol of Christ, from the brazen serpent in the wilderness. Perhaps it was the Egyptian Agatho-dæmon. M. Matter's notion was right to a certain extent as to one sect of the Ophites, the Peratæ. See Philosophumena, p. 133.

[b] On the Ophites alone, the Refutation of all Heresies promises to enlarge our knowledge; to me that promise has ended, on examination, in utter disappointment; it is darkness darkened, confusion worse confounded. Hippolytus devotes a whole book, which we have nearly perfect, to the tenets of four sects of Ophites. None of them agrees with what has been gathered from other sources, as appears from the text, which I leave unaltered. These sects are, the Naassenes, the Peratæ, the Sethians, the Justinians. Through all these run some common notions, the blending of in-

tellectual, physical, moral conceptions; their perpetual impersonation; the evolution of the creative mind; the imprisonment of mind in matter, its emancipation from its bondage; the forcible blending up of the Christian tenets concerning Christ and the Holy Ghost with these repugnant and discordant schemes. (The Serpent appears in all the four systems, but with a different character and office.) All delight in their triple form of thought, the intellectual (the $\nu o \epsilon \rho \grave{o} \nu$), the life (the $\psi \nu \chi \iota \kappa \grave{o} \nu$), the brute matter (the $\chi o \iota \kappa \grave{o} \nu$).

The Naassenes are so called from the Hebrew word Nahash, a serpent; and from Nahash they strangely derived the Greek $\nu a \acute{o} s$, a temple. Temples being universally raised throughout the world, showed the universality of Serpent-worship. With them the Serpent is the principle of moisture ($\dot{\eta}$ $\dot{\upsilon} \gamma \rho \dot{\eta}$) as with Thales the Milesian, the origin and source of all

Such, in its leading branches, was the Gnosticism of the East, which rivalled the more genuine Christianity, if not in the number of its converts, in the activity with which it was disseminated. It arose simultaneously or

things. Their great characteristic is the constant labour to identify Christianity with the Secret of all the Pagan Mysteries, Phrygian, Samothracian, Eleusinian. There is a wild confusion of the orgiastic superstition which prevailed so widely through the Roman world, the worship of Cybele, with that of Christ.

The Peratæ were distinguished (they were Orientals) by a predominant infusion of astrological notions. With them the Serpent was a sort of Intermediate Being, the Son, the Word, between the Father, the primal Monad, and Matter. Καθέζεται οὖν μέσος τῆς ὕλης καὶ τοῦ πατρὸς ὁ υἱὸς, ὁ λόγος, ὁ ὄφις ἀεὶ κινούμενος πρὸς ἀκίνητον τὸν πατέρα καὶ κινουμένην τὴν ὕλην.

With the Sethians the Serpent was the violent wind, which came out of darkness, the firstborn of the waters, and the generating principle of all things, specially of man. p. 142.

With the Justinians (this sect, of course, has no relation with 'Justin Martyr) the Serpent approaches more nearly to his function in the beginning of the book of Genesis.   But the seduction of Eve is in a coarser and grosser form (p. 155). The Serpent is also the Tempter of our Lord in the wilderness. p. 157.

I must say that throughout this book there is too much of Hippolytus, of the writer of the third century, proud of his knowledge of the Greek religion and the Greek philosophy. All these Ophites he would assume to be the earliest Gnostics (they first took the name), and so almost reaching up to the Apostolic times. But it is utterly incredible that there should have existed at that time any set of men who were equally familiar with the Old and New Testaments and the Greek poets; who appealed to the Pentateuch and the Gospels, and to Homer, Pindar, Anacreon; who had anticipated the identification of Christianity with the Secret of the Pagan Mysteries, of which they might almost seem to be the Hierophants; who had their mystic hymns in which the new and the old, the Oriental, and Greek and Christian notions, were blended and confused. Hippolytus appeals to, cites their writings, but of the age of those writings, I must presume to doubt his critical discernment.

Finally, I cannot think these smaller sects of any importance in Christian history, further than as testifying to that general fermentation of thought, that appetency for truth, that distressing and exciting want of satisfaction for the heart and soul and intellect of man, which Christianity found and stimulated to the utmost; from which it suffered to a certain extent, but from which it emerged, if not in all its primal purity, with unsubdued energy and force; by which it subjugated the world.

successively in all the great centres of Christianity, in Alexandria, in Antioch, in Edessa, in Ephesus. Many of its teachers—Valentinus, Marcion, and their followers—found their way to Rome. Their progress was especially among the higher and more opulent; and, in their lofty pretensions, they claimed a superiority over the humbler Christianity of the vulgar. But, for this very reason, Gnosticism, in itself, was diametrically opposite to the true Christian spirit: instead of being popular and universal, it was select and exclusive. It was another, in one respect a higher, form of Judaism, inasmuch as it did not rest its exclusiveness on the title of birth, but on especial knowledge (gnosis), vouchsafed only to the enlightened and inwardly designated few. It was the establishment of the Christians as a kind of religious privileged order, a theo-philosophic aristocracy, whose esoteric doctrines soared far above the grasp and comprehension of the vulgar.[c] It was a philosophy rather than a religion; at least the philosophic or speculative part would soon have predominated over the spiritual. They affected a profound and awful mystery; they admitted their disciples, in general, by slow and regular gradations. Gnostic Christianity, therefore, might have been a formidable antagonist to the prevailing philosophy of the times, but it would never have extirpated an ancient and deeply-rooted religion; it might have drained the schools of their hearers, but it never would have changed the temples into solitudes. It would have affected only the surface of society: it did not begin to work upward

Gnosticism not popular.

---

[c] Tertullian taunts the Valentinians —"nihil magis curant quam occultare quid prædicant, si tamen præ-dicant qui occultant." Tert. adv. Valent.

from its depths, nor did it penetrate to that strong under-current of popular feeling and opinion which alone operates a profound and lasting change in the moral sentiments of mankind.

With regard to Paganism, the Gnostics are accused of a compromising and conciliatory spirit, Conciliatory totally alien to that of primitive Christianity. Paganism. They affected the haughty indifference of the philosophers of their own day, or the Brahmins of India, to the vulgar idolatry ; scrupled not at a contemptuous conformity with the established worship ; attended the rites and the festivals of the Heathen ; partook of meats offered in sacrifice, and, secure in their own intellectual or spiritual purity, conceived that no stain could cleave to their uninfected spirits from this which, to most Christians, appeared a treasonable surrender of the vital principles of the faith.

This criminal compliance of the Gnostics, no doubt, countenanced and darkened those charges of unbridled licentiousness of manners with which they are almost indiscriminately assailed by the early Fathers. Those dark and incredible accusations of midnight meetings, where all the restraints of shame and of nature were thrown off, which Pagan hostility brought against the general body of the Christians, were reiterated by the Christians against these sects, whose principles were those of the sternest and most rigid austerity. They are accused of openly preaching the indifference of human action. The material nature of man was so essentially evil and malignant, that there was no necessity, as there could be no advantage, in attempting to correct its inveterate propensities. While, therefore, that nature might pursue, uncontrolled, its own innate and inalienable propensities, the serene and uncontaminated spirit of those, at least, who were enlightened by the divine ray, might remain aloof, either unconscious of, or, at least, unparticipant in, the aberrations of its grovelling consort. Such general charges, it is equally unjust to believe, and impossible to refute. The dreamy indolence of mysticism is not unlikely to degenerate into voluptuous excess. The excitement of mental, has often a strong effect on bodily, emotion. The party of the Gnostics may have contained many whose passions were too strong for their principles, or who may have made their principles the slaves of their passions; but Christian Charity and sober historical criticism concur in rejecting these general accusations. The Gnostics were, mostly, imaginative, rather than practical, fanatics; they indulged a mental, rather than corporeal, licence. The Carpocratians have been exposed to the most obloquy. But, even in their case, the charitable doubts of dispassionate historical criticism are justified by those of an ancient writer, who declares his disbelief of any irreligious, lawless, or forbidden practices among these sectaries.[d]

It was the reaction, as it were, of Gnosticism, that produced the last important modification of Christianity, during the second century, the Montanism of Phrygia. But we have, at present, proceeded in our relation of the contest between Orientalism and Christianity so far

---

[d] Καὶ εἰ μὲν πράσσεται παρ' αὐτοῖς τὰ ἄθεά, καὶ ἔκθεσμα, καὶ ἀπειρημένα, ἐγὼ οὐκ ἂν πιστεύσαιμι. Irenæus, i. 24. The Philosphumena accuses the Simonians of following the example of their master, whose Helena was his mistress. They used a coarse phrase to excuse promiscuous concubinage. But all this must, I think, be accepted with much reservation, as well as their orgies.

beyond the period to which we conducted the contest with Paganism, that we reascend at once to the commencement of the second century. Montanism, however thus remotely connected with Gnosticism, stands alone and independent as a new aberration from the primitive Christianity, and will demand our attention in its influence upon one of the most distinguished and effective of the early Christian writers.

CHAPTER VI.

Christianity during the prosperous period of the Roman Empire.

WITH the second century of Christianity commenced
Roman Em-
perors at the
commence-
ment of the
second cen-
tury. the reign of another race of Emperors. Trajan,
Hadrian, and the Antonines, were men of larger
minds, more capable of embracing the vast empire, and of taking a wide and comprehensive
survey of the interests, the manners, and the opinions
of the various orders and races of men which reposed
under the shadow of the Roman sway. They were not,
as the first Cæsars, monarchs of Rome, governing the
other parts of the world as dependent provinces; but
sovereigns of the Western World, which had gradually
coalesced into one majestic and harmonious system.
Under the military dominion of Trajan, the Empire appeared to reassume the strength and enterprise of the
conquering Republic: he had invested the whole frontier
with a defence more solid and durable than the strongest
line of fortresses, or the most impregnable wall—the
terror of the Roman arms, and the awe of Roman discipline. If the more prudent Hadrian withdrew the
advanced boundaries of the empire, it seemed in the
consciousness of strength, disdaining the occupation of
wild and savage districts, which rather belonged to the
yet unreclaimed realm of barbarism, than were fit to be
incorporated in the dominion of civilisation. Even in
the East, the Euphrates appeared to be a boundary
traced by nature for the dominion of Rome. Hadrian

was the first emperor who directed his attention to the general internal affairs of the whole population of the empire. The spirit of jurisprudence prevailed during the reign of the Antonines; and the main object of the ruling powers seemed to be the uniting under one general system of law the various members of the great political confederacy. Thus, each contributed to the apparent union and durability of the social edifice. This period has been considered by many able writers, a kind of golden age of human happiness.[a] What, then, was the effect of Christianity on the general character of the times; and how far were the Christian communities excluded from the general felicity?

It was impossible that the rapid and universal progress of a new religion should escape the notice of minds so occupied with the internal as well as the external affairs of the whole empire. But it so happened (the Christian will admire in this singular concurrence of circumstances the overruling power of a beneficent Deity) that the moderation and humanity of the Emperors stepped in, as it were, to allay at this particular crisis the dangers of a general and inevitable collision

---

[a] This theory is most ably developed by Hegewisch. See the Translation of his Essay, by M. Solvet. Paris, 1834. The silence of history, that too faithful record in general of the folly and misery, of the wars and devastating conquests of mankind, may seem a full testimony to the happiness of the æra; but this silence is perhaps mainly due to other causes. In fact, there is, properly speaking, no history of the times; and even if there were what is ordinarily received as history, it might throw but dim light on the condition of the masses of mankind throughout the vast empire. Peace was undoubtedly in itself a blessing; but how much oppression, tyranny of the government over all, of class over class, may be hid under the smooth surface of peace! The vast, comprehensive, and age-enduring fabric of Roman jurisprudence, which began to rise at this time, bears nobler witness to the wisdom of the rulers, and to the distribution of equal justice, that best guard and guarantee of human happiness, over the whole empire.

with the temporal government. Christianity itself was just in that state of advancement in which, though it had begun to threaten, and even to make most alarming encroachments on the established Polytheism, it had not so completely divided the whole race of mankind, as to force the heads of the Polytheistic party, the official conservators of the existing order of things, to take violent and decisive measures for its suppression. The temples, though, perhaps, becoming less crowded, were in few places deserted; the alarm, though, perhaps, in many towns it was deeply brooding in the minds of the priesthood, and of those connected by zeal or by interest with the maintenance of Paganism, was not so profound or so general, as imperiously to require the interposition of the civil authorities. The milder or more indifferent character of the Emperor had free scope to mitigate or to arrest the arm of persecution. The danger was not so pressing but that it might be averted: that which had arisen thus suddenly and unexpectedly (so little were the wisest probably aware of the real nature of the revolution working in the minds of men) might die away with as much rapidity. Under an Emperor, indeed, who should have united the vigour of a Trajan and the political forethought of a Hadrian with the sanguinary relentlessness of a Nero, Christianity would have had to pass a tremendous ordeal. Now, however, the collision of the new religion with the civil power was only occasional, and, as it were, fortuitous; and in these occasional conflicts with the ruling powers, we constantly appear to trace the character of the reigning sovereign.

Of these emperors, Trajan possessed the most powerful and vigorous mind—a consummate general, a humane

Characters of the Emperors favourable to the advancement of Christianity.

but active ruler: Hadrian was the profoundest statesman, the Antonines the best men. The con-
duct of Trajan was that of a military sove- *Trajan Emperor from A.D. 98 to 116.*
reign, whose natural disposition was tempered
with humanity—prompt, decisive, never unnecessarily
prodigal of blood, but careless of human life if it appeared to stand in the way of any important design, or
to hazard that paramount object of the government, the
public peace. Hadrian was inclined to a more
temporising policy. The more the Roman *Hadrian Emperor from 117 to 138.*
Empire was contemplated as a whole, the more
the coexistence of multifarious religions might appear
compatible with the general peace. Christianity might,
in the end, be no more dangerous than the other foreign
religions, which had flowed, and were still flowing in,
from the East. The temples of Isis had arisen throughout the empire, but those of Jupiter or Apollo had not
lost their votaries: the Eastern mysteries, the Phrygian,
at a later period the Mithriac, had mingled, very little
to their prejudice, with the general mass of the prevailing
superstitions. The last characteristic of Christianity
which would be distinctly understood, was its invasive
and uncompromising spirit. The elder Anto- *Antoninus Pius Emperor from 138 to 161.*
ninus may have pursued from mildness of
character the course adopted by Hadrian from
policy. The change which took place during the reign
of Marcus Aurelius may be attributed to the circumstances of the time; though the pride of philosophy, as
well as the established religion, might begin to take the
alarm.

Christianity had probably spread with partial and
very unequal success in different quarters: its converts
bore in various cities or districts a very different proportion to the rest of the population. Nowhere, perhaps,

had it advanced with greater rapidity than in the northern provinces of Asia Minor, where the inhabitants
were of very mingled descent, neither purely Greek,
nor essentially Asiatic, with a considerable proportion
of Jewish colonists, chiefly of Babylonian or Syrian, not
of Palestinian origin. It is here, in the province of Bithynia, that Polytheism first discovered the deadly enemy which was under-
mining her authority. It was here that the
first cry of distress was uttered; and complaints of
deserted temples and less frequent sacrifices were brought
before the tribunal of the government. The memorable
correspondence between Pliny and Trajan is the most
valuable record of the early Christian history during
this period.[b]   It represents to us Paganism already
claiming the alliance of power to maintain its decaying
influence; Christianity proceeding in its silent course,
imperfectly understood by a wise and polite Pagan, yet
still with nothing to offend his moral judgement, except
its contumacious repugnance to the common usages of
society. This contumacy, nevertheless, according to the
recognised principle of passive obedience to the laws of
the Empire, was deserving of the severest punishment.
The appeal of Pliny to the supreme authority
for advice as to the course to be pursued with
these new, and, in most respects, harmless delinquents,
unquestionably implies that no general practice had yet

Christianity in Bithynia and the adjacent provinces. A.D. 111, or 112.

Letter of Pliny.

---

[b] The chronology of Pagi (Critica
in Baronium) appears to me the most
trustworthy as to the date of Pliny's
letter ; so too, in opposition to Mr.
Fynes Clinton, who dates Pliny's
letter in civ., concur Mr. Greswell
and Mr. Charles Merivale. He places
it in the year cxi. or cxii. Pagi dates
the martyrdom of Ignatius, or rather
the period when he was sent to Rome,
in cxii., the time when Trajan was in
the East, preparing for his Persian
war ; but Trajan's journey to the East
was not before cxiv. or cxv.

been laid down to guide the provincial governors in such emergencies.[c] The answer of Trajan is characterised by a spirit of moderation. It betrays humane anxiety to allow all such offenders as were not forced under the cognisance of the public tribunals, to elude persecution. Nevertheless it distinctly intimates, that by some existing law, or by the ordinary power of the provincial governor, the Christians were amenable to the severest penalties, to torture, and even to capital punishment. Such punishment had already been inflicted by Pliny; as Governor he had been forced to interfere by accusations lodged before his tribunal. An anonymous libel, or impeachment, had denounced numbers of persons, some of whom altogether disclaimed, others declared that they had renounced Christianity. With that unthinking barbarity with which in those times such punishments were inflicted on persons in inferior station, two servants, females—it is possible they were deaconesses—were put to the torture, to ascertain the truth of the vulgar accusations against the Christians. On their evidence, Pliny could detect nothing further than a " culpable and extravagant superstition." [d] The only facts which he could discover were, that they had a custom of meeting together before daylight, and singing a hymn to Christ as God. They were bound together by no unlawful sacrament, but only under mutual obligation not to commit theft, robbery, adultery, or fraud. They met a second time in the day, and partook together of food, but that of a perfectly innocent kind. The test of guilt to which

Answer of Trajan.

---

[c] Pliny professes his ignorance, because he had never happened to be present at the trial of such causes.

This implies that such trials were not unprecedented.

[d] Prava et immodica superstitio.

he submitted the more obstinate delinquents, was adoration before the statues of the Gods and of the Emperor, and the malediction of Christ. Those who refused he ordered to be led out to execution.[e] Such was the summary process of the Roman Governor; and the approbation of the Emperor clearly shows that he had not exceeded the recognised limits of his authority. Neither Trajan nor the senate had before this issued any edict on the subject. The rescript to Pliny invested him with no new powers; it merely advised him, as he had done, to use his actual powers with discretion,[f] neither to encourage the denunciation of such criminals, nor to proceed without fair and unquestionable evidence. The system of anonymous delation, by which private malice might wreak itself, by false or by unnecessary charges, upon its enemies, Trajan reprobates in that generous spirit with which the wiser and more virtuous emperors constantly repressed that most disgraceful iniquity of the times.[g] But it is manifest, from the executions ordered by Pliny and sanctioned by the approbation of the Emperor, that Christianity was *already* an offence amenable to capital punishment,[h] and this, either under some existing statute, under the common law of the Empire which invested the provincial governor with the arbitrary power of life and death, or lastly, what in this instance cannot have been the case, the *summum imperium* of the Emperor.[i] While then in the individual the

---

[e] " Duci jussi " cannot bear a milder interpretation.

[f] Actum quem debuisti in excutiendis causis eorum, qui Christiani ad te delati fuerant, secutus es. Traj. ad Plin.

[g] Nam est pessimi exempli, nec nostri sæculi est.

[h] Those who were Roman citizens were sent for trial to Rome. " Alii quia cives Romani erant, adnotavi in urbem remittendos."

[i] This rescript or answer of Trajan, approving of the manner in which Pliny carried his law into execution, and suggesting other regulations for

profession of Christianity might thus, by the summary sentence of the governor and the tacit approbation of the Emperor, be treated as a capital offence, and the provincial governor might appoint the measure and the extent of the punishment, all public assemblies for the purpose of new and unauthorised worship might likewise be suppressed by the magistrate; for the police of the Empire always looked with the utmost jealousy on all associations not recognised by the law; and resistance to such a mandate would call down, or the secret holding of such meetings after their prohibition would incur, any penalty which the conservator of public order might think proper to inflict upon the delinquent. Such then was the general position of the Christians with the ruling authorities. They were guilty of a crime against the state, by introducing a new and unauthorised religion, or by holding assemblages contrary to the internal regulations of the Empire. But the extent to which the law would be enforced against them—how far Christianity would be distinguished from Judaism and other foreign religions, which were permitted the free establishment of their rites—with how much greater jealousy their secret assemblies would be watched than those of other mysteries and esoteric religions—all this would depend upon the milder or more rigid character of the governor, and the willingness or reluctance of their fellow-citizens to arraign them before the tribunal of the magistrates. This in turn would depend on the

---

his conduct, is converted by Mosheim into a new law, which from that time became one of the statutes of the Empire. " Hæc Trajani lex inter publicas Imperii sanctiones relata " (p. 234). Trajan's words expressly declare that no certain rule of proceeding can be laid down, and leave almost the whole question to the discretion of the magistrate. " Neque enim in universum aliquid, quod quasi certam formam habet, constitui potest." Traj. ad Plin.

circumstances of the place and the time; on the caprice
of their enemies; on their own discretion; on their
success and the apprehensions and jealousies of their
opponents. In general, so long as they made no visible
impression upon society, so long as their absence from
the religious rites of the city or district, or even from
the games and theatrical exhibitions which were essential parts of the existing Polytheism, caused no sensible
diminution in the concourse of the worshippers, their
unsocial and self-secluding disposition would be treated
with contempt and pity rather than with animosity.
The internal decay of the spirit of Polytheism had little
effect on its outward splendour.   The philosophic party,
who despised the popular faith, were secure in their rank
or in their decent conformity to the public ceremonial.
The theory of all the systems of philosophy was to
avoid unnecessary collision with the popular religious
sentiment: their superiority to the vulgar was flattered,
rather than offended, by the adherence of the latter to
their native superstitions.   In the public exhibitions,
the followers of all other foreign religions met, as on a
common ground.   In the theatre or the hippodrome, the worshipper of Isis or of Mithra
mingled with the mass of those who still adhered to Bacchus or to Jupiter.   Even the Jews, in
many parts, at least at a later period, in some instances
at the present, betrayed no aversion to the popular
games or amusements.   Though, in Palestine, the elder
Herod had met with a sullen and intractable resistance
in the religious body of the people against his attempt
to introduce Gentile and idolatrous games into the Holy
Land, yet it is probable that the foreign Jews were more
accommodating.   A Jewish player, named Aliturus,
stood high in the favour of Nero; nor does it appear

The Jews not
averse to
theatrical
amusements.

that he had abandoned his religion. He was still connected with his own race; and some of the priesthood did not disdain to owe their acquittal, on certain charges on which they had been sent prisoners to Rome, to the actor's interest with the Emperor or with the ruling favourite Poppæa. After the Jewish war, multitudes of the prisoners were forced to exhibit themselves as gladiators; and at a later period, the confluence of the Alexandrian Jews to the theatres, where they equalled in numbers the Pagan spectators, endangered the peace of the city. The *Christians abstain from them.* Christians alone stood aloof from exhibitions which, in their higher and nobler forms, arose out of, and were closely connected with, the Heathen religion; were performed on days sacred to the deities; introduced the deities upon the stage; and, in short, were among the principal means of maintaining in the public mind its reverence for the old mythological fables. The sanguinary diversions of the arena, and the licentious voluptuousness of some of the other exhibitions, were no less offensive to their humanity and to their modesty than those more strictly religious to their piety. Still, so long as they were comparatively few in number, and did not sensibly diminish the concourse to these scenes of public enjoyment, they would be rather exposed to individual acts of vexatious interference, of ridicule, or contempt, than become the victims of a general hostile feeling: their absence would not be resented as an insult upon the public, nor as an act of punishable disrespect against the local or more widely worshipped deity to whose honour the games were dedicated. The time at which they would be in the greatest danger from what would be thought their suspicious or disloyal refusal to join in the public rejoicings, would be precisely that which has been conjectured with much ingenuity and probability to have been the occasion of their being thus committed with the popular sentiment and with the government—the celebration of the birthday or the accession of the Emperor.[k] With the cere-monial of those days, even if, as may have been the case, the actual adoration of the statue of the Emperor was not an ordinary part of the ritual, much which was strictly idolatrous would be mingled up; and the ordinary excuse of the Christians to such charges of disaffection, that they prayed with the utmost fervour for the welfare of the Emperor, would not be admitted, either by the sincere attachment of the people and of the government to a virtuous, or their abject and adulatory celebration of a cruel and tyranni-cal, Emperor.

Danger on occasions of political rejoicings.

This crisis in the fate of Christianity—this transition from safe and despised obscurity to dangerous and obnoxious importance—would of course depend on the comparative rapidity of its progress in different quarters. In Bithynia, the province of Pliny, it had attained that height in little more than seventy years after the death of Christ. Though a humane and enlightened govern-ment might still endeavour to close its eyes upon its multiplying numbers and expanding influence, the keener sight of jealous interest, of rivalry in the command of the popular mind, and of mortified pride, already anti-cipated the time when this formidable antagonist might balance, might at length overweigh, the failing powers

---

[k] The conjecture of Pagi, that the attention of the government was directed to the Christians by their standing aloof from the festivals which celebrated the quindecennalia of Trajan (in the year 111 or 112), is extremely probable. Pagi quotes two passages of Pliny on the subject of these ge-neral rejoicings. Critica in Baron. i. 100.

of Polytheism. Under a less candid governor than
Pliny, and an Emperor less humane and dispassionate
than Trajan, the exterminating sword of persecution
would have been let loose, and a relentless and systematic edict for the suppression of Christianity would
have hunted down its followers in every quarter of the
empire.

Not only the wisdom and humanity of Trajan, but
the military character of his reign, would tend to divert
his attention from that which belonged rather to the
internal administration of the empire. It is Probable con-
far from impossible, though the conjecture nexion of the
is not countenanced by any allusion in the persecution
despatch of Pliny, that the measures adopted under Pliny
with the state
against the Christians were not entirely unconnected of the East.
with the political state of the East. The Roman Empire, in the Mesopotamian province, was held on a
precarious tenure; the Parthian kingdom had acquired
new vigour and energy, and, during great part of his
reign, the state of the East must have occupied the
active mind of Trajan. The Jewish population of Babylonia and the adjacent provinces was of no inconsiderable importance in the impending contest. There is
strong ground for supposing that the last insurrection of
the Jews, under Hadrian, was connected with a rising of
their brethren in Mesopotamia, no doubt secretly, if not
openly, fomented by the intrigues, and depending on the
support, of the king of Parthia. This was at a considerably later period; yet, during the earlier part of
the reign of Trajan, the insurrection had already commenced in Egypt and in Cyrene, and in the island of
Cyprus, and no sooner were the troops of Trajan engaged
on the eastern frontier, towards the close of his reign,
than the Jews rose up in all these provinces, and were

not subdued till after they had perpetrated and endured
the most terrific massacres.[m] Throughout the Eastern
wars of Trajan this spirit was most likely known to be
fermenting in the minds of the whole Jewish population,
not only in the insurgent districts, but in Palestine and
other parts of the empire. The whole race, which
occupied in such vast numbers the conterminous regions,
would be watched, therefore, with hostile jealousy by
the Roman governors, already prejudiced against their
unruly and ungovernable character, and awakened to
more than ordinary vigilance by the disturbed aspect of
the times. The Christians stood in a singular and ambiguous position between the Jewish and Pagan population; many of them probably descended from, and
connected with, the Jews. Their general peaceful
habits and orderly conduct would deserve the protection
of a parental government; still their intractable and persevering resistance to the religious institutions of the
Empire might throw some suspicion on the sincerity of
their civil obedience. The unusual assertion of religious,
might be too closely allied with that of political, independence. At all events, the dubious and menacing
state of the East required more than ordinary watchful-
ness, and a more rigid plan of government in the adjacent provinces; and thus the change in society, which
was working unnoticed in the more peaceful and less
Christianised West, in the East might be forced upon
the attention of an active and inquiring ruler. The
apprehensions of the inhabitants themselves would be
more keenly alive to the formation of a separate and
secluded party within their cities; and religious ani-

---

[m] Euseb. iv. 2. Dio. Cass., or | places this Jewish rebellion, A.D.
rather, Xyphilin. Orosius, l. 7. Pagi | 116.

mosity would eagerly seize the opportunity of impli-
cating its enemies in a charge of disaffection to the
existing government.   Nor is there wanting evidence
that the acts of persecution ascribed to Trajan were, in
fact, connected with the military movements of the
Emperor.   The only authentic Acts are those of Simeon,
Bishop of Jerusalem ; I cannot admit those of Ignatius,
Bishop of Antioch.[n]   In the prefatory observations to
the former, it is admitted that this martyrdom was a local
act of violence.   The more celebrated trial of Ignatius is
stated to have taken place before the Emperor himself
at Antioch, when he was preparing for his Eastern campaign.   The Emperor is represented as kindling to
anger at the disparagement of those gods on whose protection he reckoned in the impending war.   " What ! Is
our religion to be treated as senseless ?   Are the gods, on
whose alliance we rely against our enemies, to be turned
to scorn ? "[o]   But the whole interview with Trajan is
too legendary to command authority.   Nevertheless, at
that time there were circumstances which account with
singular likelihood for that sudden outburst of persecution in Antioch.   Trajan knew that the whole Jewish
world was in a state of actual, or of threatened insurrection.   It is probable that the clearest understanding,
agitated by alarm and hatred, would lose, if it had yet
attained, any distinct discernment of the difference
between Jews and Christians.   Hardly two years before,
the Christians had been denounced by a provincial
governor in the East as dangerous disturbers of the

---

[n] See them in Ruinart, Selecta et
sincera Martyrum Acta.

[o] 'Ημεῖς οὖν σοι δοκοῦμεν κατὰ
νοῦν μὴ ἔχειν θεοὺς, οἷς καὶ χρώμεθα
ξυμμάχοις πρὸς τοὺς πολεμίους.

The Jewish legends are full of acts of
personal cruelty, ascribed to Trajan,
mingled up, as usual, with historical
errors and anachronisms.   See Hist.
of Jews, ii. 418.

religion, therefore of the peace of the Empire. At this
very time an earthquake, more than usually terrible
and destructive, shook the cities of the East. Antioch
suffered its most appalling ravages—Antioch, crowded
with the legionaries prepared for the Emperor's invasion
of the East, with ambassadors and tributary kings from
all parts of the East. The city shook through all its
streets; houses, palaces, theatres, temples fell crashing
down. Many were killed: the Consul Pedo died of his
hurts. The Emperor himself hardly escaped through a
window, and took refuge in the Circus, where he passed
some days in the open air. Whence this terrible blow
but from the wrath of the Gods, who must be appeased
by unusual sacrifices? This was towards the end of
January; early in February the Christian Bishop,
Ignatius, was arrested. We know how, during this century, at every period of public calamity, whatever that
calamity might be, the cry of the panic-stricken Heathens
was, "The Christians to the lions!" It may be that, in
Trajan's humanity, in order to prevent a general massacre by the infuriated populace, or to give greater
solemnity to the sacrifice, the execution was ordered to
take place, not in Antioch, but in Rome.

From the Epistles of Ignatius [p] (I confine myself to
the three short Syriac Epistles, for which we are indebted
to Dr. Cureton) it is manifest that this was no general
persecution. Throughout his journey the "Bishop of
Antioch" is in free communication and correspondence
with the Christian communities, and the most eminent

---

[p] I owe this suggestion to the sagacity of Bunsen (Christianity and
Mankind, p. 89). But the chronology
is from Fynes Clinton, Fasti Hellenici,
who, though he quotes authorities for
the close approximation of the two
events, seems to have no thought of
their historical connexion. The description of the earthquake is from
Dion Cassius, lxviii. 24 et seqq.

Bishops of Asia Minor, who appear to be in perfect
security; Ignatius alone is in danger. Of this solitary
danger he is proud. There is throughout a wild eagerness
for martyrdom (how different from the calm serenity of
St. Paul!). As he would thus during his journey court,
he may reasonably be supposed, in Antioch to have provoked, martyrdom; at least he would not have allayed by
prudent concession the indignation and anger of the Government. He even deprecates the interference of his
Christian friends in his behalf. He fears lest their ill-
timed, and, as he thinks, cruelly officious love might by
some influence (influence which implies their own complete exemption from danger) deprive him of that glorious
crown. He is apprehensive lest their unwelcome appeal
to the Imperial clemency might meet with success.

Trajan, indeed, is absolved, at least by the almost
general voice of antiquity, from the crime of persecuting
the Christians.[q] The legend of his redemption from
purgatory, at the prayer of Pope Gregory I. (Dante,
Purgatorio, x. 47), and his appearance in heaven as one
of the five heathens to whom salvation was vouchsafed

---

[q] The recent boasted discovery of a
catacomb, near the seventh milestone
on the Via Nomentana, where Alexander, Bishop of Rome in the reign
of Trajan, who is promoted into a
martyr, was buried; with a chapel
(contemporary, as it is boldly asserted)
dedicated to his memory and worship,
is a pure religious romance. A catacomb there is, from which the remains
of S. Alexander *are said* to have been
removed by Pope Paschal, a Pope of
almost the darkest period in the Papal
annals, A.D. 817-824. Of this there
is not the shadow of a shade of historical evidence. As to the chapel (I
have visited the spot, and inspected
the ruins, and am confident that it
was never subterranean ; no part of
the catacomb). It was no doubt of
about the age of Jerome; when pil-
grimage to, and worship in, such edifices, sacred to the memory of martyrs,
who were multiplied according to the
demand, had become a passion. Excepting of Ignatius, probably of Simeon
of Jerusalem, there is no authentic martyrdom in the reign of Trajan. The
letters of Ignatius—the genuine letters
—are conclusive against any persecution of the Christians in Rome.

(Paradiso, xx. 43), would hardly have grown up, if there
had been any tradition of him as another Nero, Decius,
or Diocletian.

The cosmopolite and indefatigable mind of Hadrian

Hadrian Em- was more likely to discern with accuracy, and
peror, A.D.
117.   estimate to its real extent, the growing influence
of the new religion. Hadrian was, still more than his
predecessor, the Emperor of the West rather than the
monarch of Rome. His active genius withdrew itself
altogether from warlike enterprise and foreign conquest;
its whole care was centered on the consolidation of the
empire within its narrower and uncontested boundaries,
and on the internal regulation of the vast confederacy
of nations which were gradually becoming more and
more assimilated, as subjects or members of the great
European empire. The remotest provinces for the first
time beheld the presence of the Emperor, not at the
head of an army summoned to defend the insulted
barriers of the Roman territory, or pushing forward the
advancing line of conquest; but in more peaceful array,
providing for the future security of the frontier by impregnable fortresses; adorning the more flourishing
cities with public buildings, bridges, and aqueducts;
inquiring into the customs, manners, and even the
religion, of the more distant parts of the world; encouraging commerce; promoting the arts; in short,
improving, by salutary regulations, for this long period
of peace, the prosperity and civilisation of the whole
empire. Gaul, Britain, Greece, Syria, Egypt, Africa,
were in turn honoured by the presence, enriched by the
liberality, and benefited by the wise policy of the Emperor.[r] His personal character showed the same in-

---

[r] M. St. Croix observes (in an essay | that we have medals of twenty-five
in the Mém. de l'Académ. xlix. 409) | countries through which Hadrian tra-

cessant activity and politic versatility. On the frontier, at the head of the army, he put on the hardi- Character of hood and simplicity of a soldier; disdained any Hadrian. distinction, either of fare or of comfort, from the meanest legionary; and marched on foot, through the most inclement seasons. In the peaceful and voluptuous cities of the South he became the careless and luxurious Epicurean. Hadrian treated the established religion with the utmost respect; he officiated with solemn dignity as supreme pontiff, and at Rome affected disdain or aversion for foreign religions.[s] But his mind was essentially imbued with the philosophic spirit:[t] he was tempted by every abstruse research, and every forbidden inquiry had irresistible attraction for his curious and busy temper.[u] At Athens he was in turn the simple and rational philosopher, the restorer of the splendid temple of Jupiter Olympius, and the awe-struck worshipper in the Eleusinian mysteries.[x] In the East, he

---

velled. (Compare Eckhel, vi. 486.) He looked into the crater of Etna; saw the sun rise from Mount Casius; ascended to the cataracts of the Nile; heard the statue of Memnon. He imported exotics from the East. The journeys of Hadrian are traced, in a note to M. Solvet's translation of Hegewisch, cited above. Tertullian calls him " curiositatum omnium explorator." Apol. i. v. Eusebius, H. E. v. 5, πάντα τὰ περίεργα πολυπραγμονῶν.

[s] Sacra Romana diligentissimè curavit, peregrina contempsit. Spartian. in Hadrian.

[t] Les autres sentiments de ce prince sont très difficiles à connaître. Il n'embrassa aucun secte, et ne fut ni Académicien, ni Stoicien, encore moins

Epicurien; il parut constamment livré à cette incertitude d'opinions, fruit de la bizarrerie de son caractère, et d'un savoir superficiel ou mal digéré. St. Croix, ubi suprà.

[u] In the Cæsars of Julian, Hadrian is described in the pregnant phrase πολυπραγμονῶν τὰ ἀπόρρητα, — busied about all the secret religions.

[x] The Apology of Quadratus was presented on Hadrian's visit to Athens, when he was initiated in the Mysteries; that of Aristides when he became Epoptes, A.D. 131. Warburton connects the hostility of the celebrators of the Mysteries towards Christianity with the Apology of Quadratus, and quotes a passage from Jerome to this effect. Compare Routh's Reliquiæ Sacræ, i. 70.

aspired to penetrate the recondite secrets of magic, and professed himself an adept in judicial astrology. In the midst of all this tampering with foreign religions, he at once paid respect to and outraged the prevailing creed by the deification of Antinöus, in whose honour quinquennial games were established at Mantinea; a city built, and a temple, with an endowment for a priesthood,[y] founded and called by his name, in Egypt: his statues assumed the symbols of various deities. Acts like these, at this critical period, must have tended to alienate a large portion of the thinking class, already wavering in their cold and doubtful Polytheism, to any purer or more ennobling system of religion.

Hadrian not merely surveyed the surface of society, but his sagacity seemed to penetrate deeper into the relations of the different classes to each other, and into the more secret workings of the social system. His regulations for the mitigation of slavery were recommended, not by humanity alone, but by a wise and prudent policy.[z] It was impossible that the rapid growth of Christianity could escape the notice of a mind so inquiring as that of Hadrian, or that he could be altogether Hadrian's blind to its ultimate bearings on the social conduct towards Chris- state of the empire. Yet the generally humane tianity. and pacific character of his government would be a security against violent measures of persecution ; and the liberal study of the varieties of human opinion would induce, if not a wise and rational spirit of toleration, yet a kind of contemptuous indifference towards the most inexplicable aberrations from the prevailing opinions. The apologists for Christianity, Quadratus

---

[y] Euseb. iv. 8. Hieronym. in Catal. et Rufin.
[z] Gibbon, vol. i. ch. ii. p. 71.

and Aristides, addressed their works to the Emperor,
who does not appear to have repelled their respectful
homage.[a] The rescript which he addressed, in the
early part of his reign, to the proconsul of Asia, afforded
the same protection to the Christians against the more
formidable danger of popular animosity, which Trajan
had granted against anonymous delation. In some of the
Asiatic cities their sullen and unsocial absence from the
public assemblies, from the games, and other public
exhibitions, either provoked or gave an opportunity for
the latent animosity to break out against them. A
general acclammation would sometimes demand their
punishment. "The Christians to the lions!" was the
fierce outcry; and the names of the most prominent
or obnoxious of the community would be denounced
with the same sudden and uncontrollable hostility. A
weak or superstitious magistrate trembled before the
popular voice, or lent himself a willing instrument to
the fury of the populace. The proconsul Serenus Granianus consulted the Emperor as to the course to be
pursued on such occasions. The answer of Hadrian is
addressed to Minucius Fundanus, probably the successor
of Granianus. It enacts that, in the prosecution of
the Christians, the formalities of law should be strictly
complied with ; that they should be regularly arraigned
before the legal tribunal, not condemned on the mere
demand of the populace, or in compliance with a lawless
outcry.[b] The edict does credit to the humanity and

---

[a] See the fragments in Routh, Reliquiæ Sacræ, i. 69-78.
  [b] Justin Martyr, Apol. i. 68, 69.
Euseb. H. E. iv. 9. Mosheim, whose
opinions on the state of the Christians
are coloured by too lenient a view of
Roman toleration, considers this edict
by no means more favourable to the
Christians than that of Trajan. It
evidently offered them protection under
a new and peculiar exigency.

wisdom of Hadrian. But, notwithstanding his active and inquisitive mind, and the ability of his general

Hadrian in-
capable of
understand-
ing Christi-
anity. policy, few persons were, perhaps, less qualified to judge of the real nature of the new religion, or to comprehend the tenacious hold which it would obtain upon the mind of man. His character wanted depth and seriousness to penetrate or to understand the workings of a high, profound, and settled religious enthusiasm.[c] The graceful verses which he addressed to his departing spirit[d] contrast with the solemn earnestness with which the Christians were teaching mankind to consider the mysteries of another life. But, on the whole, the long and peaceful reign of Hadrian allowed free scope to the progress of Christianity; the increasing wealth and prosperity of the empire probably raised in the social scale that class

---

[c] The well-known letter of Hadrian gives a singular view of the state of the religious society in Egypt, as it existed, or, rather, as it appeared to the inquisitive Emperor. "I am now, my dear Servianus, become fully acquainted with that Egypt which you praise so highly. I have found the people vain, fickle, and shifting with every breath of popular rumour. Those who worship Serapis are Christians; and those who call themselves Christian bishops are worshippers of Serapis. There is no ruler of a Jewish synagogue, no Samaritan, no Christian bishop, who is not an astrologer, an interpreter of prodigies, and an anointer. The Patriarch himself, when he comes to Egypt, is compelled by one party to worship Serapis, by the other, Christ. . . . . They have but one God: him, Christians, Jews, and Gentiles, worship alike." This latter clause Casaubon understood seriously. It is evidently malicious satire. The common God is Gain. The key to the former curious statement is probably that the tone of the higher, fashionable, society in Alexandria, was to affect, either on some Gnostic or philosophic theory, that all these religions differed only in form, but were essentially the same; that all adored one Deity, all one Logos or Demiurge, under different names; all employed the same arts to impose upon the vulgar, and all were equally despicable to the real philosopher. Dr. Burton, in his History of the Church, suggested, with much ingenuity, that the Samaritans may have been the Gnostic followers of Simon Magus.

[d] Animula, vagula, blandula,
Hospes comesque corporis,
Quæ nunc abibis in loca?

among which it was chiefly disseminated; while the
better part of the more opulent would be tempted, at
least to make themselves acquainted with a religion the
moral influence of which was so manifestly favourable to
the happiness of mankind, and which offered so noble a
solution of the great problem of human philosophy, the
immortality of the soul.

The gentle temper of the first Antoninus would
maintain that milder system which was adopted   Antoninus
by Hadrian from policy or from indifference.   Pius Em-
                                                      peror, A.D.
The Emperor, whose parental vigilance scruti-   138.
nised the minutest affairs of the most remote province, could not be ignorant, though his own residence
was fixed in Rome and its immediate neighbourhood,
of the still expanding progress of Christianity. The
religion itself acquired every year a more public character. The Apology now assumed the tone of an
arraignment of the folly and unholiness of the established Polytheism; nor was this a low and concealed
murmur within the walls of its own places of assemblage, or propagated in the quiet intercourse of the
brethren. It no longer affected disguise, or dissem-
bled its hopes; it approached the foot of the throne;
it stood in the attitude, indeed, of a suppliant, claiming
the inalienable rights of conscience, but asserting in
simple confidence its moral superiority, and, in the
name of an Apology, publicly preaching its own doctrines in the ears of the sovereign and of the world.
The philosophers were joining its ranks; it was rapidly
growing up into a rival power, both of the religions and
philosophies of the world.   Yet, during a reign in which
human life assumed a value and a sanctity before unknown; in which the hallowed person of a senator

was not once violated, even by the stern hand of justice;[e] under an Emperor who professed and practised
the maxim of Scipio, that he had rather save the life of
a single citizen than cause the death of a thousand enemies;[f] who considered the subjects of the Empire as one
family, of which himself was the parent,[g] even religious
zeal would be rebuked and overawed; and the provincial
governments, which too often reflected the fierce passions
and violent barbarities of the throne, would now, in turn,
image back the calm and placid serenity of the imperial
tribunal. Edicts are said to have been issued to some of
the Grecian cities—Larissa, Thessalonica, and Athens—
and to the Greeks in general, to refrain from any unprecedented severities against the Christians. Another
rescript,[h] addressed to the cities of Asia Minor, speaks
language too distinctly Christian even for the anticipated
Christianity of disposition evinced by Antoninus. It
calls upon the Pagans to avert the anger of Heaven,
which was displayed in earthquakes and other public
calamities, by imitating the piety, rather than denouncing
the atheism, of the Christians. The pleasing vision

---

[e] Jul. Capit. Anton. Pius, Aug.
Script. p. 138.

[f] Ibid., p. 140.

[g] The reign of Antoninus the First
is almost a blank in history. The book
of Dion Cassius which contained his
reign was lost, except a small part,
when Xiphilin wrote. Xiphilin asserts
that Antoninus favoured the Christians.

[h] The rescript of Antoninus, in
Eusebius, to which Xiphilin alludes
(Euseb. iv. 13), in favour of the
Christians, is now generally given up
as spurious. The older writers disputed to which of the Antonini it belonged. Lardner argues, from the
Apologies of Justin Martyr, that the
Christians were persecuted "even to
death" during this reign. The inference is inconclusive: they were obnoxious to the law, and might endeavour to gain the law on their side,
though it may not have been carried
into execution. The general voice of
Christian antiquity is favourable to
the First Antoninus.

must, it is to be feared, be abandoned, which would represent the best of the Pagan Emperors bearing his public testimony in favour of the calumniated Christians; the man who, from whatever cause, deservedly bore the name of the Pious among the adherents of his own religion, the most wisely tolerant to the faith of the Gospel.

CHAPTER VII.

Christianity and Marcus Aurelius the Philosopher.

THE virtue of Marcus Aurelius the Philosopher was of a more lofty and vigorous character than that of his gentle predecessor. The Second Antoninus might seem the last effort of Paganism, or rather of Gentile philosophy, to raise a worthy opponent to the triumphant career of Christianity. A blameless disciple in the severest school of philosophic morality, the austerity of Marcus rivalled that of the Christians in its contempt of the follies and diversions of life; yet his native kindliness of disposition was not hardened and embittered by the severity or the pride of his philosophy.[a] With Aurelius, nevertheless, Christianity found not only a fair and high-minded competitor for the command of the human mind; not only a rival in the exaltation of the soul of man to higher views and more dignified motives, but a violent and intolerant persecutor. During his reign, the martyrologies become more authentic and credible; the distinct voice of Christian history arraigns the Philosopher, not indeed as the author of a general and systematic plan for the extirpation of Christianity, but as withdrawing even the ambiguous protection of the former Emperors, and giving free scope to the excited passions, the wounded pride, and the jealous

---

[a] Verecundus sine ignaviâ, sine tristitiâ gravis. Jul. Capit. Aug. Hist. p. 160.

interests of its enemies; neither discountenancing the stern determination of the haughty governor to break the contumacious spirit of resistance to his authority, nor the outburst of popular fury, which sought to appease the offended gods by the sacrifice of these despisers of their Deities.

Three important causes concurred in bringing about this dangerous crisis in the destiny of Chris- *Three causes of the hostility of M. Aurelius and his government to Christianity.* tianity at this particular period:—1. The change in the relative position of Christianity to the religion of the Empire; 2. The circumstances of the times; 3. The character of the Emperor.

I. Sixty years of almost uninterrupted peace, since the beginning of the second century, had opened a wide field for the free development of Chris- *I. Altered position of Christianity in regard to Paganism.* tianity. It had spread into every quarter of the Roman dominions. The Western provinces, Gaul and Africa, rivalled the East in the number, if not in the opulence, of their Christian congregations. In almost every city had gradually arisen a separate community, seceding from the ordinary habits and usages of life, at least from the public religious ceremonial; governed by its own laws; acting upon a common principle; and bound together in a kind of latent federal union throughout the empire. A close and intimate correspondence connected this new moral republic. An impulse, an opinion, a feeling, which originated in Egypt or Syria, was propagated with electric rapidity to the remotest frontier of the West. Irenæus, the Bishop of Lyons in Gaul, whose purer Greek had been in danger of corruption from his intercourse with the barbarous Celtic tribes, enters into a controversy with the speculative teachers of Antioch, Edessa, or Alexandria; while Tertullian in his rude African Latin denounces or advocates

opinions which sprang up in Pontus or in Phrygia. A
new kind of literature had arisen, propagated with the
utmost zeal of proselytism, among a numerous class of
readers, who began to close their ears against the profane fables and the unsatisfactory philosophical systems
of Paganism. While the Emperor himself condescended, in Greek of no despicable purity and elegance
for the age, to explain the lofty tenets of the Porch, and
to commend its noble morality to his subjects, the
minds of a large portion of the world were preoccupied
by writers who, in language often impregnated with
foreign and Syrian barbarisms, enforced still higher
morals, resting upon religious tenets altogether new and
incomprehensible excepting to the initiate. Their
sacred books were of still higher authority; commanded
the homage, and required the diligent and respectful
study, of all the disciples of the new faith. Nor was
this empire within the empire, this universally disseminated sect—which had its own religious rites, its own
laws, to which it appealed rather than to the statutes of
the empire; its own judges (for the Christians, wherever
they were able, submitted their disputes to their bishop
and his associate presbyters), its own financial regulations, whether for the maintenance of public worship, or
for charitable purposes; its own religious superiors, who
exercised a very different control from that of the pontiffs or sacerdotal colleges of Paganism; its own usages
and conduct; in some respects its own language—confined to one class, or to one description of Roman
subjects. Christians were to be found in the court, in
the camp, in the commercial market; they discharged
all the duties, and did not decline any of the offices, of
society. They did not altogether shun the forum,
or abandon all interest in the civil administration; they

had their mercantile transactions, in common with the rest of that class. One of their apologists indignantly repels the charge of their being useless to society : " We are no Indian Brahmins, or devotees, living naked in the woods, self-banished from civilised life. We gratefully accept, we repudiate no gift of God the Creator; we are only temperate in their use. We avoid not your forum, your markets, your baths, your shops, your forges, your inns, your fairs. We are one people with you in all worldly commerce. We serve with you as sailors, as soldiers; we are husbandmen and merchants like you. We practise the same arts; we contribute to all public works for your use."[b] Among their most remarkable distinctions, no doubt, was their admission of slaves to an equality in religious privileges. Yet there was no attempt to disorganise or correct the existing relations of society. Though the treatment of slaves in Christian families could not but be softened and humanised, as well by the evangelic temper as by this acknowledged equality in the hopes of another life, yet Christianity left the emancipation of mankind from these deeply-rooted distinctions between the free and servile races to times which might be ripe for so great and important a change.

This secession of one part of society from its accus-

---

[b] I add Tertullian's Latin : " Infructuosi in negotiis dicimur. Quo pacto homines vobiscum degentes, ejusdem victûs, habitûs, instinctûs, ejusdem ad vitam necessitatis ? Neque enim Brachmanæ, aut Indorum gymnosophistæ sumus, sylvicolæ et exules vitæ. Meminimus gratiam nos debere Deo domino creatori, nullum fructum operum ejus repudiamus, planè temperamus, ne ultra modum aut perperam utamur. Itaque non sine foro, non sine macello, non sine balneis, tabernis, officinis, stabulis, nundinis vestris, cæterisque commerciis, cohabitamus in hoc seculo : navigamus et nos vobiscum et *militamus*, et rusticamur, et mercamur; proinde miscemus artes, opera nostra publicamus usui vestro." Apologet. c. 42.

tomed religious intercourse with the rest, if in nothing
but religious intercourse, independent of the numbers
whose feelings and interests were implicated in the
support of the national religion in all its pomp and
authority, would necessarily produce estrangement,
jealousy, animosity.

As Christianity became more powerful, a vague appre-
Connexion of hension began to spread abroad among the
Christianity
with the fall Roman people that the fall of their old reli-
of the Roman
Empire.   gion might, to a certain degree, involve that
of their civil dominion; and this apprehension, it cannot
be denied, was justified, deepened, and confirmed, by
the tone of some of the Christian writings, no doubt by
the language of some Christian teachers. Idolatry was
not merely an individual, but a national, sin, which
would be visited by temporal as well as spiritual retribution. The anxiety of one at least, and that certainly
not the most discreet of the Christian apologists, to disclaim all hostility towards the temporal dignity of the
Empire, implies that the Christians were obnoxious
to this charge. The Christians are calumniated, writes
Tertullian to Scapula,[c] at a somewhat later period
(under Severus), as guilty of treasonable disloyalty to
the Emperor. As the occasion required, he exculpates
them from any leaning to Niger, Albinus, or Cassius,
the competitors of Severus, and then proceeds to make
this solemn protestation of loyalty : " The Christian is
the enemy of no man, assuredly not of the Emperor.

---

[c] Sed et circa majestatem imperii
infamamur, tamen nunquam Albi-
niani, nec Nigriani, vel Cassiani, in-
veniri potuerunt Christiani.

Christianus nullius est hostis, ne-
dum Imperatoris ; quem sciens a Deo
suo constitui, necesse est ut et ipsum
diligat, et revereatur, et honoret, et
salvum velit, cum toto Romano imperio, quousque sæculum stabit : tam-
diu enim stabit. Tertullian ad Sca-
pulam, 1.

The sovereign he knows to be ordained by God; of necessity, therefore, he loves, reveres, and honours him, and prays for his safety, with that of the whole Roman Empire, that it may endure—and endure it will—as long as the world itself."[d]   But other Christian documents, or at least documents eagerly disseminated by the Christians, speak a very different language.[e]   By many modern interpreters, the Apocalypse itself is supposed to refer, not to the fall of a predicted spiritual Rome, but of the dominant Pagan Rome, the visible Babylon of idolatry, and pride, and cruelty.   According to this view, it is a grand dramatic vaticination of the triumph of Christianity over Heathenism in its secular as well as its spiritual power.   Be this as it may, in later writings, the threatening and maledictory tone of the Apocalypse is manifestly borrowed, and directed against the total abolition of Paganism, in its civil as well as religious supremacy. Many of these forged prophetic writings belong to the reign of the Antonines, and could not emanate from any quarter but that of the more injudicious and fanatical Christians.   The second (Apocryphal) book of Esdras is of this character, the work of a Judaising Christian;[f] it refers distinctly to the reign of the twelve Cæsars,[g] and obscurely intimates, in many parts, the approaching dissolution of the existing order of things.   The doctrine of

Tone of some Christian writings confirmatory of this apprehension.

---

[d] Quousque sæculum stabit.

[e] I have been much indebted, in this passage, to the excellent work of Tschirner, 'Der Fall des Heidenthums,' a work written with so much learning, candour, and Christian temper, as to excite great regret that it was left incomplete at its author's death.

[f] The general character of the work, the nationality of the perpetual allusions to the history and fortunes of the race of Israel, betray the Jew; the passages ch. ii. 42, 48; v. 5; vii. 26, 29, are avowed Christianity. On this book read Ewald.

[g] C. xii. 14.   Compare Basnage, Hist. des Juifs, l. vii. c. 2.

the Millennium, which was as yet far from exploded or
fallen into disregard, mingled with all these prophetic
anticipations of future change in the destinies of mankind.[h] The visible throne of Christ, according to these
writings, was to be erected on the ruins of all earthly
empires : the nature of His kingdom would, of course, be
unintelligible to the Heathen : and all that he would
comprehend would be a vague notion that the empire of
the world was to be transferred from Rome, and that this
extinction of the majesty of the Empire was, in some incomprehensible manner, connected with the triumph of
the new faith.   His terror, his indignation, and his contempt, would lead to fierce and implacable animosity.
Even in Tertullian's Apology, the ambiguous word
" sæculum " might mean no more than a brief and
limited period, which was yet to elapse before the final
consummation.

But the Sibylline verses, which clearly belong to this
The Sibylline period, express, in the most remarkable manner,
books. this spirit of exulting menace at the expected
simultaneous fall of Roman idolatry and of Roman empire.   The origin of the whole of the Sibylline oracles
now extant is not distinctly apparent, either from the
style, the manner of composition, or the subject of their
predictions.[i] It is manifest that they were largely interpolated by the Christians, to a late period, and some of
the books can be assigned to no other time but the
present.[k] Much, no doubt, was of an older date.   It is

---

[h] There are apparent allusions to
the Millennium in the Sibylline verses,
particularly at the close of the eighth
book.

[i] The first book, to page 176, may
be Jewish ; it then becomes Christian,
as well as the second.   But in these
books there is little prophecy ; it is in
general the Mosaic history, in Greek
hexameters.   If there are any fragments of Heathen verses, they are in
the third book.

[k] Ad horum imperatorum (Antonini Pii cum liberis suis M. Aurelio

scarcely credible that the Fathers of this time would quote contemporary forgeries as ancient prophecies. The Jews of Alexandria, who had acquired some taste for Grecian poetry, and displayed some talent for the translation of their sacred books into the Homeric language and metre,[m] had, no doubt, set the example of versifying their own prophecies, and of ascribing them to the Sibyls, whose names were universally venerated, as revealing to mankind the secrets of futurity. They may have begun by comparing their own prophets with these ancient seers, and spoken of the predictions of Isaiah or Ezekiel as their Sibylline verses, which may have been another word for prophetic or oracular.

Almost every region of Heathenism boasts its Sibyl.[n] Poetic predictions, ascribed to these inspired women, were either published or religiously preserved in the sacred archives of cities. Nowhere were they held in such awful reverence as in Rome. The opening of the

---

et Lucio Vero) tempora videntur Sibyllarum vaticinia tantum extendi; id quod etiam e lib. v. videre licet. Note of the editor, Opsopæus, p. 688.

[m] Compare Valckenaer's learned treatise De Aristobulo Judæo. The fragments of Ezekiel Tragædus, and many passages, which are evident versions of the Jewish Scriptures, in the works of the Fathers, particularly of Eusebius, may be traced to this school. It is by no means impossible that the Pollio of Virgil may owe many of its beauties to those Alexandrian versifiers of the Hebrew prophets. Virgil, who wrought up indiscriminately into his refined gold all the ruder ore which he found in the older poets, may have seen and admired some of these verses.

He may have condescended, as he thought, to borrow the images of these religious books of the barbarians, as a modern might the images of the Vedas or of the Koran.

[n] See on the different Sibyls and the origin of the different poems the dissertation the (Excursus i. and vi.) of the new editor of the Sibylline verses, M. Alexandre, t. ii. (Paris, 1856). On the Roman Sibylline books, Excursus iii. I do not pledge myself to all M. Alexandre's historical criticism; but I wish to bear my humble testimony to the superiority of this edition over all previous ones. The editor has availed himself of the valuable suggestions of Bleek.

Sibylline books was an event of rare occurrence, and only at seasons of fearful disaster or peril. Nothing would be more tempting to the sterner or more ardent Christian, than to enlist, as it were, on his side, these authorised Pagan interpreters of futurity; to extort, it might seem, from their own oracles, this confession of their approaching dissolution. Nothing, on the other hand, would more strongly excite the mingled feelings of apprehension and animosity in the minds of the Pagans, than this profanation, as it would appear, whether they disbelieved or credited them, of the sacred treasures of prophecy. It was Paganism made to utter, in its most hallowed language, and by its own inspired prophets, its own condemnation; to announce its own immediate downfall, and the triumph of its yet obscure enemy over both its religious and temporal dominion.

The fifth and eighth books of the Sibylline oracles are those which most distinctly betray the sentiments and language of the Christians of this period.[o] In the spirit of the Jewish prophets, they denounce the folly of worshipping gods of wood and stone, of ivory, of gold, and silver; of offering incense and sacrifice to dumb and deaf deities. The gods of Egypt, and those of Greece —Hercules, Jove, and Mercury—are cut off. The whole sentiment is in the contemptuous and aggressive tone of the later, rather than the more temperate and defensive argument of the earlier, apologists for Christianity. But the Sibyls are made, not merely to denounce the fall of Heathenism, but the ruin of Heathen states and the desolation of Heathen cities. Many passages relate to Egypt, and seem to point out Alexandria, with Asia Minor, the cities of which, particularly Lao-

---

[o] Lib. v. p. 557.

dicea, are frequently noticed, as the chief staple of
these poetico-prophetic forgeries.[p] The following passage might almost seem to have been written after the
destruction of the Serapeum by Theodosius:[q] "Isis,
thrice hapless goddess, thou shalt remain alone on the
shores of the Nile, a solitary Mænad by the sands of
Acheron. No longer shall thy memory endure upon
the earth. And thou, Serapis, that restest upon thy
stones, much must thou suffer; thou shalt be the
mightiest ruin in thrice hapless Egypt; and those, who
worshipped thee for a god, shall know thee to be
nothing. And one of the linen-clothed priests shall
say, Come, let us build the beautiful temple of the true
God; let us change the awful law of our ancestors, who,
in their ignorance, made their pomps and festivals to
gods of stone and clay; let us turn our hearts, hymning
the Everlasting God, the Eternal Father, the Lord of
all, the True, the King, the Creator and Preserver of
our souls, the Great, the Eternal God."

---

[p] Θμοῦις καὶ Ξοῦις θλίβεται, καὶ κόπτεται.
Βουλὴ Ἡρακλεούς τε Διός τε καὶ Ἑρμειδο.—P. 558.
The first of these lines is mutilated.

[q] Ἰσὶ, θεὰ τριτάλαινα, μενεῖς δ' ἐπὶ χεύμασι Νείλου,
Μούνη, μαινὰς ἄτακτος, ἐπὶ ψαμάθοις Ἀχέροντος,
Κοὐκέτι σου μνεῖά γε μενεῖ κατὰ γαίαν ἅπασαν.
Καὶ σὺ Σέραπι, λίθοις ἐπικείμενε, πολλὰ μογήσεις,
Κείσῃ πτῶμα μέγιστον, ἐν Αἰγύπτῳ τριταλαίνῃ.
          *   *   *   *
Γνώσονται σε τὸ μηδὲν, ὅσοι Θεὸν ἐξύμνησαν.
Καὶ τις ἐρεῖ τῶν ἱερέων λινόσσιος ἀνὴρ·
Δεῦτε Θεοῦ τέμενος καλοῦ στήθωμεν ἀληθὲς,
Δεῦτε τὸν ἐκ προγόνων δεινὸν νόμον ἀλλάξωμεν,
Τοῦ χάριν ἢ λίθινοις καὶ ὀστρακίνοισι θεοῖσι
Πομπὰς καὶ τελετὰς ποιούμενοι οὐκ ἐνόησαν
Στρέψωμεν ψυχὰς, Θεὸν ἄφθιτον ἐξυμνοῦντες.
Αὐτὸν τὸν γενετῆρα, τὸν αἴδιον γεγαῶτα,
Τὸν πρυτανὶν πάντων, τὸν ἀληθέα, τὸν βασιλῆα.
Ψυχοτρόφον γενετῆρα, Θεὸν μέγαν, αἰὲν ἐόντα.
          Lib. v. p. 638, edit. Gall. Amstelod. 1689.

A bolder prophet, without doubt writing precisely at
this perilous crisis, dares, in the name of a Sibyl, to
connect together the approaching fall of Rome and the
gods of Rome. " O haughty Rome, the just chastisement of Heaven shall come down upon thee from on
high; thou shalt stoop thy neck, and be levelled with
the earth; and fire shall consume thee, razed to thy
very foundations; and thy wealth shall perish; wolves
and foxes shall dwell among thy ruins, and thou shalt
be desolate as if thou hadst never been. Where then
will be thy Palladium? Which of thy gods of gold, or
of stone, or of brass, shall save thee? Where then the
decrees of thy senate? Where the race of Rhea, of
Saturn, or of Jove; all the lifeless deities thou hast
worshipped, or the shades of the deified dead? When
thrice five gorgeous Cæsars [the twelve Cæsars usually
so called, with Nerva, Trajan, Hadrian], who have enslaved the world from east to west, shall be, one will
arise silver-helmed, with a name like the neighbouring
sea [Hadrian and the Hadriatic Sea]," [r] The poet describes the busy and lavish character of Hadrian, his

---

[r] "Ἥξει σοί ποτ' ἄνωθεν ἴση, ὑψαύχενε Ῥώμη,
Οὐράνιος πληγὴ, καὶ κάμψεις αὐχένα πρώτη,
Κἀξεδαφισθῆσῃ, καὶ πῦρ σε ὅλην δαπανήσει
Κεκλιμένην ἐδάφεσσιν ἐοῖς, καὶ πλοῦτος ὀλεῖται,
Καὶ σὰ θέμεθλα λύκοι, καὶ ἀλώπεκες οἰκήσουσι.
Καὶ τότ' ἔσῃ πανέρημος ὅλως, ὡς μὴ γεγονυῖα.
Ποῦ τότε Παλλάδιον; ποῖος σε θεὸς διασώσει,
Χρυσοῦς, ἢ λίθινος, ἢ χάλκεος; ἢ τότε ποῦ σοι
Δόγματα συγκλήτου; ποῦ, Ῥείης, ἠὲ Κρόνοιο,
Ἠὲ Διὸς γενεὴ, καὶ πάντων ὧν ἐσεβάσθης
Δαίμονας ἀψύχους, νεκρῶν εἴδωλα καμόντων:

*   *   *   *

Ἀλλ' ὅτε σοι βασιλεῖς χλιδανοὶ τρὶς πέντε γένωνται,
Κόσμον δουλώσαντες ἀπ' ἀντολίης μέχρι δυσμῶν,
Ἔσσετ' ἄναξ πολιόκρανος, ἔχων πέλας οὔνομα πόντου.
                                    Lib. viii. p. 679.
                                              The

curiosity in prying into all religious mysteries, and his deification of Antinöus.[s]

" After him shall reign three, *whose times shall be the last*.[t] * * * Then from the uttermost parts of the earth, whither he fled, shall the matricide [Nero] return."[u]

The ruin of Rome, and the restoration of Europe to the East, are likewise alluded to in the following passages : lib. iii. p. 404-408 ; v. 573-576 ; viii. 694, 712, 718.

There is another allusion to Hadrian, lib. v. p. 552, much more laudatory :
Ἔσται καὶ πανάριστος ἀνὴρ, καὶ πάντα νοήσει.

[s] Κόσμον ἐποπτεύων μιαρῷ ποδὶ, δῶρα πορίζων
* * *
Καὶ μαγικῶν ἀδύτων μυστήρια πάντα μεθέξει,
Παιδὰ θεὸν δεικνύσει, ἅπαντα σεβάσματα λύσει.—P. 688.

(Compare the xiith book, published by A. Mai, where the reading is ἰδίῳ ποδὶ, line 167.)

[t] Τὸν μετὰ τρεῖς ἄρξουσι, πανύστατον ἦμαρ ἔχοντες—

One of these three is to be an old man, to heap up vast treasures, in order to surrender them to the Eastern destroyer, Nero—

Ἲν ὅταν γ᾽ ἀπανέλθῃ
Ἐκ περίτων γαίης ὃ φυγας μητροκτόνος ἐλθών.
Καὶ τότε πενθήσεις, πλατὺ πόρφυρον ἡγεμονήων
Φῶς ἐκδυσαμένη, καὶ πένθιμον εἶμα φεροῦσα.
* * * *
Καὶ γὰρ ἀετοφόρων λεγεώνων δόξα πεσεῖται.
Ποῦ τότε σοι τὸ κράτος ; ποία γῆ σύμμαχος ἔσται,
Δουλωθεῖσα τεαῖς ματαιοφροσύνῃσιν ἀθέσμως ;
Πάσης γὰρ γαίης θνητῶν τότε σύγχυσις ἔσται,
Αὐτὸς παντοκράτωρ ὅταν ἐλθὼν βήμασι κρίνῃ
Ζώντων καὶ νεκύων ψυχὰς, καὶ κόσμον ἅπαντα.
* * * *
Ἐκ τοτέ σοι βρυγμὸς, καὶ σκορπισμὸς, καὶ ἅλωσις,
Πτῶσις ὅταν ἔλθῃ πόλεων, καὶ χάσματα γαίης.
Lib. viii. 688.

[u] The strange notion of the flight of Nero beyond the Euphrates, from whence he was to return as Antichrist, is almost the burthen of the Sibylline verses. Compare lib. iv. p. 520-525 ; v. 573, where there is an allusion to his theatrical tastes, 619-714. The best commentary is that of St. Augustine on the Thessalonians : " Et tunc revelabitur ille iniquus. Ego prorsus quid dixerit me fateor ignorare. Suspiciones tamen hominum, quas vel audire vel legere de hâc re potui, non tacebo. Quidam putant

And now, O king of Rome, shalt thou mourn, disrobed
of the purple laticlave of thy rulers, and clad in sack-
cloth. The glory of thy eagle-bearing legions shall
perish. Where shall be thy might? What land, which
thou hast enslaved by thy vain laurels, shall be thine
ally? For there shall be confusion on all mortals over
the whole earth, when the Almighty Ruler comes, and,
seated upon his throne, judges the souls of the quick and
of the dead, and of the whole world. There shall be
wailing and scattering abroad, and ruin, when the fall
of the cities shall come, and the abyss of earth shall
open."

In another passage, the desolation of Italy, the return
of Nero, the general massacre of kings, are portrayed
in fearful terms. The licentiousness of Rome is detailed
in the blackest colours. "Sit silent in thy sorrow,
O guilty and luxurious city; the vestal virgins shall no
longer watch the sacred fire; thy house is desolate."[x]
Christianity is then represented under the image of
a pure and heaven-descending temple, embracing the
whole human race.

---

hoc de *imperio dictum fuisse Romano;*
et propterea Paulum Apostolum non
id apertè scribere voluisse, ne calum-
niam videlicet incurreret quod Romano
imperio malè optaverit, cum spera-
retur æternum : ut hoc quod dixit,
'Jam enim mysterium iniquitatis
operatur,' Neronem voluerit intelligi,
cujus jam facta velut Antichristi vide-
bantur ; unde nonnulli ipsum resur-
recturum· et futurum Antichristum
suspicantur. Alii vero nec eum occi-
sum putant, sed subtractum potiùs, ut
putaretur occisus; et vivum occultari
in vigore ipsius ætatis, in quâ fuit
cum crederetur extinctus, donec suo

tempore reveletur, et restituatur in
regnum." According to the Sibyls,
Nero was to make an alliance with
the kings of the Medes and Persians;
return at the head of a mighty army;
accomplish his favourite scheme of
digging through the Isthmus of Corinth, and then· conquer Rome. For
the manner in which Neander traces
the germ of this notion in the Apocalypse, see Pflanzung, Der Chr. Kirche,
ii. 327. Nero is Antichrist in the
political verses of Commodianus, xli.
Compare M. Alexandre, ii. 495.

[x] Lib. v. p. 621.

Whether or not these prophecies merely embodied, for the private edification, the sentiments of the Christians, they are manifest indications of these sentiments; and they would scarcely be concealed with so much prudence and discretion as not to transpire among adversaries, who now began to watch them with jealous vigilance: if they were boldly published, for the purpose of converting the Heathen, they would be still more obnoxious to the general indignation and hatred.   However the more moderate and rational, probably the greater number, of the Christians might deprecate these dangerous and injudicious effusions of zeal, the consequences would involve all alike in the indiscriminating animosity which they would provoke; and, whether or not these predictions were contained in the Sibylline poems, quoted by all the early writers, by Justin Martyr, by Clement, and by Origen, the attempt to array the authority of the Sibyls against that religion and that empire, of which they were before considered almost the tutelary guardians, would goad the rankling aversion into violent resentment.

The general superiority assumed in any way by Christianity, directly it came into collision with the opposite party, would of itself be fatal to the peace which it had acquired in its earlier obscurity.   Of all pretensions, man is most jealous of the claim to moral superiority.

II. The darkening aspect of the times wrought up this growing alienation and hatred to open and furious hostility.   In the reign of M. Aurelius, we approach the verge of that narrow oasis of peace which intervenes between the final conquests of Rome and the recoil of repressed and threatening barbarism upon the civilisation of the world.   The public

II. Change in the circumstances of the times.

mind began to be agitated with gloomy rumours from the frontier, while calamities, though local, yet spread over wide districts, shook the whole Roman people with apprehension. Foreign and civil wars, inundations, earthquakes, pestilences, which I shall presently assign to their proper dates, awoke the affrighted empire from its slumber of tranquillity and peace.[y]

The Emperor Marcus reposed not, like his predecessor, in his Lanuvian villa, amid the peaceful pursuits of agriculture, or with the great jurisconsults of the time, meditating on a general system of legislation. The days of the Second Numa were gone by, and the Philosopher must leave his speculative school and his Stoic friends to place himself at the head of the legions. New levies invade the repose of peaceful families; even the public amusements are encroached upon; the gla-diators are enrolled to serve in the army.[z] It Terror of the Roman world. was at this unexpected crisis of calamity and terror, that Superstition, which had slept in careless and Epicurean forgetfulness of its gods, suddenly awoke, and when it fled for succour to the altar of the tutelar deity, found the temple deserted and the shrine neglected. One portion of society stood aloof in sullen disregard or avowed contempt of rites so imperiously demanded by the avenging gods. If, in the time of public distress, true religion inspires serene resignation to the Divine will, and receives the awful admonition to more strenuous and rigid virtue, Superstition shudders at the manifest anger of the gods, yet looks not within to correct the offensive guilt, but abroad, to discover some gift or

---

[y] Tillemont, Hist. des Emp. ii. 593.

[z] Fuit enim populo hic sermo, cum *sustulisset ad bellum gladiatores* quod populum sublatis voluptatibus vellet cogere ad philosophiam. Jul. Cap. p. 204.

sacrifice which may appease the Divine wrath, and bribe back the alienated favour of Heaven. Rarely does it discover any offering sufficiently costly, except human life.[a] The Christians were the public and avowed enemies of the gods; they were the self-designated victims, whose ungrateful atheism had provoked, whose blood might avert, their manifest indignation. The public religious ceremonies, the sacrifices, the games, the theatres, afforded constant opportunities of inflaming and giving vent to the paroxysms of popular fury, with which it disburthened itself of its awful apprehensions. The cry of " The Christians to the lions!" was now no longer the wanton clamour of individual or party malice; it was not murmured by the interested, and eagerly reechoed by the blood-thirsty, who rejoiced in the exhibition of unusual victims; it was the deep and general voice of fanatic terror, solemnly demanding the propitiation of the wrathful gods, by the sacrifice of these impious apostates from their worship.[b] The Christians were the authors of all the calamities which were brooding over the world, and in vain their earnest apologists appealed to the prosperity of the empire since the appearance of Christ, in the reign of Augustus, and showed that the great enemies of Christianity, the Emperors Nero and Domitian, were likewise the scourges of mankind.[c]

---

[a] Compare on similar events, paroxysms of popular religious zeal arising out of public calamities, Hartung, Religion des Römer, i. 234.

[b] The miracle of the thundering legion (see postea), after having suffered deadly wounds from former assailants, was finally transfixed by the critical spear of Moyle (Works, vol. ii.). Is it improbable that it was invented or wrought up, from a casual occurrence, into its present form, as a kind of counterpoise to the reiterated charge which was advanced against the Christians, of having caused, by their impiety, all the calamities inflicted by the barbarians on the Empire?

[c] Melito apud Routh, Reliq. Sacr. i. 111. Compare Tertullian, Apologet. v.

III. Was, then, the philosopher Aurelius superior to
the vulgar superstition? In what manner did
his personal character affect the condition of
the Christians? Did he authorise, by any new edict, a
general and systematic persecution, or did he only give
free scope to the vengeance of the awe-struck people,
and countenance the timid or fanatic concessions of the
provincial governors to the riotous demand of the
populace for Christian blood? Did he actually repeal or
suspend, or only neglect to enforce, the milder edicts of
his predecessors, which secured to the Christians a fair
and public trial before the legal tribunal?[d] The acts
ascribed to Marcus Aurelius, in the meagre and unsatisfactory annals of his reign, are at issue with the sentiments expressed in his grave and lofty Meditations.
He assumes, in his philosophical lucubrations, which he
dictated during his campaigns upon the Danube, the
tone of profound religious sentiment, but proudly dis-
claims the influence of superstition upon his mind. Yet
in Rome he either shared, or condescended to appear to
share, all the terrors of the people. The pestilence,
said to have been introduced from the East by the
soldiers, on their return from the Parthian campaign,
had not yet ceased its ravages, when the public mind
was thrown into a state of the utmost depression by the
news of the Marcomannic war. M. Aurelius, as we
shall hereafter see, did not, in his proper person, coun-

III. The cha-
racter of the
Emperor.

---

[d] There is an edict of the Emperor
Aurelian in the genuine Acts of St.
Symphorian, in which Pagi, Ruinart,
and Neander (i. 106), would read the
name of M. Aurelius instead of Aure-
lianus. Their arguments are, in my
opinion, inconclusive, and the fact that
Aurelian is named among the persecuting Emperors in the treatise ascribed to Lactantius (De Mort. Persecutor.), in which his edicts (scripta)
against the Christians are distinctly
named, outweighs their conjectural
objections.

tenance, to the utmost, the demands of the popular superstition. For all the vulgar arts of· magic, divination,
and vaticination, the Emperor declares his sovereign
contempt; yet on that occasion, besides the public religious ceremonies, to which I shall presently allude, he
is said himself to have tampered with the dealers in the
secrets of futurity; to have lent a willing ear to the
prognostications of the Chaldeans, and to the calculations of astrology. If these facts be true, and all this
were not done in mere compliance with the
general sentiment, the serene composure of
Marcus himself may at times have darkened
into terror; his philosophic apathy may not always
have been exempt from the influence of shuddering
devotion. In issuing an edict against the Christians,
Marcus may have supposed that he was consulting the
public good, by conciliating the alienated favour of the
gods. But the superiority of the Christians to all the
terrors of death appears at once to have astonished and
wounded the Stoic pride of the Emperor. Philosophy,
which was constantly dwelling on the solemn question
of the immortality of the soul, could not comprehend
the eager resolution with which the Christian departed
from life; and in the bitterness of jealousy sought out
unworthy motives for the intrepidity which it could not
emulate. "How great is that soul which is ready, if it
must depart from the body, to be extinguished, to be
dispersed, or still to subsist! And this readiness must
proceed from the individual judgement, not from mere
obstinacy, like the Christians, but deliberately, solemnly,
and without tragic display." e The Emperor did not

*Private senti-
ments of the
Emperor, in
his Medita-
tions.*

---

e The Emperor's Greek is by no
means clear in this remarkable passage. Ψιλὴν παράταξιν is usually
translated as in the text " mere ob-

choose to discern that it was in the one case the doubt,
in the other the assurance, of the eternal destiny of the
soul, which constituted the difference.   Marcus, no
doubt, could admire, not merely the dignity with which
the philosopher might depart on his uncertain but
necessary disembarkation from the voyage of life, and
the bold and fearless valour with which his own legionaries or their barbarous antagonists could confront
death on the field of battle; but, at the height of his
wisdom, he could not comprehend the exalted enthusiasm with which the Christian trusted in the immortality and blessedness of the departed soul in the
presence of God.

There can be little doubt that Marcus Antoninus
issued an edict by which the Christians were again
exposed to all the denunciations of common informers,
whose zeal was now whetted by some share, if not by
the whole, of the confiscated property of delinquents.
The most distinguished Christians of the East were
sacrificed to the base passions of the meanest of mankind, by the Emperor, who, with every moral qualifica-
tion to appreciate the new religion, closed his ears, either
in the stern apathy of Stoic philosophy, or the more
engrossing terrors of Heathen bigotry.

It is remarkable how closely the more probable
records of Christian martyrology harmonise with the
course of events, during the whole reign of M. Aurelius,

---

stinacy."   A recent writer renders it
"ostentation or parade."   I suspect
an antithesis with ἰδικῆς κρίσεως, and
that it refers to the manner in which
the Christians *arrayed* themselves as
a body against the authority of the
persecutors; and should render the
words omitted in the text ὥστε καὶ
ἄλλον πεῖσαι, and without that tragic
display which is intended to persuade
others to follow our example.   The
Stoic pride would stand alone in the
dignity of an intrepid death.

and illustrate and justify my view of the causes and
motives of their persecution.[f]

It was on the 7th March, A.D. 161, that the elder Antoninus, in the charitable words of a Christian
apologist, sank in death into the sweetest sleep,[g]   A.D. 161.
and M. Aurelius assumed the reins of empire.   He immediately associated with himself the other adopted
son of Antoninus, who took the name of L. Verus.
One treacherous year of peace gave the hope of undisturbed repose, under the beneficent sway which carried
the maxims of a severe and humane philosophy into the
administration of public affairs.   Mild to all lighter
delinquencies, but always ready to mitigate the severity
of the law, the Emperor was only inexorable to those
more heinous offences which endanger the happiness of
society.   While the Emperor himself superintended the
course of justice, the senate resumed its ancient honours.
In the second year of his reign, the horizon
began to darken. During the reign of the First   A.D. 162.
Antoninus, earthquakes which shook down some of the
Asiatic cities, and fires which ravaged those of the West,
had excited much alarm ; but these calamities assumed
a more dire and destructive character during the reign
of Aurelius.   Rome itself was first visited with a terrible

---

[f] A modern writer, M. Ripault
(Hist. Philosophique de Marc Aurèle),
ascribes to this time the memorable
passage of Tertullian's Apology :—
" Existiment omnis publicæ cladis,
omnis popularis incommodi, Christianos esse causam. Si Tiberis *ascendit
in mœnia,* si Nilus non ascendit in
arva, si cœlum stetit, *si terra movit,
si fames, si lues,* statim Christianos ad
leones." An older, more learned historian writes that—" Tout ce qui suit
les cultes de l'empire s'élève de toutes
parts contre les Chrétiens. On attri-
bue à ce qu'on appelle leur impiété,
le déchaînement des fléaux, sous les-
quelles gémissent tous les hommes
sans privilége ni exemption, sans distinction de religion." Tillemont, Hist.
des Emp., Marc. Aurèl.

[g] Quadratus apud Xiphilin. Antonin. 3.

K 2

inundation.[h] The Tiber swept away all the cattle in the neighbourhood, threw down a great number of buildings; among the rest, the granaries and magazines of corn, which were chiefly situated on the banks of the river. This appalling event was followed by a famine, which pressed heavily on the poorer population of the capital. At the same time, disturbances took place in Britain. The Catti, a German tribe, ravaged Belgium ; and the Parthian war, which commenced under most disastrous circumstances, the invasion of Syria, and the loss of three legions, demanded the presence of his colleague in the empire. Though the event was announced to be prosperous, yet intelligence of doubtful and hard-won victories seemed to intimate that the spell of Roman conquest was beginning to lose its power. [i]

After four years, Verus returned, bearing the trophies of victory ; but, at the same time, the seeds of a calamity which outweighed all the barren honours which he had won on the shores of the Euphrates. His army was infected with a pestilence, which superstition ascribed to the plunder of a temple in Seleucia or Babylonia. The rapacious soldiers had opened a mystic coffer, inscribed with magical signs, from which issued a pestilential air, which laid waste the whole world. This fable is a vivid indication of the state of the public mind.[j] More rational observation traced the

A.D. 166.
Calamities of
the Empire.

---

h Capitol. M. Antonin. p. 168.

i " Sed in diebus Parthici belli, persecutiones Christianorum, quartâ jam post Neronem vice, in Asiâ et Galliâ graves præcepto ejus extiterunt, multique sanctorum martyrio coronati sunt." This loose language of Orosius (for the persecution in Gaul, if not in Asia, was much later than the Parthian war) appears to connect the calamities of Rome with the persecutions.

j This was called the " annus calamitosus." There is a strange story in Capitolinus of an impostor who harangued the populace from the wild

fatal malady from Ethiopia and Egypt to the Eastern army, which it followed from province to province, mouldering away its strength as it proceeded, even to the remote frontiers of Gaul and the northern shores of the Rhine. Italy felt its most dreadful ravages, and in Rome itself the dead bodies were transported out of the city, not on the decent bier, but heaped up in waggons. Famine aggravated the miseries, and, perhaps, increased the virulence, of the plague.[k] Still the hopes of peace began to revive the drooping mind; and flattering medals were struck, which promised the return of golden days. On a sudden, the Empire was appalled with the intelligence of new wars in all quarters. The Moors laid waste the fertile provinces of Spain; a rebellion of shepherds withheld the harvests of Egypt from the capital. Their defeat only added to the dangerous glory of Avidius Cassius, who, before long, stood forth as a competitor for the Empire. A vast confederacy of nations, from the frontiers of Gaul to the borders of Illyricum, comprehending some of the best known and most formidable of the German tribes, with others whose dissonant names were new to the Roman ears, had arisen with a simultaneous movement.[m] The armies were wasted with the Parthian campaigns, and the still more destructive plague.

The Marcomannic has been compared with the Second Punic War, though, at the time, even in the paroxysm of terror, the pride of Rome would probably not have

---

fig-tree in the Campus Martius, and asserted that if, in throwing himself from the tree, he should be turned into a stork, fire would fall from heaven, and the *end of the world was at hand:* " ignem de cœlo lapsurum finemque mundi affore diceret." As he fell, he loosed a stork from his bosom. Aurelius, on his confession of the imposture, released him. Cap. Anton. 13.

[k] Julius Cap. Ant. Phil. 21.

[m] See the list in Capitol. p. 200.

ennobled an irruption of barbarians, however formidable,
by such a comparison. The presence of both the Emperors was imperiously demanded. Marcus, indeed,
lingered in Rome, probably to enrol the army (for
which purpose he swept together recruits from all quarters, and even robbed the arena of its bravest gladiators), certainly to perform the most solemn and costly
religious ceremonies. Every rite was celebrated which
could propitiate the Divine favour, or allay the popular
fears. Priests were summoned from all quarters; foreign
rites performed;[n] lustrations and funereal banquets for
seven days purified the infected city. It was, no doubt,
on this occasion that the unusual number of victims
provoked the sarcastic wit which insinuated that, if the
Emperor returned victorious, there would be a dearth
of oxen.[o] Precisely at this time, the Christian
martyrologies date the commencement of the
persecution under Aurelius. In Rome itself, Justin, the
apologist of Christianity, either in the same or in the
following year, ratified with his blood the sincerity of
his belief in the doctrines for which he had abandoned
the Gentile philosophy. His death is attributed to the
jealousy of Crescens, a Cynic, whose audience had been
drawn off by the more attractive tenets of the Christian
Platonist. Justin was summoned before Rusticus, one
of the philosophic teachers of Aurelius, the prefect of

Christian
martyrdoms.
A.D. 166.

---

[n] " Peregrinos ritus *impleverit*."
Such seems the uncontested reading in
the Augustan history; yet the singular
fact that at such a period the Emperor
should introduce foreign rites, as well
as the unusual expression, may raise a
suspicion that some word with an
opposite meaning is the genuine expression of the author.

[o] This early pasquinade was couched
in the form of an address from the
white oxen to the Emperor : " If you
conquer, we are undone :" Οἱ βόες οἱ
λευκοὶ Μαρκῷ τῷ Καίσαρι [χαίρειν]
Ἂν δὲ σὺ νικήσῃς, ἧμες ἀπωλόμεθα.
Amm. Marc. xxv. 4.

the city, and commanded to perform sacrifice. On his refusal, and open avowal of his Christianity, he was scourged, and put to death. It is by no means improbable that, during this crisis of religious terror, mandates should have been issued to the provinces to imitate the devotion of the capital, and everywhere to appease the offended gods by sacrifice. Such an edict, though not designating them by name, would, in its effects, and perhaps in intention, expose the Christians to the malice of their enemies. Even if the provincial governors were left of their own accord to imitate the example of the Emperor, their own zeal or loyalty would induce them to fall in with the popular current. The lofty humanity which would be superior at once to superstition, to interest, and to the desire of popularity, and which would neglect the opportunity of courting the favour of the Emperor and the populace, would be a rare and singular virtue upon the tribunal of a provincial ruler.

The persecution raged with the greatest violence in Asia Minor. It was here that the new edicts Persecution in Asia were promulgated, so far departing from the Minor. humane regulations of the former Emperors, that the prudent apologists venture to doubt their emanating from the imperial authority.[P] By these rescripts, the delators were again let loose, and were stimulated by the gratification of their rapacity out of the forfeited goods of the Christian victims of persecution, as well as of their revenge.

The fame of the aged Polycarp, whose death the sorrowing Church of Smyrna related in an epistle to the Christian community at Philomelium or Philadel-

---

[P] Melito apud Euseb. H. E. iv. 20.

phia, which is still extant, and bears every mark of
authenticity,[q] has obscured that of the other
victims of Heathen malice or superstition. Of
these victims, the names of two only have survived;
one who manfully endured, the other who timidly
apostatised in the hour of trial. Germanicus appeared;
was forced to descend into the arena; he fought gal-
lantly, until the merciful Proconsul entreated him to
consider his time of life. He then provoked the tardy
beast, and in an instant obtained his immortality. The
impression on the wondering people was that of indignation rather than of pity. The cry was redoubled,
"Away with the godless! Let Polycarp be apprehended!" The second, Quintus, a Phrygian, had
boastfully excited the rest to throw themselves in the
way of the persecution. He descended, in his haste,
into the arena; the first sight of the wild beasts so
overcame his hollow courage, that he consented to
sacrifice.

Polycarp was the most distinguished Christian of the
East; he had heard the Apostle St. John; he had long
presided, with the most saintly dignity, over the see of
Smyrna. Polycarp neither ostentatiously exposed himself, nor declined such measures for security as might
be consistent with his character. He consented to
retire into a neighbouring village, from which, on the
intelligence of the approach of the officers, he retreated
to another. His place of concealment being betrayed
by two slaves, whose confession had been extorted by
torture, he exclaimed, "The will of God be done;"
ordered food to be prepared for the officers of justice;
and requested time for prayer, in which he spent two

Polycarp.

---

[q] In Cotelerii Patres Apostolici, ii. 195.

hours. He was placed upon an ass, and, on a day of
great public concourse, conducted towards the town.
He was met by Herod the Irenarch and his father
Nicetas, who took the Bishop, with considerate respect,
into their own carriage, and vainly endeavoured to
persuade him to submit to the two tests by which the
Christians were tried, the salutation of the Emperor by
the title of Lord, and sacrifice. On his determined
refusal, their compassion gave place to contumely; he
was hastily thrust out of the chariot, and conducted to
the crowded stadium. On the entrance of the old man
upon the public scene, the excited devotion of the
Christian spectators imagined that they heard a voice
from heaven, " Polycarp, be firm ! " The Heathen, in
their vindictive fury, shouted aloud, that Polycarp had
been apprehended. The merciful Proconsul entreated
him, in respect to his old age, to disguise his name.
He proclaimed aloud that he was Polycarp; the trial
proceeded. " Swear," they said, " by the Genius of
Cæsar; retract, and say, ' Away with the godless ! ' "
The old man gazed in sorrow at the frantic and raging
benches of the spectators, rising above each other, and,
with his eyes uplifted to heaven, said, " Away with the
godless ! " The Proconsul urged him further—" Swear,
and I release thee; blaspheme Christ." " Eighty and
six years have I served Christ, and He has never done
me wrong; how can I blaspheme my King, and my
Saviour ? " The Proconsul again commanded him to
swear by the Genius of Cæsar. Polycarp replied, by
avowing himself a Christian, and by requesting a day to
be appointed on which he might explain before the
Proconsul the blameless tenets of Christianity. " Persuade the people to consent," replied the compassionate
but overawed ruler. " We owe respect to authority;

to thee I will explain the reasons of my conduct; to the populace I will make no explanation." The old man knew too well the ferocious passions raging in their minds, which it had been vain to attempt to allay by the rational arguments of Christianity. The Proconsul threatened to expose him to the wild beasts.. "'Tis well for me to be speedily released from this life of misery." He threatened to burn him alive. " I fear not the fire that burns for a moment; thou knowest not that which burns for ever and ever." The Christian's countenance was full of peace and joy, even when the herald advanced into the midst of the assemblage, and thrice proclaimed—" Polycarp has professed himself a Christian!" The Jews and Heathens (for the former were in great numbers, and especially infuriated against the Christians) replied with an overwhelming shout, " This is the teacher of all Asia, the overthrower of our gods, who has perverted so many from sacrifice and the adoration of the gods!" They demanded of the Asiarch, the president of the games, instantly to let loose a lion upon Polycarp. The Asiarch excused himself by alleging that the games were over. A general cry arose that Polycarp should be burned alive. The Jews were again as vindictively active as the Heathens in collecting the fuel of the baths, and other combustibles, to raise up a hasty yet capacious funeral pile. He was speedily unrobed; he requested not to be nailed to the stake; he was only bound to it.

The calm and unostentatious prayer of Polycarp may be considered as embodying the sentiments of the Christians of that period. " O Lord God Almighty, the Father of thy well-beloved and ever-blessed Son Jesus Christ, by whom we have received the knowledge of thee; the God of angels, powers, and of every creature

and of the whole race of the righteous who live before
thee, I thank thee that thou hast graciously thought me
worthy of this day and this hour, that I may receive a
portion in the number of thy martyrs, and drink of
Christ's cup, for the resurrection to eternal life, both of
body and soul, in the incorruptibleness of the Holy
Spirit; among whom may I be admitted this day, as a
rich and acceptable sacrifice, as thou, O true and
faithful God, hast prepared, and foreshown, and accomplished. Wherefore I praise thee for all thy mercies;
I bless thee; I glorify thee, with the eternal and
heavenly Jesus Christ, thy beloved Son, to whom, with
thee and the Holy Spirit, be glory now and for ever."

The fire was kindled in vain. It arose curving like
an arch around the serene victim, or, like a sail swelling
with the wind, left the body unharmed. To the sight
of the Christians, he resembled a treasure of gold or
silver (an allusion to the gold tried in the furnace);
and delicious odours, as of myrrh or frankincense,
breathed from his body. An executioner was sent in to
despatch the victim; his side was pierced, and blood
enough flowed from the aged body to extinguish the
flames immediately around him.[r]

The whole of this narrative has the genuine energy
of truth: the prudent yet resolute conduct of the aged
bishop; the calm and dignified expostulation of the
governor; the wild fury of the populace; the Jews
eagerly seizing the opportunity of renewing their un-
slaked hatred to the Christian name, are described with
the simplicity of nature. The supernatural part of the

---

[r] The Greek account adds a dove,
which soared from his body, as it
were his innocent departing soul. For
περίστερα, however, has been very
ingeniously substituted επ' αριστερὰ.
See Jortin's Remarks on Ecclesiastical
History, i. 316. Perhaps περὶ στερνὰ,
" around the chest." Ruinart.

transaction is no more than may be ascribed to the
high-wrought imagination of the Christian spectators,
deepening every casual incident into a wonder: the
voice from heaven, heard only by Christian ears; the
flame from the hastily piled wood, arching over the
unharmed body; the grateful odours, not impossibly
from aromatic woods, which were used to warm the
baths of the more luxurious, and which were collected
for the sudden execution; the effusion of blood, which
might excite wonder from the decrepit frame of a man
at least a hundred years old.[s]   Even the vision of
Polycarp himself,[t] by which he was forewarned of his
approaching fate, was not unlikely to arise before his
mind at that perilous crisis.   Polycarp closed the
nameless train of Asiatic martyrs.[u]

Some few years after, the city of Smyrna was visited
with a terrible earthquake; a generous sympathy was
displayed by the inhabitants of the neighbouring cities;
provisions were poured in from all quarters; homes
were offered to the houseless; carriages furnished to
convey the infirm and the children from the scene of
ruin.   They received the fugitives as if they had been
their parents or children.   The rich and the poor vied
in the offices of charity; and, in the words of the
Grecian sophist, thought that they were receiving rather
than conferring a favour.[x]   A Christian historian may

[s] According to the great master of
nature, Lady Macbeth's diseased memory is haunted with a similar circumstance, at the murder of Duncan.
"Who would have thought the old
man to have had so much blood in
him?"—*Macbeth*, act v. s. 1.

[t] The difficulty of accurately recon-

ciling the vision with its fulfilment
has greatly perplexed the writers who
insist on its preternatural origin.
Jortin, p. 307.

[u] Κατέπαυσε τὸν διωγμὸν.

[x] Tillemont, Hist. des Emp. t. ii. p.
687. The philosopher Aristides wrote
an oration on this event.

be excused if he discerns in this humane conduct the manifest progress of Christian benevolence; and that benevolence, if not unfairly ascribed to the influence of Christianity, is heightened by the recollection that the sufferers were those whose amphitheatre had so recently been stained with the blood of the aged martyr. If, instead of beholding the retributive hand of Divine vengeance in the smouldering ruins of the city, the Christians hastened to alleviate the common miseries of Christian and of Pagan with equal zeal and liberality, it is impossible not to trace at once the extraordinary revolution in the sentiments of mankind, and the purity of the Christianity which was thus superior to those passions which have so often been fatal to its perfection.

At this period of enthusiastic excitement—of Superstition on the one hand, returning in unreasoning terror to its forsaken gods, and working itself up by every means to a consolatory feeling of the Divine protection; of Religion, on the other, relying in humble confidence on the protection of an allruling Providence; when the religious parties were, it might seem, aggrandising their rival deities, and tracing their conflicting powers throughout the whole course of human affairs—to every mind each extraordinary event would be deeply coloured with supernatural influence; and whenever any circumstance really bore a providential or miraculous appearance, it would be ascribed by each party to the favouring interposition of its own god.

Such was the celebrated event which was long current in Christian history as the miracle of the thundering legion.[y] Heathen historians, medals still extant, and the

---

[y] See Moyle's Works, vol. ii. Compare Routh, Reliq. Sacræ, i. 153, with authors quoted.

column which bears the name of Antoninus at Rome,
Miracle of the concur with Christian tradition in commemo-
thundering
legion. rating the extraordinary deliverance of the
Roman army, during the war with the German nations,
from a situation of the utmost peril and difficulty. If the
Christians at any time served in the Imperial armies [z]—
if military service was a question, as seems extremely
probable, which divided the early Christians,[a] some
considering it too closely connected with the idolatrous
practices of an oath to the fortunes of Cæsar and with
the worship of the standards, which were to the rest of
the army, as it were, the household gods of battle;
while others were less rigid in their practice, and forgot
their piety in their allegiance to their sovereign and
their patriotism to their country—at no time were the
Christians more likely to overcome their scruples than
at this critical period. The armies were recruited by
unprecedented means; and many Christians, who would
before have hesitated to enrol themselves, might less
reluctantly submit to the conscription, or even think
themselves justified in engaging in what appeared
necessary and defensive warfare. There might then
have been many Christians in the armies of M. Aurelius,
—but that they formed a whole separate legion, is
manifestly the fiction of a later age. In the campaign
of the year of our Lord 174, the army advanced incautiously into a country entirely without water; and,
in this faint and enfeebled state, was exposed to a
formidable attack of the whole barbarian force. Suddenly, at their hour of most extreme distress, a copious

---

[z] Tertullian, in a passage already quoted, states distinctly, "*militamus vobiscum.*"

[a] Neander has developed this notion with his usual ability, in this part of his History of the Church.

and refreshing rain came down, which supplied their
wants; and while their half-recruited strength was still
ill able to oppose the onset of the enemy, a tremendous
storm, with lightning, and hailstones of an enormous
size, drove full upon the adversary, and rendered his
army an easy conquest to the reviving Romans.[b] Of
this awful yet seasonable interposition, the whole army
acknowledged the preternatural, the Divine, origin. By
those of darker superstition, it was attributed to the
incantations of the magician Arnuphis, who controlled
the elements to the service of the Emperor. The
medals struck on the occasion, and the votive column
erected by Marcus himself, render homage to the established deities, to Mercury and to Jupiter.[c] The more
rational Pagans, with a flattery which received the
suffrage of admiring posterity, gave the honour to the
virtues of Marcus, which demanded this signal favour
from approving Heaven.[d] The Christian, of course,
looked alone to that One Almighty God whose providence ruled the whole course of nature, and saw the
secret operation of his own prayers meeting with the
favourable acceptance of the Most High.[e] " While the
Pagans ascribed the honour of this deliverance to their
own Jove," writes Tertullian, " they unknowingly bore
testimony to the Christians' God."

---

[b] In the year after this victory
(A.D. 175), the formidable rebellion of
Avidius Cassius disturbed the East,
and added to the perils and embarrass-
ments of the Empire.

[c] Mercury, according to Pagi, appears on one of the coins relating to
this event. Compare Reading's note
in Routh, loc. cit.

[d] Lampridius (in vit.) attributes
the victory to the Chaldeans. Marcus,

De Seipso (lib. i. c. 6), allows that he
had the magician Arnuphis in his
army.

Chaldæa mago seu carmina ritu
Armavere Deos, seu, quod reor, omne
        Tonantis
Obsequium Marci mores potuere mererl.
            —Claud. vi. Cons. Hon.

[e] In Jovis nomine Deo nostro testi-
monium reddidit. Tertullian, Ad Sca-
pulam, p. 20.   Euseb. Hist. Eccl.
v. 5.

The latter end of the reign of Marcus Aurelius[f] was signalised by another scene of martyrdom, in a part of the empire far distant from that where persecution had before raged with the greatest violence, though not altogether disconnected from it by the original descent of the sufferers.[g]

Martyrs of Vienne. A.D. 177. The Christians of Lyons and Vienne appear to have been a religious colony from Asia Minor or Phrygia, and to have maintained a close correspondence with those distant communities. There is something remarkable in the connexion between these regions and the East. To this district the two Herods, Archelaus and Herod Antipas, were successively banished; and it is singular enough, that Pontius Pilate, after his recall from Syria, was exiled to the same neighbourhood.

There now appears a Christian community, corresponding in Greek with the mother Church.[h] It is by no means improbable that a kind of Jewish settlement of the attendants on the banished sovereigns of Judæa might have been formed in the neighbourhood of Vienne and Lyons, and maintained a friendly, no doubt a mercantile, connexion with their opulent brethren of Asia Minor, perhaps through the port of Marseilles. Though Christianity does not appear to have penetrated

---

If I had determined to force the events of this period into an accordance with my own view of the persecutions of M. Aurelius, I might have adopted the chronology of Dodwell, who assigns the martyrs of Lyons to the year 167; but the evidence seems in favour of the later date, 177. See Mosheim. Lardner, who commands authority, if not by his critical saga-city, by his scrupulous honesty, says, "Nor do I expect that any learned man, who has a concern for his reputation as a writer, should attempt a direct confutation of this opinion." Works, 4to edit. i. 360.

[g] Euseb. Hist. Ecc. v. 1.

[h] Epistola Viennensium et Lugdunensium, in Routh, i. 265.

into Gaul till rather a late period,[i] it may have travelled by the same course, and have been propagated
in the Jewish settlement by converts from Phrygia or
Asia Minor. Its Jewish origin is, perhaps, confirmed
by its adherence to the Judæo-Christian tenet of
abstinence from blood.[k]

The commencement of this dreadful, though local,
persecution was an ebullition of popular fury. It was
about the period when the German war, which had
slumbered during some years of precarious peace, again
threatened to disturb the repose of the empire. Southern
Gaul, though secure beyond the Rhine, was yet at no
great distance from the incursions of the German
tribes ; and it is possible that personal apprehensions
might mingle with the general fanatic terror, which
exasperated the Heathens against their Christian fellow-
citizens. The Christians were on a sudden exposed to
a general attack of the populace. Clamours soon grew
to personal violence ; they were struck, dragged about
the streets, plundered, stoned, shut up in their houses,
until the more merciful hostility of the ruling authorities gave orders for their arrest and imprisonment
until the arrival of the governor. One man of birth
and rank, Vettius Epagathus, boldly undertook their
defence against the vague charges of atheism and
impiety : he was charged with being himself a Christian,
and fearlessly admitted the honourable accusation. The
greater part of the Christian community adhered reso-

---

[i] "Serius Alpes transgressa," is the
expression of a Christian writer, Sulpicius Severus.

[k] "How can those eat infants to
whom it is not lawful to eat the blood
of brutes?" Compare, however,

Tertullian's Apology, ch. 9, and
Origen contra Celsum, viii. ; from
whence it appears that this abstinence
was more general among the early
Christians.

lutely to their belief; the few whose courage failed in
the hour of trial, and who purchased their security by
shameful submission, nevertheless did not abandon their
more courageous and suffering brethren, but, at considerable personal danger, continued to alleviate their
sufferings by kindly offices. Some Heathen slaves were
at length compelled, by the dread of torture, to confirm
the odious charges which were so generally advanced
against the Christians:—banquets on human flesh;
promiscuous and incestuous concubinage; Thyestean
feasts, and Œdipodean weddings. The extorted confessions of these miserable men exasperated even the
more moderate of the Heathens, while the ferocious
populace had now free scope for their sanguinary
cruelty. The more distinguished victims were Sanctus,
a deacon of Vienne; a new convert named Maturus,
and Attalus, of Phrygian descent, from the city of
Pergamus. They were first tortured by means too
horrible to describe—if, without such description, the
barbarity of the persecutors, and the heroic endurance
of the Christian martyrs, could be justly represented.
Many perished in the suffocating air of the noisome
dungeons; many had their feet strained to dislocation
in the stocks; the more detested victims, after all
other means of torture were exhausted, had hot plates
of iron placed upon the most sensitive parts of their
bodies.

Among these victims was the aged Bishop of Lyons,
Pothinus, now in his ninetieth year, who died in prison
after two days from the ill usage which he had received
from the populace. His feeble body had failed, but his
mind remained intrepid; when the frantic rabble
environed him with their insults, and demanded, with con-
tumelious cries, "Who is the God of the Christians?"

he calmly replied, "Wert thou worthy, thou shouldst know."

But the amphitheatre was the great public scene of popular barbarity and of Christian endurance. The martyrs were exposed to wild beasts), which, however, do not seem to have been permitted to despatch their miserable victims), and made to sit in a heated iron chair till their flesh reeked upwards with an offensive stench.

A rescript of the Emperor, instead of allaying the popular frenzy, gave ample licence to its uncontrolled violence. Those who denied the faith were to be released; those who persisted in it, condemned to death.

But the most remarkable incident in this fearful and afflicting scene, and the most characteristic of the social change which Christianity had begun to work, was this, that the chief honours of this memorable martyrdom were assigned to a female, a slave. Even the Christians themselves scarcely appear aware of the deep and universal influence of their own sublime doctrines. The mistress of Blandina, herself a martyr, trembled lest the weak body, and still more the debased condition, of the lowly associate in her trial, might betray her to criminal concession. Blandina shared in all the most excruciating sufferings of the most distinguished victims; she equalled them in the calm and unpretending superiority to every pain which malice, irritated and licensed, as it were, to exceed, if it were possible, its own barbarities on the person of a slave, could invent. She was selected by the peculiar vengeance of the persecutors, whose astonishment probably increased their malignity, for new and unprecedented tortures, which she bore with the same equable magnanimity.

Martyrdom of Blandina.

L 2

Blandina was first led forth with Sanctus, Maturus, and Attalus; and, no doubt, the ignominy of their public exposure was intended to be heightened by their association with a slave. The wearied executioners wondered that her life could endure under the horrid succession of torments which they inflicted. Blandina's only reply was, "I am a Christian, and no wickedness is practised among us."·

In the amphitheatre, she was suspended to a stake, while the combatants, Maturus and Sanctus, derived vigour and activity from the tranquil prayers which she uttered in her agony; and the less savage wild beasts kept aloof from their prey. A third time she was brought forth, for a public exhibition of suffering, with a youth of fifteen, named Ponticus. During every kind of torment, her language and her example animated the courage and confirmed the endurance of the boy, who at length expired under the torture. Blandina rejoiced at the approach of death, as if she had been invited to a wedding banquet, and not thrown to the wild beasts. She was at length released. After she had been scourged, placed in the iron chair, enclosed in a net, and, now in a state of insensibility, tossed by a bull, some more merciful barbarian transpierced her with a sword. The remains of all these martyrs, after lying long unburied, were cast into the Rhone, in order to mock and render still more improbable their hopes of a resurrection.

CHAPTER VIII.

Fourth Period.   Christianity under the successors of M. Aurelius.

SUCH was the state of Christianity at the commencement of the fourth period between its first promul- Fourth gation and its establishment under Constantine. period. The golden days of the Roman Empire had already begun to darken, and closed for ever with the reign of Marcus the Philosopher. The empire of the world became the prize of bold adventure, or the precarious gift of a lawless soldiery. During little more than Rapid suc- cession of a century, from the accession of Commodus to Emperors. that of Diocletian, more than twenty Emperors. A.D. 180 to 284. (not to mention the pageants of a day, and the competitors for the throne who retained a temporary authority over some single province) flitted like shadows along the tragic scene of the imperial palace. A long line of military adventurers, often strangers to the name, to the race, to the language of Rome—Africans and Syrians, Arabs and Goths—seized the quickly shifting sceptre of the world. The change of sovereign was almost always a change of dynasty ; or, by some strange fatality, every attempt to re-establish an hereditary succession was thwarted by the vices or imbecility of the second generation. M. Aurelius is succeeded by the brutal Commodus; the vigorous and able Severus by the fratricide Caracalla. One of the imperial historians has made the melancholy observation, that of the great men of Rome scarcely one left a son the heir of his virtues; they had either died without offspring, or had left such heirs, that it had been better for mankind if they had died leaving no posterity.[a]

In the weakness and insecurity of the throne lay the strength and safety of Christianity. During such a period, no systematic policy was pursued in any of the leading internal interests of the empire. It was a government of temporary expedients, of individual passions. The first and commanding object of each succeeding head of a dynasty was to secure his contested throne, and to centre upon himself the wavering or divided allegiance of the provinces. Many of the Emperors were deeply and inextricably involved in foreign wars, and had no time to devote to the social changes within the pale of the empire. The tumults or the terrors of the German, or Gothic, or Persian inroad, effected a perpetual diversion from the slow and silent internal aggressions of Christianity. The frontiers constantly and imperiously demanded the presence of the Emperor, and left him no leisure to attend to the feeble remonstrances of the neglected priesthood. The dangers of the civil absorbed those of the religious constitution. Thus Christianity had another century of regular and progressive advancement to arm itself for the inevitable collision with the temporal authority, till, in the reign of Diocletian, it had grown far beyond the power of the most unlimited and arbitrary despotism to arrest its invincible progress; and Constantine, whatever the motives of his conversion, no doubt adopted a wise and judicious policy in securing the alliance of, rather than continuing the strife with, an

Insecurity of the throne favourable to Christianity.

---

[a] Neminem prope magnorum virorum optimum et utilem filium reliquisse satis claret. Denique aut sine liberis viri interierunt, aut tales habuerunt plerique, ut melius fuerit de rebus humanis sine posteritate discedere. Spartiani Severus, Aug. Hist. p. 360.

adversary which divided the wealth, the intellect, if not the property and the population, of the empire.

The persecutions which took place during this interval were the hasty consequences of the personal hostility of the Emperors, not the mature and deliberate policy of a regular and permanent government. In general, the vices and the detestable characters of the persecutors would tend to vindicate the innocence of Christianity, and to enlist the sympathies of mankind in its favour, rather than to deepen the general animosity. Christianity, which had received the respectful homage of Alexander Severus, could not lose in public estimation by being exposed to the gladiatorial fury of Maximin. Some of the Emperors were almost as much strangers to the gods as to the people and to the senate of Rome. They seemed to take a reckless delight in violating the ancient majesty of the Roman religion. Foreign superstitions, almost equally new, and scarcely less offensive to the general sentiment, received the public, the pre-eminent homage of the Emperor. Commodus, though the Grecian Hercules was at once his model, his type, and his deity, was an ardent votary of the Isiac mysteries; and at the Syrian worship of the Sun, in all its foreign and Oriental pomp, Elagabalus commanded the attendance of the trembling senate.

If Marcus Aurelius was, as it were, the last effort of expiring Polytheism, or rather of ancient philosophy, to produce a perfect man according to the highest ideal conception of human reason, the brutal Commodus might appear to retrograde to the savage periods of society. Commodus was a gladiator on the throne; and if the mind, humanised either by the milder spirit of the times, or by the incipient

influence of Christianity, had begun to turn in distaste
from the horrible spectacles which flooded the arena with
human carnage, the disgust would be immeasurably
deepened by the appearance of the Emperor as the
chief actor in these sanguinary scenes. Even Nero's
theatrical exhibitions had something of the elegance of
a polished age ; the actor in one of the noble tragedies
of ancient Greece, or even the accomplished musician,
might derogate from the dignity of an Emperor, yet
might, in some degree, excuse the unseemliness of his
pursuits by their intellectual character. But the amusements and public occupations of Commodus had long
been consigned by the general contempt and abhorrence
to the meanest of mankind, to barbarians and slaves;
and were as debasing to the civilised man as unbecoming in the head of the empire.[b] The courage which
Commodus displayed in confronting the hundred lions
which were let loose in the arena, and fell by his shafts
(though in fact the Imperial person was carefully
guarded against real danger), and the skill with which
he clave with an arrow the slender neck of the giraffe,
might have commanded the admiration of a flattering
court. But when he appeared as a gladiator, gloried
in the acts, and condescended to receive the disgraceful
pay of a profession so infamous as to degrade for ever
the man of rank or character who had been forced
upon the stage by the tyranny of former Emperors, the
courtiers, who had been bred in the severe and dignified
school of the Philosopher, must have recoiled with
shame, and approved, if not envied, the more rigid
principles of the Christians, which kept them aloof from
such degrading spectacles. Commodus was an avowed

---

[b] Ælii Lampridii, Commodus, in August. Hist.

proselyte of the Egyptian religion, but his favourite god
was the Grecian Hercules. He usurped the attributes
and placed his own head on the statues of this deity,
which was the impersonation, as it were, of brute force
and corporeal strength. But a deity which might command adoration in a period of primæval barbarism,
when man lives in a state of perilous warfare with the
beasts of the forest, in a more intellectual age sinks to
his proper level. He might be the appropriate god of
a gladiator, but not of a Roman Emperor.[c]

Everything which tended to desecrate the popular
religion to the feelings of the more enlightened and
intellectual must have strengthened the cause of Christianity; the more the weaker parts of Paganism, and
those most alien to the prevailing sentiment of the
times, were obtruded on the public view, the more they
must have contributed to the advancement of that faith
which was rapidly attaining to the full growth of a rival
to the established religion. The subsequent deification
of Commodus, under the reign of Severus, in wanton
resentment against the senate,[d] prevented his odious
memory from sinking into oblivion. His insults upon
the more rational part of the existing religion could no
longer be forgotten, as merely emanating from his
personal character. Commodus advanced into a god,
after his death, brought disrepute upon the whole
Polytheism of the empire. Christianity was perpetually,

---

[c] In the new fragments of Dion Cassius recovered by M. Mai there is an
epigram pointed against the assumption of the attributes of Hercules by
Commodus. The Emperor had placed
his own head on the colossal statue of
Hercules, with the inscription—"Lu-
cius Commodus Hercules."

Διὸς παῖς Καλλίνικος Ἡρακλῆς,
Οὐκ εἰμὶ Λεύκιος, ἀλλ' ἀναγκάζουσί με.

The point is not very clear, but it seems
to be a protest of the God against being
confounded with the Emperor. Mai,
Fragm. Vatic. ii. 225.

[d] Spartiani Severus, Hist. Aug.
p. 345.

as it were, at hand, and ready to profit by every favourable juncture.   By a singular accident, the ruffian Commodus was personally less inimically disposed to the Christians than his wise and amiable father.   His favourite concubine, Marcia, in some manner connected with the Christians, mitigated the barbarity of his temper, and restored to the persecuted Christians a· long and unbroken peace, which had been perpetually interrupted by thè hostility of the populace, and the edicts of the Government in the former reign.   Christianity had no doubt been rigidly repelled from the precincts of the court during the life of Marcus, by the predominance of the philosophic faction.   From this period, a Christian party occasionally appears in Rome.   Many families of distinction and opulence professed Christian tenets, and the religion is sometimes found in connexion with the Imperial family.   Still Rome, to the last, seems to have been the centre of the Pagan interest, though other causes will hereafter appear for this curious fact in the conflict of the two religions.

Severus wielded the sceptre of the world with the

Reign of Severus. A.D. 194 to 210.

vigour of the older Empire.   But his earlier years were occupied in the establishment of his power over the hostile factions of his competitors, and by his Eastern wars; his latter by the settlement of the remote province of Britain.[e]   Severus was at one time the protector, at another the persecutor, of Christianity.   Local circumstances appear to have influenced his conduct, on both occasions, to the Christian party.   A Christian named Proculus, a dependent, probably, upon his favourite freed slave Evodus, had been so fortunate as to restore Severus to health by

---

[e] Compare Tillemont, Hist. des Empereurs, iii. part 1, p. 146.

anointing him with oil, and was received into the Imperial family, in which he retained his honourable
situation till his death. Not improbably through the
same connexion, a Christian nurse and a Christian preceptor formed the disposition of the young Infancy of
Caracalla; and, till the natural ferocity of his Caracalla.
character ripened under the fatal influence of jealous
ambition, fraternal hatred, and unbounded power, the
gentleness of his manners and the sweetness of his
temper enchanted and attached his family, his friends,
the senate, and the people of Rome. The people beheld with satisfaction the infant pupil of Christianity
turning aside his head and weeping at the barbarity
of the ordinary public spectacles, in which criminals
were exposed to wild beasts.[f] The Christian interest at
the court repressed the occasional outbursts of popular
animosity: many Christians of rank and distinction
enjoyed the avowed favour of the Emperor. Their security may partly be attributed to their calm determination not to mingle themselves up with the contending
factions for the empire. During the conflict Peaceful con-
of parties, they had refused to espouse the duct of the
cause of either Niger or Albinus. Retired Christians.
within themselves, they rendered their prompt and
cheerful obedience to the ruling Emperor. The implacable vengeance which Severus wreaked on the senate
for their real or suspected inclination to the party of
Albinus, his remorseless execution of so many of the
noblest of the aristocracy, may have placed in a stronger
light the happier fortune, and commended the unimpeachable loyalty, of the Christians. The provincial
governors, as usual, reflected the example of the court;

---

[f] Spartian. Anton. Caracalla, p. 404.

some adopted merciful expedients to avoid the necessity
of carrying the laws into effect against those Christians
who were denounced before their tribunals; while the
more venal humanity of others extorted a considerable
profit from the Christians for their security. The unlawful religion, in many places, purchased its peace at
the price of a regular tax, which was paid by other
illegal, and mostly infamous, professions. This traffic
with the authorities was sternly denounced by some of
the more ardent believers, as degrading to the religion,
and as an ignominious barter of the hopes and glories of
martyrdom.[g]

Such was the flourishing and peaceful state of Chris-
Persecution   tianity during the early part of the reign of
in the East.   Severus. In the East, at a later period, he
embraced a sterner policy. During the conflict with
Niger, the Samaritans had espoused the losing,
A.D. 202.   the Jews the successful, party. The edicts of
Severus were, on the whole, favourable to the Jews, but
the prohibition to circumcise proselytes was re-enacted
during his residence in Syria, in the tenth year of his
reign. The same prohibition against the admission of
new proselytes was extended to the Christians. But
Christianity   this edict may have been intended to allay the
not perse-   violence of the hostile factions in Syria. Of
cuted in the
West.   the persecution under Severus there are few,
if any, traces in the West.[h] It is confined to Syria,

---

[g] Sed quid non timiditas persuade-
bit, quasi et fugere scriptura permit-
tat, et redimere præcipiat. . . . Nescio
dolendum an erubescendum sit cum in
matricibus beneficiariorum et curioso-
rum, inter tabernarios et lanios et fures
balnearum et aleones et lenones, Christiani quoque vectigales continentur.

Tertull. De Fugâ, c. 13.

[h] "Nous ne trouvons rien de considé-
rable touchant les martyrs que la per-
sécution de Sevère a pu faire à Rome
et en Italie." Tillemont. St. Andeole,
and the other martyrs in Gaul (Tillemont, p. 160), are of more than suspicious authenticity.

perhaps to Cappadocia, to Egypt, and to Africa; and, in the latter provinces, appears as the act of hostile governors, proceeding upon the existing laws, rather than the consequence of any recent edict of the Emperor. The Syrian Eusebius may have exaggerated local acts of oppression, of which the sad traces were recorded in his native country, into a general persecution: he admits that Alexandria was the chief scene of Christian suffering. The date and the scene Probable of the persecution may lend a clue to its origin. causes.

From Syria, the Emperor, exactly at this time, proceeded to Egypt. He surveyed, with wondering interest, the monuments of Egyptian glory Egypt. and of Egyptian superstition,[i] the temples of Memphis, the Pyramids, the Labyrinth, the Memnonium. The plague alone prevented him from continuing his excursions into Ethiopia. The dark and relentless mind of Severus appears to have been strongly impressed with the religion of Serapis. In either character, as the great Pantheistic deity, which absorbed the attributes and functions of all the more ancient gods of Egypt, or with his more limited attributes, as the Pluto of their mythology, the lord of the realm of departed spirits, Serapis[k] was likely to captivate the imagination of Severus, and to suit those gloomier moods in which he delighted in brooding over the secrets of futurity; and, having realised the proud prognostics of greatness, which his youth had watched with hope, now began to dwell on the darker omens of decline and dissolution.[m] The hour of imperial favour was likely to be seized by the

---

[i] Spartian. Hist. Aug. p. 553.

[k] Compare De Guigniaut, Sérapis et son Origine.

[m] Spartian had the advantage of consulting the autobiography of the Emperor Severus. Had time but spared us the original, and taken the whole Augustan history in exchange!

Egyptian priesthood to obtain the mastery and to wreak
their revenge on this new foreign religion, which was
making such rapid progress throughout the provinces
and the whole of Africa. Whether or not the Emperor
actually authorised the persecution, his countenance
would strengthen the Pagan interest, and encourage
the obsequious Prefect[n] in adopting violent measures.
Lætus would be vindicating the religion of the Emperor
in asserting the superiority of Serapis ; and the superiority of Serapis could be by no means so effectually
asserted as by the oppression of his most powerful
adversaries. Alexandria was the ripe and pregnant soil
of religious feud and deadly animosity. Three hostile
parties divided the city—the Jews, the Pagans, and the
Christians. They were perpetually blending and modifying each other's doctrines, and forming schools in
which Judaism allegorised itself into Platonism, and
Platonism, having assimilated itself to the higher Egyptian mythology, soared into Christianity; and thus Platonic Christianity, from a religion, became a mystic
philosophy. They all awaited, nevertheless, the signal
for persecution, and for licence to draw off in sanguinary
factions, and to settle the controversies of the schools
by bloody tumults in the streets.[o] The perpetual syncretism of opinions, instead of leading to peace and
charity, seemed to inflame the deadly animosity; and
the philosophical spirit, which attempted to blend all

---

[n] His name was Lætus. Eusebius,
Hist. Eccl. vi. 2.

[o] Leonidas, the father of Origen,
perished in this persecution. Origen
was kept away from joining him in his
imprisonment, and, if possible, in his
martyrdom, only by the prudent stratagem of his mother, who concealed all
his clothes. The boy of seventeen sent
a letter to his father, entreating him
not to allow his parental affection for
himself and his six brothers to stand
in his way of obtaining the martyr's
crown. Euseb. vi. 2. The property
of Leonidas was confiscated to the imperial treasury. Ibid.

the higher doctrines into a lofty Eclectic system, had
no effect in harmonising the minds of the different sects
to mutual toleration and amity. It was now the triumph
of Paganism. The controversy with Christianity was
carried on by burning the priests and torturing the
virgins, until the catechetical or elementary schools of
learning, by which the Alexandrian Christians trained up
their pupils for the reception of their more mysterious
doctrines, were deserted. The young Origen alone
laboured, with indefatigable and successful activity, to
supply the void caused by the general desertion of the
persecuted teachers.[p]

The African Prefect followed the example of Lætus
in Egypt. In no part of the Roman Empire
had Christianity taken more deep and perma-   Africa.
nent root than in the province of Africa, then crowded
with rich and populous cities, and forming, with Egypt,
the granary of the Western world; but which many
centuries of Christian feud, Vandal invasion, and Mohammedan barbarism, have blasted to a thinly-peopled
desert. Up to this period, this secluded region had gone
on advancing in its uninterrupted course of civilization.
Since the battle of Thapsus, the African province had
stood aloof from the tumults and desolation which
attended the changes in the imperial dynasty. As yet
it had raised no competitor for the empire, though
Severus, the ruling monarch, was of African descent.
The single legion, which was considered adequate to
protect the remote tranquillity of the province from the
occasional incursions of the Moorish tribes, had been
found sufficient for its purpose. The Paganism of the
African cities was probably weaker than in other parts

---

[p] Euseb. Hist. Eccl. vi. 2.

of the empire. It had no ancient and sacred associations with national pride. The new cities had raised new temples, to gods foreign to the region. The religion of Carthage,[q] if it had not entirely perished with the final destruction of the city, maintained but a feeble hold upon the Italianised inhabitants. The Carthage of the Empire was a Roman city. If Christianity tended to mitigate the fierce spirit of the inhabitants of these burning regions, it acquired itself a depth and impassioned vehemence, which perpetually broke through all restraints of moderation, charity, and peace. From Tertullian to Augustine, the climate seems to be working into the language, into the essence of Christianity. Here disputes maddened into feuds; and feuds, which, in other countries, were allayed by time, or died away of themselves, grew into obstinate, implacable, and irreconcileable factions.

African Christianity had no communion with the dreamy and speculative genius of the East. It

African Christianity. sternly rejected the wild and poetic impersonations, the daring cosmogonies, of the Gnostic sects: it was severe, simple, practical, in its creed; it governed by its strong and imperious hold upon the feelings, by profound and agitating emotion. It eagerly received the rigid asceticism of the anti-materialist system, while it disdained the fantastic theories by which that system accounted for the origin of evil. The imagination had another office than that of following out its own fantastic creations; it spoke directly to the fears and to the

---

q Compare Munter, Relig. der Carthager. The worship of the Dea cœlestis, the Queen of Heaven, should perhaps be excepted. See, forward, the reign of Elagabalus. Even in the fifth century the Queen of Heaven, according to Salvian (De Gubernatione Dei, lib. viii.), shared with Christ the worship of Carthage.

passions ; it delighted in realising the terrors of the final Judgement; in arraying, in the most appalling language, the gloomy mysteries of future retribution. This character appears in the dark splendour of Tertullian's writings; engages him in contemptuous and relentless warfare against the Gnostic opinions, and their latest and most dangerous champion, Marcion; till, at length, it hardens into the severe, yet simpler, enthusiasm of Montanism. It appears, allied with the stern assertion of ecclesiastical order and sacerdotal domination, in the earnest and zealous Cyprian; it is still manifestly working, though in a chastened and loftier form, in the deep and impassioned, but comprehensive, mind of Augustine.

Tertullian alone belongs to the present period, and Tertullian is, perhaps, the representative and the perfect type of this Africanism. It is among the most remarkable illustrations of the secret unity which connected the whole Christian world, that opinions first propagated on the shores of the Euxine found their most vigorous antagonist on the coast of Africa, while a new and fervid enthusiasm, which arose in Phrygia, captivated the kindred spirit of Tertullian. Montanism harmonised with African Christianity in the simplicity of its creed, which did not depart from the predominant form of Christianity; and in the extreme rigour of its fasts. While Gnosticism outbid the religion of Jesus and his Apostles, Montanism outbid the Gnostics in its austerities;[r] it admitted marriage as a neces-

Montanism.

---

[r] The Western Churches were, as yet, generally averse to the excessive fasting subsequently introduced to so great an extent by the monastic spirit. See the curious vision of Attalus, the martyr of Lyons, in which a fellow-prisoner, Alcibiades, who had long lived on bread and water alone, was reproved for not making free use of God's creatures, and thus giving offence to the

sary evil, but it denounced second nuptials as an inexpiable sin;[s] above all, Montanism concurred with the belief of the South in resolving religion into inward emotion. There is a singular correspondence between Phrygian Heathenism and the Phrygian Christianity of Montanus and his followers. The Orgiasm, the inward rapture, the working of a divine influence upon the soul till it was wrought up to a state of holy frenzy, had continually sent forth the priests of Cybele, and females of a highly excitable temperament, into the Western provinces;[t] whom the vulgar beheld with awe, as manifestly possessed by the divinity; whom the philosophic party, equally mistaken, treated with contempt, as impostors. So, with the followers of Montanus (and women were his most ardent votaries), with Prisca and Maximilla, the apostles of his sect, the pure, and meek, and peaceful spirit of Christianity became a wild, a visionary, a frantic enthusiasm: it worked paroxysms of intense devotion; it made the soul partake of all the fever of physical excitement. As in all ages where the mild and rational faith of Christ has been too calm and serene for persons brooding to madness over their own internal emotions, it proclaimed itself a religious ad-

---

Church. The Churches of Lyons and Vienne, having been founded from Phrygia, were anxious to avoid the least imputation of Montanism. Euseb. Hist. Eccl. v. 3.

[s] The prophetesses abandoned their husbands, according to Apollonius apud Euseb. v. 18.

[t] The effect of national character and temperament on the opinions and form of religion did not escape the observation of the Christian writers. There is a curious passage on the Phrygian national character in Socrates, H. E. iv. 28:—"The Phrygians are a chaste and temperate people; they seldom swear: the Scythians and Thracians are choleric; the Eastern nations more disposed to immorality; the Paphlagonians and Phrygians to neither: they do not care for the theatre or the games; prostitution is unusual." Their suppressed passions seem to have broken out at all periods in religious emotions.

vancement, a more sublime and spiritual Christianity.
Judaism was the infancy, Christianity the youth, the
revelation of the Spirit the manhood of the human soul.
It was this Spirit, this Paraclete, which resided in all
its fulness in the bosom of Montanus; his adversaries
asserted that he gave himself out as the Paraclete; but
it is more probable that his vague and mystic language
was misunderstood, or, possibly misrepresented by the
malice of his adversaries. In Montanism the sectarian,
the exclusive spirit, was at its height; and this claim to
higher perfection, this seclusion from the vulgar race of
Christians, whose weakness had been too often shown in
the hour of trial; who had neither attained the height
of his austerity, nor courted martyrdom, nor refused all
ignominious compromises with the persecuting authorities with the unbending rigour which he demanded,
would still further commend the claims of Montanism to
the homage of Tertullian.

During the persecution under Severus, Tertullian
stood forth as the apologist of Christianity; Apology of
and the tone of his Apology is characteristic Tertullian.
not only of the man, but of his native country,
while it is no less illustrative of the altered position of
Christianity. The address of Tertullian to Scapula, the
Prefect of Africa, is no longer in the tone of tranquil
expostulation against the barbarity of persecuting blameless and unoffending men, still less that of humble
supplication. Every sentence breathes scorn, defiance,
menace. It heaps contempt upon the gods of Paganism;
it avows the determination of the Christians to expel
the *dæmons* from the respect and adoration of mankind.
It condescends not to exculpate the Christians from
being the cause of the calamities which had recently
laid waste the province; the torrent rains which had

swept away the harvests; the fires which had heaped with ruin the streets of Carthage; the sun which had been preternaturally eclipsed, when at its meridian, during an assembly of the province at Utica. All these portentous signs are unequivocally ascribed to the vengeance of the Christians' God, visiting the guilt of obstinate idolatry. The persecutors of the Christians are warned by the awful examples of Roman dignitaries who had been stricken blind, and eaten with worms, as the chastisement of Heaven for their injustice and cruelty to the worshippers of Christ. Scapula himself is sternly admonished to take warning by their fate; while the orator, by no means deficient, at the same time, in dexterous address, reminds him of the humane policy of others:—" Your cruelty will be our glory. Thousands of both sexes, and of every rank, will eagerly crowd to martyrdom, exhaust your fires, and weary your swords. Carthage must be decimated; the principal persons in the city, even, perhaps, your own most intimate friends and kindred, must be sacrificed. Vainly will you war against God. Magistrates are but men, and will suffer the common lot of mortality; but Christianity will endure as long as the Roman Empire, and the duration of the Empire will be coeval with that of the world." [u]

History, even Christian history, is confined to more general views of public affairs, and dwells too exclusively on what may be called the high places of human life; but whenever a glimpse is afforded of lowlier, and of more common life, it is, perhaps, best fulfilling its office of presenting a lively picture of the times, if it allows

---

[u] I would recommend to my readers the fair and just contrast between Tertullian and Origen in Mons. Albert de Broglie's L'Eglise et l'Empire, pp. 121-126.

itself occasionally some more minute detail, and illustrates the manner in which the leading events of
particular periods affected individuals not in the highest
station.

Of all the histories of martyrdom, none is so unex-
aggerated in its tone and language, so entirely
unencumbered with miracle; none abounds in
such exquisite touches of nature, or, on the
whole, from its minuteness and circumstantiality,
breathes such an air of truth and reality, as that of
Perpetua and Felicitas, two African females. Their
death is ascribed, in the Acts, to the year of the accession
of Geta, [x] the son of Severus. Though there was no
general persecution at that period, yet, as the
Faithful held their lives, at all times, liable
to the outburst of popular resentment, or the caprice of
an arbitrary proconsul, there is much probability that a
time of general rejoicing might be that in which the
Christians, who were always accused of a disloyal reluctance to mingle in the popular festivities, and who
kept aloof from the public sacrifices on such anniver-

Martyrdom of Perpetua and Felicitas.

A.D. 202.

---

[x] The external evidence to the authenticity of these Acts is not quite
equal to the internal. They were first
published by Lucas Holstenius, from
a MS. in the Convent of Monte Casino;
re-edited by Valesius at Paris, and by
Ruinart, in his Acta Sincera Martyrum, p. 90, who collated two other
MSS. There appear, however, strong
indications that the Acts of these
African Martyrs are translated from
the Greek; at least it is difficult otherwise to account for the frequent un-
translated Greek words and idioms
in the text. The following are ex-

amples: c. iii., turbarum beneficio,
χαρὶν· c. iv., bene venisti, tegnon,
τεκνὸν· c. viii., in oramate, a vision,
ὁράματι· diadema, or diastema, an
interval, διαστῆμα· c. x., afe, ἀφὴ·
xii., agios, agios, agios.

There are indeed some suspicious
marks of Montanism which perhaps
prevented these Acts from being more
generally known.

It is not quite clear where these
martyrs suffered. Valesius supposed
Carthage; others, in one of the two
towns called Tuburbium which were
situated in Proconsular Africa.

saries, would be most exposed to persecution. The youthful catechumens, Revocatus and Felicitas, Saturninus and Secundulus, were apprehended, and with them Vivia Perpetua, a woman of good family, liberal education, and honourably married. Perpetua was about twenty-two years old; her father and mother were living; she had two brothers,—one of them, like herself, a catechumen,—and an infant at her breast. The history of the persecution is related by Perpetua herself, and is said to have been written by her own hand :—"When we were in the hands of the persecutors, my father, in his tender affection, persevered in his endeavours to pervert me from the faith.[y] 'My father, this vessel, be it a pitcher, or any thing else, can we call it by any other name?' 'Certainly not,' he replied. 'Nor can I call myself by any other name but that of Christian.' My father looked as if he could have plucked my eyes out; but he only harassed me, and departed, persuaded by the arguments of the devil. Then, after being a few days without seeing my father, I was enabled to give thanks to God, and his absence was tempered to my spirit. After a few days we were baptized, and the waters of baptism seemed to give power of endurance to my body. Again a few days, and we were cast into prison. I was terrified; for I had never before seen such total darkness. O miserable day!—from the dreadful heat of the prisoners crowded together, and the insults of the soldiers. But I was wrung with solicitude for my infant. Two of our deacons, however, by the payment of money, obtained our removal for some hours in the day to a more open part of the prison. Each of

---

[y] Dejicere, "to cast me down," is the expressive phrase, not uncommon among the early Christians.

the captives then pursued his usual occupation; but I
sat and suckled my infant, who was wasting away with
hunger. In my anxiety, I addressed and consoled my
mother, and commended my child to my brother; and
I began to pine away at seeing them pining away on
my account. And for many days I suffered this anxiety,
and accustomed my child to remain in the prison with
me; and I immediately recovered my strength, and was
relieved from my toil and trouble for my infant, and
the prison became to me like a palace; and I was
happier there than I should have been anywhere else.

"My brother then said to me, 'Perpetua, you are exalted to such dignity, that you may pray for a vision, and
it shall be shown you whether our doom is martyrdom
or release.'" This is the language of Montanism; but
the vision is exactly that which might haunt the slumbers
of the Christian in a high state of religious enthusiasm;
it showed merely the familiar images of the faith,
arranging themselves into form. She saw a lofty ladder
of gold, ascending to heaven; around it were swords,
lances, hooks; and a great dragon lay at its foot, to
seize those who would ascend. Saturus, a distinguished
Christian, went up first; beckoned her to follow; and
controlled the dragon by the name of Jesus Christ.
She ascended, and found herself in a spacious garden,
in which sat a man with white hair, in the garb of a
shepherd, milking his sheep,[z] with many myriads around
him. He welcomed her, and gave her a morsel of
cheese; and "I received it with folded hands, and ate
it; and all the saints around exclaimed, 'Amen.' I
awoke at the sound, with the sweet taste in my mouth,

---

[z] Bishop Münter, in his 'Sinnbilder
der alten Christen,' refers to this passage, to illustrate one of the oldest bas
reliefs of Christian art. H. i. p. 62.

and I related it to my brother; and we knew that our martyrdom was at hand, and we began to have no hope in this world."

"After a few days, there was a rumour that we were to be heard. And my father came from the city, wasted away with anxiety, to pervert me; and he said, 'Have compassion, O my daughter! on my grey hairs; have compassion on thy father, if he is worthy of the name of father. If I have thus brought thee up to the flower of thine age; if I have preferred thee to all thy brothers, do not expose me to this disgrace. Look on thy brother; look on thy mother, and thy aunt; look on thy child, who cannot live without thee. Do not destroy us all.' Thus spake my father, kissing my hands in his fondness, and throwing himself at my feet; and in his tears he called me not his daughter, but his mistress (domina). And I was grieved for the grey hairs of my father, because he alone, of all our family, did not rejoice in my martyrdom; and I consoled him, saying, 'In this trial, what God wills, will take place. Know that we are not in our own power, but in that of God.' And he went away sorrowing.

"Another day, while we were at dinner, we were suddenly seized and carried off to trial; and we came to the town. The report spread rapidly, and an immense multitude was assembled. We were placed at the bar; the rest were interrogated, and made their confession. And it came to my turn; and my father instantly appeared with my child, and he drew me down the step, and said in a beseeching tone, 'Have compassion on your infant;' and Hilarianus the procurator, who exercised the power of life and death for the Proconsul Timinianus, who had died, said, 'Spare the grey hairs of your parent; spare your infant; offer sacrifice for the welfare of the Emperor.' And I answered, 'I will not sacrifice.' 'Art thou a Christian?' said Hilarianus. I answered, 'I am a Christian.' And while my father stood there to persuade me, Hilarianus ordered him to be thrust down, and beaten with rods. And the misfortune of my father grieved me ; and I was as much grieved for his old age as if I had been scourged myself. He then passed sentence on us all, and condemned us to the wild beasts; and we went back in cheerfulness to the prison. And because I was accustomed to suckle my infant, and to keep it with me in the prison, I sent Pomponius the deacon to seek it from my father. But my father would not send it; but, by the will of God, the child no longer desired the breast, and I suffered no uneasiness lest at such a time I should be afflicted by the sufferings of my child, or by pains in my breasts."

Her visions now grow more frequent and vivid. The name of her brother Dinocrates suddenly occurred to her in her prayers. He had died at seven years old, of a loathsome disease, no doubt without Christian baptism. She had a vision in which Dinocrates appeared in a place of profound darkness, where there was a pool of water, which he could not reach on account of his small stature. In a second vision, Dinocrates appeared again; the pool rose up and touched him, and he drank a full goblet of the water. "And when he was satisfied, he went away to play, as infants are wont, and I awoke; and I knew that he was translated from the place of punishment."[a]

Again a few days, and the keeper of the prison, profoundly impressed by their conduct, and beginning to

---

[a] This is evidently a kind of purgatory.

discern "the power of God within them," admitted
many of the brethren to visit them, for mutual consolation. "And as the day of the games approached, my
father entered, worn out with affliction, and began to
pluck his beard, and to throw himself down with his
face upon the ground, and to wish that he could hasten
his death, and to speak words which might have moved
any living creature. And I was grieved for the sorrows
of his old age." The night before they were to be
exposed in the arena, she dreamed that she was changed
to a man; fought and triumphed over a huge and terrible Egyptian gladiator; and she put her foot upon his
head, and she received the crown, and passed out of the
Vivarian Gate, and knew that she had triumphed not
over man but over the devil. The vision of Saturus,
which he related for their consolation, was more splendid.
He ascended into the realms of light, into a beautiful
garden, and to a palace, the walls of which were light;
and there he was welcomed, not only by the angels,
but by all the friends who had preceded him in the
glorious career. It is singular that, among the rest,
he saw a bishop and a priest, between whom there
had been some dissensions; and while Perpetua was
conversing with them, the angels interfered and
insisted on their perfect reconciliation. Some kind of
blame seems to be attached to the Bishop Optatus,
because some of his flock appeared as if they came from
the factions of the circus, with the spirit of mortal
strife not yet allayed.

The narrative then proceeds to another instance of
the triumph of faith over the strongest of human
feelings, the love of a young mother for her offspring.
Felicitas was in the eighth month of her pregnancy.
She feared, and her friends shared in her apprehension,

that, on that account, her martyrdom might be delayed. They prayed together, and her travail came on. In her agony at that most painful period of delivery, she gave way to her sufferings. "How then," said one of the servants of the prison, "if you cannot endure these pains, will you endure exposure to the wild beasts?" She replied, "I bear now my own sufferings; then, there will be One within me who will bear my sufferings for me, because I shall suffer for his sake." She brought forth a girl, of whom a Christian sister took the charge.

Perpetua maintained her calmness to the end. While they were treated with severity by a tribune, who feared lest they should be delivered from the prison by enchantment, Perpetua remonstrated with a kind of mournful pleasantry, and said that, if ill-used, they would do no credit to the birthday of Cæsar: the victims ought to be fattened for the sacrifice. But their language and demeanour were not always so calm and gentle; the words of some became those of defiance— almost of insult; and this is related with as much admiration as the more tranquil sublimity of the former incidents. To the people who gazed on them, in their importunate curiosity, at their agapè, they said, "Is not to-morrow's spectacle enough to satiate your hate? To-day you look on us with friendly faces; to-morrow you will be our deadly enemies. Mark well our countenances, that you may know them again on the day of judgement." And to Hilarianus, on his tribunal, they said, "Thou judgest us, but God will judge thee." At this language, the exasperated people demanded that they should be scourged. When taken out to the execution, they declined, and were permitted to decline, the profane dress in which they were to be clad; the men, that of the priests of Saturn ; the women, that of the priestesses of Ceres.[b] They came forward in their simple attire, Perpetua singing psalms. The men were exposed to leopards and bears; and the women were hung up naked in nets, to be gored by a furious cow. But even the excited populace shrank with horror at the spectacle of two young and delicate women, one recently recovered from childbirth, in this state. They were recalled by acclamation, and in mercy brought forward again, clad in loose robes.[c] Perpetua was tossed, her garment was rent; but, more conscious of her wounded modesty than of pain, she drew the robe over the part of her person which was exposed. She then calmly clasped up her hair, because it did not become a martyr to suffer with dishevelled locks, the sign of sorrow. She then raised up the fainting and mortally wounded Felicitas, and, the cruelty of the populace being for a time appeased, they were permitted to retire. Perpetua seemed rapt in ecstasy, and, as if awaking from sleep, inquired when she was to be exposed to the beast. She could scarcely be made to believe what had taken place ; her last words tenderly admonished her brother to be steadfast in the faith. I may close the scene by intimating that all were speedily released from their sufferings, and entered into their glory. Perpetua guided with her own hand the merciful sword of the gladiator which relieved her from her agony.

This African persecution, which laid the seeds of future schisms and fatal feuds, lasted till, at least, the

---

b This was an unusual circum- stance; and ascribed to the devil.

c I am not sure that I am correct in this part of the version; it appears to me to be the sense. "Ita revocatæ discinguntur" is paraphrased by Lucas Holstenius, "revocatæ et discinctis in- dutæ."

second year of Caracalla.   From its close, except
during the short reign of Maximin, Christianity
enjoyed uninterrupted peace till the reign
of Decius.[d]   But during this period occurred
a remarkable event in the religious history of Rome.
The pontiff of one of the wild forms of the Nature-
worship of the East appeared in the city of Rome as Emperor.   The ancient rites of Baalpeor, but little changed
in the course of ages, intruded themselves into the
sanctuary of the Capitoline Jove, and offended at once
the religious majesty and the graver decency of Roman
manners.[e]   Elagabalus derived his name from
the Syrian appellative of the Sun; the had
been educated in the precincts of the temple; and the
Emperor of Rome was lost and absorbed in the priest of
an effeminate superstition.   The new religion did not
steal in under the modest demeanour of a stranger,
claiming the common rights of hospitality as the national
faith of a subject people : it entered with a public pomp,
as though to supersede and eclipse the ancestral deities
of Rome.   The god Elagabalus was conveyed in solemn
procession through the wondering provinces; his symbols were received with all the honour of the Supreme
Deity.   The conical black stone, which was adored at
Emesa, was, no doubt, in its origin, one of those obscene
symbols which appear in almost every form of the
Oriental Nature-worship.   The rudeness of ancient art
had allowed it to remain in less offensive shapelessness;
and, not improbably, the original symbolic meaning had
become obsolete.   The Sun had become the visible type

*Caracalla.
Geta.
A.D. 211-217.*

*Elagabalus
Emperor.
A.D. 218.*

---

[d] From 212 to 249:—Caracalla, 211; Macrinus, 217; Elagabalus, 218; Alexander Severus, 222 ; Maximin and the Gordians, 235-244; Philip, 244; Decius, 249.

[e] Lampridii Heliogabalus. Dion Cassius, lib. lxxix.; Herodian, v.

of Deity, and the object of adoration. The mysterious principle of generation, of which, in the primitive religion of nature, he was the type and image, gave place to the noblest object of human idolatry—the least debasing representative of the Great Supreme. The idol of Emesa entered Rome in solemn procession; a magnificent temple was built upon the Palatine Hill; a number of altars stood round, on which every day the most sumptuous offerings — hecatombs of oxen, countless sheep, the most costly aromatics, the choicest wines—were offered. Streams of blood and wine were constantly flowing down; while the highest dignitaries of the Empire—commanders of legions, rulers of provinces, the gravest senators, appeared as humble ministers, clad in the loose and flowing robes and linen sandals of the East, among the lascivious dances and the wanton music of Oriental drums and cymbals. These degrading practices were the only way to civil and military preferment. The whole senate and equestrian order stood around; and those who played ill the part of adoration, or whose secret murmurs incautiously betrayed their devout indignation (for this insult to the ancient religion of Rome awakened some sense of shame in the degenerate and servile aristocracy), were put to death. The most sacred and patriotic sentiments cherished, above all the hallowed treasures of the city, the Palladium, the image of Minerva. Popular veneration worshipped, in distant awe, the unseen deity; for profane eye might never behold the virgin image. The inviolability of the Roman dominion was inseparably connected with the uncontaminated sanctity of the Palladium. The Syrian declared his intention of wedding the ancient tutelary goddess to his foreign deity. The image was publicly brought forth; exposed to the sullying gaze of the multitude; solemnly wedded, and insolently repudiated by the unworthy stranger. A more appropriate bride was found in the kindred Worship of the Sun in Rome. Syrian deity, worshipped under the name of Astarte in the East, in Carthage as the Queen of Heaven—Venus Urania, as translated into the mythological language of the West. She was brought from Carthage. The whole city—the whole of Italy—was commanded to celebrate the bridal festival; and the nuptials of the two foreign deities might appear to complete the triumph over the insulted divinities of Rome.

Nothing was sacred to the voluptuous Syrian. He introduced the manners as well as the religion of the East; his rapid succession of wives imitated the polygamy of an Oriental despot; and his vices not merely corrupted the morals, but insulted the most sacred feelings, of the people. He tore a vestal virgin from her sanctuary, to suffer his polluting embraces; he violated the sanctuary itself; attempted to make himself master of the mystic coffer in which the sacred deposit was enshrined : it was said that the pious fraud of the priesthood deceived him with a counterfeit, which he dashed to pieces in his anger. It was openly asserted that the worship of the Sun, under his name of Elagabalus, was to supersede all other worship. If we may believe the biographies in the Augustan history, a more ambitious scheme of a universal religion had dawned upon the mind of the Emperor. Religious innovations meditated by Elagabalus. The Jewish, the Samaritan, even the Christian, were to be fused and recast into one great system, of which the Sun was to be the central object of adoration.[f] At all events, the deities of Rome

---

[f] Id agens ne quis Romæ Deus nisi Heliogabalus coleretur. Dicebat præ- | terea, Judæorum et Samaritanorum religiones, et Christianam devotionem,

were actually degraded before the public gaze into humble ministers of Elagabalus. Every year of the Emperor's brief reign, the god was conveyed from his Palatine temple to a suburban edifice of still more sumptuous magnificence. The statue passed in a car drawn by six horses. The Emperor of the world, his eyes stained with paint, ran and danced before it with antic gestures of adoration. The earth was strewn with gold dust ; flowers and chaplets were scattered by the people, while the images of all the other gods, the splendid ornaments and vessels of all their temples, were carried, like the spoils of subject nations, in the annual ovation of the Phœnician deity. Even human sacrifices, and, if we may credit the monstrous fact, the most beautiful sons of the noblest families, were offered on the altar of this Moloch of the East.[g]

It impossible to suppose that the weak and crumbling edifice of Paganism was not shaken to its base by this extraordinary revolution. An ancient religion cannot thus be insulted without losing much of its majesty : its hold upon the popular veneration is violently torn asunder. With its more sincere votaries, the general animosity to foreign, particularly to Eastern, religions, might be inflamed or deepened ; and Christianity might share in some part of the detestation excited by the excesses of a superstition so opposite in its nature. But others whose faith had been shaken, and whose moral feelings revolted, by a religion whose essential character was sensuality, and whose licentious tendency had been so disgustingly illustrated by the unspeakable pollutions

---

illuc transferendam, ut omnium cultu-rarum secretum Heliogabali sacerdo-tium teneret. p. 461.

     [g] Cædit et humanas hostias, lectis ad hoc pueris nobilibus et decoris per omnem Italiam patrimis et matrimis, credo ut major esset utrique parenti dolor. Lamprid. Heliogabalus.

of its imperial patron, would hasten to embrace that
purer faith which was most remote from the religion of
Elagabalus.

From the policy of the Court, as well as the pure and
amiable character of the successor of Elaga- Alexander
balus, the more offensive parts of this foreign Severus
superstition disappeared with their imperial A.D. 222.
patron.   But the old Roman religion was not reinstated
in its jealous and unmingled dignity.   Alexander Severus had been bred in another school ; and the influence which swayed him, during the earlier part at
least of his reign, was of a different character from that
which had formed the mind of Elagabalus.   It was the
mother of Elagabalus who, however she might blush
with shame at the impurities of her effeminate son, had
consecrated him to the service of the deity in Emesa.
The mother of Alexander Severus, the able, perhaps
crafty and rapacious, Mammæa, had at least Mammæa.
held intercourse with the Christians of Syria.
She had conversed with the celebrated Origen, and
listened to his exhortations, if without conversion, still not
without respect.   Alexander, though he had neither the
religious education, the pontifical character, nor the
dissolute manners of his predecessor, was a Syrian,
wth no hereditary attacnment to the Roman form of
Paganism.   He seems to have affected a kind of univer-
salism : he paid decent respect to the gods of the
Capitol ; he held in honour the Egyptian worship, and
enlarged the temples of Isis and Serapis.   In his own
palace, with respectful indifference, he enshrined, as it
were, as his household deities, the representatives of
the different religious or theophilosophic systems which
were prevalent in the Roman Empire,—Orpheus, Abraham, Christ, and Apollonius of Tyana.   The first of

these represented the wisdom of the Mysteries, the purified Nature-worship, which had laboured to elevate the popular mythology into a noble and coherent allegorism. It is singular that Abraham, rather than Moses, was placed at the head of Judaism : it is possible that the traditionary sanctity which attached to the first parent of the Jewish people, and of many of the Arab tribes, and which was afterwards embodied in the Mohammedan Koran, was floating in the East, and would comprehend, as it were, the opinions not only of the Jews, but of a much wider circle of the Syrian natives.[h] In Apollonius was centred the more modern Theurgy, the magic which commanded the intermediate spirits between the higher world and the world of man; the more spiritual polytheism which had released the subordinate deities from their human form, and maintained them in constant intercourse with the soul of man. Christianity, in the person of its founder, even where it did not command authority as a religion, had nevertheless lost the character under which it had so long and so unjustly laboured, of animosity to mankind. Though He was considered but as one of the sages who shared in the homage paid to their beneficent wisdom, the followers of Jesus had now lived down all the bitter hostility which had so generally prevailed against them. The homage of Alexander Severus may be a fair test of the general sentiment of the more intelligent Heathen of his time.[1] It is clear that the exclusive spirit of

[h] This might seem to confirm the theory of Sprenger as to the widespread Abrahamic religion, Monotheism, called Hanyferey, prevalent in Arabia at the time of the coming of Mohammed. Leben des Mohammed, B. i. c. i.

[1] Jablonski wrote a very ingenious essay to show that Alexander Severus was converted to *Gnostic* Christianity. Opuscula, vol. iv. Compare Heyne, Opuscula, vi. p. 169, et seqq.

Greek and Roman civilisation is broken down: it is
not now Socrates or Plato, Epicurus or Zeno, who are
considered the sole guiding intellects of human wisdom. These Eastern *barbarians* are considered rivals,
if not superior, to the philosophers of Greece. The
world is betraying its irresistible yearning towards a
religion; and these are the first overtures, as it were,
to more general submission.

In the reign of Alexander Severus, at least, commenced the great change in the outward appearance of Christianity. Christian bishops   Change in
the relation
were admitted, even at the court, in a recog-   of Christi-
nised official character; and Christian churches anity to
society.
began to rise in different parts of the empire, and to
possess endowments in land.[k] To the astonishment of
the Heathen, the religion of Christ had as yet appeared
without temple or altar; the religious assemblies had been
held in privacy : it was yet a domestic worship. Even
the Jew had his public synagogue or his more secluded
proseucha ; but where the Christians met was indicated
by no separate and distinguished dwelling; the cemetery
of their dead, the sequestered grove, the private chamber, contained their peaceful assemblies. Their privacy
was as once their security and their danger. On the
one hand, there was no well-known edifice in which the
furious and excited rabble could surprise the   First
Christian
general body of the Christians, and wreak its   churches.
vengeance by indiscriminate massacre; on the other, the

---

[k] Tillemont, as Gibbon observes, assigns the date of the earliest Christian
churches to the reign of Alexander
Severus ; Mr. Moyle to that of Gallienus. The difference is very slight, and,
after all, the change from a private
building, set apart for a particular
use, and a public one of no architectural pretensions, may have been almost
imperceptible. The passage of Lampridius appears conclusive in favour of
Tillemont.

jealousy of the Government against all private associations would be constantly kept on the alert; and a religion without a temple was so inexplicable a problem to Pagan feeling, that it would strengthen and confirm all the vague imputations of Atheism, or of criminal licence in these mysterious meetings which seemed to shun the light of day. Their religious usages must now have become much better known, as Alexander borrowed their mode of publishing the names of those who were proposed for ordination, and established a similar proceeding with regard to all candidates for civil office; and a piece of ground, in Rome, which was litigated by a company of victuallers, was awarded by the Emperor himself to the Christians, upon the principle that it was better that it should be devoted to the worship of God in any form, than applied to a profane and unworthy use.[m]

These buildings were no doubt, as yet, of modest height and unpretending form; but the religion was thus publicly recognised as one of the various forms of worship which the Government did not prohibit from opening the gates of its temples to mankind.

The progress of Christianity during all this period, though silent, was uninterrupted. The miseries which were gradually involving the whole Roman Empire, from the conflicts and the tyranny of a rapid succession of masters—from taxation becoming more grinding and burdensome—and from the still multiplying inroads and expanding devastations of the barbarians, assisted its progress. Many took refuge in a religion which promised beatitude in a future state of being, from the inevitable evils of this life.

---

[m] Ælii Lampridii Alexander Severus.

But in no respect is the progress of Christianity more evident and remarkable than in its influence on Heathenism itself. Though philosóphy, which had long been the antagonist and most dangerous enemy of the popular religion, now made apparently common cause with it against the common enemy, Christianity, yet there had been an unperceived *Influence of Christianity on Heathenism.* and amicable approximation between the two religions. Heathenism, as interpreted by philosophy, almost found favour with some of the more moderate Christian apologists; while, as we have seen, in the altered tone of the controversy, the Christians have rarely occasion to defend themselves against those horrible charges of licentiousness, incest, and cannibalism, which, till recently, their advocates had been constrained to notice. The Christians endeavoured to enlist the earlier philosophers in their cause; they were scarcely content with asserting that the nobler Grecian philosophy might be designed to prepare the human mind for the reception of Christianity; they were almost inclined to endow these sages with a kind of prophetic foreknowledge of its more mysterious doctrines. " I have explained," says the Christian in Minucius Felix, " the opinions of almost all the philosophers, whose most illustrious glory it is that they have worshipped one God, though under various names; so that one might suppose, either that the Christians of the present day are philosophers, or that the philosophers of old were already Christians."[n]

But these advances on the part of Christianity were

---

[n] According to Justin Martyr (Apolog. 5), Socrates was instructed through the Word, the Word which afterwards took the form of man, and was called Jesus Christ. (Compare Clem. Alex. Isagoge ad Hypotup., apud Bunsen, Analecta, i. 169). I am here again considerably indebted to Tschirner, Fall des Heidenthums, pp. 334-401.

more than met by Paganism. The Heathen religion,
which prevailed at least among the more enlightened
Pagans during this period, and which, differently modified, more fully developed, and, as we shall hereafter
find, exalted still more from a philosophy into a religion,
Change in   Julian endeavoured to reinstate as the esta-
Heathenism. blished faith, was almost as different from that
of the older Greeks and Romans, or even that which
prevailed at the commencement of the Empire, as it
was from Christianity. It worshipped in the same temples; it performed, to a certain extent, the same rites;
it actually abrogated the local worship of no one of the
multitudinous deities of Paganism. But over all this,
which was the real religion, both in theory and practice,
in the older times, had risen a kind of speculative
Theism, to which the popular worship acknowledged its
humble subordination. On the great elementary principle of Christianity, the Unity of the Supreme God, this
approximation had long been silently made. Celsus, in
his celebrated controversy with Origen, asserts that this
philosophical notion of the Deity is perfectly reconcileable
with Paganism. "We also can place a Supreme Being
above the world and above all human things, and approve
and sympathise in whatever may be taught of a spiritual
rather than material adoration of the gods; for, with
the belief in the gods worshipped in every land and by
every people, harmonises the belief in a Primal Being, a
Supreme God, who has given to every land its guardian,
to every people its presiding deity. The unity of the
Supreme Being, and the consequent unity of the design
of the universe, remains, even if it be admitted that
each people has its gods, whom it must worship in a
peculiar manner, according to their peculiar character;
and the worship of all these different deities is reflected

back to the Supreme God, who has appointed them, as
it were, his delegates and representatives. Those who
argue that men ought not to serve many masters impute
human weakness to God. God is not jealous of the
adoration paid to subordinate deities; He is superior in
his nature to degradation and insult. Reason itself might
justify the belief in the inferior deities, which are the objects of the established worship. For, since the Supreme
God can only produce that which is immortal and imperishable, the existence of mortal beings cannot be
explained, unless we distinguish from him those inferior
deities, and assert them to be the creatures of mortal
beings and of perishable things." [o]

From this time, Paganism has changed not merely
some of its fundamental tenets, but its general Paganism
character; it has become serious, solemn, de- serious.
vout. In Lucian, unbelief seemed to have reached its
height, and as rapidly declined. The witty satirist of
Polytheism had, no doubt, many admirers; he had no
imitators. A reaction has taken place; none of the
distinguished statesmen of the third century boldly
and ostentatiously, as in the times of the later Republic,
display their contempt for religion. Epicureanism has
lost, if not its partisans, its open advocates. The most
eminent writers treat religion with decency if not with
devout respect; no one is ambitious of passing for a
despiser of the gods. And with faith and piety broke
forth all the aberrations of religious belief and devout
feeling, wonder-working mysticism, and dreamy enthusiasm, in their various forms. [p]

This was the commencement of that new Platonism
which, from this time, exercised a supreme authority, to

---

[o] Origen contra Celsum, lib. vii.   [p] Tschirner, p. 401.

the extinction of the older forms of Grecian philosophy,
and grew up into a dangerous antagonist of Christianity.
It aspired to be a religion as well as a philosophy, and
gradually incorporated more and more of such religious
elements from the creeds of the Oriental philosophers as
would harmonise with its system.   It was extravagant,
but it was earnest; wild, but serious.   It created a kind
of literature of its own.   The Life of Apollonius
of Tyana was a grave romance, in which it
embodied much of its Theurgy, its power of connecting
the invisible with the visible world; its wonder-working,
through the intermediate dæmons at its command, which
bears possibly, but not clearly, an intentional, certainly
a close, resemblance to the Gospels.   It seized and
moulded to its purpose the poetry and philosophy of
older Greece.   Such of the mythic legends as it could
allegorise, it retained with every demonstration of reverence; the rest it either allowed quietly to fall into
oblivion, or repudiated as lawless fictions of the poets.
The manner in which poetry was transmuted into moral
and religious allegory is shown in the treatise
of Porphyrius on the Cave of the Nymphs in
the Odyssey.   The skill, as well as the dreamy mysticism,
with which this school of writers combined the dim traditions of the older philosophy and the esoteric doctrines
of the Mysteries, to give the sanction of antiquity to their
own vague but attractive and fanciful theories, appears
in the Life of Pythagoras, and in the work on
the Mysteries, by a somewhat later writer,
Iamblichus.

After all, however, this philosophic Paganism could
exercise no very extensive influence.   Its votaries were probably far inferior in number
to those of any one of the foreign religions introduced into

Apollonius of Tyana.

Porphyrius.

Life of Pythagoras.

Philosophic Paganism not popular.

the Greek and Roman part of the empire; and its strength perhaps consisted in the facility with which it coalesced with any one of those religions, or blended them up together in one somewhat discordant syncretism. The same man was philosopher, Hierophant at Samothrace or Eleusis, and initiate in the rites of Cybele, of Serapis, or of Mithra. Of itself this scheme was far too abstract and metaphysical to extend beyond the schools of Alexandria or of Athens. Though it prevailed afterwards in influencing the Heathen fanaticism of Julian, it eventually retarded but little the extinction of Heathenism. It was merely a sort of refuge for the intellectual few— a self-complacent excuse, which enabled them to assert, as they supposed, their own mental superiority, while they were endeavouring to maintain or to revive the vulgar superstition, which they-themselves could not but in secret contemn. The more refined it became, the less was it suited for common use, and the less it harmonised with the ordinary Paganism. Thus that which, in one respect, elevated it into a dangerous rival of Christianity, at the same time deprived it of its power. It had borrowed much from Christianity, or, at least, had been tacitly modified by its influence; but it was the speculative rather than the practical part, that which constituted· its sublimity rather than its popularity, in which it approximated to the Gospel. We shall encounter this new Paganism again before long, in its more perfect and developed form.

The peace which Christianity enjoyed under the virtuous Severus was disturbed by the violent _{Maximin.} accession of a Thracian savage.[q] It was enough _{A.D. 235.} to have shared in the favour of Alexander to incur the

---

q Euseb. Hist. Ecc. vi. 28.

brutal resentment of Maximin. The Christian bishops, like all the other polite and virtuous courtiers of his peaceful predecessor, were exposed to the suspicions and the hatred of the rude and warlike Maximin. Christianity, however, suffered, though in a severer degree, the common lot of mankind.

The short reign of Gordian was uneventful in Christian history. The Emperors, it has been justly observed, who were born in the Asiatic provinces were, in general, the least unfriendly to Christianity. Their religion, whatever it might be, was less uncongenial to some of the forms of the new faith; it was a kind of Eclecticism of different Eastern religions, which, in general, was least inclined to intolerance: at any rate, it was uninfluenced by national pride, which was now become the main support of Roman Paganism.

Gordian.
A.D. 238-244.

Philip, the Arabian,[r] is claimed by some of the earliest Christian writers as a convert to the Gospel. But the extraordinary splendour with which he celebrated the great religious rites of Rome refutes at once this statement. Yet it might be fortunate that a sovereign of his mild sentiments towards the new faith filled the throne at a period when the secular games, which commemorated the thousandth year of Rome, were celebrated with unexampled magnificence. The majesty, the eternity, of the empire were intimately connected with the due performance of these solemnities. To their intermission, after the reign of Diocletian, the Pagan historian ascribes the decline of Roman greatness.[s] The second millennium of Rome commenced with no flattering signs; the times were gloomy and menacing; and the

Philip.
A.D. 244.

Secular games.
A.D. 247.

---

[r] Euseb. vi. 34.   [s] Zosimus, ii. 7.

general and rigid absence of the Christians from these
sacred national creremonies, under a sterner or more
bigoted Emperor, would scarcely have escaped the
severest animadversions of the Government. Even
under the present circumstances, the danger of popular
tumult would be with difficulty avoided or restrained.
Did patriotism and national pride incline the Roman
Christians to make some sacrifice of their severer principles; to compromise for a time their rigid aversion to
idolatry, which was thus connected with the peace and
prosperity of the state?

The persecution under Decius, both in extent and
violence, is the most uncontested of those Decius.
which the ecclesiastical historians took pains A.D. 249-251.
to raise to the mystic number of the ten plagues of
Egypt. It was almost the first measure of a reign
which commenced in successful rebellion, and ended,
after two years, in fatal defeat. The Goths delivered
the Christians from their most formidable oppressor;
yet the Goths may have been the innocent authors of
their calamities. The passions and the policy of the
Emperor were concurrent motives for his hostility. The
Christians were now a recognised body .in the state;
however carefully they might avoid mingling in the
political factions of the empire, they were necessarily of
the party of the Emperor whose favour they had enjoyed.
His enemies became their enemies. Maximin persecuted those who had appeared at the court of Alexander
Severus; Decius hated the adherents, as he supposed
the partisans, of the murdered Philip.[t] The Gothic war
shook to the centre the edifice of Roman greatness.
Roman Paganism discovered in the relaxed morals of

---

[t] Euseb. vi. 39.

the people one of the causes of the decline of the empire ; it demanded the revival of the censorship. Causes of the This indiscriminating feeling would mistake, Decian perse-cution. in the blindness of aversion and jealousy, the great silent corrective of the popular morality for one of the principal causes of depravation. The partial protection of a foreign religion by a foreign Emperor (now that Christianity had begun to erect temple against temple, altar against altar, and the Christian bishop met the pontiff on equal terms around the imperial throne) would be considered among the most flagrant departures from the sound wisdom of ancient. Rome. The descendant of the Decii, however his obscure Pannonian birth might cast a doubt on his hereditary dignity, was called upon to restore the religion as well as the manners of Rome to their ancient austere purity ; to vindicate their insulted supremacy from the rivalship of an Asiatic and modern superstition. The persecution of Decius endeavoured to purify Rome itself from the presence of these degenerate enemies to her prosperity. Fabianus, Bi-shop of Rome. The bishop Fabianus was one of the first vic-tims of his resentment ;[u] and the Christians did not venture to raise a successor to the obnoxious office during the brief reign of Decius.

The example of the capital was followed in many of the great cities of the empire. In the turbulent and sanguinary Alexandria, the zeal of the populace outran that of the Emperor, and had already commenced a violent local persecution.[x] Antioch lamented the loss of her bishop, Babylas, whose relics were afterwards

---

[u] The Cav. de Rossi has found the name of Fabianus (I have read it myself), the first authentic martyr Pope in the real cemetery of Callistus, which his sagacity discovered, and his labours have explored. More on the Catacombs hereafter.

[x] Euseb. vi. 40, 41.

worshipped in what was still the voluptuous grove of
Daphne.[y] Origen was exposed to cruel torments, but
escaped with his life. But Christian enthusiasm, by
being disseminated over a wider sphere, had
naturally lost some of its first vigour. With
many, it was now a hereditary faith, not embraced by the ardent conviction of the individual, but instilled into the mind, with more or less
depth, by Christian education. The Christian writers
now begin to deplore the failure of genuine Christian
principles, and to trace the Divine wrath in the affliction
of the Churches. Instead of presenting, as it were, a
narrow, but firm and unbroken, front to the enemy, a
much more numerous, but less united and less uniformly
resolute, force now marched under the banner of Christianity. Instead of the serene fortitude with which they
formerly appeared before the tribunal of the magistrate,
many now stood pale, trembling, and reluctant, neither
ready to submit to the idolatrous ceremony of sacrifice,
nor prepared to resist even unto death. The fiery zeal
of the African Churches appears to have been most
subject to these paroxysms of weakness;[z] it was there
that the fallen (the Lapsi) formed a distinct and too
numerous class, whose readmission into the privileges of
the Faithful became a subject of fierce controversy;[a]
and the Libellatici, who had purchased a billet of immunity from the rapacious Government, formed another
party, and were held in no less disrepute by those who,
in the older spirit of the faith, had been ready or eager
to obtain the crown of martyrdom.

*Enthusi-
asm of
Christi-
anity less
strong.*

---

[y] Read the Sermons of Chrysostom
on S. Babylas.

[z] Dionysius apud Eusebium, vi. 14.

[a] The severer opinion was called the
heresy of Novatian ; charity and ortho-

doxy, on this occasion, concurred.
Euseb. vi. sub fin., vii. 4, 5. Another
controversy arose on the rebaptizing
heretics, in which Cyprian took the lead
of the severer party. Euseb. vii. 3.

Carthage was disgraced by the criminal weakness even of some among her clergy. A Council was held to decide this difficult point; and the decisions of the Council were tempered by moderation and humanity. None were irrevocably and for ever excluded from the pale of salvation; but they were absolved, according to the degree of criminality which might attach to their apostasy. Those who had sacrificed—the most awful and scarcely expiable offence!—required long years of penitence and humility; those who had only weakly compromised their faith, by obtaining or purchasing billets of exemption from persecution, were admitted to shorter and easier terms of reconciliation.[b]

Valerian, who ascended the throne three years after the death of Decius, had been chosen by Decius to revive, in his person, the ancient and honourable office

---

[b] The horror with which those who had sacrificed were beheld by the more rigorous of their brethren may be conceived from the energetic language of Cyprian: " Nonne quando ad Capitolium sponte ventum est, quando ultro ad obsequium diri facinoris accessum est, labavit gressus, caligavit aspectus, tremuerunt viscera, brachia conciderunt? Nonne sensus obstupuit, lingua hæsit, sermo defecit? . . Nonne ara illa, quo moriturus accessit, rogus illi fuit? Nonne diaboli altare quod fœtore tætro fumare et redolere conspexerat, velut funus et bustum vitæ suæ horrere, ac fugere debebat. . . . Ipse ad aram hostia, victima ipse venisti. Immolâsti illio-salutem tuam, spem tuam, fidem tuam funestis illis ignibus concremâsti." Cyprian, De Lapsis. Some died of remorse; with some the guilty food acted as poison. But the following was the most extraordinary occurrence, of which Cyprian declares himself to have been an eyewitness. An infant had been abandoned by its parents in their flight. The nurse carried it to the magistrate. Being too young to eat meat, bread, steeped in wine offered in sacrifice, was forced into its mouth. Immediately that it returned to the Christians, the child, which could not speak, communicated the sense of its guilt by cries and convulsive agitations. It refused the sacrament (then administered to infants), closed its lips, and averted its face. The deacon forced it into its mouth. The consecrated wine would not remain in the contaminated body, but was cast up again.—In what a high-wrought state of enthusiasm must men have been who would relate and believe such statements as miraculous?

of Censor; and the general admiration of his virtues
had ratified the appointment of the Emperor. Valerian.
It was no discredit to Christianity that the A.D. 254.
commencement of the Censor's reign, who may be supposed to have examined with more than ordinary care
its influence on the public morals, was favourable to
their cause. Their security was restored, and, for a
short time, persecution ceased. The change which took
place in the sentiments and conduct of Valerian is
attributed to the influence of a man deeply versed in
magical arts.[c] The censor was enslaved by a superstition which the older Romans would have beheld with
little less abhorrence than Christianity itself. It must
be admitted, that Christian superstition was too much
inclined to encroach upon the province of Oriental
magic; and the more the elder Polytheism decayed,
the more closely it allied itself with this powerful agent
in commanding the fears of man. With all classes,
from the Emperor who employed their mystic arts to
inquire into the secrets of futurity, to the peasant who
shuddered at their power, the adepts in those dark
and forbidden sciences were probably more influential
opponents of Christianity than the ancient and established
priesthood.

Macrianus is reported to have obtained such complete
mastery over the mind of Valerian, as to induce him to
engage in the most guilty mysteries of magic to trace
the fate of the empire in the entrails of human victims.
The edict against the Christians, suggested by
the animosity of Macrianus, allowed the com- A.D. 257.
munity to remain in undisturbed impunity; but it
subjected to the penalty of death all the bishops who

---

c Euseb. vii. 10.

refused to conform, and confiscated all the endowments
of their churches into the public treasury.

The dignity of one of its victims conferred a melan-
Cyprian, Bishop of Carthage. choly celebrity on the persecution of Valerian.
The most distinguished prelate at this time
in Western Christendom was Cyprian, Bishop of Carthage. If not of honourable birth or descent, for this
appears doubtful, his abilities had raised him to eminence
and wealth. He taught rhetoric at Carthage, and,
either by this honourable occupation or by some other
means, had acquired an ample fortune. Cyprian was
advanced in life when he embraced the doctrines of
Christianity; but he entered on his new career, if with
the mature reason of age, with the ardour and freshness
of youth. His wealth was devoted to pious and charitable uses; his rhetorical studies, if they gave clear-
ness and order to his language, by no means chilled its
fervour or constrained its vehemence. He had the
African temperament of character, and, if it may be so
said, of style; the warmth, the power of communicating
its impassioned sentiments to the reader; perhaps not
all the pregnant conciseness, nor all the energy, of
Tertullian, but, at the same time, little of his rudeness
and obscurity. Cyprian passed rapidly through the
steps of Christian initiation, almost as rapidly through
the first gradations of the clerical order. On the vacancy
of the bishopric of Carthage, his reluctant diffidence was
overpowered by the acclamations of the whole city, who
environed his house, and compelled him by their friendly
violence to assume the distinguished and, it might be,
dangerous office. He yielded, to preserve the peace of
Carthage.[d]

-----

[d] Epist. xiv.

Cyprian entertained the loftiest notions of the episcopal authority. The severe and inviolable unity of the outward and visible Church appeared to him an integral part of Christianity; and the rigid discipline enforced by the episcopal order the only means of maintaining that unity. The pale which enclosed the Church from the rest of mankind was drawn with the most relentless precision. The Church was the ark, and all without it were left to perish in the unsparing deluge.[e] The growth of heretical discord or disobedience was inexpiable, even by the blood of the transgressor. He might bear the flames with equanimity; he might submit to be torn to pieces by wild beasts—there could be no martyr *without* the Church. Tortures and death bestowed not the crown of immortality; they were but the just retribution of treason to the faith.[f]

The fearful times which arose during his episcopate tried these stern and lofty principles, as the questions which arose out of the Decian persecutions did his judgement and moderation. Cyprian, who embraced without hesitation the severer opinion with regard to the rebaptizing heretics, notwithstanding his awful horror of the guilt of apostasy, acquiesced in, if he did not dictate, the more temperate decisions of the Car-

---

[e] Si potuit evadere quisquam, qui extra arcam Noe fuit, et qui extra ecclesiam foris fuerit, evadit. Cyprian, de Unitate Ecclesiæ.

[f] Esse martyr non potest, qui in ecclesiâ non est.

Ardeant licet flammis et ignibus traditi, vel objecti bestiis animas suas ponant, non erit illa fidei corona, sed pœna perfidiæ, nec religiosæ virtutis exitus gloriosus, sed desperationis in-

teritus. De Unit. Eccles.

Et tamen neque hoc baptisma (sanguinis) heretico prodest, quamvis Christum confessus, et extra ecclesiam fuerit occisus. Epist. lxxiii.

"Though I give my body to be burned, and have not charity, it profiteth me nothing." 1 Cor. xiii. 3.— Is there no difference between the spirit of St. Paul and of Cyprian?

thaginian synod concerning those whose weakness had
betrayed them either into the public denial, or a timid
dissimulation, of the faith.

The first rumour of persecution designated the Bishop
of Carthage for its victim. " Cyprian to the lions!" was
the loud and unanimous outcry of infuriated Paganism.
Cyprian withdrew from the storm, not, as his subsequent
courageous behaviour showed, from timidity; but neither
approving that useless and sometimes ostentatious pro-
digality of life, which betrayed more pride than humble
acquiescence in the Divine will; possibly from the truly
charitable reluctance to tempt his enemies to an irre-
trievable crime. He withdrew to some quiet and secure
retreat, from which he wrote animating and consolatory
letters to those who had not been so prudent or so
fortunate as to escape the persecution. His letters
describe the relentless barbarity with which the Christians were treated; they are an authentic and contemporary statement of the sufferings which the Christians
endured in defence of their faith. If highly coloured
by the generous and tender sympathies or by the ardent
eloquence of Cyprian, they have nothing of legendary
extravagance. The utmost art was exercised to render
bodily suffering more acute and intense; it was a continued strife between the obstinacy and inventive cruelty
of the tormentor, and the patience of the victim.[g]
During the reign of Decius, which appears to have been

---

[g] Tolerâstis usque ad consumma-
tionem gloriæ durissimam questionem,
nec cessistis suppliciis, sed vobis potius
supplicia cesserunt.

Steterunt tuti torquentibus fortiores,
et pulsantes et laniantes ungulas pul-
sata ac laniata membra vicerunt. In-
expugnabilem fidem superare non potuit sæviens diu plaga repetita quamvis ruptâ compage viscerum ; torquen-
tur in servis Dei jam non membra,
sed vulnera. Cyprian, Epist. viii. ad
Martyres. Compare Epist. lxii.

one continued persecution, Cyprian stood aloof in his undisturbed retreat. He returned to Carthage probably at the commencement of Valerian's reign, and had a splendid opportunity of Christian revenge upon the city which had thirsted for his blood. A plague Plague in Carthage. ravaged the whole Roman world, and its most destructive violence thinned the streets of Carthage. It went spreading on from house to house, especially those of the lower orders, with awful regularity. The streets were strewn with the bodies of the dead and the dying, who vainly appealed to the laws of nature and humanity for that assistance of which those who passed them by might soon stand in need. General distrust spread through society. Men avoided or exposed their nearest relatives; as if, by excluding the dying, they could exclude death.[h] No one, says the Deacon Pontius, writing of the population of Carthage in general, did as he would be done by. Cyprian addressed the Christians in the most earnest and effective language. He exhorted them to show the sincerity of their A.D. 252. Conduct of Cyprian and the Christians. belief in the doctrines of their Master, not by confining their acts of kindliness to their own brotherhood, but by extending them indiscriminately to their enemies. The city was divided into districts; offices were assigned to all the Christians; the rich lavished their wealth, the poor their personal exertions; and men, perhaps just emerged from the mine or the prison, with the scars or mutilations of their recent tortures upon their bodies, were seen exposing their lives, if possible, to a more honourable martyrdom; as before the voluntary victims of Christian faith, so now of

---

[h] Pontius, in Vitâ Cypriani. Horrere omnes, fugere, vitare contagium; exponere suos impie; quasi cum illo peste morituro, etiam mortem ipsam aliquis posset excludere.

Christian charity. Yet the Heathen party, instead of
being subdued, persisted in attributing this terrible
scourge to the impiety of the Christians, which provoked
the angry gods; nor can we wonder if the zeal of Cyprian
retorted the argument, and traced rather the retributive
justice of the Almighty to the wanton persecutions
inflicted on the unoffending Christians.

Cyprian did not again withdraw on the commencement of the Valerian persecution. He was
summoned before the proconsul, who communicated his instructions from the Emperor, to compel
all those who professed foreign religions to offer sacrifice. Cyprian refused, with tranquil determination. He
was banished from Carthage. He remained in his
pleasant retreat rather than place of exile, in the small
town of Ceribis, near the sea-shore, in a spot shaded
with verdant groves, and with a clear and healthful
stream of water. It was provided with every comfort,
and even luxury, in which the austere nature of Cyprian
would permit itself to indulge.[1] But when his hour
came, the tranquil and collected dignity of Cyprian in
no respect fell below his lofty principles.

On the accession of a new proconsul, Galerius Maximus, Cyprian was either recalled or permitted
to return from his exile. He resided in his
own gardens, from whence he received a summons to
appear before the proconsul. He would not listen to
the earnest solicitations of his friends, who entreated
him again to consult his safety by withdrawing to some
place of concealment. His trial was postponed for a

Cyprian's retreat.

Return to Carthage.

---

[1] "If," says Pontius, who visited
his master in his retirement, "instead
of this sunny and agreeable spot, it had
been a waste and rocky solitude, the
angels which fed Elijah and Daniel
would have ministered to the holy
Cyprian."

day; he was treated, while in custody, with respect and
even delicacy. But the intelligence of the apprehension of Cyprian drew together the whole city; the
Heathen, eager to behold the spectacle of his martyrdom, the Christians, to watch in their affectionate zeal
at the doors of his prison. In the morning, he had to
walk some distance, and was violently heated by the
exertion. A Christian soldier offered to procure him
dry linen, apparently from mere courtesy, but, in
reality, to obtain such precious relics, steeped in the
" bloody sweat" of the martyr. Cyprian intimated
that it was useless to seek remedy for inconveniences
which, perhaps, would that day pass away for ever.
After a short delay, the proconsul appeared. The examination was brief:—" Art thou Thascius Cyprian, the
bishop of so many impious men? The most sacred Emperor commands thee to sacrifice." Cyprian answered,
" I will not sacrifice." " Consider well," rejoined the
proconsul. " Execute your orders," answered Cyprian;
" the case admits of no consideration."

Galerius consulted with his Council, and then reluctantly [J] delivered his sentence. " Thascius Cyprian,
thou hast lived long in thy impiety, and assembled
around thee many men involved in the same wicked
conspiracy. Thou hast shown thyself an enemy alike
to the gods and the laws of the empire; the pious
and sacred Emperors have in vain endeavoured to recall
thee to the worship of thy ancestors. Since, then, thou
hast been the chief author and leader of these most
guilty practices, thou shalt be an example to those
whom thou hast deluded to thy unlawful assemblies.

[J] In the Acta, " vix ægrè " is the expression; it may, however, mean that
he spoke with difficulty, on account of
his bad health.

Thou must expiate thy crime with thy blood." Cyprian
said, "God be thanked."[k]   The Bishop of Carthage
was carried into a neighbouring field and beheaded.
He maintained his serene composure to the last.   It was
remarkable that but a few days afterwards the proconsul
died.   Though he had been in bad health, this circumstance was not likely to be lost upon the Christians.

Everywhere, indeed, the public mind was no doubt
strongly impressed with the remarkable fact, which
Miserable   the Christians would lose no opportunity of
death of the
persecutors of   enforcing on the awe-struck attention, that
Christianity.   their enemies appeared to be the enemies of
Heaven.   An early and a fearful fate appeared to be
the inevitable lot of the persecutors of Christianity.
Their profound and earnest conviction that the hand of
Divine Providence was perpetually and visibly interposing in the affairs of men would not be so deeply
imbued with the spirit of their Divine Master, as to
suppress the language of triumph, or even of vengeance,
when the enemies of their God and of themselves either
suffered defeat and death, or, worse than an honourable
death, a cruel and insulting captivity.   The death of
Decius, according to the Pagan account, had been
worthy of the old Republic.   He was environed by the
Goths; his son was killed by an arrow; he cried aloud,
that the loss of a single soldier was nothing to the glory
of the empire; he renewed the battle, and fell valiantly.
The Christian writers strip away all the more ennobling

---

[k] I have translated this sentence, as
the Acts of Cyprian are remarkable for
their simplicity, and total absence of
later legendary ornament; and particularly for the circumstantial air of
truth with which they do justice to the
regularity of the whole proceeding.
Compare the Life of Cyprian by the
Deacon Pontius; the Acts, in Ruinart,
p. 216; Cave's Lives of the Apostles,
&c., art. "Cyprian."

incidents. According to their account, having been decoyed by the enemy, or misled by a treacherous friend, into a marsh where he could neither fight nor fly, he perished tamely, and his unburied body was left to the beasts and carrion fowls.[m] The captivity of Valerian, the mystery which hung over his death, allowed ample scope to the imagination of those whose national hatred of the barbarians would attribute the most unmanly ferocity to the Persian conqueror, and of those who would consider their God exalted by the most cruel and debasing sufferings inflicted on the oppressor of the Church. Valerian, it was said, was forced to bend his back that the proud conqueror might mount his horse, as from a footstool; his skin was flayed off (according to one more modern account, while he was alive), stuffed, and exposed to the mockery of the Persian rabble.

The luxurious and versatile Gallienus restored peace to the Church. The edict of Valerian was rescinded; the bishops resumed their public functions; the buildings were restored, and their property, which had been confiscated by the state, restored to the rightful owners.[n] *Gallienus alone. A.D. 260.*

The last transient collision of Christianity with the Government before its final conflict under Diocletian, took place, or was at least threatened, during the administration of the great Aurelian. The reign of Aurelian, occupied by warlike campaigns in every part of the world, left little time for attention to the internal police, or the religious interests, of the empire. The mother of Aurelian was priestess of the Sun at Sirmium, and the Emperor built a temple to *Aurelian. A.D. 271-275.*

---

[m] Orat. Constant. apud Euseb. c. xxiv. Lactant. de Mort. Persec.

[n] Euseb. vii. 13; x. 23.

that deity, his tutelary god, at Rome. But the dangerous wars of Aurelian required the concurrent aid of all the deities who took an interest in the fate of Rome. The sacred ceremony of consulting the Sibylline books, in whose secret and mysterious leaves were written the destinies of Rome, took place at his command. The severe Emperor reproaches the senate for their want of faith in these mystic volumes, or of zeal in the public service, as though they had been infected by the principles of Christianity.[°]

But there were no hostile measures taken against Christianity in the early part of his reign; and he was summoned to take upon himself the extraordinary office of arbiter in a Christian controversy. A new empire seemed rising in the East, under the warlike Queen of Palmyra. Zenobia extended her protection, with politic indifference, to Jew, to Pagan, and to Christian. It might also appear that a kindred spiritual ambition animated her favourite, Paul of Samosata, the Bishop of Antioch, and that he aspired to found a new religion, adapted to the kingdom of Palmyra, by blending together the elements of Paganism, of Judaism, and of Christianity. Ambitious, dissolute, and rapacious, according to the representation of his adversaries, Paul of Samosata had been advanced to the important see of Antioch; but the zealous vigilance of the neighbouring bishops soon discovered that Paul held opinions, as to the mere human nature of the Saviour, more nearly allied to Judaism than to the Christian creed. The pride, the wealth, the state of Paul, no less offended the feelings, and put to shame

Paul of Samosata.

---

* Read the Life of Aurelian by Vopiscus, one of the best, at least most careful, in that unequal collection.

the more modest demeanour and the humbler pretensions
of former prelates. He had obtained, either from the
Roman authorities or from Zenobia, a civil magistracy,
and prided himself more on his title of ducenary than
of Christian bishop. He passed through the streets
environed by guards, and preceded and followed by
multitudes of attendants and supplicants, whose petitions he received and read with the stately bearing of
a public officer rather than the affability of a prelate.
His conduct in the ecclesiastical assemblies was equally
overbearing : he sat on a throne, and, while he indulged himself in every kind of theatric gesture, resented the silence of those who did not receive him
with applause, or pay homage to his dignity. His
magnificence disturbed the modest solemnity of the
ordinary worship. Instead of the simpler music of the
Church, the hymns, in which the voices of the worshippers mingled in fervent, if less harmonious, unison, Paul
organised a regular choir, in which the soft tones of
female voices, in their more melting and artificial ca-
dences, sometimes called to mind the voluptuous rites
of Paganism, and could not be heard without shuddering
by those accustomed to the more unadorned ritual.[p]
The Hosannas, sometimes introduced as a kind of salutation to the bishop, became, it was said, the chief part
of the service, which was rather to the glory of Paul
than of the Lord. This introduction of a new and
effeminate ceremonial would of itself, with its rigid
adversaries, have formed a ground for the charge of
dissolute morals, against which may be fairly urged
the avowed patronage of the severe Zenobia.[q] But the

---

[p] Ὦν καὶ ἀκουσας ἄν τις φρίξειεν.
Such is the expression in the decree of
excommunication issued by the bishops.

Euseb. vii. 30.
[q] Compare Routh, Reliq. Sacr. ii.
505.

pomp of Paul's expenditure did not interfere with the
accumulation of considerable wealth, which he extorted
from the timid zeal of his partisans, and, it was said, by
the venal administration of the judicial authority of his
episcopate, perhaps of his civil magistracy. But Paul
by no means stood alone; he had a powerful party
among the ecclesiastical body, the chorepiscopi of the
country districts, and the presbyters of the city. He
set at defiance the synod of bishops, who pronounced
a solemn sentence of excommunication;[r] and, secure
under the protection of the Queen of Palmyra, if her
ambition should succeed in wresting Syria, with its
noble capital, from the power of Rome, and in maintaining her strong and influential position between the
conflicting powers of Persia and the Empire, Paul
might hope to share in her triumph, and establish his
degenerate but splendid form of Christianity in the
very seat of its primitive Apostolic foundation. Paul
had staked his success upon that of his warlike pa-
troness; and on the fall of Zenobia, the bishops appealed to Aurelian to expel the rebel against their
authority, and the partisan of the Palmyrenes, who had
taken arms against the majesty of the empire, from his
episcopal dignity at Antioch. Aurelian did not altogether refuse to interfere in this unprecedented cause,
but, with laudable impartiality, declined any actual
cognisance of the affair, and transferred the sentence
from the personal enemies of Paul, the Bishops of Syria,
to those of Rome and Italy. By their sentence, Paul
was degraded from his episcopate.

The sentiments of Aurelian changed towards Christi-

---

[r] See the sentence in Eusebius, vii. 30, and in Routh, Reliquiæ Sacræ, ii.
465, et seq.

anity near the close of his reign. The severity of his
character, reckless of human blood, would not, if committed in the strife, have hesitated at any measures
to subdue the rebellious spirit of his subjects. Sanguinary edicts were issued, though his death prevented
their general promulgation ; and in the fate of Aurelian
the Christians discovered another instance of the Divine
vengeance, which appeared to mark their enemies with
the sign of inevitable and appalling destruction.

Till the reign of Diocletian, the Churches reposed in
undisturbed but enervating security.

CHAPTER IX.

The Persecution under Diocletian.

THE final contest between Paganism and Christianity drew near. Almost three hundred years had elapsed since the divine Author of the new religion had entered upon his mortal life in a small village in Pales-

A.D. 284.

tine;[a] and now, having gained so powerful an ascendancy over the civilised world, the Gospel was to undergo its last and most trying ordeal, before it should assume the reins of empire, and become the established religion of the Roman world. It was to sustain the deliberate and systematic attack of the temporal authority, arming, in almost every part of the empire, in defence of the ancient Polytheism. At this crisis, it is important to survey the state of Christianity, as well as the character of the sovereign and of the government, which made this ultimate and most vigorous attempt to suppress the triumphant progress of the new faith.

Peace of the Christians.

The last fifty years, with a short interval of menaced, probably of actual, persecution, during the reign of Aurelian, had passed in peace and security. The Christians had become not merely a public, but an imposing and influential, body ; their separate existence had been recognised by the law of Gallienus; their churches had arisen in most of the cities of the empire ; as yet, probably, with no great pre-

---

[a] Diocletian began his reign A.D. 284. The commencement of the persecution is dated A.D. 303.

tensions to architectural grandeur, though no doubt
ornamented by the liberality of the worshippers, and
furnished with vestments, and with chalices, lamps, and
chandeliers of silver. The number of these buildings
was constantly on the increase, or the crowding multitudes of proselytes demanded the extension of the
narrow and humble walls. The Christians no longer
declined, or refused to aspire to, the honours of the
state. They filled offices of distinction, and even of
supreme authority, in the provinces, and in the army;
they were exempted, either by tacit connivance or direct
indulgence, from the accustomed sacrifices. Progress of
Among the more immediate attendants on the Christianity.
Emperor, two or three openly professed the Christian
faith. Prisca the wife, and Valeria, the daughter of
Diocletian and wife of Galerius, were suspected, if not
avowed, partakers of the Christian mysteries.[b] If it be
impossible to form the most remote approximation to
their relative numbers with that of the Pagan population, it is equally erroneous to estimate their strength
and influence by numerical calculation. All political
changes are wrought by a compact, organised, and disciplined minority. The mass of mankind are shown by
experience, and appear fated by the constitution of our
nature, to follow any vigorous impulse from a determined and incessantly aggressive few.

The long period of prosperity had produced in the
Christian community its usual consequences, Relaxation of
some relaxation of morals: but Christian charity Christian
had probably suffered more than Christian morals—
of Christian
purity. The more flourishing and extensive charity.
the community, the more the pride, perhaps the

---

b Euseb. Ecc. Hist. viii. 1.

temporal advantages, of superiority, predominated over the Christian motives which led men to aspire to the supreme functions in the Church.   Sacerdotal domination began to exercise its awful powers, and the bishop to assume the language and the authority of the vicegerent of God.   Feuds distracted the bosom of the peaceful communities, and disputes sometimes proceeded to open violence.   Such is the melancholy confession of the Christians themselves, who, according to the spirit of the times, considered the dangers and the afflictions to which they were exposed in the light of divine judgements;   and deplored, perhaps with something of the exaggeration of religious humiliation, the visible decay of holiness and peace.[c]   But it is the strongest proof of the firm hold of a party, whether religious or political, upon the public mind, when it may offend with impunity against its own primary principles.   That which at one time is a sign of incurable weakness or approaching dissolution, at another seems but the excess of healthful energy and the evidence of unbroken vigour.

The acts of Diocletian are the only trustworthy history of his character.   The son of a slave, or, at all events,
Diocletian.   born of obscure and doubtful parentage, who could force his way to sovereign power, conceive and accomplish the design of reconstructing the whole empire, must have been a man, at least, of strong political courage, of profound, if not always wise and statesmanlike views.   In the person of Diocletian, the Emperor of Rome became an Oriental monarch.   The old republican forms were disdainfully cast aside; consuls and tribunes gave way to new officers, with adulatory and un-Roman appellations.   Diocletian him-

---

[c] Euseb. Ecc. Hist. viii. 1.

self assumed the new title of Dominus or Lord, which gave offence even to the servile and flexible religion of his Pagan subjects, who reluctantly, at first, paid the homage of adoration to the master of the world.

Nor was the ambition of Diocletian of a narrow or personal character. With the pomp, he did not affect the solitude, of an Eastern despot. The necessity of the state appeared to demand the active and perpetual presence of more than one person invested with sovereign authority, who might organise the decaying forces of the different divisions of the empire, against the menacing hosts of barbarians on every frontier. Two Augusti and two Cæsars shared the dignity and the cares of the public administration[d]— a measure, if expedient for the security, fatal to the prosperity, of the exhausted provinces, which found themselves burdened with the maintenance of four imperial establishments. A new system of taxation was imperatively demanded, and relentlessly introduced,[e] while the Emperor seemed to mock the bitter and ill-suppressed murmurs of the provinces, by his lavish expenditure in magnificent and ornamental buildings. That was attributed to the avarice of Diocletian, which arose out of the change in the form of government, and in some degree out of his sumptuous taste in that particular department, the embellishment, not of Rome only, but of the chief cities of the empire—Milan, Carthage, and Nicomedia. At one time, the all-pervading government aspired, after a season of scarcity, to regulate

Diocletian. Change in the state of the empire.

---

[d] In the Leben Constantins des Grossen, by Manso, there is a good discussion on the authority and relative position of the Augusti and the Cæsars.

[e] The extension of the rights of citizenship to the whole empire by Caracalla made it impossible to maintain the exemptions and immunities which that privilege had thus lavishly conferred.

the prices of all commodities, and of all interchange,
whether of labour or of bargain and sale, between man
and man. This singular and gigantic effort of well-
meaning but mistaken despotism has come to light in
the present day.[f]

Among the innovations introduced by Diocletian,
Neglect of none, perhaps, was more closely connected with
Rome. the interests of Christianity than the virtual
degradation of Rome from the capital of the empire, by
the constant residence of the Emperor in other cities.
Though the old metropolis was not altogether neglected
in the lavish expenditure of the public wealth upon new
edifices, either for the convenience of the people or the
splendour of public solemnities, yet a larger share fell
to the lot of other towns, particularly of Nicomedia.[g]
In this city, the Emperor more frequently displayed the
new state of his imperial court, while Rome was rarely
honoured by his presence. Nor was his retreat, when
wearied with political strife, on the Campanian coast, in
the Bay of Baiæ, which the older Romans had girt with
their splendid seats of retirement and luxury; it was
on the Illyrian and barbarous side of the Adriatic that
the palace of Diocletian arose, and his agricultural
establishment spread its narrow belt of fertility. The
removal of the seat of government more clearly discovered the magnitude of the danger to the existing
institutions from the progress of Christianity. The East
was, no doubt, more fully peopled with Christians than
any part of the Western world, unless, perhaps, the
province of Africa; at all events, their relative rank,

---

[f] Edict of Diocletian, published and
illustrated by Col. Leake. It is alluded
to in the Treatise De Mortibus
Persecut. C. vii.

[g] Ita semper dementabat, Nicode-
miam studens urbi Romæ coæquare.
De Mort. Persecut. C. vii.

wealth, and importance, much more nearly balanced
that of the adherents of the old Polytheism.[h] In Rome,
the ancient majesty of the national religion must still
have kept down in comparative obscurity the aspiring
rivalry of Christianity. The Prætor still made way for
the pontifical order, and submitted his fasces to the
vestal virgin, while the Christian bishop pursued his
humble and unmarked way. The modest church or
churches of the Christians lay hid, no doubt, in some
sequestered street or in the obscure Transteverine region,
and did not venture to contrast themselves with the
stately temples on which the ruling people of the world
and the sovereigns of mankind had for ages lavished
their treasures. However the church of the metropolis
of the world might maintain a high rank in Christian
estimation, might boast its antiquity, its Apostolic origin,
or at least of being the scene of Apostolic martyrdom,
and might number many distinguished proselytes in all
ranks, even in the imperial court ; still Paganism, in
this stronghold of its most gorgeous pomp, its hereditary
sanctity, its intimate connexion with all the institutions, and its incorporation with the whole ceremonial

---

[h] Tertullian, Apolog. c. 37. Mr.
Coneybeare (Bampton Lectures, page
345) has drawn a curious inference
from a passage in this chapter of Tertullian, that the majority of those who
had a right of citizenship in those
cities had embraced the Christian faith,
while the mobs were its most furious
opponents. It appears unquestionable
that the strength of Christianity lay in
the middle, perhaps the mercantile,
classes. The last two books of the
Paidagogos of Clement of Alexandria,
the most copious authority for Christian
manners at that time, inveigh against
the vices of an opulent and luxurious
community : splendid dresses, jewels,
gold and silver vessels, rich banquets,
gilded litters and chariots, and private
baths. The ladies kept Indian birds,
Median peacocks, monkeys, and Maltese
dogs, instead of maintaining widows
and orphans; the men had multitudes
of slaves. The sixth chapter of the
third book—" that the Christian alone
is rich"—would have been unmeaning
if addressed to a poor community.

of public affairs; in Rome, must have maintained at
least its outward supremacy.[1] But, in comparison with
the less imposing dignity of the municipal government
or the local priesthood, the Bishop of Antioch or Nicomedia was a far greater person than the predecessor of
the popes among the consulars and the senate, the
hereditary aristocracy of the old Roman families or
the ministers of the ruling Emperor. In Nicomedia, the
Christian church, an edifice at least of considerable
strength and solidity, stood on an eminence commanding
the town, and conspicuous above the palace of the
sovereign.

Diocletian might seem born to accomplish that revolution which took place so soon after, under the reign
of Constantine. The new constitution of the empire
might appear to require a reconstruction of the religious
system. The Emperor, who had not scrupled to accom-
modate the form of the government, without respect to
the ancient majesty of Rome, to the present position of
affairs—to degrade the capital itself into the rank of a
provincial city—and to prepare the way, at least, for the
removal of the seat of government to the East, would
Religion of   have been withheld by no scruples of venera-
Diocletian.   tion for ancient rites or ancestral ceremonies,
if the establishment of a new religion had appeared

---

[1] In a letter of Cornelius, bishop of
Rome, written during or soon after the
reign of Decius, the ministerial establishment of the Church in Rome is thus
stated:—One bishop; forty-six presbyters; seven deacons; seven sub-
deacons; forty-two acolyths or attendants; fifty-two exorcists, readers, and
doorkeepers; fifteen hundred widows
and poor. Euseb. vi. 43.

Optatus, lib. ii., states that there
were more than forty churches in Rome
at the time of the persecution of Diocletian. It has been usual to calculate
one church for each presbyter; which
would suppose a falling-off, at least no
increase, during the interval. But
some of the presbyters reckoned by
Cornelius may have been superannu-
ated, or in prison, and their place supplied by others.

to harmonise with his general policy. But his mind was not yet ripe for such a change ; nor perhaps his knowledge of Christianity and its profound and unseen influence, sufficiently extensive. In his assumption of the title Jovius, while his colleague took that of Herculius, Diocletian gave a public pledge of his attachment to the old Polytheism. Among the cares of his administration, he by no means neglected the purification of the ancient religions.[k] In Paganism itself, New Paganism. that silent but manifest change, of which we have already noticed the commencement, had been creeping on. The new philosophic Polytheism which Julian attempted to establish on the ruins of Christianity was still endeavouring to supersede the older poetic faith of the Heathen nations. It had not even yet come to sufficient maturity to offer itself as a formidable antagonist to the religion of Christ. This new Paganism, as has been observed, arose out of the alliance of the philosophy and the religion of the old world. These once implacable adversaries had reconciled their differences, and coalesced against the common enemy. Christianity itself had no slight influence upon the formation of the new system ; and now an Eastern element, more and more strongly dominant, mingled with the whole, and lent it, as it were, a visible object of worship. From Christianity, the new Paganism had adopted the Unity of the Deity ; and scrupled not to degrade all the gods of the older world into subordinate dæmons or ministers. The Christians had Worship of incautiously held the same language: both the Sun. concurred in the name of dæmons ; but the Pagans used the phrase in the Platonic sense, as good, but sub-

---

[k] Veterrimæ religiones castissimè curatæ.   Aurel. Vict. de Cæsar.

ordinate, spirits; while the same term spoke to the Christian ear as expressive of malignant and diabolic agency. But the Jupiter Optimus Maximus was not the great Supreme of the new system. The universal deity of the East, the Sun, to the philosophic was the emblem or representative, to the vulgar, the Deity. Diocletian himself, though he paid so much deference to the older faith as to assume the title of Jovius, as belonging to the Lord of the world, yet, on his accession, when he would exculpate himself from all concern in the murder of his predecessor Numerian, appealed in the face of the army to the all-seeing deity of the Sun. It is the oracle of Apollo of Miletus, consulted by the hesitating Emperor, which is to decide the fate of Christianity. The metaphorical language of Christianity had unconsciously lent strength to this new adversary; and, in adoring the visible orb, some, no doubt, supposed that they were not departing far from the worship of the "Sun of Righteousness." [m]

But though it might enter into the imagination of an imperious and powerful sovereign to fuse together all these conflicting faiths, the new Paganism was beginning to advance itself as the open and most dangerous adversary of the religion of Christ. Hierocles, the great Hierophant of the Platonic Paganism, is distinctly named as the author of the persecution under Diocletian. [n]

Thus, then, an irresistible combination of circumstances tended to precipitate the fatal crisis. The whole

---

[m] Hermogenes, one of the older heresiarchs, applied the text " he has placed his tabernacle in the sun " to Christ, and asserted that Christ had put off his body in the sun. Pantænus ap. Routh, Reliquiæ Sacræ, i. 339.

[n] Another philosophic writer published a work against the Christians. See Fleury, p. 452, from Tertullian.

political scheme of Diocletian was incomplete, unless some distinct and decided course was taken with these self-governed corporations, who rendered, according to the notions of the time, such imperfect allegiance to the sovereign power. But the cautious disposition of Diocletian, his deeper insight, perhaps, into the real nature of the struggle which would take place; his advancing age, and, possibly, the latent and depressing influence of the malady which may then have been hanging over him, and which, a short time after, brought him to the brink of the grave;[o] these concurrent motives would induce him to shrink from violent measures; to recommend a more temporising policy; and to consent, with difficult reluctance, to the final committal of the imperial authority in a contest in which the complete submission of the opposite party could only be expected by those who were altogether ignorant of its strength. The imperial power had much to lose in an unsuccessful contest; it was likely to gain, if successful, only a temporary and external conquest. On the one hand, it was urged by the danger of permitting a vast and self-governed body to coexist with the general institutions of the empire; on the other, if not a civil war, a contest which would array one part of almost every city of the empire against the other in domestic hostility, might appear even of more perilous consequence to the public welfare.

The party of the old religion, now strengthened by

---

[o] The charge of derangement, which rests on the authority of Constantine, as related by Eusebius, is sufficiently confuted by the dignity of his abdication, the placid content with which he appeared to enjoy his peaceful retreat, the respect paid to him by his turbulent and ambitious colleagues; and the involuntary influence which he still appeared to exercise over the affairs of the empire.

the accession of the philosophic faction, risked nothing,
and might expect much, from the vigorous,
systematic, and universal intervention of the
civil authority. It was clear that nothing
less would restore its superiority to the decaying cause
of Polytheism. Nearly three centuries of tame and
passive connivance, or of open toleration, had only increased the growing power of Christianity, while it had
not in the least allayed that spirit of moral conquest
which avowed that its ultimate end was the total extinction of idolatry.

Sentiments of the philoso- phic party.

But in the army, the parties were placed in more
inevitable opposition; and in the army commenced the
first overt acts of hostility, which were the prognostics
of the general persecution.[p] Nowhere did the old
Roman religion retain so much hold upon the mind as
among the sacred eagles. Without sacrifice to the
givers of victory, the superstitious soldiery would advance, divested of their usual confidence, against the
enemy; and defeat was ascribed to some impious omission in the ceremonial of propitiating the gods. The
Christians now formed no unimportant part in the
army: though permitted by the ruling authorities to
abstain from idolatrous conformity, their contempt of
the auspices which promised, and of the rites which
insured, the divine favour, would be looked upon with
equal awe and animosity. The unsuccessful general,
and the routed army, would equally seize every excuse
to cover the misconduct of the one, or the cowardice of
the other. In the pride of victory, the present deities
of Rome would share the honour with Roman valour:

---

p Ἐκ τῶν ἐν στρατείαις ἀδελφῶν καταρχομένου τοῦ διωγμοῦ.   Euseb.
viii. 1.   Compare ch. iv.

the assistance of the Christians would be forgotten in defeat; the resentment of the gods, to whom that defeat would be attributed, would be ascribed by the Pagans to the impiety of their godless comrades. An incident of this kind took place, during one of his campaigns, in the presence of Diocletian. The army was assembled around the altar; the sacrificing priest in vain sought for the accustomed signs in the entrails of the victim; the sacrifice was again and again repeated, but always with the same result. The baffled soothsayer, trembling with awe or with indignation, denounced the presence of profane strangers. The Christians had been seen to make, perhaps boasted that they had made, the sign of the cross, and put to flight the impotent dæmons of idolatrous worship. They were apprehended, and commanded to sacrifice; and a general edict was issued that all who refused to pay honour to the martial deities of Rome should be expelled from the army. It is far from improbable that frequent incidents of this nature may have occurred; if in the unsuccessful campaign of Galerius in the East, nothing was more likely to embitter the mind of that violent Emperor against the whole community. Nor would this animosity be allayed by the success with which Galerius retrieved his former failure. While the impiety of the Christians would be charged with all the odium of defeat, they would never be permitted to participate in the glories of victory.

During the winter of the year of Christ 302–3, the great question of the policy to be adopted towards the Christians was debated, first in a private conference between Diocletian and Galerius. Diocletian, though urged by his more vehement partner in the empire, was averse from sanguinary proceedings, from bloodshed and confusion; he was in-

Deliberations concerning Christianity.

clined to more temperate measures, which would degrade
the Christians from every post of rank or authority, and
expel them from the palace and the army.   The palace
itself was divided by conflicting factions.   Some of the
chief officers of Diocletian's household openly professed
Christianity; his wife and his daughter were at least
favourably disposed to the same cause; while the mother
of Galerius, a fanatical worshipper, probably of Cybele,
was seized with a spirit of proselytism, and celebrated
almost every day a splendid sacrifice, followed by a
banquet, at which she required the presence of the
whole court.   The pertinacious resistance of the Christians provoked her implacable resentment; and her
influence over her son was incessantly employed to
inflame his mind to more active animosity.

Diocletian at length consented to summon a council,
Council.   formed of some persons versed in the administration of the law, and some military men.
Of these, one party were already notoriously hostile to
Christianity;[q] the rest were courtiers, who bent to every
intimation of the imperial favour.   Diocletian still
prolonged his resistance,[r] till, either to give greater
solemnity to the decree, or to identify their measures
more completely with the cause of Polytheism, it was
determined to consult the oracle of Apollo at Miletus.
The answer of the oracle might be anticipated; and
Diocletian submitted to the irresistible united authority

---

[q] Hierocles, the philosopher, was
probably a member of this council.
Mosheim, p. 922.

[r] According to the unfriendly representation of the author of the treatise
De Mort. Pers., whose view of Diocletian's character is confirmed by Eutro-

pius, it was the crafty practice of Diocletian to assume all the merit of
popular measures as emanating from
himself alone, while, in those which
were unpopular, he pretended to act
altogether by the advice of others.

of his friends, of Galerius, and of the God, and contented himself with moderating the severity of the edict. Galerius proposed that all who refused to sacrifice should be burned alive: Diocletian stipulated that there should be no loss of life.

A fortunate day was chosen for the execution of the imperial decree. The feast of Terminalia was inseparably connected with the stability of the Roman power; that power which was so manifestly endangered by the progress of Christianity. At the dawn of day, the Prefect of the city appeared at the door of the church in Nicomedia, attended by the officers of the city and of the court. The doors were instantly thrown down; the Pagans beheld with astonishment the vacant space, and sought in vain for the statue of the deity. The sacred books were instantly burned, and the rest of the furniture of the building plundered by the tumultuous soldiery. The Emperors commanded from the palace a full view of the tumult and spoliation, for the church stood on a height at no great distance; and Galerius wished to enjoy the spectacle of a conflagration of the building. The more prudent Diocletian, fearing that the fire might spread to the splendid edifices which adjoined it, suggested a more tardy and less imposing plan of demolition. The pioneers of the Prætorian guard advanced with their tools, and in a few hours the whole building was razed to the ground.

The Christians made no resistance, but awaited in silent consternation the promulgation of the fatal edict. On the next morning it appeared. It was framed in terms of the sternest and most rigorous proscription, short of the punishment of death. It comprehended all ranks and orders under its sweeping and inevitable

Edict of persecution.

Its publication.

Its execution in Nicomedia.

provisions. Throughout the empire, the churches of
the Christians were to be levelled with the ground; the
public existence of the religion was thus to be annihilated. The sacred books were to be delivered, under
pain of death, by their legitimate guardians, the bishops
and presbyters, to the imperial officers, and publicly
burnt. The philosophic party thus hoped to extirpate
those pernicious writings with which they in vain contested the supremacy of the public mind.

The property of the churches, whether endowments
in land or furniture, was confiscated; all public assemblies, for the purposes of worship, prohibited; the
Christians of rank and distinction were degraded from
all their offices, and declared incapable of filling any
situation of trust or authority; those of the plebeian
order were deprived of the right of Roman citizenship,
which secured the sanctity of their persons from corporal
chastisement or torture; slaves were declared incapable
of claiming or obtaining liberty; the whole race were
placed without the pale of the law, disqualified from
appealing to its protection in case of wrong, as of personal injury, of robbery, or adultery; while they were
liable to civil actions, bound to bear all the burdens of
the state, and amenable to all its penalties. In many
places, an altar was placed before the tribunal of justice,
on which the plaintiff was obliged to sacrifice, before
his cause could obtain a hearing.[s]

No sooner had this edict been affixed in the customary
place, than it was torn down by the hand of a
rash and indignant Christian, who added insult
to his offence by a contemptuous inscription: "Such are
the victories of the Emperors over the Goths and Sar-

Edict torn
down.

---

[s] Euseb. viii. 2. De Mort. Persecut. apud Lactantium.

matians."[t] This outrage on the Imperial majesty was
expiated by the death of the delinquent, who avowed
his glorious crime. Although less discreet Christians
might secretly dignify the sufferings of the victim with
the honours of martyrdom, they could only venture to
approve the patience with which he bore the agony of
being roasted alive by a slow fire.[u]

The prudence or the moderation of Diocletian had
rejected the more violent and sanguinary counsels of
the Cæsar, who had proposed that all who refused to
sacrifice should be burned alive. But his personal
terrors triumphed over the lingering influence of compassion or justice. On a sudden, a fire burst Fire in the
out in the palace of Nicomedia, which spread palace at Nicomedia.
almost to the chamber of the Emperor. The real origin
of this fatal conflagration is unknown; and notwithstanding the various causes to which it was ascribed by
the fears, the malice, and the superstition of the different
classes, we may probably refer the whole to accident.
It may have arisen from the hasty or injudicious construction of a palace built but recently. One account
ascribes it to lightning. If this opinion obtained general
belief among the Christian party, it would, no doubt, be
considered, by many, a visible sign of the Divine vengeance, on account of the promulgation of the imperial
edict. The Christians were accused by the indignant
voice of the Heathen; they retorted, by throwing the
guilt upon the Emperor Galerius, who had practised (so
the ecclesiastical historian suggests) the part of a secret
incendiary, in order to criminate the Christians and
alarm Dioclesian into his more violent measures.[x]

The obvious impolicy of such a measure, as the

---

[t] Mosheim, De Reb. Christ.   [u] Euseb. viii. 5.   [x] Euseb. viii. 6.

chance of actually destroying both their imperial enemies
in the fire must have been very remote, and as it could
only darken the subtle mind of Diocletian with the
blackest suspicions and madden Galerius to more
unmeasured hostility, must acquit the Christians of any
such design, even if their high principles, their sacred
doctrines of peaceful submission under the direst persecution, did not place them above all suspicion. The
only Christian who would have incurred the guilt, or
provoked upon his innocent brethren the danger inseparable from such an act, would have been some
desperate fanatic, like the man who tore down the edict.
And such a man would have avowed and gloried in the
act; he would have courted the ill-deserved honours of
martyrdom. The silence of Constantine may clear
Galerius of the darker charge of contriving, by these
base and indirect means, the destruction of a party
against which he proceeded with undisguised hostility.
Galerius, however, as if aware of the full effect with
which such an event would work on the mind of Diocletian immediately left Nicomedia, declaring that he
could not consider his person safe within that city.

The consequences of this fatal conflagration were
disastrous, to the utmost extent which their worst
enemies could desire, to the whole Christian community.
The officers of the household, the inmates of the palace,
were exposed to the most cruel tortures, by the order,
it is said in the presence, of Diocletian. Even the
females of the Imperial family were not exempt, if from
the persecution, from that suspicion which demanded
the clearest evidence of their Paganism. Prisca and
Valeria were constrained to pollute themselves with
sacrifice ; the powerful eunuchs, Dorotheus and Gor-
gonius and Andreas, suffered death ; Anthimus, the

Bishop of Nicomedia, was beheaded. Many were executed, many burnt alive, many laid bound, with stones round their necks, in boats, rowed into the midst of the lake, and thrown into the water.

From Nicomedia, the centre of the persecution, the imperial edicts were promulgated, though with less than the usual rapidity, through the East. Letters were despatched requiring the co-operation of the Western Emperors, Maximian, the associate of Diocletian, and the Cæsar Constantius, in the restoration of the dignity of the ancient religion, and the suppression of the hostile faith. Constantius made a show of concurrence in the measures of his colleagues; he commanded the demolition of the churches,•but abstained from all violence against the persons of the Christians.[y] Gaul alone, his favoured province, was not defiled by Christian blood. The fiercer temper of Maximian only awaited the signal, and readily acceded, to carry into effect the barbarous edicts of his colleagues.

In almost every part of the world, Christianity found itself at once assailed by the full force of the civil power, constantly goaded on by the united influence of the Pagan priesthood and the philosophic party. Nor was Diocletian, now committed in the desperate strife, content with the less tyrannical and sanguinary edict of Nicomedia. Vague rumours of insurrection, some tumultuary risings in regions which were densely peopled with Christians, and even the enforced assumption of

The persecution becomes general.

April 18.

---

[y] Eusebius, whose panegyric on Constantine throws back some of its adulation upon his father, makes Constantius a Christian, with the Christian service regularly performed in his palace. Vit. Constant. c. 33. The exaggeration of this statement is exposed by Pagi, ad ann. 303, n. viii. Mosheim, De Rebus ante Const. Mag. p. 929-935.

the purple by two adventurers, one in Armenia, another in Antioch, seemed to countenance the charges of political ambition, and the design of armed and vigorous resistance.

It is the worst evil of religious contests that the civil power cannot retract without the humiliating confession of weakness, and must go on increasing in the severity of its measures. It soon finds that there is no success short of the extermination of the adversary; and it has but the alternative of acknowledged failure or this internecine warfare. The demolition of the churches might remove objects offensive to the wounded pride of the dominant Polytheism; the destruction of the sacred books might gratify the jealous hostility of the philosophic party; but not a single community was dissolved. The precarious submission of the weaker Christians only confirmed the more resolute opposition of the stronger and more heroic adherents of Christianity.

Edict followed edict, rising in regular gradations of angry barbarity. The whole clergy were declared enemies of the state; they were seized wherever a hostile Prefect chose to put forth his boundless authority; and bishops, presbyters, and deacons were crowded into the prisons intended for the basest malefactors. A new rescript prohibited the liberation of any of these prisoners, unless they should consent to offer sacrifice.

During the promulgation of these rescripts, Diocletian celebrated his triumph in Rome; he held a conference with the Cæsar of Africa, who entered into his rigorous measures. On his return to Nicomedia, he was

Illness.

seized with that long and depressing malady which, whether or not it affected him with temporary derangement, secluded him within the impenetrable precincts of the palace, whose sacred secrets were forbidden to be betrayed to the popular ear. This rigid concealment gave currency to every kind of gloomy rumour. The whole Roman world awaited with mingled anxiety, hope, and apprehension, the news of his dissolution. Diocletian, to the universal astonishment, appeared again in the robes of empire; to the still greater general astonishment, he appeared only to lay them aside, to abdicate the throne, and to retire to the peaceful occupation of his palace and agricultural villa on the Illyrian shore of the Adriatic. His colleague Maximian, with ill-dissembled reluctance, followed the example of his associate, patron, and coadjutor in the empire.

And abdication of Diocletian. A.D. 304.

The great scheme of Dioclesian, the joint administration of the empire by associate Augusti, with their subordinate Cæsars, if it had averted for a time the dismemberment of the empire, and had infused some vigour into the provincial governments, had introduced other evils of appalling magnitude; but its fatal consequences were more manifest directly the master hand was withdrawn which had organised the new machine of government. Fierce jealousy succeeded at once among the rival Emperors to decent concord; all subordination was lost; and a succession of civil wars between the contending sovereigns distracted the whole world. The earth groaned under the separate tyranny of its many masters; and, according to the strong expression of a rhetorical writer, the grinding taxation had so exhausted the proprietors and the cultivators of the soil, the merchants, and the artisans, that none remained to tax but beggars.[z] The sufferings of the Christians, however, still inflicted with unremitting

General misery.

---

[z] De Mort. Persecut. c. xxiii.

barbarity, were lost in the common sufferings of mankind. The rights of Roman citizenship, which had been violated in their persons, were now universally neglected ; and, to extort money, the chief persons of the towns, the unhappy decurions, who were responsible for the payment of the contributions, were put to the torture. Even the punishment, the roasting by a slow fire,—invented to force the conscience of the devout Christians,—was borrowed, in order to wring the reluctant impost from the unhappy provincial.

The abdication of Diocletian left the most implacable
Galerius Emperor of the East. enemy of Christianity, Galerius, master of the East ; and in the East the persecution of the Christians, as well as the general oppression of the
Maximin Daias. subjects of the empire, continued in unmitigated severity. The nephew of Galerius the Cæsar, Maximin Daias, was the legitimate heir to his relentless violence of temper, and to his stern hostility to the Christian name. In the West, the assumption of the purple by Maxentius, the son of the abdicated Maximian (Herculius), had no unfavourable effect on the situation of the Christians. They suffered only with the rest
Maxentius. of their fellow-subjects from the vices of Maxentius. If their matrons and virgins were not secure from his lust, it was the common lot of all who, although of the highest rank and dignity, might attract his insatiable passions. If a Christian matron, the wife of a senator, submitted to a voluntary death[a] rather than to the loss of her honour, it was her beauty, not
Constantine. her Christianity, which marked her out as the victim of the tyrant. It was not until Constantine began to develope his ambitious views of reuniting

---

a Euseb. viii. 14.

the dismembered monarchy, that Maxentius threw himself, as it were, upon the ancient gods of Rome, and identified his own cause with that of Polytheism.

At this juncture all eyes were turned towards the elder son of Constantius. If not already recognised by the prophetic glance of devout hope as the first Christian sovereign of Rome, he seemed placed by providential wisdom as the protector, as the head, of the Christian interest. The enemies of Christianity were his; and if he was not, as yet, bound by the hereditary attachment of a son to the religion of his mother Helena, his father Constantius had bequeathed him the wise example of humanity and toleration. Placed as a hostage in the hands of Galerius, Constantine had only escaped from the honourable captivity of the Eastern court, where he had been exposed to constant peril of his life, by the promptitude and rapidity of his movements. He had fled, and during the first stages maimed the post-horses which might have been employed in his pursuit. During the persecution of Diocletian, Constantius alone, of all the Emperors, by a dexterous appearance of submission, had screened the Christians of Gaul from the common lot of their brethren. Nor was it probable that Constantine would render, on this point, more willing allegiance to the sanguinary mandates of Galerius. At present, however, Constantine stood rather aloof from the affairs of Italy and the East; and till the resumption of the purple by the elder Maximian, his active mind was chiefly employed in the consolidation of his own power in Gaul, and the repulse of the German barbarians who threatened the frontier of the Rhine.

Notwithstanding that the persecution had now lasted for six or seven years, in no part of the world did

Christianity betray any signs of vital decay. It was far too
deeply rooted in the minds of men, far too ex-

A.D. 309.
tensively promulgated, far too vigorously organized, not to endure this violent but unavailing shock. If
its public worship was suspended, the believers met in
secret, or cherished in the unassailable privacy of the
heart the inalienable rights of conscience. If it suffered
numerical loss, the body was not weakened by the
severance of its more feeble and worthless members.
Sufferings   The inert resistance of the general mass wearied
of the Chris-
tians.   out the vexatious and harassing measures of the
Government. Their numbers secured them against
general extermination; but, of course, the persecution
fell most heavily upon the most eminent of the body;
upon men who were deeply pledged by the sense of
shame and honour, even if, in any case, the nobler
motives of conscientious faith and courageous confidence
in the truth of the religion were wanting, to bear with
unyielding heroism the utmost barbarities of the persecutor. Those who submitted performed the hated ceremony with visible reluctance, with trembling hand,
averted countenance, and deep remorse of heart; those
who resisted to death were animated by the presence of
multitudes who, if they dared not applaud, could scarcely
conceal their admiration. Women crowded to kiss the
hems of their garments, and their scattered ashes, or
unburied bones, were stolen away by the devout zeal of
their adherents, and already began to be treasured as
incentives to faith and piety. It cannot be supposed
that the great functionaries of the state, the civil or
military governors, could be so universally seared to
humanity, or so incapable of admiring these frequent
examples of patient heroism, as not either to mitigate in
some degree the sufferings which they were bound to

inflict, or even to feel some secret sympathy with the blameless victims whom they condemned. That sympathy might ripen, at a more fortunate period, into sentiments still more favourable to the Christian cause.

The most signal and unexpected triumph of Christianity was over the author of the persecution. While victory and success appeared to follow that party in the state which, if they had not as yet openly espoused the cause of Christianity, had unquestionably its most ardent prayers in their favour, the enemies of the Christians were smitten with the direst calamities, and the Almighty appeared visibly to exact the most awful vengeance for their sufferings. Galerius himself was forced, as it were, to implore mercy; not indeed in the attitude of penitence, but of profound humiliation, at the foot of the Christian altar. In the eighteenth year of his reign, the great persecutor lay expiring of a most loathsome malady. A deep and fetid ulcer preyed on the lower regions of his body, and ate them away into a mass of living corruption. It is certainly singular that the disease, vulgarly called being " eaten of worms," should have been the destiny of Herod the Great, of Galerius, and of Philip II. of Spain. Physicians were sought from all quarters; every oracle was consulted in vain; that of Apollo suggested a cure which aggravated the virulence of the disease. Not merely the chamber, the whole palace, of Galerius is described as infected by the insupportable stench which issued from his wound; while the agonies which he suffered might have satiated the worst vengeance of the most unchristian enemy.

From the dying bed of Galerius issued an edict, which, while it condescended to apologise for the past severities against the Christians, under the specious plea of regard for the public welfare Edict of Galerius, A.D. 311, April 30.

and the unity of the state—while it expressed compassion for his deluded subjects, whom the Government
was unwilling to leave in the forlorn condition of being
absolutely without a religion—admitted to the fullest
extent the total failure of the severe measures for the
suppression of Christianity.[b] It permitted the free and
public exercise of the Christian religion. Its close was
still more remarkable; it contained an earnest request
to the Christians to intercede for the suffering Emperor
in their supplications to their God. Whether this edict
was dictated by wisdom, by remorse, or by superstitious
terror; whether it was the act of a statesman, convinced
by experience of the impolicy, or even the injustice, of
his sanguinary acts; whether, in the agonies of his
excruciating disease, his conscience was harassed by the
thought of his tortured victims; or, having vainly
solicited the assistance of his own deities, he would
desperately endeavour to propitiate the favour, or, at
least, allay the wrath, of the Christians' God; the whole
Roman world was witness of the public and humiliating
acknowledgment of defeat extorted from the dying
Emperor. A few days after the promulgation of the
edict, Galerius expired.

The edict was issued from Sardica, in the name of
A.D. 311. Galerius, of Licinius, and of Constantine. It
May. accorded with the sentiments of the two latter:
Maximin II. alone, the Cæsar of the East, whose peculiar
jurisdiction extended over Syria and Egypt, rendered
but an imperfect and reluctant obedience to the decree
of toleration. His jealousy was, no doubt, excited by
the omission of his name in the preamble to the edict;
and he seized this excuse to discountenance its promul-

---

b Euseb. H. E. viii. 17.

gation in his provinces. Yet for a time he suppressed
his profound and inveterate hostility to the Conduct of
Christian name. He permitted unwritten orders Maximin in the East.
to be issued to the municipal governors of the towns, and
to the magistrates of the villages, to put an end to all
violent proceedings. The zeal of Sabinus, the Prætorian
Prefect of the East, supposing the milder sentiments of
Galerius to be shared by Maximin, seems to have outrun
the intentions of the Cæsar. A circular rescript appeared
in the name of Sabinus, echoing the tone, though it did
not go quite to the length, of the imperial edict. It
proclaimed that " it had been the anxious wish of the
divinity of the most mighty Emperors to reduce the
whole empire to pay a harmonious and united worship
to the immortal gods. But their clemency had at length
taken compassion on the obstinate perversity of the
Christians, and determined on desisting from their
ineffectual attempts to force them to abandon their
hereditary faith." The magistrates were instructed to
communicate the contents of this letter to each other.
The governors of the provinces, supposing at once that
the letter of the Prefect contained the real sentiments
of the Emperor, with merciful haste despatched orders
to all persons in subordinate civil or military command,
the magistrates both of the towns and the villages, who
acted upon them with unhesitating obedience.[c]

The cessation of the persecution showed at once its
extent. The prison doors were thrown open ; the mines
rendered up their condemned labourers. Everywhere
long trains of Christians were seen hastening to the
ruins of their churches and visiting the places sanctified
by their former devotion. The public roads, the streets,

---

[c] Euseb. ix. 1.

and market-places of the towns were crowded with long processions, singing psalms of thanksgiving for their deliverance. Those who had maintained their faith under these severe trials passed triumphant in conscious, even if lowly pride, amid the flattering congratulations of their brethren; those who had failed in the hour of affliction hastened to reunite themselves with their God, and to obtain readmission into the flourishing and re-united fold. The Heathens themselves were astonished, it is said, at this signal mark of the power of the Christians' God, who had thus unexpectedly wrought so sudden a revolution in favour of his worshippers.[d]

But the cause of the Christians might appear not yet sufficiently avenged. The East, the great scene of persecution, was not restored to prosperity or peace. It had neither completed nor expiated the eight years of relentless persecution. The six months of ap-
Maximin hostile to Christianity.
parent reconciliation were occupied by the Cæsar Maximin in preparing measures of more subtile and profound hostility. The situation of Maximin himself was critical and precarious. On the death of
A.D. 311.
Galerius, he had seized on the government of the whole of Asia, and the forces of the two Emperors, Licinius and Maximin, watched each other on either side of the Bosphorus, with jealous and ill-dissembled hostility. Throughout the West, the Em-perors were favourable, or at least not inimical, to Christianity. The political difficulties, even the vices of Maximin, enforced the policy of securing the support of a large and influential body; he placed himself at the head of the Pagan interest in the East. A deliberate scheme was laid for the advancement of one party in

---

d Euseb. H. E. ix. 1.

the popular favour for the depression of the other. Measures were systematically taken to enfeeble the influence of Christianity, not by the authority of Government, but by poisoning the public mind, and infusing into it a settled and conscientious animosity. False Acts of Pilate were forged, intended to cast discredit on the Divine founder of Christianity; they were disseminated with the utmost activity. The streets of Antioch and other Eastern cities were placarded with the most calumnious statements of the origin of the Christian faith. The instructors of youth were directed to introduce them as lessons into the schools, to make their pupils commit them to memory; and boys were heard repeating, or grown persons chanting, the most scandalous blasphemies against the object of Christian adoration.[e] In Damascus, the old arts of compelling or persuading women to confess that they had been present at the rites of the Christians, which had ended in lawless and promiscuous licence, were renewed. The confession of some miserable prostitutes was submitted to the Emperor, published by his command, and disseminated throughout the Eastern cities, although the Christian rites had been long celebrated in those cities with the utmost publicity.[f]

The second measure of Maximin was the reorganisation of the Pagan religion in all its original Reorganisation of pomp, and more than its ancient power. A Paganism. complete hierarchy was established on the model of the Christian episcopacy. Provincial pontiffs, men of the highest rank, were nominated; they were inaugurated

---

[e] In the speech attributed to S. Lucianus, previous to his martyrdom at Nicomedia, there is an allusion to these Acts of Pilate, which shows that they had made considerable impression on the public mind. Routh, Reliquiæ Sacræ, iii. 286.

[f] Euseb. viii. 14.

with a solemn and splendid ceremonial, and were distinguished by a tunic of white. The Emperor himself
assumed the appointment to the pontifical offices in the
different towns, which had in general rested with the
local authorities. Persons of rank and opulence were
prevailed on to accept these sacred functions, and were
thus committed, by personal interest and corporate
attachment, in the decisive struggle. Sacrifices were
performed with the utmost splendour and regularity,
and the pontiffs were invested with power to compel the
attendance of all the citizens. The Christians were liable
to every punishment or torture, short of death. The
Pagan interest having thus become predominant in the
greater cities, addresses were artfully suggested, and
voted by the acclaiming multitude, imploring the interference of the Emperor to expel these enemies of the
established religion from their walls. The rescripts of
the Emperor were engraved on brass, and suspended in
the public parts of the city. The example was set by
Antioch, once the head-quarters, and still, no doubt, a
stronghold of Christianity. Theotecnus, the logistes or
chamberlain of the city, took the lead. A splendid
image was erected to Jupiter Philius, and dedicated
with all the imposing pomp of mystery, perhaps of
Eastern magic.[g] As though they would enlist that
strong spirit of mutual attachment which bound the
Christians together, the ancient Jupiter was invested
in the most engaging and divine attribute of the God of
Christianity—he was the God of Love. Nicomedia,
the capital of the East, on the entrance of the Emperor,
presented an address to the same effect as those which
had been already offered by Antioch, Tyre, and other

---

[g] Euseb. ix. 2, 3.

cities; and the Emperor affected to yield to this simultaneous expression of the general sentiment.

The first overt act of hostility was a prohibition to the Christians to meet in their cemeteries, where probably their enthusiasm was wrought to the utmost height by the sacred thoughts associated with the graves of their martyrs. *Persecutions in the dominions of Maximin.* But the policy of Maximin, in general, confined itself to vexatious and harassing oppression, and to other punishments, which inflicted the pain and wretchedness without the dignity of dying for the faith: the persecuted had the sufferings, but not the glory, of martyrdom. Such, most likely, were the general orders of Maximin, though, in some places, the zeal of his officers may have transgressed the prescribed limits, it must not be said, of humanity. The Bishop and two inhabitants of Emesa, and Peter the Patriarch of Alexandria, obtained the honours of death. Lucianus, the Bishop of Antioch, was sent to undergo a public examination at Nicomedia; he died in prison. The greater number of victims suffered the less merciful punishment of mutilation or blinding. The remonstrances of Constantine were unavailing; the Emperor persisted in his cruel course; and is said to have condescended to an ingenious artifice to afflict the sensitive consciences of some persons of the higher orders who escaped less painful penalties. His banquets were served with victims previously slain in sacrifice, and his Christian guests were thus unconsciously betrayed into a crime which the authority of St. Paul had not yet convinced the more scrupulous believers to be a matter of perfect indifference.[h]

The Emperor, in his public rescript in answer to the

---

[h] Euseb. ix. 7.

address from the city of Tyre, had, as it were, placed
the issue of the contest on an appeal to Heaven.
The gods of Paganism were asserted to be
the benefactors of the human race ; through
their influence, the soil had yielded its annual
increase ; the genial air had not been parched by fatal
droughts ; the sea had neither been agitated with tem-
pests nor swept by hurricanes ; the earth, instead of
being rocked by volcanic convulsions, had been the
peaceful and fertile mother of its abundant fruits.
Their own neighbourhood spoke the manifest favour of
these benignant deities, in its rich fields waving with
harvests, its flowery and luxuriant meadows, and in
the mild and genial temperature of the air. A city so
blest by its tutelary gods, in prudence as well as in
justice, would expel those traitorous citizens whose impiety endangered these blessings, and would wisely
purify its walls from the infection of their heaven-
despising presence.

But peace and prosperity by no means ensued upon
the depression of the Christians. Notwithstanding the embellishment of the Heathen
temples, the restoration of the Polytheistic ceremonial
in more than ordinary pomp, and the nomination of
the noblest citizens to the pontifical offices, every kind
of calamity—tyranny, war, pestilence, and famine—
depopulated the Asiatic provinces. Not the least
scourge of the Pagan East was the Pagan Emperor
himself. Christian writers may have exaggerated, they
can scarcely have invented, the vices of Maximin. His
lusts violated alike the honour of noble and plebeian
families. The eunuchs, the purveyors for his
passions, traversed the provinces, marked out
those who were distinguished by fatal beauty, and con-

The Pagans appeal to the flourishing state of the East.

Reverse.
A.D. 312.

Tyranny of Maximin.

ducted these extraordinary perquisitions with the most insolent indignity : where milder measures would not prevail, force was used. Nor was tyranny content with the gratification of its own licence : noble virgins, after having been dishonoured by the Emperor, were granted in marriage to his slaves ; even those of the highest rank were consigned to the embraces of a barbarian husband. Valeria, the widow of Galerius, and the daughter of Diocletian, was first insulted by proposals of marriage from Maximin, whose wife was still living, and then forced to wander through the Eastern provinces in the humblest disguise, till, at length, she perished at Thessalonica by the still more unjustifiable sentence of Licinius.

The war of Maximin with Armenia was wantonly undertaken in a spirit of persecution. This earliest Christian kingdom was attached, in all the zeal of recent proselytism, to the new religion. That part which acknowledged the Roman sway was commanded to abandon Christianity ; and the legions of Rome were employed in forcing the reluctant kingdom to obedience.[1]

War with Armenia.

But these were foreign calamities. Throughout the dominions of Maximin the summer rains did not fall ; a sudden famine desolated the whole East ; corn rose to an unprecedented price.[k] Some large villages were entirely depopulated ; many opulent families were reduced to beggary, and persons in a decent station sold their children as slaves. The rapacity of the Emperor aggravated the general misery. The granaries of individuals were seized, and their stores

Famine.

<hr>

[1] Euseb. ix. 8.

[k] The statement in the text of Eusebius, as it stands, is utterly incredible—a measure of wheat at 2500 attics (drachms), from 70*l.* to 80*l.*

closed up by the imperial seal. The flocks and herds
were driven away, to be offered in unavailing sacrifices
to the gods. The court of the Emperor, in the mean
time, insulted the general suffering by its excessive
luxury; his foreign and barbarian troops lived in a kind
of free quarters, in wasteful plenty, and plundered on
all sides with perfect impunity. The scanty
Pestilence. and unwholesome food produced its usual effect,
a pestilential malady. Carbuncles broke out all over
the bodies of those who were seized with the disorder,
but particularly attacked the eyes, so that multitudes
became helplessly and incurably blind. The houses
of the wealthy, which were secure against the famine,
seemed particularly marked out by the pestilence. The
hearts of all classes were hardened by the extent of the
calamity. The most opulent, in despair of diminishing
the vast mass of misery, or of relieving the swarms
of beggars who filled every town and city, gave up the
fruitless endeavour. The Christians alone took a nobler
and evangelic revenge upon their suffering enemies.
They were active in allaying those miseries of which
they were the common victims. The ecclesiastical historian claims no exemption for the Christians from the
general calamity, but honourably boasts that they alone
displayed the offices of humanity and brotherhood.
They were everywhere, tending the living, and burying
the dead. They distributed bread; they visited the infected houses; they scared away the dogs which preyed,
in open day, on the bodies in the streets, and rendered
to those bodies the decent honours of burial. The myriads
who perished, and were perishing, in a state of absolute
desertion, could not but acknowledge that Christianity
was stronger than love of kindred. The fears and the
gratitude of mankind were equally awakened in their

favour : the fears which could not but conclude these
calamities to be the vengeance of Heaven for the persecutions of its favoured people ; the gratitude to those
who thus repaid good for evil in the midst of a hostile
and exasperated society.[m]

Before we turn our attention to the West, and follow
the victorious career of Constantine to the reconsolida-
tion of the empire in his person, and the triumph of
Christianity through his favour, it may be more consistent with the distinct view of these proceedings to violate
in some degree the order of time, and follow to its close
the history of the Christian persecutions in the East.

Maximin took the alarm, and endeavoured, too late,
to retrace his steps. He issued an edit, in Maximin
which he avowed the plain principles of tole- retracts his
persecuting
ration, and ascribed his departure from that edit.
salutary policy to the importunate zeal of his capital
and of other cities, which he could not treat with disrespect, but which had demanded the expulsion of the
Christians from their respective territories. He commanded the suspension of all violent measures, and
recommended only mild and persuasive means to win
back these apostates to the religion of their forefathers.
The Christians, who had once been deluded by a show
of mercy, feared to reconstruct their fallen edifices,
or to renew their public assemblies, and awaited, in
trembling expectation, the issue of the approaching
contest with Licinius.[n]

The victory of Constantine over Maxentius had left
him master of Rome. Constantine and Licinius reigned
over all the European provinces; and the public
edict for the toleration of Christianity, issued in the

---

m Euseb. ix. 9.   n Euseb. viii. 14.

name of these two Emperors, announced the policy of
the Western Empire.

After the defeat of Maximin by Licinius, his obscure
death gave ample scope for the credulous if not inventive malice of his enemies to ascribe to his last
moments every excess of weakness and cruelty, as well
as of suffering. He is said to have revenged his baffled

A.D. 313.   hopes of victory on the Pagan priesthood, who
Death of   had incited him to the war, by a promiscuous
Maximin.   massacre of all within his power. His last
imperial act was the promulgation of another edict,[o]
still more explicitly favourable to the Christians, in
which he not merely proclaimed an unrestricted liberty
of conscience, but restored the confiscated property of
their churches. His bodily sufferings completed the
dark catalogue of persecuting Emperors who had
perished under the most excruciating torments; his
body was slowly consumed by an internal fire.[p]

With Maximin expired the last hope of Paganism to

The new   maintain itself by the authority of the Govern-
Paganism   ment. Though Licinius was only accidentally
falls with
Maximin.   connected with the Christian party, and afterwards allied himself for a short time to the Pagan
interest, at this juncture his enemies were those of
Christianity; and his cruel triumph annihilated at once
the adherents of Maximin, and those of the old religion.
The new hierarchy fell at once; the chief magistrates
of almost all the cities were executed; for even where
they were not invested in the pontifical offices, it was
under their authority that Paganism had renewed its
more imposing form, and sank with them into the com-

---

[o] Edict of toleration issued from Nicomedia, A.D. 313, 13th June.
[p] Euseb. ix. 9.

mon ruin. The arts by which Theotecnus of Antioch,
the chief adviser of Maximin, had imposed upon the
populace of that city by mysterious wonders, were detected and exposed to public contempt, and the author
put to death. Tyre, which had recommended itself to
Maximin by the most violent hostility to the Christian
name, was constrained to witness the reconstruction of
the fallen church in far more than its original
grandeur. Eusebius, afterwards the Bishop of *Rebuilding of the church of Tyre.*
Cæsarea and the historian of the Church, pro-
nounced an inaugural discourse on its reconstruction.
His description of the building is curious in itself, as the
model of an Eastern church, and illustrates the power
and opulence of the Christian party in a city which had
taken the lead on the side of Paganism. Nor would
the Christian orator venture greatly to exaggerate the
splendour of a building which stood in the midst of, and
provoked, as it were, a comparison with, temples of high
antiquity and unquestioned magnificence.

The Christian church was built on the old site ; for,
though a more convenient and imposing space might
have been found, the piety of the Christians clung with
reverence to a spot consecrated by the most holy associations ; and their pride, perhaps, was gratified in
restoring to more than its former grandeur the edifice
which had been destroyed by Pagan malice. The whole
site was environed with a wall ; a lofty propylæon,
which faced the rising sun, commanded the attention
of the passing Pagan, who could not but contrast the
present splendour with the recent solitude of the place ;
and afforded an imposing glimpse of the magnificence
within. The intermediate space between the propylæon
and the church, was laid out in a cloister with four
colonnades, enclosed with a palisade of wood. The

centre square was open to the sun and air, and two
fountains sparkled in the midst, and reminded the worshipper, with their emblematic purity, of the necessity
of sanctification. The uninitiate proceeded no farther
than the cloister, but might behold at this modest
distance the mysteries of the sanctuary. Several other
vestibules, or propylæa, intervened between the cloister
and the main building. The three gates of the church
fronted the East, of which the central was the loftiest
and most costly, "like a queen between her attendants."
It was adorned with plates of brass and richly sculptured
reliefs. Two colonnades, or aisles, ran along the main
building, above which were windows, which lighted the
edifice; other buildings for the use of the ministers
adjoined.   Unfortunately, the pompous eloquence of
Eusebius would not condescend to the vulgar details
of measurements, and dwells only in vague terms of
wonder at the spaciousness, the heaven-soaring loftiness,
the splendour of the interior. The roof was of beams
from the cedars of Lebanon, the floor inlaid with marble.
In the centre rose the altar, which had already obtained
the name of the place of sacrifice; it was guarded from
the approach of the profane by a trellis of the most
slender and graceful workmanship. Lofty seats were
prepared for the higher orders, and benches for those of
lower rank were arranged with regularity throughout
the building.   Tyre, no doubt, did not stand alone in
this splendid restoration of her Christian worship; and
Christianity, even before her final triumph under Constantine, before the restitution of her endowments, and
the munificent imperial gifts, possessed sufficient wealth
at least to commence these costly undertakings.

BOOK III.

———◆◇◆———

CHAPTER I.

Constantine.

THE reign of Constantine the Great forms one of the epochs in the history of the world. It is the Reign of Con- æra of the dissolution of the Roman Empire; stantine. the commencement, or rather consolidation, of a kind of Eastern despotism, with a new capital, a new patriciate, a new constitution, a new financial system, a new, though as yet imperfect, jurisprudence, and, finally, a new religion. Already, in the time of Diocletian, Change in the Italy had sunk into a province; Rome into empire. *one* of the great cities of the empire. The declension of her importance had been gradual, but inevitable; her supremacy had been shaken by that slow succession of changes which had imperceptibly raised the relative weight and dignity of other parts of the empire, and of the empire itself, as a whole, until she ceased to be the central point of the administration of public affairs. Rome was no longer the heart of the social Degradation system, from which emanated all the life and of Rome. power which animated and regulated the vast and unwieldy body, and to which flowed in the wealth and the homage of the obedient world. The admission of the whole empire to the rights of Roman citizenship by Caracalla had dissolved the commanding spell which centuries of glory and conquest had attached to the majesty of the Roman name. To be a Roman was no longer a privilege ; it gave no distinctive rights, its exemptions were either taken away, or vulgarised by being made common to all except the servile order. The secret once betrayed that the imperial dignity might be conferred elsewhere than in the imperial city, lowered still more the pre-eminence of Rome. From that time, the seat of government was at the head of the army. If the Emperor, proclaimed in Syria, in Illyria, or in Britain, condescended, without much delay, to visit the ancient capital, the trembling senate had but to ratify the decree of the army, and the Roman people to welcome, with submissive acclamations, their new master.

Diocletian had consummated the degradation of Rome, by transferring the residence of the court to Nicomedia. He had commenced the work of reconstructing the empire upon a new basis. Some of his measures were vigorous, comprehensive, and tending to the strength and consolidation of the social edifice ; but he had introduced a principle of disunion, more than powerful enough to counteract all the energy which he had infused into the executive government. His fatal policy of appointing co-ordinate sovereigns, two Augusti, with powers avowedly equal, and two Cæsars, with authority nominally subordinate, but which, in able hands, would not long have brooked inferiority, had nearly dismembered the solid unity of the empire. As yet, Unity of the empire still the influence of the Roman name was commanding and awful ; the provinces were accustomed to consider themselves as parts of one political confederacy ; the armies marched still under the same banners, were united by discipline, and as yet by the unforgotten inheritance of victory from their all-subduing ancestors. In all parts of the world, every vestige of civil independence had long been effaced; centuries of servitude had destroyed every dangerous memorial of ancient dynasties or republican constitutions. Hence, therefore, the more moderate- ambition of erecting an independent kingdom never occurred to any of the rival Emperors ; or, if the separation had been attempted, if a man of ability had endeavoured to partition off one great province, dependent upon its own resources, defended by its own legions, or by a well-organised force of auxiliary barbarians, the age was not yet ripe for such a daring innovation. The whole empire would have resented the secession of any member from the ancient confederacy, and turned its concentrated force against the recreant apostate from the majestic unity of Imperial Rome. Yet, if this system had long prevailed, the disorganising must have finally triumphed over the associating principle : separate interests would have arisen ; a gradual departure from the uniform order of administration must have taken place ; a national character might have developed itself in different quarters ; and the vast and harmonious edifice would have split asunder into distinct, and insulated, and at length hostile, kingdoms.

Nothing less than a sovereign whose comprehensive mind could discern the exigencies of this critical period, nothing less than a conqueror who rested on the strength of successive victories over his competitors for the supremacy, could have reunited, and in time, under one vigorous administration, the dissolving elements of the empire.

Such a conqueror was Constantine : but, reunited, the empire imperiously demanded a complete civil reorganisation. It was not the foundation of the new capital which wrought the change in the state of the empire, it was the state of the empire which required a new capital. The ancient system of government, emanating entirely from Rome, and preserving, with sacred reverence, the old republican forms, had lost its awe ; the world acknowledged the master wherever it felt the power. The possession of Rome added no great weight to the candidate for empire, while its pretensions embarrassed the ruling sovereign.[a] The powerless senate, which still expected to ratify the imperial decrees ; the patrician order, which had ceased to occupy the posts of honour, and danger, and distinction ; the turbulent populace, and the prætorian soldiery, who still presumed to assert their superiority over the legions who were bravely contesting the German or the Persian frontier ; the forms, the intrigues, the interests, the factions of such a city, would not be permitted by an Emperor accustomed to rule with absolute dominion in Treves, in Milan, or in Nicomedia, to clog the free movements of his administration. The disso-

New nobility. lution of the prætorian bands by Constantine, on his victory over Maxentius, though necessary to the peace, was fatal to the power, of Rome. It cut off one of her great though dearly-purchased distinctions. Around the Asiatic, or the Illyrian, or the Gaulish court, had gradually arisen a new nobility, if not hitherto distinguished by title, yet, by service or by favour, possessing the marked and acknowledged confidence of the

---

[a] Galerius (if we are to trust the hostile author of the De Mort. Persecut.) had never seen Rome before his invasion of Italy, and was unacquainted with its immense magnitude. Galerius, according to the same doubtful authority, threatened, after his flight from Italy, to change the name of the empire from Roman to Dacian — (c. xxvii.)

Emperor, and filling all offices of power and of dignity—a nobility independent of patrician descent, or the tenure of property in Italy. Ability in the field or in the council, or even court intrigue, would triumph over the claims of hereditary descent; and all that remained was to decorate with title, and organise into a new aristocracy, those who already possessed the influence and the authority of rank. With Emperors of provincial or barbarous descent naturally arose a race of military or civil servants, strangers to Roman blood and to the Roman name. The will of the sovereign became the fountain of honour. New regulations of finance, and a jurisprudence, though adhering closely to the forms and the practice of the old institutions, new in its spirit and in the scope of many of its provisions, embraced the whole empire in its comprehensive sphere. It was no longer Rome which legislated for the world, but the legislation which comprehended Rome among the cities subject to its authority. The laws were neither issued nor ratified, they were only submitted to, by Rome.

The Roman religion sank with the Roman supremacy. The new empire welcomed the new religion as its ally and associate in the government of the human mind. The empire lent its countenance, its sanction, at length its power, to Christianity. Christianity infused throughout the empire a secret principle of association, which, long after it had dissolved into separate and conflicting masses, held together, nevertheless, the loose and crumbling confederacy, and, at length, itself assuming the lost or abdicated sovereignty, compressed the whole into one system under a spiritual dominion. The Papal, after some interval of confusion and disorganisation, succeeded the Imperial autocracy over the European world.

State of the religion of Rome.

Of all historical problems, none has been discussed with
a stronger bias of opinion, of passion, and of prejudice, according to the age, the nation, the creed
of the writer, than the conversion of Constantine, and the establishment of Christianity as the religion
of the empire. Hypocrisy, policy, superstition, divine
inspiration, have been in turn assigned as the sole or
the predominant influence which, operating on the mind
of the Emperor, decided at once the religious destiny of
the empire. But there is nothing improbable in supposing that Constantine was actuated by concurrent, or
even conflicting, motives; all of which united in enforcing the triumph of Christianity. There is nothing
contradictory in the combination of the motives themselves, particularly if we consider them as operating
with greater strength, or with successive paroxysms, as
it were, of influence, during the different periods in the
life of Constantine, on the soldier, the statesman, and
the man. The soldier, at a perilous crisis, might appeal,
without just notions of his nature, to the tutelary power
of a deity to whom a considerable part of his subjects,
and perhaps of his army, looked up with faith or with
awe. The statesman may have seen the absolute
necessity of basing his new constitution on religion; he
may have chosen Christianity as obviously possessing
the strongest, and a still strengthening, hold upon the
minds of his people. He might appreciate, with profound political sagacity, the moral influence of Christianity, as well as its tendency to enforce peaceful, if
not passive, obedience to civil government. At a later
period, particularly if the circumstances of his life threw
him more into connexion with the Christian priesthood,
he might gradually adopt as a religion that which had
commanded his admiration as a political influence. He

Motives for the conversion of Constantine.

might embrace, with ardent attachment, yet, after all, by no means with distinct apprehension, or implicit obedience to all its ordinances, that faith which alone seemed to survive amid the wreck of all other religious systems.

A rapid but comprehensive survey of the state of Christianity at this momentous period will explain the position in which it stood in relation to the civil government, to the general population of the empire, and to the ancient religion; and throw a clear and steady light upon the manner in which it obtained its political as well as its spiritual dominion over the Roman world.

The third century of Christianity had been prolific in religious revolutions.   In the East, the silent Revival of progress of the Gospel had been suddenly ism. arrested; Christianity had been thrown back with irresistible violence on the Roman territory.   An ancient religion, connected with the great political changes in the sovereignty of the Persian kingdom, revived in all the vigour and enthusiasm of a new creed; it was received as the associate and main support of the state. A hierarchy, numerous, powerful, and opulent, with all the union and stability of a hereditary caste, strengthened by large landed possessions, was reinvested with an authority almost co-ordinate with that of the sovereign.   The restoration of Zoroastrianism, as the established and influential religion of Persia, is perhaps the only instance of the vigorous revival of a Pagan religion.[b]   Of the native religion of the Parthians,

---

[b] The materials for this view of the restoration of the Persian religion are chiefly derived from the following sources:—Hyde, De Religione Persa-rum; Anquetil du Perron; Zenda-vesta, 3 vols.; the German translation of Du Perron, by Kleuker, with very valuable volumes of appendix (An-

little, if anything, is known. They were a Scythian race, who overran and formed a ruling aristocracy over the remains of the older Persian, and the more modern Grecian civilisation. The Scythian, or Tartar, or Turcoman tribes, who have perpetually, from China westward, invaded and subdued the more polished nations, have never attempted to force their rude and shapeless deities, their more vulgar Shamanism, or even the Buddhism which in its simpler form has prevailed among them to a great extent, on the nations over which they have ruled. The ancient Magian priesthood remained, if with diminished power, in great numbers, and not without extensive possessions in the eastern provinces of the Parthian empire. The temples raised by the Greek successors of Alexander, whether to Grecian deities, or blended with the Tsabaism or the Nature-worship of Babylonia or Syria, continued to possess their undiminished honours, with their ample endowments and their sacerdotal colleges. Some vestiges of the deification of the kings of the line of Arsaces seem to be discerned, but with doubtful certainty.

The earliest legendary history of Christianity assigns Parthia as the scene of Apostolic labours ; it was the province of St. Thomas. But in the intermediate region, the great Babylonian province, there is the strongest evidence that Christianity had made an early, a rapid, and a successful progress. It was the residence, at least for a certain period, of the Apostle St. Peter.[c] With what success it conducted its contest with Judaism, it is impossible to conjecture ; for Judaism, which, after

---

hang); De Guigniaut's Translation of Creuzers Symbolik ; Malcolm's History of Persia ; Heeren, Ideen.
Some of these sources were not open to Gibbon when he composed his brilliant chapter on this subject.

[c] Compare note to vol. i. p. 63.

the second rebellion in the reign of Hadrian, maintained but a permissive and precarious existence in
Palestine, flourished in the Babylonian province with
something of a national and independent character.
The Resch-Glutha, or Prince of the Captivity, far surpassed in the splendour of his court the Patriarch of
Tiberias; and the activity of their schools of learning in
Nahardea, in Sura, and in Pumbeditha, is attested by
the vast compilation of the Babylonian Talmud.[d]   Nor
does the Christianity of this region appear to have suffered from the persecuting spirit of the Magian hierarchy
during the earlier conflicts for the Mesopotamian provinces between the arms of Rome and Persia.   Though
one bishop ruled the united communities of Seleucia
and Ctesiphon, the numbers of Christians in the rest of
the province were probably far from inconsiderable.

It was in the ancient dominions of Darius and of
Xerxes that the old religion of Zoroaster reassumed its power and authority.   No sooner
had Ardeschir Babhegan (the Artaxerxes of
the Greeks) destroyed the last remains of the
foreign Parthian dynasty, and reorganised the
dominion of the native Persian kings, from
the borders of Charismia to the Tigris (the Persian
writers assert to the Euphrates),[e] than he hastened to
environ his throne with the Magian hierarchy, and to
re-establish the sacerdotal order in all its former dignity.
But an ancient religion, which has sunk into obscurity,
will not regain its full influence over the popular mind,
unless reinvested with divine authority: intercourse with
heaven must be renewed; the sanction and ratification
of the deity must be public and acknowledged.   Wonder

Restoration of Persian monarchy by Ardeschir Babhegan.

Of the religion of Zoroaster.

---

[d] See History of the Jews, ii. 485, &c.   [e] Malcolm's History of Persia, i. 72.

and miracle are as necessary to the revival of an old, as to the establishment of a new, religion. In the records of the Zoroastrian faith, which are preserved in the ancient language of the Zend, may be traced many singular provisions which bear the mark of great antiquity, and show the transition from a pastoral to an agricultural life.[f] The cultivation of the soil; the propagation of fruit-trees, nowhere so luxuriant and various as in the districts which probably gave birth to the great religious legislator of the East, Balk, and the country of the modern Afghans, and the destruction of noxious animals, are among the primary obligations enforced on the followers of Zoroaster. A grateful people might look back with the deepest veneration on the author of a religious code so wisely beneficent; the tenth of the produce would be no disproportionate offering to the priesthood of a religion which had thus turned civilisation into a duty, and given a Divine sanction to the first principles of human wealth and happiness. But a new impulse was necessary to a people which had long passed this state of transition, and were only reassuming the possessions of their ancestors, and reconstructing their famous monarchy. Zoroastrianism, like all other religions, had split into numerous sects; and an authoritative exposition of the Living Word of Zoroaster could alone restore its power and its harmony to the re-established Magianism of the realm of Ardeschir.

Vision of Erdiviraph. Erdiviraph was the Magian, designated, by his blameless innocence from his mother's womb, to renew the intercourse with the Divinity, and to unfold, on the authority of inspiration, the secrets of

---

[f] Compare Heeren, Ideen, and Rhode, die Heilige Sage des Zendvolks. But | see throughout the work of Dr. Haug, cited in Chap. I.

heaven and hell. Forty (according to one account, eighty thousand) of the Magian priesthood, the Archimage, who resided in Bactria, the Desters and the Mobeds, had assembled to witness and sanction the important ceremony. They were successively reduced to 40,000, to 4000, to 400, to 40, to 7 : the acknowledged merit of Erdiviraph gave him the pre-eminence among the seven.[g] Having passed through the strictest ablutions, and drunk a powerful opiate, he was covered with a white linen, and laid to sleep. Watched by seven of the nobles, including the king, he slept for seven days and nights; and, on his reawakening, the whole nation listened with believing wonder to his exposition of the faith of Oromazd, which was carefully written down by an attendant scribe, for the benefit of posterity.[h]

A hierarchy which suddenly regains its power, after centuries of obscurity, perhaps of oppression, will not be scrupulous as to the means of giving strength and permanence to its dominion. *Intolerance of the Magian hierarchy.* With Ardeschir, the restoration of the Persian people to their rank among the nations of the earth, by the reinfusion of a national spirit, was the noble object of ambition ; the re-establishment of a national religion, as the strongest and most enduring bond of union, was an essential part of his great scheme ; but a national religion, thus associated with the civil polity, is necessarily exclusive, and impatient of the rivalry of other creeds. Intolerance lies in the very nature of a religion

---

[c] All these numbers, it should be observed, are multiples of 40, the in= definite number throughout the East. (See Bredow's Dissertation, annexed to the new edition of Syncellus ; Byzant, Hist. Bonn.) The recusants of Zoroas-trianism (vid. infrà) are in like manner reduced to seven, the sacred number with the Zoroastrian, as with the religion of the Old Testament.

[h] Hyde (fi om Persian authorities), De Relig. Pers. p. 278 et seqq.

which, dividing the whole world into the realm of two
conflicting principles, raises one part of mankind into a
privileged order, as followers of the Good principle, and
condemns the other half as the irreclaimable slaves of
the Evil One.   The national worship is identified with
that of Oromazd ; and the kingdom of Oromazd must be
purified from the intrusion of the followers of Ahriman.
The foreign relations, so to speak, of the Persian
monarchy, according to their old poetical history, are
strongly coloured by their deep-rooted religious opinions.
Their implacable enemies, the pastoral Tartar or Turcoman tribes, inhabit the realm of darkness, and at times
invade and desolate the kingdom of light, till some
mighty monarch, Kaiomers, or some redoubtable hero,
Rustan, reasserts his majesty, and revenges the losses,
of the kingdom of Oromazd.   Iran and Turan are the
representatives of the two conflicting worlds of light
and darkness. In the same spirit, to expel, to persecute,
the followers of other religions, was to expel, to trample
on, the followers of Arhiman.   This edict of Ardeschir
closed all the temples but those of the fire-worshippers,
—only eighty thousand followers of Ahriman, including
the worshippers of foreign religions, and the less orthodox believers in Zoroastrianism, remained to infect the
purified region of Oromazd.[i]   Of the loss sustained by
Destruction   Christianity during this conflict, in the proof Christian-
ity in Persia.   per dominions of Persia, and the number of
churches which shared the fate of the Parthian and

---

[i] Gibbon, in his chapter on the restoration of the Persian monarchy and
religion, has said that in this conflict
" the sword of Aristotle (such was the
name given by the Orientals to the
Polytheism and philosophy of the
Greeks) was easily broken."   I suspect
this expression to be an anachronism ;
it is clearly post-Mohammedan and
from a Mohammedan author.   Gibbon
has likewise quoted authorities for the
persecution of Artaxerxes which relate
to those of his descendants.

Grecian temples, there is no record. The persecutions by the followers of Zoroaster are to be traced, at a later period, only in Armenia and in the Babylonian province; but Persia, from this time until the fiercer persecutions of their own brethren forced the Nestorian Christians to overleap every obstacle, presented a stern and insuperable barrier to the progress of Christianity.[k] It cut off all connexion with the Christian communities (if communities there were) in the remoter East.[m]

Ardeschir bequeathed to his royal descendants the solemn charge of maintaining the indissoluble union of the Magian religion with the state: "Never forget that, as a king, you are at once the protector of religion and of your country. Consider the altar and the throne as inseparable; they must always sustain each other. A sovereign without religion is a tyrant; and a people who have none, may be deemed the most monstrous of societies. Religion may exist without a state, but a state cannot exist without religion: it is by holy laws that a political association can alone be bound. You should be to your people an example of piety and virtue, but without pride or ostentation."[n] The kings of the race of Sassan accepted and fulfilled the sacred trust; the Magian hierarchy encircled and supported the kingly power of Persia.

Connexion of the throne and the hierarchy.

---

[k] Sozomen, indeed, asserts that Christianity was first introduced into the Persian dominions at a later period, from their intercourse with Osroene and Armenia. But it is very improbable that the active zeal of the Christians in the first ages of the religion should not have taken advantage of the mild and tolerant government of the Parthian kings. "Parthians and Elamites," i. e. Jews inhabiting those countries, are mentioned as among the converts on the day of Pentecost. Sozomen, ii. 8.

[m] The date of the earliest Christian communities in India is judiciously discussed in Bohlen, Das alte Indien, i. 369 to the end.

[n] Malcolm's Hist. of Persia, i. 74, from Ferdusi.

They formed the great council of the state. Foreign religions, if tolerated, were watched with jealous severity. Magianism was established at the point of the sword in those parts of Armenia which were subjugated by the Persian kings. When Mesopotamia was included within the pale of the Persian dominions, the Jews were, at times, exposed to the severest oppressions; the burial of the dead was peculiarly offensive to the usages of the fire-worshippers. Mani was alike rejected, and persecuted by the Christian and the Magian priesthood; and the barbarous execution of the Christian bishops, who ruled over the Babylonian sees, demanded at a later period the interference of Constantine.[o]

But while Persia thus fiercely repelled Christianity from its frontier, upon that frontier arose a Christian state.[p] Armenia was the first country which embraced Christianity as the religion of the king, the nobles, and the people. During the early ages of the empire, Armenia had been an object of open contention, or of political intrigue, between the conflicting powers of Parthia and Rome. The adoption of Christianity as the religion of the state, while it united the interests of the kingdom, by a closer bond, with the Christian empire of Rome (for it anticipated the honour of being the first Christian state by only a few years), added, to its perilous situation on the borders of the two empires, a new cause for the implacable hostility of Persia. Every successful invasion, and every subtle negotiation to establish the Persian predominance in Armenia, was marked by the most relentless and

Armenia the first Christian kingdom.

---

[o] Sozomen, ii. 9, 10. Compare, on these persecutions of the Christians, Kleuker, Anhang zum Zendavesta, p. 292 et seq., with Assemanni, Act. Martyr. Or. et Occid. Romæ, 1748.

[p] St. Martin, Mémoires sur l'Arménie, i. 405, 406, &c. Notes to Le Beau, Hist. des Empereurs, i. 76.

sanguinary persecutions, which were endured with the combined dignity of Christian and patriotic heroism by the afflicted people. The Vartobed, or Patriarch, was always the first victim of Persian conquest, the first leader to raise the fallen standard of independence.

The Armenian histories, written, almost without exception, by the priesthood, in order to do honour to their native country by its early reception of Christianity, have included the Syrian kingdom of Edessa within its borders, and assigned a place to the celebrated Abgar in the line of their kings. The personal correspondence of Abgar with the Divine author of Christianity is, of course, incorporated in this early legend. But though, no doubt, Christianity had made considerable progress, at the commencement of the third century, the government of Armenia was still sternly and irreconcileably Pagan. Khosrov I. imitated the cruel and impious Pharaoh. He compelled the Christians, for a scanty stipend, to labour on the public works. Many obtained the glorious crown of martyrdom.[q]

A.D. 214.

Gregory the Illuminator was the Apostle of Armenia. The birth of Gregory was darkly connected with the murder of the reigning king, the almost total extirpation of the royal race, and the subjugation of his country to a foreign yoke. He was the son of Anah, the assassin of his sovereign. The murder of Khosrov, the valiant and powerful king of Armenia, is attributed to the jealous ambition of Ardeschir, the first king of Persia.[r] Anah, of a noble Armenian race, was bribed, by the promise of vast

Gregory the Illuminator.

---

q Father Chamich, History of Armenia, i. 153, translated by Avdall.
r Moses Choren. 64, 71 ; Chamich, Hist. Armén. i. 154, and other authorities. St. Martin, Mémoires sur l'Arménie, i. 303, &c.

wealth and the second place in the empire, to conspire against the life of Khosrov. Pretending to take refuge in the Armenian dominions from the persecution of King Ardeschir, he was hospitably received in the city of Valarshapat. He struck theking to the heart, and

Murder of Khosrov.

fled. The Armenian soldiery, in their fury, pursued the assassin, who was drowned, during his flight, in the river Araxes. The vengeance of the soldiers wreaked itself upon his innocent family;[s] the infant Gregory alone was saved by a Christian nurse, who took refuge in Cæsarea. There the future Apostle was baptized, and (thus runs the legend) by divine revelation received the name of Gregory. Ardeschir reaped all the advantage of the treachery of Anah, and Armenia sank into a Persian province. The conqueror consummated the crime of his base instrument; the whole family of Khosrov was put to death, except Tiridates, who fled to the Roman dominions, and one sister, Khosrovedught, who was afterwards instrumental in the introduction of Christianity into the kingdom. Tiridates served with distinction in the Roman armies of Diocletian, and seized the favourable opportunity of reconquering his hereditary throne. The re-establishment of Armenia as a friendly power was an important event in the Eastern policy of Rome; the simultaneous conversion of the empire and its Eastern ally to the new religion strengthened the bonds of union by a common religious interest.

Gregory re-entered his native country in the train

Tiridates, King of Armenia.

of the victorious Tiridates. But Tiridates was a bigoted adherent to the ancient religion of his country. This religion appears to have been a

---

[s] According to St. Martin, two children of Anah were saved.

mingled form of corrupt Zoroastrianism and Grecian, or rather Oriental, Nature-worship, with some rites of Scythian origin. Their chief deity was Aramazd, the Ormuzd of the Magian system, but their temples were crowded with statues, and their altars reeked with animal sacrifices; usages revolting to the purer Magianism of Persia.[t] The Babylonian impersonation of the female principle of generation, Anaitis or Anahid, was one .of their most celebrated divinities; and at the funeral of their great King Artaces many persons had immolated themselves, after the Scythian or Getic custom, upon his body.

It was in the temple of Anaitis, in the province of Ekelias, that Tiridates offered the sacrifice of thanksgiving for his restoration to his hereditary throne. He commanded Gregory to assist in the idolatrous worship. The Christian resolutely refused, and endured, Persecution according to the Armenian history, twelve dif- of Gregory. ferent kinds of torture. It was disclosed to the exasperated monarch, that the apostate from the national religion was son to the assassin of his father. Gregory was plunged into a deep dungeon, where he languished for fourteen years, supported by the faithful charity of a Christian female. At the close of the fourteen years, a pestilence, attributed by the Christian party to the Divine vengeance, wasted the kingdom of Armenia. The virgin sister of Tiridates, Khosrovedught (the daughter of Khosrov) had embraced the faith of the Gospel. By Divine revelation (thus speaks the piety of the priestly historians), she advised the immediate release of Gregory. What Heaven had commanded, Heaven had approved by wonders. The King himself, afflicted by the malady.

---

[t] Chamich, i. 145.

was healed by the Christian missionary. The pestilence
Conversion of the King. ceased. The king, the nobles, the people, almost
simultaneously submitted to baptism. Armenia
became at once a Christian kingdom. Gregory took
the highest rank, as Archbishop of the kingdom. Priests
were invited from Greece and Syria; four hundred
bishops were consecrated; churches and religious houses
arose in every quarter; the Christian festivals and days
of religious observance were established by law.

But the severe truth of history must make the melancholy acknowledgement that the Gospel did not finally
triumph without a fierce and sanguinary strife. The
province of Dara, the sacred region of the Armenians,
crowded with their national temples, made a stern and
Persecution by the Christians. determined resistance. The priests fought for
their altars with desperate courage, and it was
only with the sword that churches could be planted in
that irreclaimable district.[u] In the war waged by
Maximin against Tiridates, in which the ultimate aim
of the Roman Emperor, according to Eusebius, was the
suppression of Christianity, he may have been invited
and encouraged by the rebellious Paganism of the subjects of Tiridates.

Towards the close of the third century, while there-
Manicheism. ligion of the East was undergoing these signal
revolutions, and the antagonistic creeds of
Magianism and Christianity were growing up into power-

---

[u] In the very curious extract from
the contemporary Armenian historian
Zenob, there is an account of this civil
war. The following inscription commemorated the decisive battle :—

The first battle in which men bravely fought.
The leader of the armies was Argan, the
chief of the Priesthood,

Who lies here in his grave,
and with him 1038 men.
And this battle we fought for the Godhead
of Kisáne and for Christ.

See Zeitschrift für die Kunde des
Morgenlandes, vol. i. 253, 378, et
seqq.

ful and hostile systems, and assuming an important influence on the political affairs of Asia; while the East and
the West thus began that strife of centuries which subsequently continued in a more fierce and implacable form in
the conflict between Christianity and Mohammedanism;
a bold and ambitious adventurer in the career
of religious change[x] attempted to unite the   Mani.
conflicting elements; to reconcile the hostile genius of
the East and of the West; to fuse together, in one
comprehensive scheme, Christianity, Zoroastrianism, and
apparently the Buddhism of India. It is singular to
trace the doctrines of the most opposite systems and of
remote regions assembled together and harmonised in
the vast Eclecticism of Mani.[y] From his native
Persia he derived his Dualism, his antagonistic Various sources of his
worlds of light and darkness; and from Ma- doctrines.
gianism, likewise, his contempt of outward temple and
splendid ceremonial. From Gnosticism, or rather from
universal Orientalism, he drew the inseparable admixture
of physical and moral notions, the eternal hostility

---

[x] Besides the original authorities, I
have consulted, for Mani and his doctrines, Beausobre, Hist. du Manichéisme; D'Herbelot, art. Mani; Lardner,
Credibility of Gospel History; Mosheim,
De Reb. Christ. ante Const. Magnum;
Matter, Hist. du Gnosticime, ii. 351. I
had only seen Baur's able Manichaische
Religions System, after this chapter
was written. I had anticipated, though
not followed out so closely, the relationship to Buddhism, much of which,
however, is evidently the common
groundwork of all Orientalism.

[y] Augustine, in various passages,
but most fully in what is given as an
extract from the book of the Founda-

tion, De Nat. Boni, p. 515. Compare
Beausobre, vol. ii. 386, who seems to
consider it an abstract from some forged
or spurious work. Probably much of
Mani's system was allegorical, but how
much, his disciples probably did not,
and his adversaries would not, know.
See also the most curious passage about
the Manichean metempsychosis, in the
statement of Tyrbo, in the Disputatio
Archelai et Manetis, apud Routh, Reliquiæ Sacræ, vol. iv.
  The most singular fact is that these
obstinate idolaters were of Indian
descent, and were distinguished by
long hair.

between Mind and Matter, the rejection of Judaism, and the identification of the God of the Old Testament with the Evil Spirit, the distinction between Jesus and the Christ, with the Docetism, or the unreal death of the incorporeal Christ. From Cabalism, through Gnosticism, came the primal man, the Adam Cædmon of that system, and (if it be a genuine part of this system) the assumption of beautiful human forms, those of graceful boys and attractive virgins, by the powers of light, and their union with the male and female spirits of darkness. From India, he took the Emanation theory (all light was a part of the Deity, and in one sense the soul of the world), the metempsychosis, the triple division of human souls (the one the pure, which reascended at once, and was reunited to the primal light; the second the semi-pure, which, having passed through a purgatorial process, returned to earth, to pass through a second ordeal of life; the third, of obstinate and irreclaimable evil): from India, perhaps, came his Homophorus, as the Greeks called it, his Atlas, who supported the earth upon his shoulders, and his Splenditenens, the circumambient air. From Chaldea, he borrowed the power of astral influences; and he approximated to the solar worship of expiring Paganism: Christ, the Mediator, like the Mithra of his countryman, had his dwelling in the sun.[z]

From his native country Mani derived the simple diet of fruits and herbs; from the Buddhism of India, his respect for animal life, which was to be slain neither for food nor for sacrifice;[a] from all the anti-materialist

---

[z] D'Herbelot, voc. "Mani."

[a] Ibid. Augustine says that they wept when they plucked vegetables for food, for in them also there was a certain portion of life, which, according to Mani, was a part of the

sects or religions, the abhorrence of every sensual indulgence, even the bath as well as the banquet; the proscription, or, at least, the disparagement of marriage.
And the whole of these foreign and extraneous tenets,
his creative imagination blended with his own form of
Christianity; for, so completely are they mingled, that
it is difficult to decide whether Christianity or Magianism
formed the groundwork of Mani's system. From Christianity he derived not, perhaps, a strictly Nicene, but
more than an Arian, Trinity. His own system was the
completion of the imperfect revelation of the Gospel.
He was a *man* invested with a divine mission,—the
Paraclete (for Mani appears to have distinguished between
the Paraclete and the Holy Spirit), who was to consummate the great work auspiciously commenced, yet un-
fulfilled by the mission of Jesus.[b] Mani had twelve
apostles. His Ertang, or Gospel, was intended to supersede the four Christian Evangelists, whose works, though
valuable, he averred had been interpolated with many
Jewish fables. The Acts, Mani altogether rejected, as
announcing the descent of the Paraclete on the Apostles.[c]
On the writings of St. Paul he pronounced a more

Deity. " Dicitis enim dolorem sentire fructum, cum de arbore carpitur,
sentire dum conciditur, cum teritur,
cum coquitur, cum manditur. Cujus,
porro dementiæ est, pios se videri velle,
quod ab animalium interfectione se
temperent, cum omnes suas escas eas-
dem animas habere dicunt, quibus ut
putant, viventibus, tanta vulnera et
manibus et dentibus ingerant." Augustin. contra Faust., lib. vi. p. 205,
206. This is pure Buddhism.

b Lardner, following Beausobre, considers the account of Mani's predeces-

sors, Scythianus and Terebinthus, or
Buddha, idle fictions. The virgin birth
assigned to Buddha, which appears to
harmonise with the great Indian My-
thos of the origin of Buddhism, might
warrant a conjecture that this is an
Oriental tradition of the Indian origin
of some of Mani's doctrines, dictated by
Greek ignorance. I now find this conjecture followed out and illustrated
with copious learning by Baur.

c Lardner (v. 11. 183) suggests
other reasons for the rejection of the
Acts.

favourable sentence. But his Ertang, it is said, was
not merely the work of a prophet, but of a painter; for,
among his various accomplishments, Mani excelled in
His paint- that art. It was richly illustrated by pictures,
ings.   which commanded the wonder of the age;
while his followers, in devout admiration, studied the
tenets of their master in the splendid images, as well as
in the sublime language, of the Marvellous Book. If
this be true, since the speculative character of Mani's
chief tenets, their theogonical, if it may be so said,
extramundane character, lay beyond the proper province
of the painter (the imitation of existing beings, and that
idealism which, though elevating its objects to an unreal
dignity or beauty, is nevertheless faithful to the truth
of nature), this imagery, with which his book was illuminated, was probably a rich system of Oriental sym-
bolism, which may have been transmuted by the blind
zeal of his followers, or the misapprehension of his
adversaries, into some of his more fanciful tenets. The
religion of Persia was fertile in these emblematic figures,
if not their native source; and in the gorgeous illuminated manuscripts of the East, often full of allegorical
devices, we may discover, perhaps, the antitypes of the
Ertang of Mani.[d]

Mani (I blend together and harmonise as far as possible the conflicting accounts of the Greeks and Asiatics)

---

[d] It appears, I think, from Augustine, that all the splendid images of the
sceptred king crowned with flowers,
the Splenditenens and the Homophorus,
were allegorically interpreted: "Si non
sunt ænigmata rationis, phantasmata
sunt cogitationis, aut vecordia furoris.
Si vero ænigmata esse dicuntur." Contra
Faust. xv. p. 277. The extract from
the "amatory song" (Contra Faust.
xv. 5), with the twelve ages (the great
cycle of 12,000 years) singing and
casting flowers upon the everlasting
sceptred king; the twelve gods (the
signs of the zodiac), and the hosts of
angels, is evidently the poetry, not the
theology, of the system.

was of Persian birth,[e] of the sacred race of the Magi. He
wore the dress of a Persian of distinction, the
lofty Babylonian sandals, the mantle of azure   Life of Mani.
blue, the parti-coloured trousers, and he bore the ebony
staff in his hand.[f] He was a proficient in the learning
of his age and country, a mathematician, and had made
a globe; he was deeply skilled, as appears from his system,
in the theogonical mysteries of the East, and so well
versed in the Christian Scriptures that he was said to
have been, and indeed he may at one time have been,
a Christian priest, in the province of Ahoriaz that bordered on Babylonia.[g] He began to propagate his
doctrines during the reign of Shah-poor, but the son of
Ardeshir would endure no invasion upon the established
Magianism.[h] Mani fled from the wrath of his sovereign
into Turkesthan ; from thence he is said to have
visited India, and even China.[i] In Turkesthan, he
withdrew himself from the society of men, like Mohammed in the cave of Hira,[k] into a grotto, through which
flowed a fountain of water, and in which provision for a
year had been secretly stored. His followers believed

---

[e] His birth is assigned by the Chronicle of Edessa to the year 239. Beausobre, i.

[f] Beausobre, who is inclined to admit
the genuineness of this description, in
the Acts of Archelaus, has taken pains
to show that there was nothing differ-
ing from the ordinary Persian dress.
Vol. i. p. 97, &c.

[g] In the Acts of Archelaus, he is
called a barbarous Persian, who understood no Greek, but disputed in Syriac.
c. 36.

[h] Malcolm, i. 79.

[i] Abulpharag, Dynast. p. 82.   See

Lardner, p. 167.

[k] Lardner considers the story of the
cave a later invention borrowed from
Mohammed. The relation of this circumstance by Mohammedan authors
leads me to the opposite conclusion.
They would rather have avoided than
invented points of similitude between
their prophet and " the impious Sad-
ducee," as he is called in the Koran.
But see Baur's very ingenious and
probable theory, which resolves it into
a myth, and connects it with the Mithraic and still earlier astronomical or
religious legends.

that he had ascended into heaven, to commune with the Deity. At the end of the year, he reappeared, and displayed his Ertang, embellished with its paintings, as the Divine revelation.[m]

In the theory of Mani, the one Supreme, who hovered in inaccessible and uninfluential distance over the whole of the Gnostic systems, the Brahm of the Indians, and the more vague and abstract Zeruane Akerene of Zoroastrianism, holds no place. The groundwork of his system is an original and irreconcileable Dualism.[n] The two antagonistic worlds of light and darkness, of spirit and matter, existed from eternity, separate, unmingled, unapproaching, ignorant of each other's existence.[o] The kingdom of light was held by God the Father, who "rejoiced in his own proper eternity, and comprehended in himself wisdom and vitality:" his most glorious kingdom was founded in a light and blessed region, which could not be moved nor shaken. On one side of his most illustrious and holy territory was the land of darkness, of vast depth and extent,

---

[m] Beausobre (i. 191, 192) would find the Cascar at which, according to the extant, but much contested, report, the memorable conference between Archelaus and Mani was held, at Cashgar in Turkesthan. But, independent of the improbability of a Christian bishop settled in Turkesthan, the whole history is full of difficulties, and nothing is less likely than that the report of such a conference should reach the Greek or Syrian Christians through the hostile territory of Persia.

[n] Epiphanius gives these words as the commencement of Mani's work (in twenty-two books) on the Mysteries: Ἦν Θεὸς καὶ ὕλη, φῶς καὶ σκότος,

ἀγαθὸν καὶ κακὸν, τοῖς πᾶσιν ἄκρως ἐναντία, ὡς κατὰ μηδὲν ἐπικοινοῦν θάτερον θατέρῳ. Epiphan. Hærat. lxvi. 14.

[o] Hæ quidem in exordio fuerunt duæ substantiæ a sese diversæ. Et luminis quidem imperium tenebat Deus Pater, in suâ sanctâ stirpe perpetuus, in virtute magnificus, naturâ ipsâ verus, æternitate propriâ semper exsultans, continens apud se sapientiam et sensus vitales . . . Ita autem fundata sunt ejusdem splendidissima regna super lucidam et beatam terram, ut a nullo unquam aut moveri aut concuti possint. Apud August. contra Ep. Manich. c. 13, n. 16.

inhabited by fiery bodies, and pestiferous races of beings.[p]
Civil dissensions agitated the world of darkness; the
defeated faction fled to the heights or to the extreme
verge of their world.[q] They beheld with amazement,
and with envy, the beautiful and peaceful regions of
light.[r] They determined to invade the delightful realm;
and the primal man, the archetypal Adam, was formed
to defend the borders against this irruption of the hostile
powers. He was armed with his five elements, opposed
to those which formed the realm of darkness. The
primal man was in danger of discomfiture in the long
and fearful strife, had not Oromazd, the great power of
the world of light, sent the living spirit to his assistance.[s]
The powers of darkness retreated; but they bore away
some particles of the divine light, and the extrication of
these particles (portions of the Deity, according to the
subtile materialism of the system) is the object of the
long and almost interminable strife of the two principles.
Thus, part of the Divinity was interfused through the
whole of matter; light was, throughout all visible existence, commingled with darkness.[t] Mankind was the

[p] The realm of darkness was divided
into five distinct circles, which may
remind us of Dante's hell. 1. Of
infinite darkness, perpetually emanating, and of inconceivable stench. 2.
Beyond these, that of muddy and turbid waters, with their inhabitants; and
3. within, that of fierce and boisterous
winds, with their prince and their
parents. 4. A fiery but corruptible
region (the region of destroying fire),
with its leaders and nations. 5. In
like manner, further within, a place
full of smoke and thick gloom, in which
dwelt the dreadful sovereign of the
whole, with innumerable princes

around him, of whom he was the soul
and the source. Ep. Fundament. ap.
Augustin. cont. Manich. c. 14, n. 19.

[q] The world of darkness, according
to one statement, cleft the world of
light like a wedge (Augustin. contr.
Faust. iv. 2); according to another
(Titus Bostrensis, i. 7), it occupied
the southern quarter of the universe.
This, as Baur observes, is Zoroastrianism. Bundehesch, part iii. p. 62.

[r] Theodoret, Hæret. Fab. i. 26.

[s] Epiphan. Hæret. lxvi. 76. Titus
Bostrensis, Augustin. de Hæret. c. 46.

[t] The celestial powers, during the
long process of commixture, assumed

creation or the offspring of the great principle of darkness, after this stolen and ethereal light had become
incorporated with his dark and material being. Man
was formed in the image of the primal Adam; his
nature was threefold, or perhaps dualistic; the body,
the concupiscent or sensual soul (which may have been
the influence of the body on the soul), and the pure,
celestial, and intellectual spirit. Eve was of inferior,
of darker, and more material origin; for the creating
Archon, or spirit of evil, had expended all the light, or
soul, upon man. Her beauty was the fatal tree of
Paradise, for which Adam was content to fall. It was
by this union that the sensual or concupiscent soul
triumphed over the pure and divine spirit;[u] and it was
by marriage, by sexual union, that the darkening race
was propagated. The intermediate, the visible world,
which became the habitation of man, was the creation
of the principle of good, by his spirit. This primal
principle subsisted in trinal unity (whether from eternity
might, perhaps, have been as fiercely agitated in the
Manichean as in the Christian schools); the Christ, the
first efflux of the God of Light, would have been defined
by the Manichean as in the Nicene Creed, as Light of
Light; he was self-subsistent, endowed with all the
perfect attributes of the Deity, and his dwelling was in

---

alternately the most beautiful forms
of the masculine and feminine sex, and
mingled with the powers of darkness,
who likewise became boys and virgins;
and from their conjunction proceeded
the still commingling world. This is
probably an allegory, perhaps a paint-
ing. There is another fanciful poetic
image of considerable beauty, and, possibly, of the same allegoric character.
The pure elementary spirits soared upwards in "their ships of light," in
which they originally sailed through
the stainless element; those which
were of a hotter nature were dragged
down to earth; those of a colder and
more humid temperament were exhaled
upwards to the elemental waters. The
ships of light are, in another view, the
celestial bodies.

[u] De Mor. Manichæor. c. 19. Acta
Archelai, c. 10.

the sun.[x] He was the Mithra of the Persian system;
and the Manichean doctrine was Zoroastrianism under
Christian appellations.[y] There is an evident difference
between the Jesus and the Christos throughout the
system; the Jesus Patibilis seems to be the imprisoned
and suffering light.

The Spirit, which made up the triple being of the
primal principle of good, was an all-pervading æther,
the source of life and being; which, continually stimu-
lating the disseminated particles of light, was the animating principle of the worlds. He was the creator of
the intermediate world, the scene of strife, in which the
powers of light and darkness contested the dominion
over man; the one assisting the triumph of the particle
of light which formed the intellectual spirit, the other
embruting and darkening the imprisoned light with the
corruption and sensual pollutions of matter. But the
powers of darkness obtained the mastery, and man was
rapidly degenerating into the baser destiny; the Homophorus, the Atlas on whose shoulders the earth rests,
began to tremble and totter under his increasing burden.[z]

---

[x] According to the creed of Faustus,
his *virtue* dwelt in the sun, his *wisdom*
in the moon. Apud August. lib. xxx.
p. 333.

[y] The Manicheans were Trinitarians,
or at least used Trinitarian language.
Angustin. contra Faust. c. xx. " Nos
Patris quidem Dei omnipotentis, et
Christi filii ejus, et Spiritus Sancti
unum idemque sub triplici appellatione
colimus numen; sed Patrem quidem
ipsum lucem incolere summam ac prin-
cipalem, quam Paulus alias inaccessi-
bilem vocat; Filium vero in hac se-
cunda ac visibili luce consistere, qui
quoniam sit et ipse geminus, ut eum

Apostolus novit, Christum dicens esse
Dei virtutem et Dei sapientiam, virtutem quidem ejus in sole habitare
credimus, sapientiam vero in luna:
necnon et Spiritus Sancti, qui est ma-
jestas tertia, aëris hunc omnem ambi-
tum sedem fatemur ac diversorium,
cujus ex viribus ac spiritali profusione
terram quoque concipieutem, gignere
patibilem Jesum, qui est vita et salus
hominum, qui suspensus ex ligno."

[z] Homophorus and his ally, the
Splenditenens, who assists him in maintaining the earth in its equilibrium, is
one of the most incongruous and least
necessary parts of the Manichean system.

Then the Christ descended from his dwelling in the sun; assumed a form *apparently* human; the Jews, incited by the Prince of Darkness, crucified his phantom form; but He left behind his Gospel, which dimly and imperfectly taught what was now revealed in all its full effulgence by Mani the Persian.

The celestial bodies, which had been formed by the living spirit of the purer element, were the witnesses and co-operators in the great strife.[a]   To the sun, the dwelling of the Christ, were drawn up the purified souls, in which the principle of light had prevailed, and passed onward for ablution in the pure water, which forms the moon; and then, after fifteen days, returned to the source of light in the sun.   The spirits of evil, on the creation of the visible world, lest they should fly away, and bear off into irrecoverable darkness the light which was still floating about, had been seized by the living spirit, and bound to the stars.   Hence the malignant influences of the constellations; hence all the terrific and destructive fury of the elements.   While the soft and refreshing and fertilising showers are the distillation

---

Is the origin of these images the notion of supporters of the earth which are so common in the East? Are any of these fables older than the introduction of Manicheism? Is it the old Indian fable under another form? or is it the Greek Atlas? I am inclined to look to India for the origin.

Beausobre's objection, that such a fiction is inconsistent with Mani's mathematical knowledge, and his formation of a globe, is of no inconsiderable weight, if it is not mere poetry.

[a] Lardner has well expressed the Manichean notion of the formation of the celestial bodies, which were made, the sun of the *good* fire, the moon of the *good* water. " In a word, not to be too minute, the Creator formed the sun and moon out of those parts of the light which had preserved their original purity. The visible or inferior heavens (for now we do not speak of the supreme heaven) and the rest of the planets were formed of those parts of light which were but little corrupted with matter. The rest he left in our world, which are no other than those parts of light which had suffered most by the contagion of matter." Lardner's Works, 4to ed., ii. 193.

of the celestial spirit, the thunders are the roarings, the lightning the flashing wrath, the hurricane the furious breath, the torrent and destructive rains the sweat, of the Dæmon of darkness. This wrath is peculiarly excited by the extrication of the passive Jesus, who was said to have been begotten upon the all-conceiving Earth, from his power, by the pure Spirit. The passive Jesus is an emblem, in one sense, it would seem, or type of mankind; more properly, in another, of the imprisoned deity or light. For gradually the souls of men were drawn upwards to the purifying sun; they passed through the twelve signs of the zodiac to the moon, whose waxing and waning was the reception and transmission of light to the sun, and from the sun to the Fountain of Light. Those which were less pure passed again through different bodies, gradually became defæcated, during this long metempsychosis; and there only remained a few obstinately and inveterately embrued in darkness, whom the final consummation of the visible world would leave in the irreclaimable society of the evil powers. At that consummation, the Homophorus would shake off his load; the world would be dissolved in fire;[b] the powers of darkness cast back for all eternity to their primæval state; the condemned souls would be kneaded up for ever in impenetrable matter, while the purified souls, in martial hosts, would surround the frontier of the region of light, and for ever prohibit any new irruption from the antagonistic world of darkness.

The worship of the Manicheans was simple: they built no altar, they raised no temple, they had no images, they had no imposing ceremonial. Pure and simple prayer was their only form of adoration;[c] they

---

b Acta Disput. c. ii. Epiphan. c. 58.

c Faustus expresses this sentiment

very finely: " Item Pagani aris, delu-
bris, simulacris, atque incenso Deum

did not celebrate the birth of Christ, for of his birth they denied the reality; their Paschal feast, as they equally disbelieved the reality of Christ's passion, though kept holy, had little of the Christian form. Prayers addressed to the sun, or at least with their faces directed to that tabernacle in which Christ dwelt—hymns to the great principle of light, exhortations to subdue the dark and sensual element within, and the study of the marvellous Book of Mani—constituted their devotion. They observed the Lord's day; they administered baptism, probably with oil; for they seem (though this point is obscure) to have rejected water-baptism; they celebrated the Eucharist; but as they abstained altogether from wine, they probably used pure water or water mingled with raisins.[d] Their manners were austere, and ascetic; they tolerated, but hardly tolerated, marriage, and that only among the inferior orders:[e] the theatre, the banquet, even the bath, were severely proscribed. Their diet was of fruits and herbs; they shrank with abhorrence from animal food; and, with Buddhist nicety, would tremble at the guilt of having extinguished the principle of life, the spark, as it were, of celestial light, in the meanest creature. This involved them in the strangest absurdities and contradictions, which are pressed against them by their antagonists with unrelent-

colendum putant. Ego ab his in hoc quoque multum diversus incedo, qui ipsum me, si modo sim dignus, rationabile Dei templum puto. Vivum vivæ majestatis simulacrum Christum filium ejus accipio ; aram, mentem puris artibus et disciplinis imbutam. Honores quoque divinos ac sacrificia in solis orationibus, et ipsis puris et simplicibus pono." Faust. apud August. xx. 3.

They bitterly taunted the Catholics with their Paganism, their sacrifices, their agapæ, their idols, their martyrs, their Gentile holidays and rites. Ib.

[d] August. contra Faust. Disput. i. 2, 3.

[e] St. Augustine accuses them of breaking the Fifth Commandment. "Tu autem doctrinâ dæmoniacâ didicisti inimicos deputare parentes tuos, quod

ing logic.[f] They admitted penitence for sin, and laid the fault of their delinquencies on the overpowering influence of matter.[g] Mani suffered the fate of all who attempt to reconcile conflicting parties without power to enforce harmony between them. He was disclaimed and rejected with

---

te per concubitum in carne ligaverint, et hoc modo utique deo tuo immundas compedes imposuerint." Adv. Faust. lib. xv. p. 278. "Opinantur et prædicant diabolum fecisse atque junxisse masculam et feminam." Idem, lib. xix. p. 331, "Displicet 'crescite et multiplicamini,' ne Dei vestri multiplicentur ergastula," &c. Adv. Secundum, c. 21.

'Απέχεσθαι γάμων καὶ ἀφροδισίων καὶ τεκνοποιίας, ἵνα μὴ ἐπιπλεῖον ἡ δύναμις ἐνοικήσῃ τῇ ὕλῃ κατὰ τὴν τοῦ γένους διαδοχήν. Alexand. Lycop. c. 4.

They asserted, indeed, that their doctrines went no farther in this respect than those of the Catholic Christians. Faustus, 30. c. 4. Their opposition to marriage is assigned as among the causes of the enmity of the Persian king. "Rex vero Persarum, cum vidisset tam Catholicos et Episcopos, quam Manichæos Manetis sectarios, a nuptiis abstinere, in Manichæos quidem sententiam mortis tulit. Ad Christianos vero idem edictum manavit. Quum igitur Christiani ad regem confugissent, jussit ille discrimen quale inter utrosque esset, sibi exponi." Apud Asseman. Biblioth. Orient. vii. 220.

There were, however, very different rules of diet and of manners for the elect and the auditors, much resembling those of the monks and other

Christians among the Catholics. See quotations in Lardner, ii. 156.

[f] St. Augustine's Treatise de Mor. Manichæor. is full of these extraordinary charges. In the Confessions (iii. 10), he says that the fig wept when it was plucked, and the parent tree poured forth tears of milk ; " that particles of the true and Supreme God were imprisoned in an apple, and could not be set free but by the touch of one of the elect. If eaten, therefore, by one not a Manichean, it was a deadly sin ; and hence they are charged with making it a sin to give any thing which had life to a poor man not a Manichean. . . . . . They showed more compassion to the fruits of the earth than to human beings." They abhorred husbandry, it is said, as continually wounding life, even in clearing a field of thorns ; "so much more were they friends of gourds than of men."

[g] An acknowledgement of the blamelessness of their manners is extorted from St. Augustine ; at least he admits that, as far as his knowledge as a hearer, he can charge them with no immorality. Contr. Fortunat. in init. In other parts of his writings, especially in the tract De Morib. Manichæor., he is more unfavourable. But see the remarkable passage, Contra Faust. v. i., in which the Manichean contrasts his *works* with the *faith* of the orthodox Christian.

every mark of indignation and abhorrence by both. On his return from exile,[h] indeed, he was received with respect and favour by the reigning sovereign, Hormouz, the son of Shahpoor, who bestowed upon him a castle named Arabion. In this point alone the Greek and Oriental accounts coincide. It was from his own castle that Mani attempted to propagate his doctrines among the Christians in the province of Babylonia. The fame of Marcellus, a noble Christian soldier, for his charitable acts in the redemption of hundreds of captives, designated him as a convert who might be of invaluable service to the cause of Manicheism. According to the Christian account, Mani experienced a signal discomfiture in his conference with Archelaus, bishop of Cascar.[l] But his dispute with the Magian Hierarchy had a more fearful termination. It was an artifice of the new king Baharam to tempt the dangerous teacher from his castle. He was seized, flayed alive, and his skin, stuffed with straw, placed over the gate of the city of Shahpoor.

Death of Mani.

But wild as may appear the doctrines of Mani, they expired not with their author. The anniversary of his death was hallowed by his mourning disciples.[k] The sect was organized upon the Christian model: he left

---

[h] According to Malcolm, he did not return till the reign of Baharam.

[l] Some of the objections of Beausobre to this conference appear insuperable. Allow a city named Cascar; can we credit the choice of Greek, even Heathen, rhetoricians and grammarians as assessors in such a city and in such a contest? Archelaus, it must indeed be confessed, plays the sophist; and if Mani had been no more powerful as a reasoner, or as a speaker, he would hardly have distracted the East and West with his doctrines. It is not improbably an imaginary dialogue in the form, though certainly not in the style, of Plato. See the best edition of it, in Routh's Reliquiæ Sacræ.

[k] Augustin. contr. Epist. Manichæi, c. 9. The day of Mani's death was kept holy by his followers, because he *really* died; the crucifixion neglected, because Christ had but *seemingly* expired on the cross.

his twelve apostles, his seventy-two bishops,[m] his priesthood. His distinction between the Elect[n] or the Perfect, and the Hearers or Catechumens, offered an exact image of the orthodox Christian communities ; and the latter were permitted to marry, to eat animal food, and to cultivate the earth.[o] In the East and in the West the doctrines spread with the utmost rapidity ; and the deep impression which they made upon the mind of man may be estimated by Manicheism having become, almost throughout Asia and Europe, a by-word of religious animosity. In the Mohammedan world the tenets of the Sadducean, the impious Mani, are branded as the worst and most awful impiety. In the West the progress of the believers in this most dangerous of Heresiarchs was so successful that the followers of Mani were condemned to the flames or to the mines, and the property of those who introduced the "execrable usages and foolish laws of the Persians" into the peaceful empire of Rome, confiscated to the imperial treasury. One of the edicts of Diocletian was aimed at their suppression.[p] St. Augustine

Propagation of his religion.

---

[m] Augustin. de Hæres. c. 46.

[n] The strangest notion was, that vegetables used for food were purified, that is, the divine principle of life and light separated from the material and impure, by passing through the bodies of the Elect. " Præbent alimenta electis suis, ut divina illa substantia in eorum ventre purgata, impetret eis veniam, quorum traditur oblatione purganda." Augustin. de Hæres, c. 46. It was a merit in the hearers to make these offerings. Compare Confess. iv. 1.

[o] Auditores, qui appellantur apud eos, et carnibus vescuntur, et agros colunt, et si voluerint, uxores habent,

quorum nihil faciunt qui vocantur Electi. Augustin. Epist. ccxxxvii.

[p] See the edict in Routh, iv. p. 285. Some doubt has been thrown on its authenticity. It is questioned by S. Basnage and by Lardner, though admitted by Beausobre. I cannot think the ignorance which it betrays of the "true principles of the Manichees," the argument adduced by Lardner, of the least weight. Diocletian's predecessors were as little acquainted with the "true principles of Christianity," yet condemned them in their public proceedings.

himself [q] with difficulty escaped the trammels of their
creed, to become their most able antagonist; and in
every century of Christianity, Manicheism, when its real
nature was as much unknown as the Copernican system,
was a proverb of reproach against all sectaries who
departed from the unity of the Church.

The extent of its success may be calculated by the
implacable hostility of all other religions to the doctrines of Mani : the causes of that success are more
difficult to conjecture. Manicheism would rally under
its banner the scattered followers of the Gnostic sects:
but Gnosticism was never, it would seem, popular ;
while Manicheism seems to have had the power of exciting a fanatic attachment to its tenets in the lower
orders. The severe asceticism of their manners may
have produced some effect ; but in this respect they
could not greatly have outdone monastic Christianity ;
and the distinct and definite impersonations of their
creed, always acceptable to a rude and imaginative
class, were encountered by formidable rivals in the
dæmonology and the more complicated form of worship
which was rapidly growing up among the Catholics.[r]

---

[q] There is something very beautiful
in the language of St. Augustine, and
at the same time nothing can show
more clearly the strong hold which
Manicheism had obtained on the Christian world. "Illi in vos sæviant, qui
nesciunt cum quo labore verum in-
veniatur, et quam difficile caveantur
errores. Illi in vos sæviant qui
nesciunt quam rarum et arduum sit
carnalia phantasmata piæ mentis sere-
nitate superare. . . . . Illi in vos
sæviant, qui nesciunt quibus suspiriis
et gemitibus fiat, ut ex quantula-

cunque parte possit intelligi Deus.
Prostremo illi in vos sæviant, qui
nunquam tali errore decepti sint, quali
vos deceptos vident." Contr. Epist.
Manichæi, c. 2. But the spirit of
controversy was too strong for the
charity and justice of Augustine. The
tract which appears to me to give the
fairest view of the real controversy, is
the Disputatio contra Fortunatum.

[r] The Manicheans were legally condemned under Valentinian and Valens.
The houses in which they held their
meetings were confiscated to the state

In the Eastern division of the Roman Empire, Christianity had obtained a signal victory. It had subdued by patient endurance the violent hostility of Galerius; it had equally defied the insidious policy of Maximin; it had twice engaged in a contest with the civil government, and twice come forth in triumph. The edict of toleration had been extorted from the dying Galerius; and the Pagan Hierarchy, and more splendid Pagan ceremonial, with which Maximin attempted to raise up a rival power, fell to the ground on his defeat by Licinius, which closely followed that of Maxentius by Constantine. The Christian communities had publicly reassembled; the churches were rising in statelier form in all the cities; the bishops had reassumed their authority over their scattered but undiminished flocks. Though, in the one case, indignant animosity and the desire of vindicating the severity of their measures against a sect dangerous for its numbers as well as its principles, in the other the glowing zeal of the martyr may be suspected of some exaggeration, yet when a public imperial edict, and the declarations of the Christians themselves, assert the numerical predominance of the Christian party, it is impossible to doubt that their numbers, as well as their activity, were imposing and formidable. In a rescript of Maximin, the Emperor states that it had been forced on the observation of his august fathers,

Triumph of Christianity.

Numbers of the Christians.

(Cod. Theodos. xvi. 3). By Theodosius, they were declared infamous, and incapable of inheriting by law, xvi. 17. The condemnation of the Manicheans in Rome, by Pope Leo I., the Great (The Manicheans in Sicily—Greg. M. Epist. iv. 6); their revival in the Middle Ages, and their extensive dissemination, at least as to their leading principles; the undying obstinacy of their tenets—is one of the most curious chapters in Christian history. See Latin Christianity, i. 171, iv. 91, &c.

T 2

Diocletian and Maximian, that almost all mankind had abandoned the worship of their ancestors, and united themselves to the Christian sect;[s] and Lucianus, a presbyter of Antioch, who suffered martyrdom under Maximin, asserts in his last speech that the greater part of the world had rendered its allegiance to Christianity; entire cities, and even the rude inhabitants of country districts.[t] These statements refer more particularly to the East; and in the East various reasons would lead to the supposition that the Christians bore a larger proportion to the rest of the population than in the other parts of the empire, except perhaps in Africa. The East was the native country of the new religion; the substratum of Judaism, on which it rested, was broader; and Judaism had extended its own conquests much

Different state of the East with regard to the propagation of Christianity.

---

[s] Σχεδὸν ἄπαντας ἀνθρώπους, καταλειφθείσης τῆς τῶν θεῶν θρησκείας, τῷ ἔθνει τῶν Χριστιανῶν συμμεμιχότας. Apud Euseb. Hist. Ec. ix. 9.

[t] " Pars pœne mundi jam major huic veritati adstipulatur ; urbes integræ ; aut si in his aliquid suspectum videatur, contestatur de his etiam agrestis manus, ignara figmenti." This speech, it is true, is only contained in the Latin translation of Eusebius by Rufinus. But there is a calm character in its tone, which avouches its authenticity. The high authority of Porson and Dr. Routh requires the addition of the following note : " Præstitisse aliis multitudine his quoque temporibus Christianos, scriptum extat apud Porphyrium, qui eos alicubi nominavit τοὺς πλείονας, ut me olim fecit certiorem eruditissimus Porsonus." Routh, Re-

liquiæ Sacræ, iii. 293. Gibbon has attempted to form a calculation of the relative numbers of the Christians (see ch. xv. vol. ii. p. 363, with my note) ; he is, perhaps, inclined to underrate the proportion which they bore to the Heathens. Yet, notwithstanding the quotations above, and the high authority of Porson and of Routh, I should venture to doubt their being the majority, except, possibly, in a few Eastern cities. In fact, in a population so fluctuating as that of the empire at this time, any accurate calculation would have been nearly impossible. M. Beugnot agrees very much with Gibbon ; and, I should conceive, with regard to the West, is clearly right, though I shall allege presently some reasons for the more rapid progress of Christianity in the West of Europe.

farther by proselytism, and had thus prepared the way
for Christianity. In Egypt and in the Asiatic provinces
all the early modifications of Christian opinions, the
Gnostic sects of all descriptions, had arisen ; showing, as
it were, by their fertility the exuberance of religious
life and the congeniality of the soil to their prolific
vegetation. The constitution of society was, in some
respects, more favourable than in Italy to the development of the new religion. But it may be questioned
whether the Western *provinces* did not at last offer the
most open field for its free and undisputed course. In
the East, the civilisation was Greek, or, in the remoter
regions, Asiatic. The Romans assumed the sovereignty,
and the highest offices of the government were long held
by men of Italian birth. Some of the richer patricians
possessed extensive estates in the different provinces,
but below this the native population retained its own
habits and usages. Unless in the mercantile towns,
which were crowded with foreign settlers from all quarters, who brought their manners, their customs, and
their deities, the whole society was Greek, Syrian, or
Egyptian. Above all, there was a native religion ; and
however this loose confederacy of religious republics, of
independent colleges or fraternities of the local or the
national priesthoods, might only be held together by
the bond of common hostility to the new faith, yet
everywhere this religion was ancient, established, conformed to the habits of the people, endeared by local
vanity, strengthened by its connexion with municipal
privileges, recognised by the homage and sanctioned
by the worship of the civil authorities. The Roman
prefect, or pro-consul, considered every form of Paganism as sufficiently identified with that of Rome to
demand his respect and support: everywhere he found

deities with the same names or attributes as those of the imperial city; and everywhere, therefore, there was an alliance, seemingly close and intimate, between the local religion and the civil government.

In the Western provinces, Gaul, Spain, and Britain, but more particularly in Gaul, the constitution of society was very different. It was Roman, formed by the influx of colonists from different quarters, and the gradual adoption of Roman manners by the natives. It had grown up on the wane of Paganism. There was no old, or established, or national religion. The ancient Druidism had been proscribed as a dark and inhuman superstition, or had gradually worn away before the progress of Roman civilisation. Out of Italy, the gods of Italy were, to a certain degree, strangers; the Romans, as a nation, built no temples in their conquered provinces: the munificence of an individual, sometimes, perhaps, of the reigning Cæsar, after having laid down the military road, built the aqueduct, or encircled the vast arena of the amphitheatre, might raise a fane to his own tutelary divinity.[u] Of the foreign settlers, each brought his worship; each set up his gods; vestiges of every kind of religion, Greek, Asiatic, Mithraic, have been discovered in Gaul, but none was dominant or exclusive. This state of society would require or welcome, or at all events offer less resistance to the propagation of a new faith. After it had once passed the Alps,[x] Christianity made rapid progress; and the father of Constantine may have been guided no

Of the West.

---

[u] Eumenius, in his panegyric on Constantine, mentions two temples of Apollo; of one, " the most beautiful in the world," the site is unknown: it is supposed to have been at Lyons or Vienne; the other was at Autun. Eumen. Paneg. xxi., with the note of Cellarius.

[x] Serius trans alpes religione Dei susceptâ? Sulpic. Sever. H. E. lib. ii.

less by policy than humanity, in his reluctant and merciful execution of the persecuting edicts of Diocletian and Galerius.

Such was the position of Christianity when Constantine commenced his struggle for universal empire. In the East, though rejected by the ancient rival of Rome, the kingdom of Persia, it was acknowledged as the religion of the state by a neighbouring nation. In the Roman provinces, it was emerging victorious from a period of the darkest trial; and though still threatened by the hostility of Maximin, that hostility was constrained to wear an artful disguise, and, when it ventured to assume a more open form, was obliged to listen, at least with feigned respect, to the remonstrances of the victorious Constantine. In the North, at least in that part from which Constantine derived his main strength, it was respected and openly favoured by the Government. Another striking circumstance might influence the least superstitious mind, and is stated by the ecclesiastical historian not to have been without effect on Constantine himself. Of all the Emperors who had been invested with the purple, either as Augusti or Cæsars, during the persecution of the Christians, his father alone, the protector of Christianity, had gone down to an honoured and peaceful grave.[y]   Diocletian, indeed, still lived,

---

[y] Euseb. Vit. Const. i. 21; Socrat. Eccles. Hist. i. 11. The language of the Ecclesiastical Historian Socrates is remarkable. Constantine, he says, was meditating the liberation of the empire from its tyrants: καὶ ὡς ἦν ἐν τηλικαύτῃ φροντίδι, ἐπενόει τίνα θεὸν ἐπίκουρον πρὸς τὴν μάχην καλέσειε, κατὰ νοῦν δὲ ἐλάμβανεν,

ὡς οὐδὲν ὤναντο οἱ περὶ Διοκλητιανὸν, περὶ τοὺς ἑλλήνων θεοὺς διακείμενοι, ἤυρισκεν τε ὡς ὁ αὗτου πατὴρ, Κονστάντιος, ἀποστραφεὶς τὰς Ἑλλήνων θρησκείας, εὐδαιμονέστερον τὸν βίον διήγαγεν. It was in this mood of mind that he saw the vision of the cross. Socr. Eccl. Hist. i. 2.

but in what, no doubt, appeared to most of his former
End of the
persecutors
of Christi-
anity. subjects, an inglorious retirement. However
the philosophy of the abdicated Emperor might
teach him to show the vegetables of his garden,
as worthy of as much interest to a mind of real dignity
as the distinctions of worldly honour; however he may
have been solicited by a falling and desperate faction
to resume the purple, his abdication was no doubt, in
general, attributed to causes less dignified than the contempt of earthly grandeur. Conscious derangement of
mind (a malady inseparably connected, according to the
religious notions of Jew, Pagan, probably of Christian
during that age, with the divine displeasure), or remorse
of conscience, was reported to embitter the calm decline
of Diocletian's life. Instead of an object of envy, no
doubt, in the general sentiment of mankind, he was
thought to merit only aversion or contempt.[z] Maximian
(Herculius), the colleague of Diocletian, after resuming
the purple, engaging in base intrigues, or open warfare,
against his son Maxentius, and afterwards against his
protector Constantine, had anticipated the sentence of
the executioner. Severus had been made prisoner, and
forced to open his own veins. Galerius, the chief author
of the persecution, had experienced the most miserable
fate; he had wasted away with a slow and agonising
and loathsome disease. Maximin alone remained, hereafter to perish in miserable obscurity. Nor should it be
forgotten that the great persecutor of the Christians
had been the jealous tyrant of Constantine's youth.

---

[z] It is curious how undying are such prejudices. I remember that M. Crétineau Joly somewhere asserts that Clement XIV. (Ganganelli) was the only Pope who ever died in a state of derangement (Boniface VIII.?). I doubt both his historical facts, but the assertion is remarkable.

Constantine had preserved his liberty, perhaps his life, only by the boldness and rapidity of his flight from the court of Galerius.[a]

Under all these circumstances, Constantine was advancing against Rome. The battle of Verona had decided the fate of the empire : the vast forces of Maxentius had melted away before the sovereign of Gaul; but Rome, the capital, was still held with the obstinacy of despair by the voluptuous tyrant Maxentius. Constantine appeared on the banks of the Tiber, though invested with the Roman purple, yet a foreign conqueror. Many of his troops were Barbarians, Kelts, Germans, Britons ; yet, in all probability, there were many of the Gaulish Christians in his army. Maxentius threw himself upon the gods, as well as upon the people of Rome ; he attempted with desperate earnestness to rally the energy of Roman valour under the awfulness of the Roman religion.

War of Constantine against Maxentius.

A.D. 312.

During the early part of his reign, Maxentius, intent upon his pleasures, had treated the religious divisions of Rome with careless indifference, or had endeavoured to conciliate the Christian party by conniving at their security. His deification of Galerius had been, as it were, an advance to the side of Paganism. The rebellion of Africa, which he revenged by the devastation of Carthage, was likely to bring him into

Religion of Maxentius.

---

[a] In his letter to Sapor, King of Persia, Constantine himself acknowledges the influence of these motives on his mind : ὃν πολλοὶ τῶν τῇδε βασιλευσάντων, μανιώδεσι πλάναις ὑπαχθέντες, ἐπεχείρησαν ἀρνήσασθαι, ἀλλ᾽ ἐκείνους ἅπαντας τοιοῦτον τιμωρὸν τέλος κατανάλωσεν, ὡς πᾶν τὸ μετ᾽ ἐκείνους ἀνθρώπων γένος, τὰς ἐκείνων συμφορὰς ἀντ᾽ ἄλλου παραδείγματος, ἐπαράτους τοῖς τὰ ὅμοια ζηλοῦσι τίθεσθαι. Apud Theodoret. Ecc. Hist. i. c. 25.

hostile contact with the numerous Christians of that province. In Rome itself an event had occurred which, however darkly described, was connected with the antagonistic religious parties in the capital. A fire had broken out in the temple of the Fortune of Rome. The tutelary deity of the Roman greatness—an awful omen in this dark period of decline and dissolution!—was in danger. A soldier—it is difficult to ascribe such temerity to any but a Christian fanatic—uttered some words of insult against the revered, and it might be alienated, goddess. The indignant populace rushed upon the traitor to the majesty of Rome, and summoned the prætorian cohorts to wreak their vengeance on all who could be supposed to share in the sentiments of the apostate soldier. Maxentius is accused by one Christian and one Pagan historian of having instigated the tumult; by one Pagan he is said to have used his utmost exertions to allay its fury. Both statements may be true; though at first he may have given free scope to the massacre, at a later period he may have taken alarm, and attempted to restore the peace of the city.[b] Of the direct hostility of Maxentius to Christianity, the evidence is dubious and obscure. A Roman matron preferred the glory, or the crime, of suicide, rather than submit to his lustful embraces. But it was the beauty, no doubt, not the religion of Sophronia,

[b] The silence of Eusebius as to the Christianity of the soldier, may be thought an insuperable objection to this view. But in the first place, the Eastern bishop was but imperfectly informed on the affairs of Rome, and might hesitate, if aware of the fact, to implicate the Christian name with that which was so long one of the most serious and effective charges against the faith, its treacherous hostility to the greatness of Rome. The words of the Pagan Zosimus are very strong:— Βλάσφημα ῥήματα κατὰ τοῦ θείου στρατιωτῶν τις ἀφεὶς, καὶ τοῦ πλήθους διὰ τὴν πρὸς τὸ θείον εὐσέβειαν ἐπελθόντος ἀναιρεθείς. Zos. Hist. ii. 13.

which excited the passions of Maxentius, whose licentiousness comprehended almost all the noble families of
Rome in its insulting range.[c]   The Papal history, not
improbably resting on more ancient authority, represents
Maxentius as degrading the Pope Marcellus to the
humble function of a groom.   The predecessor of the
Gregories and Innocents swept the Imperial stable.[d]

The darkening and more earnest Paganism of Maxentius is more clearly disclosed by the circum-   His Pagan-
stances of his later history.   He had ever   ism.
listened with trembling deference to the expounders of
signs and omens.   He had suspended his expedition
against Carthage, because the signs were not propitious.[e]
Before the battle of Verona, he commanded the Sybil-
line books to be consulted.   " The enemy of the Romans
will perish," answered the prudent and ambiguous oracle;
but who could be the enemy of Rome but the foreign
Constantine, descending from his imperial residence at
Treves, with troops levied in the barbarous provinces,
and of whom the gods of Rome, though not yet declaredly hostile to their cause, might entertain a jealous
suspicion?

On the advance of Constantine, Maxentius redoubled
his religious activity.   He paid his adoration at the
altars of all the gods; he consulted all the diviners of
future events.[f]   He had shut himself in his palace; the
adverse signs made him take refuge in a private house.[g]
Darker rumours were propagated in the East: he is
reported to have attempted to read the secrets of futurity

---

[c] Euseb. Vit. Const. i. 33, 34.
[d] Anastasius, Vit. Marcell.; Pla-
tina, Vit. Pontificum in Marcello.
[e] Zosimus, ii. 14.

[f] Euseb. Vit. Const. i. 21; speaks
of his κακοτέχνους καὶ γοητικὰς
μαγγανείας.
[g] Zosimus, ii. 14.

in the entrails of pregnant women;[h] to have sought an
alliance with the infernal deities, and endeavoured by
magical formularies to avert the impending danger.
However the more enlightened Pagans might disclaim
the weak, licentious, and sanguinary Maxentius, as the
representative either of the Roman majesty or the
Roman religion, in the popular mind, probably, an intimate connexion united the cause of the Italian sovereign
with the fortunes and the gods of Rome. It is possible
that Constantine might attempt to array against this
imposing barrier of ancient superstition the power of
the new and triumphant faith: he might appeal, as it
were, to the God of the Christians against the gods of
the capital. His small, though victorious, army might
derive courage in their attack on the fate-hallowed city,
from whose neighbourhood Galerius had so recently
returned in discomfiture, from a vague notion that they
were under the protection of a tutelar deity, of whose
nature they were but imperfectly informed, and whose
worshippers constituted no insignificant part of their
barbarian army.

Up to this period all that we know of Constantine's
Religion of religion would imply that he was outwardly,
Constantine. and even zealously, Pagan. In a public oration his panegyrist extols the magnificence of his offerings to the gods. His victorious presence was not merely
expected to restore more than their former splendour to
the Gaulish cities, ruined by barbaric incursions, but
sumptuous temples were to arise at his bidding, to propitiate the deities, particularly Apollo, his tutelary God.[i]

---

[h] Euseb. Vit. Const. i. 36.

[i] Merito igitur augustissima illa
delubra tantis donariis honorâsti, ut
jam vetera non quærant. Jam omnia

vocare ad se templa videntur, præci-
pueque Apollo noster, cujus ferven-
tibus aquis perjuria puniuntur, quæ
te maxime oportet odisse. Nec magis

The medals struck for these victories are covered with the symbols of Paganism. Eusebius himself admits that Constantine was at this time in doubt which religion he should embrace, and, after his vision, required to be instructed in the doctrines of Christianity.[k]

The scene in which the memorable vision of Constantine is laid varies widely in the different accounts. Several places in Gaul lay claim to the honour of this momentous event in Christian history. If we assume the most probable period for such an occurrence, whatever explanation we adopt of the vision itself, it would be at this awful crisis in the destiny of Constantine and of the world, before the walls of Rome; an instant when, if we could persuade ourselves that the Almighty Ruler, *in such a manner*, interposed to proclaim the fall of Paganism and the establishment of Christianity, it would have been a public and a solemn occasion, worthy of the Divine interference. Nowhere, on the other hand, was the high-wrought imagination of Constantine so likely to be seized with religious awe, and to transform some extraordinary appearance in the heavens into the sign of the prevailing Deity of Christ; nowhere, lastly, would policy more imperiously require some strong religious impulse to counterbalance the hostile terrors of Paganism, embattled against him.

Eusebius,[m] the Bishop of Cæsarea, asserts that Constantine himself made, and confirmed by an oath, the extraordinary statement, which was received with im-

---

Jovi Junonique recubantibus terra submisit, quam circa tua, Constantine, vestigia urbes et templa consurgunt. Eumenii Panegyr. cxxi.

[k] Ἐννοεῖ δῆτα ὁποῖον δέοι θεὸν ἐπιγραψάσθαι βοηθόν. Euseb. Vit.

Constant. c. 27-32.

[m] Vit. Const. i. 28. The recent editor of Eusebius has well called the life of Constantine a Christian Cyropædia.

plicit veneration during many ages of Christianity, but
which the severer judgement of modern historical inquiry has called in question, has investi-
gated with the most searching accuracy, and almost
universally destroyed its authority with rational men; yet,
it must be admitted, found no satisfactory explanation of
its origin.[n]   While Constantine was meditating in grave

---

[n] The silence, not only of all contemporary history (the legend of Arte-
mius, abandoned even by Tillemont,
does not deserve the name), but of
Eusebius himself, in his Ecclesiastical
History, gives a most dangerous advantage to those who altogether reject
the story. But on whom is the invention of the story to be fathered?
On Eusebius? who, although his conscience might not be delicately scrupulous on the subject of pious fraud,
is charged with no more than the
suppression of truth, not with the
direct invention of falsehood. Or, on
Constantine himself? Could it be
with him a deliberate fiction to command the higher veneration of the
Christian party? Or was his imagination at the time, or was his memory
in his later days, deceived by some
inexplicable illusion?

The first excursus of Heinichen, in
his edition of Eusebius, contains the
fullest, and, on the whole, the most
temperate and judicious discussion of
this subject, so inexhaustibly interesting, yet so inexplicable, to the historical inquirer. There are three leading theories, variously modified by
their different partisans: 1. A real
miracle. 2. A natural phænomenon,
presented to the imagination of the
Emperor. 3. A deliberate invention

on the part of the Emperor, or of
Eusebius. The first has few partisans
in the present day. " Ut enim mira-
culo Constantinum a superstitione
gentili avocatum esse, nemo facile
hac ætate adhuc credet." Heinichen,
p. 522. Independent of all other
objections, the moral difficulty in the
text is to me conclusive. The third
has its partisans, but appears to me
to be absolutely incredible. But the
general consent of the more learned
and dispassionate writers seems in
favour of the second, which was first,
I believe, suggested by F. Albert
Fabricius. In this concur Schroeck,
the German Church historian, Neander,
Manso, Heinichen, and, in short, all
modern writers who have any claim
to historical criticism.

The great difficulty which encum-
bers the theory which resolves it into
a solar halo or some natural phænomenon is the legend ἐν τούτῳ νίκᾳ,
which no optical illusion can well explain, if it be taken literally. The
only rational theory is to suppose
that this was the inference drawn by
the mind of Constantine, and embodied
in these words; which, from being
inscribed on the Labarum, or on the
arms or any other public monument,
as commemorative of the event, gradually grew into an integral part of

earnestness the claims of the rival religions,—on one hand the awful fate of those who had persecuted Christianity, on the other the necessity of some divine assistance to counteract the magical incantations of his enemy, —he addressed his prayers to the One great Supreme. On a sudden, a short time after noon, appeared a bright cross in the heavens, just above the sun, with this inscription, " By this, conquer." Awe seized himself and the whole army, who were witnesses of the wonderful phænomenon. But of the signification of the vision Constantine was altogether ignorant. Sleep fell upon his harassed mind, and during his sleep Christ himself appeared, and enjoined him to make a banner in the shape of that celestial sign, under which his arms would be for ever crowned with victory.

Constantine immediately commanded the famous Labarum to be made,—the Labarum which for a long time was borne at the head of the Imperial armies, and venerated as a sacred relic at Constantinople. The shaft of this celebrated standard was cased with gold ; above the transverse beam, which formed the cross, was wrought in a golden crown the monogram, or rather the device of two letters, which signified the name of Christ. And so for the first time the meek and peaceful Jesus became a God of battle, and the cross, the holy sign of Christian redemption, a banner of bloody strife.

---

the original vision.

The later and more poetic writers adorn the shields and the helmets of the whole army with the sign of the cross.

Testis Christicolæ ducis adventantis ad urbem
Mulvius, exceptum Tiberina in stagna tyrannum
Præcipitans, quanam victricia viderit arma

Majestate regi, quod signum dextera vindex
Prætulerit, quali radiarint stemmate pila.
Christus purpureum, gemmanti textus in auro,
Signabat labarum, *clypeorum insignia Christus*
Scripserat : ardebat summis crux addita cristis.

Prudent. in Symmachum, v. 482.

Euseb. Vit. Const. i. 28 ; H. E. ix. 9. Zosimus, ii. 15. Manso, Leben Constantins, p. 41, seqq.

This irreconcileable incongruity between the symbol
of universal peace and the horrors of war, in my judgement, is conclusive against the miraculous or supernatural character of the transaction.° Yet the admission
of Christianity, not merely as a controlling power, and
the most effective auxiliary of civil government (an
office not unbecoming its divine origin), but as the animating principle of barbarous warfare, argues at once
the commanding influence which it had obtained over
the human mind, as well as its degeneracy from its pure
and spiritual origin. The unimpeached and unquestioned authority of this miracle during so many centuries,
shows how completely, in the association which took
place between Barbarism and Christianity, the former
maintained its predominance. This was the first advance
to the military Christianity of the Middle Ages, a modification of the pure religion of the Gospel, if directly
opposed to its genuine principles, still apparently indis-
pensable to the social progress of men; through which
the Roman Empire and the barbarous nations, which
were blended together in the vast European and
Christian system, must necessarily have passed, before
they could arrive at a higher civilisation and a purer
Christianity.

° I was agreeably surprised to find
that Mosheim concurred in these sentiments, for which I will readily encounter the charge of Quakerism.

"Hæccine oratio servatori generis
humani, qui peccata hominum morte
suâ expiavit; hæccine oratio illo digna
est, qui pacis auctor mortalibus est, et
suos hostibus ignoscere vult. . . . . .
Caveamus ne veterum Christianorum
narrationibus de ætatis suæ miraculis
acrius defendendis in ipsam majestatem
Dei, et sanctissimam religionem, quæ
non hostes, sed non ipsos debellare docet,
injurii simus." De Reb. ante Const. 985.
When the Empress Helena, among the
other treasures of the tomb of Christ,
found the nails which fastened him to
the cross, Constantine turned them
into a helmet and bits for his war-
horse.   Socrates, i. 17.   True or
fabulous, the story is characteristic
of the *Christian* sentiment then prevalent.

The fate of Rome and of Paganism was decided in the battle of the Milvian Bridge; the eventual result was the establishment of the Christian empire. But to Constantine himself, if at this time Christianity had obtained any hold upon his mind, it was now the Christianity of the warrior, as subsequently it was that of the statesman. It was the military commander who availed himself of the assistance of any tutelar divinity who might insure success to his daring enterprise.

Christianity, in its higher sense, appeared neither in the acts nor in the decrees of the victorious Constantine after the defeat of Maxentius. Though his general conduct was tempered with a wise clemency, yet the execution of his enemies and the barbarous death of the infant son of Maxentius, still showed the same relentless disposition which had exposed the barbarian chieftains, whom he had taken in his successful campaign beyond the Rhine, in the arena at Treves.[p] The Emperor still maintained the same proud superiority over the conflicting religions of the empire, which afterwards appeared at the foundation of the new metropolis. Even in the Labarum, if the initiated eyes of the Christian soldiery could discern the sacred symbol of Christ indistinctly glittering above the cross, there appeared, either embossed on the beam below, or embroidered on the square purple banner which depended from it, the bust of the Emperor and those of his family, to whom the heathen part of his army might pay their homage of veneration. Constantine, though he does not appear to have ascended to

Conduct of Constantine after his victory over Maxentius.

---

[p] One of these barbarous acts was selected by the panegyrical orator as a topic of the highest praise. "Puberes, qui in manus venerunt et quorum nec perfidia erat apta militiæ nec ferocia severitati, ad pœnas spectaculo dati, sævientes bestias multitudine suâ fatigarunt." Eumenii Panegr. c. xii.

the Capitol, to pay his homage and to offer sacrifice [q] to
Jupiter the best and greatest, and the other tutelary
deities of Rome (in general the first act of a victorious
emperor), yet did not decline to attend the sacred games.[r]
Among the acts of the conqueror in Rome, was the restoration of the Pagan temples; among his imperial
titles he did not decline that of the Pontifex Maximus.[s]
The province of Africa, in return for the bloody head of
their oppressor Maxentius, was permitted to found a
college of priests in honour of the Flavian family.

The first public edict of Constantine in favour of
Christianity is lost; that issued at Milan in the
Edict of Constantine from Milan. joint names of Constantine and Licinius, is
the great charter of the liberties of Christianity.[t]
But it is an edict of full and unlimited toleration, and
no more. It recognises Christianity as one of the legal
forms by which the Divinity may be worshipped.[u] It

---

[q] Euseb. Vit. Const. i. 51. Le
Beau, Histoire du Bas Empire, l. ii.
c. xvi.

[r] Nec quidquam aliud homines,
diebus munerum sacrorumque lu-
dorum, quam te ipsum spectare potuerunt. Incert. Paneg. c. xix.

[s] Zosimus, iv. 36.

[t] The edict, or rather the copy,
sent by Licinius to the Prefect of
Bithynia in Lactantius, De Mort. Pers.
xlviii.

[u] Decree of Milan, A.D. 313. "Hæc
ordinanda esse credidimus, ut daremus
et Christianis et omnibus liberam potestatem sequendi religionem quam
quisque voluisset, quod quidem *divinitas* in sede cœlesti nobis atque
omnibus qui sub potestate nostrâ sunt
constituti, placata ac propitia possit
existere." [This divinitas, I conceive,

was that equivocal term for the Supreme Deity, admitted by the Pagan
as well as the Christian. What Zosimus called τὸ θεῖον] etiam aliis religionis suæ vel observantiæ potestatem
similiter apertam, et liberam, pro
quiete temporis nostri esse concessam,
ut in colendo quod quisque delegerit,
habeat liberam facultatem, quia (no-
lumus detrahi) honori neque cuiquam
religioni aliquid a nobis.

I will transcribe, however, the observations of Kestner on this point:
"Multi merito observârunt, animum
illud ostendere (sc. decretum Medio-
lense) ab antiqua religione minime
alienum. Observandum vero, parum
hoc decretum valere, ut veram Constantini mentem inde intelligamus.
Non solus quippe illius auctor fuit,
sed Licinius quoque—Huic autem—

performs an act of justice in restoring all the public buildings and the property which had been confiscated by the persecuting edicts of former emperors. Where the churches or their sites remained in the possession of the imperial treasury, they were restored without any compensation; where they had been alienated, the grants were resumed; where they had been purchased, the possessors were offered an indemnity for their enforced and immediate surrender, from the state. The prefects were to see the restitution carried into execution without delay and without chicanery. But the same absolute freedom of worship was secured to all other religions; and this proud and equitable indifference is to secure the favour of the divinity to the reigning emperors. The whole tone of this edict is that of imperial clemency, which condescends to take under its protection an oppressed and injured class of subjects, rather than that of an awe-struck proselyte, esteeming Christianity the one true religion, and already determined to enthrone it as the dominant and established faith of the empire.

The earlier laws of Constantine, though in their effects favourable to Christianity, claimed some deference, as it were, to the ancient religion in the ambiguity of their language, and the cautious terms in which they interfered with the liberty of Paganism. The rescript commanding the celebration of the Chris-

Earlier laws of Constantine.

---

etsi iis (Christianis) non sincerus erat amicus, parcere debuit Constantinus; neque cæteris displicere voluit subditis, qui antiquam religionem profiterentur. Quamvis igitur etiam religionis indole plenius jam fuisset imbutus, ob rerum tamen, quæ id temporis erant, conditionem, manifestare mentem non potuisset. Kestner, Disp. de commut. quam, Constant. M. auct. societas subiit Christiana. Compare Heinichen, Excurs. in Vit. Const. p. 513.

tian Sabbath, bears no allusion to its peculiar sanctity as a Christian institution. It is the day of the Sun, which is to be observed by the general veneration; the courts were to be closed, and the noise and tumult of public business and legal litigation were no longer to violate the repose of the sacred day. But the believer in the new Paganism, of which the solar worship was the characteristic, might acquiesce without scruple in the sanc-

Sanctity of the Sunday. tity of the first day of the week. The genius of Christianity appears more manifestly in the single civil act, which was exempted from the general restriction on public business. The courts were to be open for the manumission of slaves on the hallowed day.[x] In the first aggression on the freedom of Paganism, though the earliest law speaks in a severe and vindictive tone, a second tempers the stern language of the former statute, and actually authorises the superstition against which it is directed, as far as it might be supposed beneficial to mankind. The itinerant soothsayers and diviners, who exercised their arts in private houses, formed no recognised part of the old religion.

Against Divination. Their rites were supposed to be connected with all kinds of cruel and licentious practices—with magic and unlawful sacrifices. They performed their ceremonies at midnight among tombs, where they evoked the dead; or in dark chambers, where they made libations of the blood of the living. They were darkly rumoured not to abstain, on occasions, from human blood, to offer children on the altar, and to read the secrets of futurity in the palpitating entrails of human victims. These unholy practices were proscribed by the old Roman law and the old Roman religion.

---

[x] Cod. Theodos. ii. viii. 1.   Vit. Constant. iv. 18.   Zosimus, i. 8.

This kind of magic was a capital offence by the laws of the Twelve Tables. Secret divinations had been interdicted by former emperors,—by Tiberius and by Diocletian.[y] The suppression of these rites by Constantine might appear no more than a strong regulation of police for the preservation of the public morals.[z] The soothsayer who should presume to enter a private house to practise his unlawful art, was to be burned alive; those who received him were condemned to the forfeiture of their property and to exile. But in the public temple, according to the established rites, the priests and seers might still unfold the secrets of futurity; the people were recommended to apply to them rather than to the unauthorised diviners, and this permission was more explicitly guaranteed by a subsequent rescript.[a] Those arts which professed to avert the thunder from the house, the hurricane and the desolating shower from the fruitful field, were expressly sanctioned as beneficial to the husbandman. Even in case of the royal palace being struck by lightning, the ancient ceremony of propitiating the Deity was to be practised, and the haruspices were to declare the meaning of the awful portent.[b]

Yet some acts of Constantine, even at this early period, might encourage the expanding hopes of the Christians that they were destined before long to receive more than impartial justice from the Emperor. His acts of liberality were

Constantine's encouragement of Christianity.

---

[y] " Haruspices secreto ac sine testibus consuli vetuit." Suetonius, Tib. c. 63. " Ars mathematica damnabilis est et interdicta omnino." Compare Beugnot, i. 79.

[z] It was addressed to Maximus, prefect of the city. Cod. Theod. xi. 8, 2.

[a] Adite aras publicas atque delubra, et consuetudinis vestræ celebrate solemnia: nec enim prohibemus præteritæ usurpationis officia liberâ luce tractari. Cod. Theodos. xi. 16.

[b] Cod. Theodos. ix. 16, xvi. 10.

beyond those of a sovereign disposed to redress the
wrongs of an oppressed class of his subjects; he not
merely enforced by his edict the restoration of their
churches and estates, he enabled them, by his own
munificence—his gift of a large sum of money to the
Christians of Africa—to rebuild their ruined edifices,
and restore their sacred rites with decent solemnity.[c]

Churches in Rome. Many of the churches in Rome claim the first
Christian Emperor for their founder. The
most distinguished of these, and, at the same time, those
which are best supported in their pretensions to antiquity, stood on the sites now occupied by the Lateran
and by St. Peter's. If it could be ascertained at what
period in the life of Constantine these churches were
built, some light might be thrown on the history of his
personal religion. For, the Lateran being an imperial
palace, the grant of a basilica within its walls for the
Christian worship (for such we may conjecture to have
been the first church), was a kind of direct recognition,
if not of his own regular personal attendance, at least of
his admission of Christianity within his domestic circle.[d]
The palace was afterwards granted to the Christians,
the first patrimony of the Popes. The Vatican suburb
seems to have been the favourite place for the settlement of foreign religions. It was thickly peopled with
Jews from an early period;[e] and remarkable vestiges of
the worship of Cybele, which appear to have flourished
side by side, as it were, with that of Christianity, remained to the fourth, or the fifth, century.[f] The site of

---

[c] See the original grant of 3000
folles to Cæcilian, bishop of Carthage,
in Eusebius, Eccl. Hist. x. 6.

[d] The Lateran was the residence of
the Princess Fausta; it is called the
Domus Faustæ in the account of the

first synod held to decide on the Donatist schism. Optat. i. 23. Fausta
may have been a Christian.

[e] Basnage, vii. 210, Hist. of Jews.

[f] Bunsen und Platner, Roms' Be-
schreibung, i. p. 23.

St. Peter's Church was believed to occupy the spot hallowed by his martyrdom ; and the Christians must have felt no unworthy pride in employing the materials of Nero's Circus, the scene of the sanguinary pleasures of the first persecutor, on a church dedicated to the memory of his now honoured, if not absolutely worshipped, victim.

With the protection, the Emperor assumed the control over the affairs of the Christian communities: to the cares of the public administration was added a recognised supremacy over the Christian Church.   The extent to which Christianity now prevailed is shown by the importance at once assumed by the Christian bishops, who brought not only their losses and their sufferings during the persecution of Diocletian, but, unhappily, likewise their quarrels, before the imperial tribunal.   From his palace at Treves, Constantine had not only to assemble military councils to debate on the necessary measures for the protection of the German frontier and the maintenance of the imperial armies, and councils of finance to remodel and enforce the taxation of the different provinces, but likewise synods of Christian bishops to decide on the contests which had grown up in the remote and unruly province of Africa. The Emperor himself is said frequently to have appeared without his imperial state, and, with neither guards nor officers around him, to have mingled in the debate, and expressed his satisfaction at their unanimity, whenever that rare virtue adorned their counsels.[g]

For Constantine, though he could give protection,

---

[g] Euseb. Vit. Const. I. xliv. χαίροντα δεικνὺς ἑαυτὸν τῇ κοινῇ πάντων ὁμονοίᾳ.   Eusebius says too that he conducted himself as the bishop of the bishops.

could not give peace to Christianity. It is the nature of man, that whatever powerfully moves, agitates to excess the public mind. With new views of those subjects which make a deep and lasting impression, new passions awaken. The profound stagnation of the human mind during the government of the earlier Cæsars had been stirred in its inmost depths by the silent underworking of the new faith. Momentous questions, which, up to that time, had been entirely left to a small intellectual aristocracy, had been calmly debated in the villa of the Roman senator or the grove sacred to philosophy, or discussed by sophists whose frigid dialectics wearied without exciting the mind, had been gradually brought down to the common apprehension. The nature of the Deity; the state of the soul after death; the equality of mankind in the sight of the Deity — even questions which are beyond the verge of human intellect; the origin of evil; the connexion of the physical and moral world—had become general topics; they were, for the first time, the primary truths of a popular religion, and naturally could not withdraw themselves from the alliance with popular passions. These passions, as Christianity increased in power and influence, came into more active operation; as they seized on persons of different temperament, instead of being themselves subdued to Christian gentleness, they inflamed Christianity, as it appeared to the world, into a new and more indomitable principle of strife and animosity. Mankind, even within the sphere of Christianity, retrograded to the sterner Jewish character: and in its spirit, as well as in its language, the Old Testament began to dominate over the Gospel of Christ.

The first civil wars which divided Christianity were those of Donatism and the Trinitarian controversy.

The Gnostic sects, in their different varieties, and the Manichean, were rather rival religions than Christian factions. Though the adherents of these sects professed to be disciples of Christianity, yet they had their own separate constitutions, their own priesthood, their own ceremonial. Donatism was a fierce and implacable schism in an established community. It was embraced with all the wild ardour, and maintained with the blind obstinacy, of the African temperament. It originated in a disputed appointment to the episcopal dignity at Carthage. The Bishop of Carthage, if in name inferior (for everything connected with the ancient capital still maintained its superior dignity in the general estimation), stood higher, probably, in proportion to the extent of his influence and the relative numbers of his adherents, as compared with the Pagan population, than any Christian dignitary in the West. The African Churches had suffered more than usual oppression during the persecution of Diocletian, not improbably during the invasion of Maxentius. External force, which in other quarters compressed the body into closer and more compact unity, in Africa left behind it a fatal principle of disorganisation. These rival claims to the see of Carthage brought the opponent parties into inevitable collision.

The pontifical offices of Paganism, ministering in a ceremonial to which the people were either indifferent or bound only by habitual attachment, calmly descended in their hereditary course, were nominated by the municipal magistracy, or attached to the higher civil offices. They awoke no ambition, they caused no contention; they did not interest society enough to disturb it. But the growth of the sacerdotal power was a necessary consequence of the

Dissensions of Christianity.

Donatism.

Christian hierarchy different from Pagan priesthood.

development of Christianity. The hierarchy asserted
(they were believed to possess) the power of sealing the
eternal destiny of man. From a post of danger, which
modest piety was compelled to assume by the unsought
and unsolicited suffrages of the whole community, a
bishopric had become an office of dignity, influence, and,
at times, of wealth. The prelate ruled not now so much
by his admitted superiority in Christian virtue, as by
the inalienable authority of his office. He opened or
closed the door of the church, which was tantamount to
an admission or an exclusion from everlasting bliss; he
uttered the sentence of excommunication, which cast
back the trembling delinquent among the lost and
perishing Heathen. He had his throne in the most distinguished part of the Christian temple; and though yet
acting in the presence and in the name of his college of
presbyters, yet he was the acknowledged head of a large
community, over whose eternal destiny he held a vague,
but not therefore less imposing and awful, dominion.
Among the African Christians, perhaps by the commanding character of Cyprian, in his writings at least,
the episcopal power is elevated to its utmost height.
No wonder that, with the elements of strife fermenting
in the society, and hostile parties already arrayed against
each other, the contest for this commanding post should
often be commenced with blind violence, and carried on
with irreconcileable hostility.[h]

In every community, no doubt, had grown up a
severer party, who were anxious to contract the pale of
salvation to the narrowest compass; and a more liberal

---

[h] The principal source of information concerning the Donatist controversy is the works of Optatus, with
the valuable collection of documents
subjoined to them; and for their later
history, various passages in the works
of St. Augustine.

class, who were more lenient to the infirmities of their brethren, and would extend to the utmost limits the beneficial effects of the Redemption. The fiery ordeal of the persecution tried the Christians of Africa by the most searching test, and drew more strongly the line of demarcation. Among the summary proceedings of the persecution, which were carried into effect with unrelenting severity by Anulinus, the Prefect of Africa (the same who, by a singular vicissitude in political affairs, became the instrument of Constantine's munificent grants to the churches of his province),[i] none was more painful to the feelings of the Christians than the demand of the unconditional surrender of the furniture of their sacred edifices, their chalices, their ornaments, above all, the sacred writings.[k] The bishop and his priests were made responsible for the full and unreserved delivery of these sacred possessions. Some from timidity, others considering that by such concessions it might be prudent to avert more dangerous trials, and that such treasures, sacred as they were, might be replaced in a more flourishing state of the church, complied with the demands of the magistrate; but, by their severer brethren, who, with more uncompromising courage, had refused the least departure from the tone of unqualified resistance, these men were branded with the ignominious name of Traditors.[m] This became the strong, the impassable, line of demarcation between

The Traditors.

---

[i] See the grant of Constantine referred to above.

[k] There is a very curious and graphic account of the rigorous perquisition for the sacred books in the Gesta apud Zenophilum in Routh, vol. iv. p. 103. The codices appear to have been under the care of the readers, who were of various ranks, mostly, however, in trade. There were a great number of codices, each probably containing one book of the Scriptures.

[m] The Donatists invariably called the Catholic party the Traditors. See Sermo Donatista and the Acts of Donatist Martyr.

the contending factions. To the latest period of the conflict, the Donatists described the Catholic party by that odious appellation.

The primacy of the African Church was the object of ambition to these two parties: an unfortunate vacancy at this time kindled the smouldering embers of strife.

Contest for the see of Carthage.

Mensurius had filled the see of Carthage with prudence and moderation during these days of emergency. He was accused by the sterner zeal of Donatus, a Numidian bishop, of countenancing at least the criminal concessions of the Traditors. It was said that he had deluded the Government by a subtle stratagem; he had substituted certain heretical writings for the genuine Scriptures; had connived at their seizure, and calmly seen them delivered to the flames. The Donatists either disbelieved, or despised as a paltry artifice, this attempt to elude the glorious danger of resistance. But, during the life of Mensurius, his character and station had overawed the hostile party. Mensurius was summoned to Rome, to answer on a charge of the concealment of the deacon Felix, accused of a political offence—the publication of a libel against the Emperor. On his departure, Mensurius entrusted to the deacons of the community the valuable vessels of gold and silver belonging to the church, of which he left an accurate inventory in the hands of a pious and aged woman. Mensurius died on his return to Carthage. Cæcilian, a deacon of the church,. was raised by the unanimous suffrages of the clergy and people to the see of Carthage. He was consecrated by Felix, Bishop of Apthunga. His first step was to demand the vessels of the church. By the advice of Botrus and Celeusius, two of the deacons, competitors it is said with Cæcilian for the see, they were refused to a bishop irregularly elected, and consecrated by a notorious Traditor. A Spanish female, of noble birth and of opulence, accused of personal hostility to Cæcilian, animated the Carthaginian faction; but the whole province assumed the right of interference with the appointment to the primacy, and Donatus, Bishop of Casæ Nigræ, placed himself at the head of the opponent party.

The commanding mind of Donatus swayed the countless hierarchy which crowded the different provinces of Africa. The Numidian bishops took the lead; Secundus, the primate of Numidia, at the summons of Donatus, appeared in Carthage at the head of seventy of his bishops. This self-installed Council of Carthage proceeded to cite Cæcilian, who refused to recognise its authority. The Council declared his election void. The consecration by a bishop guilty of tradition, was the principal ground on which his election was annulled. But darker charges were openly advanced, or secretly murmured, against Cæcilian; charges which, if not entirely ungrounded, show that the question of tradition had, during the persecution, divided the Christians into fierce and hostile factions. He was said to have embittered the last hours of those whose more dauntless resistance put to shame the timorous compliance of Mensurius and his party. He had taken his station, with a body of armed men, and precluded the pious zeal of their adherents from obtaining access to the prison of those who had been seized by the Government;[n] he had prevented, not merely the consolatory and inspiriting visits of kinsmen and friends, but even the introduction of food and other comforts, in their state of starving destitution. The Carthaginian

Appeal to the civil power.

---

[n] Optatus, i. 22.

faction proceeded to elect Majorinus to the vacant see. Both parties appealed to the civil power; and Anulinus, the Prefect of Africa, who during the reign of Diocletian had seen the Christians dragged before his tribunal, and whose authority they then disclaimed with uncompromising unanimity, now saw them crowding in hostile factions to demand his interference in their domestic discords.

The cause was referred to the imperial decision of Constantine. At a later period the Donatists, being worsted in the strife, bitterly reproached their adversaries with this appeal to the civil tribunal, "What have Christians to do with kings, or bishops with palaces?"[o] Their adversaries justly recriminated, that they had been as ready as themselves to request the intervention of the Government. Constantine delegated the judgement in their cause to the bishops of Gaul;[p] but the first council was composed of a great majority of Italian bishops; and Rome, for the first time, witnessed a public trial of a Christian cause before an assembly of bishops, presided over by her prelate. The Council was formed of the three Gallic bishops of Cologne, of Autun, and of Arles. The Italian bishops (we may conjecture that these were considered the more

Council of Rome.

---

[o] Optatus, i. 22.

[p] Augustine, writing when the episcopal authority stood on a level nearer to or even higher than the throne, asserts that Constantine did not dare to assume a cognisance over the election of a bishop. "Constantinus non ausus est de causâ episcopi judicare." Epist. cv. n. 8. Natural equity as well as other reasons would induce Constantine to delegate the affair to a Christian commission. The account of Optatus ascribes to Constantine speeches which it is difficult to reconcile with his public conduct as regards Christianity at this period of his life. The Council of Rome was held A.D. 313, 2nd October.

The decrees of the Council of Rome and of Arles, with other documents on the subject, may be found in the fourth volume of Routh.

important sees, or were filled by the most influential
prelates) were those of Milan, Cesena, Quintiano, Rimini,
Florence, Pisa, Faenza, Capua, Benevento, Terracina,
Præneste, Tres Tabernæ, Ostia, Ursinum (Urbinum),
Forum Claudii.

Cæcilian and Donatus appeared each at the head of
ten bishops of his party. Both denounced their adversaries as guilty of the crime of tradition. The partisans
of Donatus rested their appeal on the invalidity of an
ordination by a bishop, Felix of Apthunga, who had
been guilty of that delinquency. The party of Cæcilian
accused almost the whole of the Numidian bishops, and
Donatus himself, as involved in the same guilt. It was
a wise and temperate policy in the Catholic party, to
attempt to cancel all embittering recollections of the
days of trial and infirmity; to abolish all distinctions,
which on one part led to pride, on the other to degradation; to reconcile, in those halcyon days of prosperity,
the whole Christian world in one harmonious confederacy.
This policy was that of the Government. At this early
period of his Christianity, if he might yet be called a
Christian, Constantine was little likely to enter into
the narrow and exclusive principles of the Donatists.
As Emperor, Christianity was recommended to his favour
by the harmonising and tranquillising influence which it
exercised over a large body of the people. If it broke
up into hostile feuds, it lost its value as an ally or an
instrument of civil government. But it was exactly
this levelling of all religious distinctions, this liberal and
comprehensive spirit, that would annihilate the less important differences, which struck at the vital principle
of Donatism. They had confronted all the malice of the
persecutor, they had disdained to compromise any principle, to concede the minutest point; and were they to

abandon a superiority so hardly earned, and to acquiesce
in the readmission of all those who had forfeited their
Christian privileges to the same rank? Were they not
to exercise the high function of readmission into the
fold with proper severity? The decision of the Council
was favourable to the cause of Cæcilian. Donatus appealed to the Emperor, who retained the heads of both
parties in Italy, to allow time for the province to regain
its quiet. In defiance of the Emperor, both the leaders
fled back to Africa, to set themselves at the head of
their respective factions. The patient Constantine summoned a new, a more remote
council at Arles. Cæcilian and the African bishops
were cited to appear in that distant province; public
vehicles were furnished for their conveyance at the Emperor's charge; each bishop was attended by two of his
inferior clergy, with three domestics. The Bishop of
Arles presided in this Council, which confirmed the
judgement of that in Rome.

A.D. 314.
1st Aug.

A second Donatus now appeared upon the scene, of
more vigorous and more persevering character, greater
ability, and with all the energy and self-confidence which
enabled him to hold together the faction. The party
now assumed the name of Donatists. On the death of
Majorinus, Donatus succeeded to the dignity of Anti-
Bishop of Carthage: the whole African province continued to espouse the quarrel; the authority of the
Government, which had been invoked by both parties, was
scornfully rejected by that against which the award was
made. Three times was the decision repeated in favour
of the Catholic party, at Rome, at Arles, and at Milan;
each time was more strongly established the
self-evident truth, which has been so late recognised by the Christian world, the incompetency of any

A.D. 316.

Council to reconcile religious differences. The suffrages of the many cannot bind the consciences, or enlighten the minds, or even overcome the obstinacy, of the few. Neither party can yield without abandoning the very principles by which they have been constituted a party.

A commission issued to Ælius, Prefect of the district, to examine the charge against Felix, Bishop of Apthunga, gave a favourable verdict.[q] An imperial commission of two delegates to Carthage, ratified the decision of the former councils. At every turn the Donatists protested against the equity of the decrees; they loudly complained of the unjust and partial influence exercised by Osius, Bishop of Cordova, over the mind of the Emperor. At length the tardy indignation of the Government had recourse to violent measures. The Donatist bishops were driven into exile, their churches destroyed or sold, and the property seized for the imperial revenue. The Donatists defied the armed interference, as they had disclaimed the authority, of the Government. This first development of the principles of Christian sectarianism was as stern, as inflexible, and as persevering, as in later times. The Donatists drew their narrow pale around their persecuted sect, and asserted themselves to be the only elect people of Christ; the only people whose clergy could claim an unbroken apostolical succession, vitiated in all other communities of Christians by the inexpiable crime of tradition. Wherever they obtained possession of a church they burned the altar; or, where wood was scarce, scraped off the infection of heretical communion; they melted the cups, and sold, it was said, the sanctified metal for profane, perhaps for Pagan; uses; they rebaptized all

Donatists persecuted.

---

[q] See the Acta Purgationis Felicis, in Routh, iv. 71.

who joined their sect; they made the virgins renew
their vows; they would not even permit the bodies of
the Catholics to repose in peace, lest they should pollute the common cemeteries. The implacable faction
darkened into a sanguinary feud. For the first time
human blood was shed in conflicts between followers of
the Prince of Peace. Each party recriminated on the
other, but neither denies the barbarous scenes of massacre and licence which devastated the African cities.
The Donatists boasted of their martyrs, and the cruelties
of the Catholic party rest on their own admission: they
deny not, they proudly vindicate their barbarities—" Is
the vengeance of God to be defrauded of its victims?" [r]
—and they appeal to the Old Testament to justify, by
the examples of Moses, of Phineas, and of Elijah, the
Christian duty of slaying by thousands the renegades,
or the unbelievers.

In vain Constantine at length published an edict of
peace: the afflicted province was rent asunder
till the close of his reign, and during that of
his son, by this religious warfare. For, on the other hand,
the barbarous fanaticism of the Circumcellions
involved the Donatist party in the guilt of insurrection, and connected them with revolting atrocities,
which they were accused of countenancing, of exciting,
if not actually sanctioning by their presence. That
which in the opulent cities, or the well-ordered commu-

A.D. 321.

The Circum-
cellions.

---

[r] This damning passage is found
in the work of the Catholic Optatus:
" Quasi omnino in vindictam Dei nullus
mereatur occidi." Compare the whole
chapter, iii. 6. An able writer (Mr.
Bright) (History of the Church) has
objected to his statement. I adhere to
it. There is a very strong description
of the persecutions which they endured
from the Catholics in the letter put
in by the Donatist bishop Habet
Deum in the conference held during
the reign of Honorius. Apud Dupin.
No. 258. in fine.

nities, led to fierce and irreconcileable contention, grew up among the wild borderers on civilisation into fanatical frenzy. Where Christianity has outstripped civilisation, and has not had time to effect its beneficent and humanising change, whether in the bosom of an old society, or within the limits of savage life, it becomes, in times of violent excitement, instead of a pacific principle to assuage, a new element of ungovernable strife. The long peace which had been enjoyed by the province of Africa, and the flourishing corn-trade which it conducted as the granary of Rome and of the Italian provinces, had no doubt extended the pursuits of agriculture into the Numidian, Gætulian, and Mauritanian villages. The wild tribes had gradually become industrious peasants, and among them Christianity had found an open field for its exertions, and the increasing agricultural settlements had become Christian bishoprics. But the savage was yet only half-tamed; and no sooner had the flames of the Donatist conflict spread into these peaceful districts, than the genuine Christian was lost in the fiery marauding child of the desert. Maddened by oppression, wounded in his religious feelings by the expulsion and persecution of the bishops, from his old nature he resumed the fierce spirit of independence, the contempt for the laws of property, and the burning desire of revenge. Of his new religion he retained only the perverted language, or rather that of the Old Testament, with an implacable hatred of all hostile sects; a stern ascetic continence, which perpetually broke out into paroxysms of unbridled licentiousness; and a fanatic passion for martyrdom, which assumed the acts of a kind of methodical insanity.

The Circumcellions commenced their ravages during the reign of Constantine, and continued in arms during

that of his successor Constans. No sooner had the
provincial authorities received instructions to reduce the
province by force to religious unity, than the Circumcellions, who had at first confined their ravages to
disorderly and hasty incursions, broke out into open
revolt.[s] They defeated one body of the imperial troops,
and killed Ursacius, the Roman general. They abandoned, by a simultaneous impulse, their agricultural
pursuits; they proclaimed themselves the instruments
of Divine justice, and the protectors of the oppressed;
they first asserted the wild theory of the civil equality
of mankind, which has so often, in later periods of the
world, become the animating principle of Christian
fanaticism; they proclaimed the abolition of slavery;
they thrust the proud and opulent master from his
chariot, and made him walk by the side of his slave,
who, in his turn, was placed in the stately vehicle; they
cancelled all debts, and released the debtors; their
most sanguinary acts were perpetrated in the name of
religion, and Christian language was profaned by its
association with their atrocities. Their leaders were
the Captains of the Saints;[t] the battle hymn, "Praise
to God!" Their weapons were not swords, for Christ
had forbidden the use of the sword to Peter, but huge
and massy clubs, with which they beat their miserable
victims to death.[u] They were bound by vows of the
severest continence, but the African temperament, in

---

[s] The Circumcellions were unacquainted with the Latin language,
and are said to have spoken only the
Punic of the country.

[t] Augustine asserts that they were
led by their clergy, v. xi. p. 575.

[u] The Donatists anticipated our
Puritans in those strange religious
names which they assumed. Habet
Deum appears among the Donatist
bishops in a conference held with the
Catholics at Carthage, A.D. 411. See
the report of the conference in the
Donatistan Monumenta collected by
Dupin, at the end of his edition of
Optatus.

its state of feverish excitement, was too strong for the bonds of fanatical restraint; the companies of the Saints not merely abused the privileges of war by the most licentious outrages on the females, but were attended by troops of drunken prostitutes whom they called their sacred virgins. But the most extraordinary development of their fanaticism, was their Passion for rage for martyrdom. When they could not martyrdom. obtain it from the sword of the enemy, they inflicted it upon themselves. The ambitious martyr declared himself a candidate for the crown of glory: he then gave himself up to every kind of revelry, pampering, as it were, and fattening the victim for sacrifice. When he had wrought himself to the pitch of frenzy, he rushed out, and, with a sword in one hand and money in the other, he threatened death and offered reward to the first comer who would satisfy his eager longings for the glorious crown. They leaped from precipices; they went into the Pagan temples to provoke the vengeance of the worshippers.

Such are the excesses to which Christianity is constantly liable, as the religion of a savage and uncivilised people; but, on the other hand, it must be laid down as a political axiom equally universal, that this fanaticism rarely bursts out into disorders dangerous to society, unless goaded and maddened by persecution.[x]

Donatism was the fatal schism of one province of Christendom: the few communities formed on these rigid principles in Spain and in Rome died away in neglect; but however diminished its influence, it distracted the African province for three centuries, and

---

[x] Compare the persecution at the end of Dupin's edition of Optatus. Tillemont, vi. 147.

was only finally extirpated with Christianity itself, by the all-absorbing progress of Mohammedanism. At one time Constantine resorted to milder measures, and issued an edict of toleration. But in the reign of Constans, the persecution was renewed with more unrelenting severity. Two imperial officers, Paul and Macurius, were sent to reduce the province to religious unity. The Circumcellions encountered them with obstinate valour, but were totally defeated in the sanguinary battle of Bagnia. In the later reigns, when the laws against heresy became more frequent and severe, the Donatists were named with marked reprobation in the condemnatory edicts. Yet, in the time of Honorius, they boasted, in a conference with the Catholics, that they equally divided at least the province of Numidia, and that the Catholics only obtained a majority of bishops by the unfair means of subdividing the sees. This conference was held in the vain, though then it might not appear ungrounded, hope of reuniting the great body of the Donatists with the Catholic communion. The Donatists, says Gibbon, with his usual sarcasm, and more than his usual truth, had received a practical lesson on the consequences of their own principles. A small sect, the Maximinians, had been formed within their body, who asserted themselves to be the only genuine Church of God, denied the efficacy of the sacraments, disclaimed the apostolic power of the clergy, and rigidly appropriated to their own narrow sect the merits of Christ, and the hopes of salvation. But neither this fatal warning, nor the eloquence of St. Augustine, wrought much effect on the Puritans of Africa; they still obstinately denied the legality of Cæcilian's ordination; still treated their adversaries as the dastardly traditors of the Sacred Writings; still dwelt apart in the unquestioning conviction that they were the sole subjects of the kingdom of Heaven; that to them alone belonged the privilege of immortality through Christ, while the rest of the world, the unworthy followers of Christ, not less than the blind and unconverted Heathen, were perishing in their outcast and desperate state of condemnation.

ʸ Donatists are mentioned at the end of the sixth century (see Gregory the Great, Epist. i. 72-75, ii. 33), and are still powerful enough to eject the Catholics from their churches. Greg. Epist. iii. 32-35, v. 63.

CHAPTER II.

Constantine becomes sole Emperor.

BY the victory over Maxentius, Constantine had be-
The East come master of half the Roman world. Chris-
still Pagan. tianity, if it had not contributed to the success,
shared the advantage of the triumph. By the Edict of
Milan the Christians had resumed all their former
rights as citizens, their churches were reopened, their
public services recommenced, and their silent work of
aggression on the hostile Paganism began again under
the most promising auspices. The equal favour with
which they were beheld by the sovereign, appeared both
to their enemies and to themselves an open declaration
on their side. The public acts, the laws, and the medals
of Constantine,[a] show how the lofty eclectic indifferentism of the Emperor, which extended impartial protection over all the conflicting faiths, or attempted to
mingle together their least inharmonious elements,
gradually but slowly gave place to the progressive influence of Christianity. Christian bishops appeared as
regular attendants upon the court; the internal dissensions of Christianity became affairs of state. The Pagan

---

[a] Eckhel supposes that the Heathen symbols disappeared from the coins of Constantine after his victory over Licinius. Doctr. Num. in Constant.

I may add here another observation of this great authority on such sub-jects: " Excute universam Constantini monetam, nunquam in eâ aut Christi imaginem aut Constantini effigiem cruce insignem reperies . . . . In nonnullis jam monogramma Christi ☧ ☧ inseritur labaro aut vexillo, jam in areâ nummi solitariè excubat, jam aliis, ut patebit, comparet modis."

party saw, with increasing apprehension for their own authority and the fate of Rome, the period of the secular games, on the due celebration of which depended the duration of the Roman sovereignty, pass away unhonoured.[b] It was an extraordinary change in the constitution of the Western world, when the laws of the empire issued from the court of Treves, and Italy and Africa awaited the changes in their civil and religious constitution, from the seat of government on the barbarous German frontier. The munificent grant of Constantine for the restoration of the African churches, had appeared to commit him in favour of the Christian party, and had perhaps indirectly contributed to inflame the dissensions in that province.

A new law recognised the clerical order as a distinct and privileged class. It exempted them from the onerous municipal offices, which had begun to press heavily upon the more opulent inhabitants of the towns. It is the surest sign of misgovernment, when the higher classes shrink from the posts of honour and of trust. During the more flourishing days of the empire, the Decurionate, the chief municipal dignity, had been the great object of provincial ambition. The Decurions formed the Senates of the towns; they supplied the magistrates from their body, and had the right of electing them.[c]

Under the new financial system introduced by Diocletian, the Decurions were made responsible for the full amount of taxation imposed by the cataster or assess-

A.D. 315.

Clerical order recognised by the law.

---

[b] Zosimus, l. ii. c. 1.

[c] Savigny Römische Recht, i. 18. Compare the whole book of the Theodosian Code, De Decurionibus. Per- sons concealed their property to escape serving the public offices. Cod. Theod. iii. 1-8.

ment on the town and district. As the payment became more burthensome or difficult, the tenants, or even the proprietors, either became insolvent or fled their country. But the inexorable revenue still exacted from the Decurions the whole sum assessed on their town or district. The office itself grew into disrepute, and the law was obliged to force that upon the reluctant citizen of wealth or character, which had before been an object of eager emulation and competition.[d] The Christians obtained the exemption of their ecclesiastical order from these civil offices. The exemption was grounded on the just plea of its incompatibility with their religious duties.[e] The Emperor declared, in a letter to Cæcilian, Bishop of Carthage, that the Christian priesthood ought not to be withdrawn from the worship of God, which is the principal source of the prosperity of the empire. The effect of this immunity shows the oppressed and disorganised state of society.[f] Numbers of persons, in order to secure this exemption, rushed at once into the clerical order of the Christians; and this manifest abuse demanded an immediate modification of the law. None were to be admitted into the sacred order except on the vacancy

A.D. 320. of a religious charge, and then those only whose
Exemption poverty exempted them from the municipal
from the De-
curionate. functions.[g] Those whose property imposed upon them the duty of the Decurionate, were ordered to

---

[d] See two dissertations of Savigny on the taxation of the empire, in the Transactions of the Berlin Academy, and translated in the Cambridge Classical Researches.

[e] The officers of the royal household, and their descendants, had the same exemption, which was likewise extended to the Jewish archisynagogi or elders. Le Beau, 165. Cod. Theodos. xvi. 8, 2.

The priests and the Flamines, with the Decurions, were exempt from certain inferior offices, Cod. Theodos. xii. v. 2.

[f] See the various laws on this subject, Codex Theodos. xvi. 2, 3, 6-11.

[g] Cod. Theodos. xvi. 2, 17, 19.

abandon their religious profession. Such was the despotic power of the sovereign, to which the Christian Church still submitted, either on the principle of passive obedience, or in gratitude for the protection of the civil authority. The legislator interfered without scruple in the domestic administration of the Christian community, and the Christians received the Imperial edicts in silent submission. The appointment of a Christian, the celebrated Lactantius, to superintend the education of Crispin, the eldest son of the Emperor, was at once a most decisive and most influential step towards the public declaration of Christianity as the religion of the Imperial family. Another important law, the groundwork of the vast property obtained by the Church, gave it the fullest power to receive the bequests of the pious. Their right of holding property had been admitted apparently by Alexander Severus, annulled by Diocletian, and was now conceded in the most explicit terms by Constantine.[h]

But half the world remained still disunited from the dominion of Constantine and of Christianity. The first war with Licinius had been closed by the battles of Cibalæ and Mardia, and a new parti- Licinius. tion of the empire. It was succeeded by a hollow and treacherous peace of nine years.[i] The favour shown by Constantine to his Christian subjects, seems to have thrown Licinius upon the opposite interest. The Edict of Milan had been issued in the joint names of the two

Wars with Licinius.

---

[h] Habeat unusquisque licentiam, sanctissimo Catholicæ venerabilique concilio, decedens bonorum, quod placet, relinquere. Non sint cassa judicia. Nihil est, quod magis hominibus debetur, quam ut supremæ voluntatis, postquam aiiud jam velle non possint, liber sit status, et licens, quod iterum non redit, imperium. C. Th. xvi. 2, 4, De Episcopis. This law is assigned to the year 321.

[i] 314 to 323.

Emperors. In his conflict with Maximin, Licinius had
avenged the oppressions of Christianity on their most
relentless adversary. But when the crisis approached
which was to decide the fate of the whole empire, as
Constantine had adopted every means of securing their
cordial support, so Licinius repelled the allegiance of
his Christian subjects by disfavour, by mistrust, by expulsion from offices of honour, by open persecution, till,
in the language of the ecclesiastical historian, the world
was divided into two regions, those of day and of night.[k]
The vices as well as the policy of Licinius might disin-

Licinius be-
comes more
decidedly
Pagan.
cline him to endure the importunate presence
of the Christian bishops in his court; but he
might disguise his hostile disposition to the
churchmen under his declared dislike of eunuchs and of
courtiers,[m]—the vermin, as he called them, of the
palace. The stern avarice of Licinius would be contrasted to his disadvantage with the profuse liberality
of Constantine; his looser debaucheries with the severer
morals of the Western Emperor. Licinius proceeded to
purge his household troops of those whose inclination to
his rival he might, not without reason, mistrust; none
were permitted to retain their rank who refused to
sacrifice. He prohibited the synods of the clergy, which
he naturally apprehended might degenerate into conspi-
racies in favour of his rival. He confined the bishops to
the care of their own dioceses.[n] He affected, in his care
for the public morals, to prohibit the promiscuous
worship of men and women in the churches;[o] and in-

---

[k] Euseb. Vita Constant. i. 49.

[m] Spadonum et Aulicorum omnium
vehemens domitor, tineas soricesque
palatii eos appellans. Aur. Vict. Epit.

[n] Vit. Constant. i. 41.

[o] Vit. Constant. Women were to
be instructed by the Deaconesses alone.
Vit. Const. i. 53.

sulted the sanctity of the Christian worship, by commanding that it should be celebrated in the open air. The edict prohibiting all access to the prisons, though a strong and unwilling testimony to the charitable exertions of the Christians, and by their writers represented as an act of wanton and unexampled inhumanity, was caused probably by a jealous policy, rather than by wanton cruelty of temper. It is quite clear that the prayers of the Christians, perhaps more worldly weapons, were armed in favour of Constantine. The Eastern Churches would be jealous of their happier Western brethren, and naturally would be eager to bask in the equal sunshine of Imperial favour. At length, either fearing the effect of their prayers with the Deity whom they addressed,[p] or their influence in alienating the minds of their votaries from his own cause to that of him who, in the East, was considered the champion of the Christian cause, Licinius commanded the Christian churches in Pontus to be closed; he destroyed some of them, perhaps for defiance of his edicts. Some acts of persecution took place; the Christians fled again into the country, and began to conceal themselves in the woods and caves. Many instances of violence, some of martyrdom, occurred,[q] particularly in Pontus. There

---

[p] Συντελεῖσθαι γὰρ οὐκ ἡγεῖτο ὑπὲρ αὐτοῦ τὰς εὐχὰς, συνειδότι φαύλῳ τοῦτο λογιζόμενος, ἀλλ' ὑπὲρ τοῦ θεοφιλοῦς βασιλέως πάντα πράττειν ἡμᾶς καὶ τὸν θεὸν ἱλεοῦσθαι πέπειστο. Euseb. x. 8.

[q] Sozomen, H. E. i. 7, asserts that many of the clergy, as well as bishops, were martyred. Dodwell, however, observes (De Paucitate Martyrum, 91), " Caveant fabulatores ne quos alios sub Licinio martyres faciant præterquam episcopos." Compare Ruinart. There is great difficulty about Basileus, Bishop of Amasa. He is generally reckoned by the Greek writers as a martyr (see Pagi ad an. 316, n. x.); but he is expressly stated by Philostorgius (lib. i.), confirmed by Athanasius (Orat. 1, contra Arianos), to have been present at the Council of Nicæa some years afterwards.

was a wide-spread apprehension that a new and general
persecution was about to break out, when the Emperor
of the West moved, in the language of the Christian
historian, to rescue the whole of mankind from the
tyranny of one.[r]

Whether or not, in fact, Licinius avowed the imminent war to be a strife for mastery between the two
religions, the decisive struggle between the ancient
gods of Rome and the new divinity of the Christians;[s]
whether he actually led the chief officers and his most
eminent political partisans into a beautiful consecrated
grove, crowded with the images of the gods; and appealed, by the light of blazing torches, and amid the
smoke of sacrifice, to the gods of their ancestors against
his atheistic adversaries, the followers of a foreign and
unknown deity, whose ignominious sign was displayed in
the van of their armies; nevertheless, the propagation of
such stories shows how completely, according to their
own sentiments, the interests of Christianity were identified with the cause of Constantine.[t] On both sides
were again marshalled all the supernatural terrors
which religious hope or superstitious awe could summon. Diviners, soothsayers, and Egyptian magicians,
animated the troops of Licinius.[u] The Christians in
the army of Constantine attributed all his success to
the prayers of the pious bishops who accompanied his
army, and especially to the holy Labarum, whose bearer
passed unhurt among showers of fatal javelins.[x]

---

[r] Vit. Const. ii. 5.

[s] Ὑπαχθεὶς τισὶν ὑπισχνουμένοις
αὐτῷ κρατήσειν, εἰς ἑλληνισμὸν
ἐτράπη. Sozomen, i. 7.

Sacrifices and divinations were resorted to, and promised to Licinius

universal empire.
[t] Vit. Constant. ii. 4.
[u] Euseb. Vit. Constant. i. 49.
[x] Eusebius declares that he heard this
from the lips of Constantine himself.
One man, who in his panic gave up

The battle of Hadrianople, and the naval victory of Crispus, decided the fate of the world, and the Battle of
Hadrianople. establishment of Christianity as the religion of A.D. 323. the empire. The death of Licinius reunited the whole Roman world under the sceptre of Constantine.

Eusebius ascribes to Constantine, during this battle, an act of Christian mercy, at least as unusual as the appearance of the banner of the cross at the head of the Roman army. He issued orders to spare the lives of his enemies, and offered rewards for all captives brought in alive. Even if this be not strictly true, its exaggeration or invention, or even its relation as a praiseworthy act, shows the new spirit which was working in the mind of man.[y]

Among the first acts of the sole Emperor of the world, were the repeal of all the edicts of Licinius against the Christians, the release of all prisoners from the dungeon or the mine or the servile and humiliating occupations to which some had been contemptuously condemned in the manufactories conducted by women; the recall of all the exiles; the restoration of all who had been deprived of their rank in the army, or in the civil service; the restitution of all property of which they had been despoiled,—that of the martyrs to the legal heirs, where there were no heirs, to the Church. The property of the churches was not only restored, but the power to receive donations in land, already granted to the Western churches, was extended to the Eastern. The Emperor himself set the example of giving back all that had been confiscated to the state.

Constantine issued two edicts, recounting all these exemptions, restitutions, and privileges—one addressed

---

the cross to another, was immediately transfixed in his flight. No one actu- | ally around the cross was wounded.
[y] Vit. Const. ii. 13.

to the Churches, the other to the cities of the East; the latter alone is extant. Its tone might certainly indicate that Constantine considered the contest with Licinius as, in some degree, a war of religion. His own triumph and the fate of his enemies are adduced as unanswerable evidences to the superiority of that God whose followers had been so cruelly persecuted. The restoration of the Christians to all their property and immunities, was an act not merely of justice and humanity, but of gratitude to the Deity.

But Constantine now appeared more openly to the whole world as the head of the Christian community. He sat, not in the Roman senate deliberating on the affairs of the empire, but presiding in a council of Christian bishops, summoned from all parts of the world, to decide, as of infinite importance to the Roman Empire, a contested point of the Christian faith. The council was held at Nicæa, one of the most ancient of the Eastern cities. The transactions of the Council, the questions which were agitated before it, and the decrees which it issued, will be postponed for the present, in order that this important controversy, which so long divided Christianity, may best be related in a continuous narrative : we pass to the following year.

A.D. 325.

Up to this period Christianity had seen much to admire, and little that it would venture to disapprove, in the public acts or in the domestic character of Constantine. His offences against the humanity of the Gospel would find palliation, or rather vindication and approval, in a warrior and a sovereign. The age was not yet so fully leavened with Christianity as to condemn the barbarity of that Roman pride which exposed without scruple the brave captive chieftains of the German tribes in the amphitheatre.

Conduct of Constantine to his enemies.

Again, after the triumph of Constantine over Maxentius,
this bloody spectacle had been renewed at Treves, on a
new victory of Constantine over the *Barbarians*. The
extirpation of the family of a competitor for the empire
would pass as the usual, perhaps the necessary, policy
of the times. The public hatred would applaud the
death of the voluptuous Maxentius, and that of his
family would be the inevitable consequences of his guilt.
Licinius had provoked his own fate by resistance to the
will of God and his persecution of the religion of Christ.
Nor was the fall of Licinius followed by any general
proscription; his son lived for a few years to be the
undistinguished victim of a sentence which involved
others in whom the public mind took far deeper interest.
Licinius himself was permitted to live a short time at
Thessalonica.[z] It is said by some that his life was
guaranteed by a solemn oath, and that he was permitted
to partake of the hospitality of the conqueror.[a] Yet his
death, though the brother-in-law of Constantine, was but
an expected event.[b] The tragedy which took place in
the family of Constantine betrayed to the surprised and
anxious world, that, if his outward demeanour showed

---

[z] Le Beau (Hist. du Bas Empire,
i. 220) recites with great fairness
the varying accounts of the death of
Licinius, and the motives which are
said to have prompted it. But he
proceeds to infer that Licinius *must*
have been guilty of some new crime,
to induce Constantine to violate his
solemn oath.

[a] Contra religionem sacramenti
Thessalonicæ privatus occisus est.
Eutrop. lib. x.

[b] Eusebius says that he was put to
death by the laws of war, and openly
approves of his execution and that of
the other enemies of God. Νόμῳ
πολέμου διακρίνας τῇ πρεπούσῃ παρε-
δίδου τιμωρίᾳ . . . καὶ ἀπώλλυντο,
τὴν προσήκουσαν ὑπέχοντες δίκην,
οἱ τῆς θεομαχίας σύμβουλοι. How
singularly does this contrast with the
passage above! See p. 319 (Vit.
Const. ii. 13) bigotry and mercy advancing hand in hand—the sterner
creed overpowering the Gospel.

respect or veneration for Christianity, its milder doctrines had made little impression on the unsoftened
Paganism of his heart.

Crispus, the son of Constantine by Minervina, his
first wife, was a youth of high and brilliant
promise. In his early years his education had
been entrusted to the celebrated Lactantius,
and there is reason to suppose that he was imbued
by his eloquent preceptor with the Christian doctrines; but the gentler sentiments instilled by the new
faith had by no means unnerved the vigour or tamed
the martial activity of youth. Had he been content
with the calmer and more retiring virtues of the Christian, without displaying the dangerous qualifications of
a warrior and a statesmen, he might have escaped the
fatal jealousy of his father, and the arts which were no
doubt employed for his ruin. In his campaign against
the Barbarians, Crispus had shown himself a worthy son
of Constantine, and his naval victory over the fleet of
Licinius had completed the conquest of the empire.
The conqueror of Maxentius and of Licinius, the undisputed master of the Roman world, might have been
expected to stand superior to that common failing of
weak monarchs, a jealous dread of the heir to their
throne. The unworthy fears of Constantine were betrayed by an edict inconsistent with the early promise
of his reign. He had endeavoured, soon after his
accession, to repress the odious crime of delation; a
rescript now appeared, inviting, by large reward and
liberal promise of favour, those informations which he
had before nobly disdained; and this edict seemed to
betray the apprehensions of the Government, that some
widely ramified and darkly organised conspiracy was
afoot. But if such conspiracy existed, the Government

A.D. 326.

Crispus, son of Constantine.

refused, by the secrecy of its own proceedings, to enlighten the public mind.

Rome itself, and the whole Roman world, heard with horror and amazement, that in the midst of the solemn festival, which was celebrating with the utmost splendour the twentieth year of the Emperor's reign, his eldest son had been suddenly seized, and, either without trial, or after a hurried examination, had been transported to the shore of Istria, and had perished by an obscure death.[c] Nor did Crispus fall alone; the young Licinius, the nephew of Constantine, who had been spared after his father's death and vainly honoured with the title of Cæsar, shared his fate. The sword of justice or of cruelty, once let loose, raged against those who were suspected as partisans of the dangerous Crispus, or as implicated in the wide-spread conspiracy, till the bold satire of an eminent officer of state did not scruple, in some lines privately circulated, to compare the splendid but bloody times with those of Nero.[d]

But this was only the first act of the domestic tragedy ; the death of the Emperor's wife Fausta, the partner of twenty years of wedlock, the mother of his three surviving sons, increased the general horror. She was suffocated in a bath, which had been heated to an insupportable degree of temperature. Many rumours

Death of Crispus.

April, A.D. 326.

Death of Fausta.

---

[c] Vict. Epit. in Constantino. Eutrop. lib. x. Zosimus, ii. c. 29. Sidonius, v. Epist. 8. Of the ecclesiastical historians, Philostorgius (lib. ii. 4) attributed the death of Crispus to the arts of his stepmother. He adds a strange story, that Constantine was poisoned by his brothers in revenge for the death of Crispus. Sozomen, while he refutes the notion of the connexion of the death of Crispus with the conversion of Constantine, admits the fact, l. i. c. 5.

[d] The Consul Albinus,—

Saturni aurea sæcla quis requiret ?
Sunt hæc gemmea sed Neroniana.
Sid. Apoll. v. 8.

were propagated throughout the empire concerning this
dark transaction, of which the real secret was no doubt
concealed, if not in the bosom, within the palace of
Constantine. The awful crimes which had thrilled the
scene of ancient tragedy, were said to have polluted the
imperial chamber. The guilty step-mother had either,
like Phædra, revenged the insensibility of the youthful
Crispus by an accusation of incestuous violence, or the
crime, actually perpetrated, had involved them both in
the common guilt and ruin. In accordance with the
former story, the miserable Constantine had discovered
too late the machinations which had stained his hand
with the blood of a guiltless son: in the agony of his
remorse he had fasted forty days; he had abstained
from the use of the bath; he had proclaimed his own
guilty precipitancy, and the innocence of his son, by
raising a golden statue of the murdered Crispus, with
the simple but emphatic inscription, "To my unfortunate son." The Christian mother of Constantine,
Helena, had been the principal agent in the detection
of the wicked Fausta; it was added, that, besides her
unnatural passion for her step-son, she was found to
have demeaned herself to the embraces of a slave.

It is dangerous to attempt to reconcile with probability these extraordinary events, which so often surpass,
in the strange reality of their circumstances, the wildest
fictions. But, according to the ordinary course of things,
Crispus would appear the victim of political rather than
of domestic jealousy. The innocent Licinius might be
an object of suspicion, as implicated in a conspiracy
against the power but not against the honour of Constantine. The removal of Crispus opened the succession
of the throne to the sons of Fausta. The passion of
maternal ambition is much more consistent with human

nature than the incestuous love of a step-mother, advanced in life and with many children, towards her husband's son. The guilt of compassing the death of Crispus, whether by the atrocious accusations of a Phædra, or by the more vulgar arts of common court intrigue, might come to light at a later period ; and the indignation of the Emperor at having been deluded into the execution of a gallant and blameless son, the desire of palliating to the world and to his own conscience his own criminal and precipitate weakness by the most unrelenting revenge on the subtlety with which he had been circumvented, might madden him to a second act of relentless barbarity.[e]

But at all events the unanimous consent of the Pagan, and most of the Christian authorities, as well as the expressive silence of Eusebius, indicates the unfavourable impression made on the public mind by these household barbarities. But the most remarkable circumstance is, the advantage which was taken of this event by the Pagan party to throw a dark shade over the conversion of Constantine to the Christian religion. Zosimus has preserved this report ; but there is good reason for supposing that it was a rumour, eagerly propagated at the time by the more desponding votaries of Paganism.[f] In the deep agony of remorse, Constantine eagerly inquired of the ministers of the ancient religions, whether their lustrations could purify the soul from the blood of a son. The unaccommodating priesthood acknowledged the inefficacy of their rites in a case of such inexpiable atrocity,[g] and Constantine

Pagan account of this event.

---

[e] Gibbon has thrown doubts on the actual death of Fausta, vol. iii. p. 110.

[f] See Heyne's note on this passage of Zosimus.

[g] According to Sozomen, whose narrative, as Heyne observes (note on

remained to struggle with the unappeased and un-atoned horrors of conscience. An Egyptian, on his journey from Spain, passed through Rome, and, being admitted to the intimacy of some of the females about the court, explained to the Emperor that the religion of Christ possessed the power of cleansing the soul from all sin. From that time Constantine placed himself entirely in the hands of the Christians, and abandoned altogether the sacred rites of his ancestors.

If Constantine at this time had been long an avowed and sincere Christian, this story falls to the ground; but if, according to my view, there was still something of ambiguity in the favour shown by Constantine to Christianity, if it still had something rather of the sagacious statesman than of the serious proselyte, there may be some slight groundwork of truth in this fiction. Constantine may have relieved a large portion of his subjects from grievous oppression, and restored their plundered property; he may have made munificent donations for the maintenance of their ceremonial; he may have permitted the famous Labarum to exalt the courage of his Christian soldiery; he may have admitted their represen-

---

Zosimus, p. 552), proves that this story was not the invention of Zosimus, but rather the version of the event current in the Pagan world, it was not a Pagan priest, but a Platonic philosopher, named Sopater, who thus denied the efficacy of any rite or ceremony to wash the soul clean from filial blood. It is true that neither the legal ceremonial of Paganism, nor the principles of the later Platonism, could afford any hope or pardon to the murderer. Julian, speaking of Constantine (in Cæsar.), insinuates the facility with which Christianity admitted the μιαίφονος, as well as other atrocious delinquents, to the divine forgiveness.

The bitterness with which the Pagan party judged of the measures of Constantine, is shown in the turn which Zosimus gives to his edict discouraging divination: "Having availed himself of the advantages of divination, which had predicted his own splendid successes, he was jealous lest the prophetic art should be equally prodigal of its glorious promises to others."

tatives to his court, endeavoured to allay their fierce feuds
in Africa, and sanctioned by his presence the meeting of
the Council of Nicæa to decide on the new controversy
which began to distract the Christian world; he may
have proclaimed himself, in short, the worshipper of
the Christians' God, whose favourites seemed likewise
to be those of fortune, and whose enemies were devoted
to ignominy and disaster (such is his constant language) : [h] but of the real character and the profounder
truths of the religion he may still have been entirely,
or, perhaps, in some degree disdainfully, ignorant; the
lofty indifferentism of the Emperor predominated over
the obedience of the convert towards the new faith.

But it was now the *man*, abased by remorse, by the
terrors of conscience, it may be by superstitious horrors,
who sought refuge against the divine Nemesis, the
avenging Furies, which haunted his troubled spirit.   It
would be the duty as well as the interest of an influential Christian to seize on the mind of the royal proselyte,
and, while it was thus prostrate in its weakness, to enforce
more strongly the *personal* sense of religion upon the
afflicted soul.   And if the Emperor was understood to
have derived the slightest consolation under this heavy
burden of conscious guilt from the doctrines of Christianity—if his remorse and despair were allayed or
assuaged—nothing was more likely than that Paganism,
which constantly charged Christianity with receiving
the lowest and most depraved of mankind among its

---

[h] It is remarkable in all the pro-
clamations and documents which
Eusebius assigns to Constantine, some
even written by his own hand, how
almost exclusively he dwells on this
worldly superiority of the God adored
by the Christians over those of the
Heathen, and the visible *temporal* advantages which attend on the worship
of Christianity. His own victory and
the disasters of his enemies are his
conclusive evidences of Christianity.

proselytes, should affect to assume the tone of superior
moral dignity, to compare its more uncompromising
moral austerity with the easier terms on which Christianity *appeared* to receive the repentant sinner. In
the bitterness of wounded pride and interest at the loss
of an imperial worshipper, it would revenge itself by
ascribing his change exclusively to the worst hour of
his life, and to the least exalted motive. It is a greater
difficulty, that, subsequent to this period, the mind of
Constantine appears to have relapsed in some degree to
its imperfectly unpaganised Christianity. His conduct
became ambiguous as before, floating between a decided
bias in favour of Christianity, and an apparent design
to harmonise with it some of the less offensive parts of
Heathenism. Yet it is by no means beyond the
common inconsistency of human nature, that, with the
garb and attitude, Constantine should throw off the
submission of a penitent. His mind, released from its
burthen, might resume its ancient vigour, and assert its
haughty superiority over the religious, as well as over
the civil allegiance of his subjects. A new object of
ambition was dawning on his mind ; a new and absorbing impulse was given to all his thoughts—the foundation of the second Rome, the new imperial city on the
Bosphorus.

Nor was this sole and engrossing object altogether
unconnected with the sentiments which arose out of
this dark transaction. Rome had become hateful to
Constantine ; for, whether on this point identifying herself with the Pagan feeling, and taunting the crime of
the Christian with partial acrimony, or pre-surmising
the design of Constantine to reduce her to the second
city of the empire, Rome assumed the unwonted liberty
of insulting the Emperor. The pasquinade which com-

pared his days to those of Nero was affixed to the gates of the palace; and so galling was the insolence of the populace, that the Emperor is reported to have consulted his brothers on the expediency of calling out his guards for a general massacre. Milder councils prevailed; and Constantine took the more tardy, but more deep-felt, revenge of transferring the seat of empire from the banks of the Tiber to the shroes of the Bosphorus.

CHAPTER III.

Foundation of Constantinople.

THE foundation of Constantinople marks one of the
Foundation
of Constanti-
nople
great periods of change in the annals of the world. Both its immediate [a] and its remoter connexion with the history of Christianity, are among those results which contributed to its influence on the destinies of mankind. The removal of the seat of empire from Rome might, indeed, at first appear to strengthen the decaying cause of Paganism. The senate became the sanctuary, the aristocracy of Rome, in general, the unshaken adherents of the ancient religion. But its more remote and eventual consequences were favourable to the consolidation and energy of the Christian power in the West. The absence of a secular competitor allowed the Papal authority to grow up and to develope its secret strength. By the side of the imperial power, perpetually contrasted with the pomp and majesty of the throne, constantly repressed in his slow but steady advancement to supremacy or obliged to contest every point with a domestic antagonist, the Pope would hardly have gained more political importance than the Patriarch of Constantinople. The extinction of the Western empire, which indeed had long held

---

[a] Constantine seized the property of some of the temples, for the expense of building Constantinople, but did not change the established worship; so says Libanius.

Τῆς κατὰ νόμους δὲ θεραπείας ἐκίνησεν οὐδὲ ἐν. vol. ii. p. 162.

its court in Milan or Ravenna rather than in the ancient capital, its revival only beyond the Alps, left all the awe which attached to the old Roman name, or which followed the possession of the imperial city, to gather round the tiara of the Pontiff. In any other city the Pope would in vain have asserted his descent from St. Peter; the long habit of connecting together the name of Rome with supreme dominion, silently co-operated in establishing the spiritual despotism of the Papal See.

Even in its more immediate influence, the rise of Constantinople was favourable to the progress *favourable to* of Christianity. It removed the seat of govern- *Christianity.* ment from the presence of those awful temples to which ages of glory had attached an inalienable sanctity, and with which the piety of all the greater days of the Republic had associated the supreme dominion and the majesty of Rome. It broke the last link which combined the pontifical and the imperial character. The Emperor of Constantinople, even if he had remained a Pagan, would have lost that power which was obtained over men's minds by his appearing in the chief place in all the religious pomps and processions, some of which were as old as Rome itself. The senate, and even the people, might be transferred to the new city; the deities of Rome clung to their native home, and would have refused to abandon their ancient seats of honour and worship.

Constantinople arose, if not a Christian, certainly not a Pagan city. The new capital of the world *Constanti-* had no ancient deities, whose worship was in- *nople a* *Christian* separably connected with her more majestic *city.* buildings and solemn customs. The temples of old Byzantium had fallen with the rest of the public edifices, when

Severus, in his vengeance, razed the rebellious city to the ground. Byzantium had resumed sufficient strength and importance to resist a siege by Constantine himself in the earlier part of his reign ; and some temples had reappeared during the reconstruction of the city.[b] The fanes of the Sun, of the Moon, and of Aphrodite, were permitted to stand in the Acropolis, though deprived of their revenues.[c] That of Castor and Pollux formed part of the Hippodrome, and the statues of those deities who presided over the games stood undisturbed till the reign of Theodosius the Younger.[d]

Once determined to found a rival Rome on the shores of the Bosphorus, the ambition of Constantine was absorbed by this great object. No expense was spared to raise a city worthy of the seat of empire— no art or influence to collect inhabitants worthy of such a city. Policy forbade any measure which would alienate the minds of any class or order who might add to the splendour or swell the population of Byzantium, and policy was the ruling principle of Constantine in the conduct of the whole transaction. It was the Emperor whose pride was now pledged to the accomplishment of his scheme with that magnificence which became the second founder of the empire, rather than the exclusive patron of one religious division of his subjects. Constantinople was not only to bear the name, it was to wear an exact resemblance of the elder Rome. The habitations of men, and the public buildings for business,

Building of the city.

---

[b] There is a long list of these temples in V. Hammer's Constantinopel und die Bosporus, i. p. 189, &c. Many of them are named in Gyllius, but it does not seem clear at what period they ceased to exist. The Paschal Chronicle, referred to by V. Hammer, says nothing of their conversion into churches by Constantine.

[c] Malala, Constantinus, x.

[d] Zosimus, ii. 31.

for convenience, for amusement, or for splendour, demanded the first care of the founder. The imperial palace arose, in its dimensions and magnificence equal to that in the older city. The skill of the architect was lavished on the patrician mansions, which were so faithfully to represent to the nobles, who obeyed the imperial invitation, the dwellings of their ancestors in the ancient Capitol, that their wondering eyes could scarcely believe their removal; their Penates might seem to have followed them.[e] The senate-house, the Augusteum, was prepared for their counsels. For the mass of the people, markets and fountains and aqueducts, theatres and hippodromes, porticoes, basilicæ, and forums, rose with the rapidity of enchantment. One class of buildings alone was wanting. If some temples were allowed to stand, it is clear that no new sacred edifices were erected to excite and gratify the religious feelings of the Pagan party, and the building of the few churches which are ascribed to the pious munificence of Constantine, seems slowly to have followed the extraordinary celerity with which the city was crowded with civil edifices.[f] A century after—a century during which Christianity had been

---

[e] Sozomen, ii. 3. In the next reign, however, Themistius admits the reluctance of the senators to remove: προτοῦ μὲν ὑπ' ἀνάγκης ἐτιμᾶτο ἡ γερουσία, καὶ ἡ τιμὴ τιμωρίας ἐδόκει μηδ'οτιοῦν διαφέρειν. Orat. Protrep. p. 57.

[f] Of the churches built by Constantine, one was dedicated to S. Sophia (the supreme Wisdom), the other to Eirene, Peace: a philosophic Pagan might have admitted the propriety of dedicating temples to each of these abstract names. The conse-

crating to individual saints was of a later period. Soz. ii. 3. The ancient Temple of Peace, which afterwards formed part of the Santa Sophia, was appropriately transformed into a Christian church. The Church of the Twelve Apostles appears, from Eusebius (Vit. Const. iv. 58), to have been built in the last year of Constantine's reign and of his life, as a burial place for himself and his family. Sozomen, indeed, says that Constantine embellished the city πολλοῖς καὶ μεγίστοις εὐκτηρίοις οἴκοις.

recognised as the religion of the empire—the metropolis contained only fourteen churches, one for each of its wards or divisions. Yet Constantine by no means neglected those measures which might connect the new city with the religious feelings of mankind. Heaven inspired, commanded, sanctified the foundation of the second Rome. The ancient ritual of Roman Paganism contained a solemn ceremony, which dedicated a new city to the protection of the Deity.

An imperial edict announced to the world that Constantine, by the command of God, had founded the eternal city.[g] When the Emperor walked, with a spear in his hand, in the front of the stately procession which was to trace the boundaries of Constantinople, the attendants followed in wonder his still advancing footsteps, which seemed as if they never would reach the appointed limit. One of them, at length, humbly inquired how much farther he proposed to advance. " When he that goes before me," replied the Emperor, " shall stop." But, however the Deity might have intimated his injunctions to commence the work, or whatever the nature of the invisible guide which, as he declared, thus directed his steps, this vague appeal to the Deity would impress with the same respect all his subjects, and by its impartial ambiguity offend none. In earlier times the Pagans would have bowed down in homage before this manifestation of the nameless tutelar deity of the new city; at the present period they had become familiarised, as it were, with the concentration of Olympus into one Supreme Being.[h] The Christians

Ceremonial of the foundation.

---

[g] On the old ceremony of founding a city, see Hartung, Religion der Römer, i. 114.

[h] The expression of the Pagan

Zosimus shows how completely this language had been adopted by the Heathen: πᾶς γὰρ χρόνος τῷ θείῳ βραχὺς, ἀεί τε ὄντι, καὶ ἐσομένῳ.

would of course assert the exclusive right of the one true
God to this appellation, and attribute to his inspiration
and guidance every important act of the Christian Emperor.[i]

But if splendid temples were not erected to the decaying deities of Paganism, their images were set up,
mingled indeed with other noble works of art, in all the
public places of Constantinople.   If the inhabitants were
not encouraged, at least they were not forbidden, to pay
divine honours to the immortal sculptures of Phidias
and Praxiteles, which were brought from all quarters to
adorn the squares and baths of Byzantium. The whole
Roman world contributed to the splendour of Constantinople. The tutelar deities of all the cities of Greece
(their influence of course much enfeebled by their removal from their local sanctuaries) were assembled:
the Minerva of Lyndus, the Cybele of Mount Dindymus
(which was said to have been placed there by the Argo-
nauts), the Muses of Helicon, the Amphitrite of Rhodes,
the Pan consecrated by united Greece after the defeat
of the Persians, the Delphic Tripod. The Dioscuri
overlooked the Hippodrome. At each end of the principal forum were two shrines, one of which held the
statue of Cybele, but deprived of her lions and her
hands, from the attitude of command distorted into that
of a suppliant for the welfare of the city : in the other
was the Fortune of Byzantium.[k] To some part of the

He is speaking of an oracle, in which
the Pagan party discovered a prediction of the future glory of Byzantium.
One letter less would make it the sentence of a Christian appealing to prophecy.

[i] At a later period the Virgin Mary
obtained the honour of having inspired
the foundation of Constantinople, of
which she became the tutelary guardian,
I had almost written, Deity.

[k] Euseb. Vit. Const. iii. 54. Sozomen, ii. 5. Codinus, de Orig. C. P.
30-62. Le Beau, i. 30.

Eusebius

Christian community this might appear to be leading, as it were, the gods of Paganism in triumph; the Pagans were shocked on their part by their violent removal from their native fanes, and their wanton mutilation. Yet the Christianity of that age, in full possession of the mind of Constantine, would sternly have interdicted the decoration of a Christian city with these *idols ;* the workmanship of Phidias or of Lysippus would have found no favour, when lavished on images of the Dæmons of Paganism.

The ceremonial of the dedication of the city [m] was attended by still more dubious circumstances. After a most splendid exhibition of chariot games in the Hippodrome, the Emperor moved in a magnificent car through the most public part of the city, encircled by all his guards in the attire of a religious ceremonial and bearing torches in their hands. The Emperor himself held a golden statue of the Fortune of the city in his hands. An imperial edict enacted the annual celebration of this rite. On the birthday of the city the gilded statue of himself, thus bearing the same golden image of Fortune, was annually to be led through the Hippodrome to the foot of the imperial throne, and to receive the adoration of the reigning Emperor. The lingering attachment of Constantine to the favourite superstition of his earlier days, may be traced on still better authority.

Eusebius would persuade his readers that these statues were set up in the public places to excite the general contempt. Zosimus admits with bitterness that they were mutilated from want of respect to the ancient religion. ii. 31. Compare Socr. Ec. Hist. 1-16.

Read, too (some lines are worth reading), the description by Christodorus of the statues in the public gymnasium of Zeuxippus. Deiphobus is fine. There are also, in strange assemblage, Venus (Cypris), Julius Cæsar, Plato, Hercules, and Homer. Antholog. Palat. i. 37.

[m] Paschal Chronicle, p. 529, edit. Bonn.

The Grecian worship of Apollo had been exalted into the Oriental veneration of the Sun, as the visible representative of the Deity; and of all the statues which were introduced from different quarters, none were received with greater honour than those of Apollo. In one part of the city stood the Pythian, in the other the Sminthian deity.[n] The Delphic Tripod, which, according to Zosimus, contained an image of the god, stood upon the column of the three twisted serpents, supposed to represent the mythic Python. But on a still loftier, the famous pillar of porphyry, stood an image in which (if we are to credit modern authority, and the more modern our authority, the less likely is it to have invented so singular a statement) Constantine dared to mingle together the attributes of the Sun, of Christ, and of himself.[o] According to one tradition, this pillar was based, as it were, on another superstition. The venerable Palladium itself, surreptitiously conveyed from Rome, was buried beneath it, and thus transferred the eternal destiny of the old to the new capital. The pillar, formed of marble and of porphyry, rose to the height of 120 feet. The colossal image on the top was that of Apollo, either from Phrygia or from Athens. But the head of Constantine had been substituted for that of the god. The sceptre proclaimed the dominion of the world, and it held in its hand the globe, emblematic of universal empire. Around the head, instead of rays, were fixed the nails of the true cross. Is this Paganism approximating to Christianity, or Christianity degenerating into Paganism? Thus Constantine, as

Statue of Constantine.

---

[n] Euseb. Vit. Const. iii. 54.

[o] The author of the Antiq. Constantinop. apud Banduri. See Von Hammer, Constantinopel und die Bosporus, i. 162. Philostorgius says that the Christians worshipped this image. ii. 17.

founder of the new capital, might appear to some still
to maintain the impartial dignity of Emperor of the
world, presiding with serene indifference over the various
nations, orders, and religious divisions which peopled his
dominions; admitting to the privileges and advantages
of citizens in the new Rome all who were tempted to
make their dwelling around her seat of empire.

Yet, even during the reign of Constantine, no doubt,
Progress of   the triumphant progress of Christianity tended
Christianity.   to efface or to obscure these lingering vestiges
of the ancient religion. If here and there remained a
shrine or temple belonging to Polytheism, built in proportion to the narrow circuit and moderate population
of old Byzantium, the Christian churches, though far
from numerous, were gradually rising, in their dimensions more suited to the magnificence and populousness
of the new city, and in form proclaiming the dominant
faith of Constantinople. The Christians were most
likely to crowd into a new city; probably their main
strength still lay in the mercantile part of the community : interest and religion would combine in urging
them to settle in this promising emporium of trade,
where their religion, if it did not reign alone and exclusive, yet maintained an evident superiority over its
decaying rival. Those of the old aristocracy who were
inclined to Christianity, would be much more loosely
attached to their Roman residences, and would be most
inclined to obey the invitation of the Emperor, while
the large class of the indifferent would follow at the
same time the religious and political bias of the sovereign. Where the attachment to the old religion was
so slight and feeble, it was a trifling sacrifice to ambition
or interest to embrace the new; particularly where
there was no splendid ceremonial, no connexion of the

priestly office with the higher dignity of the state; nothing, in short, which could enlist either old reverential feelings, or the imagination, in the cause of Polytheism. The sacred treasures, transferred from the Pagan temples to the Christian city, sank more and more into national monuments, or curious remains of antiquity; their religious significance was gradually forgotten; they became, in the natural process of things, a mere collection of works of art.

In other respects Constantinople was not a Roman city. An amphitheatre, built on the restoration of the city after the siege of Severus, was permitted to remain, but it was restricted to exhibitions of wild beasts; the first Christian city was never disgraced by the bloody spectacle of gladiators.[p] There were theatres indeed, but it may be doubted whether the noble religious drama of Greece ever obtained popularity in Constantinople. The chariot race was the amusement which absorbed all others; and to this, at first, as it was not necessarily connected with the Pagan worship, Christianity might be more indulgent. How this taste grew into a passion, and this passion into a frenzy, the later annals of Constantinople bear melancholy witness. Beset with powerful enemies without, oppressed by a tyrannous government within, the people of Constantinople thought of nothing but the colour of their faction in the Hippodrome, and these more engrossing and

The Amphitheatre.

---

[p] An edict of Constantine (Cod. Theod. xv. 12), if it did not altogether abolish these sanguinary shows, restricted them to particular occasions. "Cruenta spectacula in otio civili, et domesticâ quiete non placent." Criminals were to be sent to the mines. But it would seem that captives taken in war might still be exposed in the amphitheatre. In fact these bloody exhibitions resisted some time longer the progress of Christian humanity.

maddening contentions even silenced the animosity of
religious dispute.

During the foundation of Constantinople, the Emperor
might appear to the Christians to have relapsed from
the head of the Christian division of his subjects, into
the common sovereign of the Roman world. In this
respect, his conduct did not ratify the promise of his
earlier acts in the East. He had not only restored
Christianity, depressed first by the cruelties of Maximin,
and afterwards by the violence of Licinius, but in many
cases he had lent his countenance, or his more active
assistance, to the rebuilding their churches on a more
imposing plan. Yet, to all outward appearance, the
world was still Pagan : every city seemed still to repose
under the tutelary gods of the ancient religion ; every-
Ancient   where the temples rose above the buildings of
temples.   men : if here and there a Christian church, in
its magnitude, or in the splendour of its architecture,
might compete with the solid and elegant fanes of antiquity, the Christians had neither ventured to expel
them from their place of honour, or to appropriate to
their own use those which were falling into neglect or
decay. As yet there had been no invasion but on the
opinions and moral influence of Polytheism.

The temples, indeed, of Pagan worship, though subsequently, in some instances, converted to Christian
uses, were not altogether suited to the ceremonial of
Christianity.[q] The Christians might look on their
stateliest buildings with jealousy—hardly with envy.
Whether raised on the huge substructures, and in the

---

[q] Compare an excellent memoir by
M. Quatremère ·de Quincy on the
means of lighting the ancient temples
(Mém. de l'Institut, iii. 171), and
Hope on Architecture.

immense masses of the older Asiatic style, as at Baalbec,
or the original Temple at Jerusalem ; whether built on
the principles of Grecian art, when the secret of vault-
ing over a vast building seems to have been unknown ;
or, after the general introduction of the arch by the
Romans had allowed the roof to spread out to ampler
extent,—still the actual enclosed temple was rarely of
great dimensions.[r]   The largest among the Greeks
were hypæthral, open to the sky.[s]   If we judge from
the temples crowded together about the Forum, those
in Rome contributed to the splendour of the city rather
by their number than by their size.   The rites of Polytheism, in fact, collected together their vast assemblages,
rather as spectators than as worshippers.[t]   The altar
itself, in general, stood in the open air, in the court
before the temple, where the smoke might find free
vent, and rise in its grateful odour to the heavenly
dwelling of the gods.   The body of the worshippers,
therefore, stood in the courts, or the surrounding porticoes.   They might approach individually, and make
their separate libation or offering, and then retire to a
convenient distance, where they might watch the movements of the ministering priest, receive his announcement of the favourable or sinister signs discovered in
the victim, or listen to the hymn, which was the only
usual form of adoration or prayer.   However Chris-

---

[r] M. Quatremère de Quincy gives
the size of some of the ancient temples :
Juno at Agrigentum, 116 (Paris) feet ;
Concord, 120 ; Pæstum, 110 ; Theseus,
100 ; Jupiter at Olympia, or Minerva
at Athens,   220-230 ;   Jupiter at
Agrigentum,   322 ;   Selinus,   320 ;
Ephesus, 350 ; Apollo Dindymus at
Miletus, 360. p. 195.

[s] The real hypæthral temples were
to particular divinities : Jupiter Ful-
gurator, Cœlum, Sol, Luna.

[t] Eleusis, the scene of the mysteries,
of all the ancient temples had the
largest nave ; it was " turbæ theatralis
capacissimum." Vitruv. vii. Ὄχλον
θεάτρου δέξασθαι δυνάμενον. Strabo.

tianity might admit gradations in its several classes of
worshippers, and assign its separate station according
to the sex, or the degree of advancement in the religious
initiation; however the penitents might be forbidden,
until reconciled with the Church, or the catechumens
before they were initiated into the community, to penetrate beyond the outer portico, or the first inner division in the church; yet the great mass of a Christian
congregation must be received within the walls of the
building; and the service consisting not merely in ceremonies performed by the priesthood, but in prayers, to
which all present were expected to respond, and in oral
instruction, the actual edifice therefore required more
ample dimensions.

In many towns there was another public building, the
Basilica, or Hall of Justice,[u] singularly adapted
for the Christian worship. This was a large
chamber, of an oblong form, with a plain flat exterior wall.
The pillars, which in the temples were without, stood
within the basilica; and the porch, or that which in the
temple was an outward portico, was contained within the
basilica. This hall was thus divided by two rows of
columns into a central avenue, with two side aisles. The
outward wall was easily pierced for windows, without
damaging the symmetry or order of the architecture. In
the one the male, in the other the female, appellants to
justice waited their turn.[x] The three longitudinal avenues

---

[u] Le Basilique fut l'édifice des
anciens, qui convint à la célébration
de ses mystères. La vaste capacité
de son intérieur, les divisions de son
plan, les grandes ouvertures, qui in-
troduisaient de toutes parts la lumière
dans son enceinte, le tribunal qui
devint la place des célébrans, et du
chœur, tout se trouva en rapport avec
les pratiques du nouveau culte. Q. de
Quincy, p. 173. See Hope on Architecture, p. 87.

[x] According to Bingham (lviii. c. 3),
the women occupied galleries in each

were crossed by one in a transverse direction, elevated
a few steps, and occupied by the advocates, notaries,
and others employed in the public business. At the
farther end, opposite to the central avenue, the building
swelled out into a semicircular recess, with a ceiling
rounded off; it was called *absis* in the Greek, and in
Latin *tribunal.* Here sat the magistrate with his assessors, and hence courts of justice were called tribunals.

The arrangement of this building coincided with remarkable propriety with the distribution of a Christian
congregation.[y] The sexes retained their separate places
in the aisles; the central avenue became the nave, so
called from the fanciful analogy of the church to the
ship of St. Peter. The transept, the $B\tilde{\eta}\mu a$, or choros,
was occupied by the inferior clergy and the singers.[z]
The bishop took the throne of the magistrate, and the
superior clergy ranged on each side on the seats of the
assessors.

Before the throne of the bishop, either within or on
the verge of the recess, stood the altar. This was
divided from the nave by the cancelli, or rails, from
whence hung curtains, which, during the celebration of
the communion, separated the participants from the
rest of the congregation.

As these buildings were numerous, and attached to
every imperial residence, they might be bestowed at
once on the Christians, without either interfering with
the course of justice, or bringing the religious feelings
of the hostile parties into collision.[a] Two, the Sessorian

---

aisle above the men. This sort of
separation may have been borrowed
from the synagogue; probably the
practice was not uniform.

[y] Some few churches were of an

octagonal form ; some in that of a
cross. See Bingham, l. viii. c. 3.

[z] Apost. Const. l. ii. c. 57.

[a] There were eighteen at Rome ;
many of these basilicæ had become

and the Lateran, were granted to the Roman Christians by Constantine. And the basilica appears to have been the usual form of building in the West, though, besides the porch, connected with, or rather included within, the building, which became the Narthex, and was occupied by the catechumens and the penitents, and in which stood the piscina, or font of baptism—there was in general an outer open court, surrounded with colonnades. This, as we have seen in the description of the church at Tyre, was general in the East, where the churches retained probably more of the templar form; while in Constantinople, where they were buildings raised from the ground, Constantine appears to have followed the form of the basilica.

By the consecration of these basilicas to the purposes of Christian worship, and the gradual erection of large churches in many of the Eastern cities, Christianity began to assume an outward form and dignity commensurate with its secret moral influence. In imposing magnitude, if not in the grace and magnificence of its architecture, it rivalled the temples of antiquity. But as yet it had neither the power, nor, probably, the inclination, to array itself in the spoils of Paganism. Its aggression was still rather that of fair competition than of hostile destruction. It was content to behold the silent courts of the Pagan fanes untrodden but by a few casual worshippers; altars without victims; thin wreaths of smoke rising where the air used to be clouded with the reek of hecatombs;

Relative position of Christianity and Paganism.

---

exchanges, or places for general business. Among the Roman basilicæ P. Victor reckons, the Basilicæ Argentariorum. Ciampini, tom. i. p. 8.

Some basilicæ were of a very large size. One is described by the younger Pliny, in which 180 judges were seated, with a vast multitude of advocates and auditors. Plin. Epist. vi. 33.

the priesthood murmuring in bitter envy at the throngs which passed by the porticoes of their temples towards the Christian church. The direct interference with the freedom of Pagan worship seems to have been confined to the suppression of those Eastern rites which were offensive to public morals. Some of the Syrian temples retained the obscene ceremonial of the older Nature-worship. Religious prostitution, and other monstrous enormities, appeared under the form of divine adoration. The same rites which had endangered the fidelity of the ancient Israelites shocked the severe purity of the Christians. A temple in Syria of the female principle of generation, which the later Greeks identified with their Aphrodite, was defiled by these unspeakable pollutions; it was levelled to the ground by the Emperor's command; the recesses of the sacred grove laid open to the day, and the rites interdicted.[b] A temple of Æsculapius at Ægæ, in Cilicia, fell under the same proscription. The miraculous cures, pretended to be wrought in this temple, where the suppliants passed the night, appear to have excited the jealousy of the Christians; and this was, perhaps, the first overt act of hostility against the established Paganism.[c] In many other places the frauds of the priesthood were detected by the zealous incredulity of the Christians; and Polytheism, feebly defended by its own party, at least left to its fate by the Government, assailed on all quarters by an active and persevering enemy, endured affront, exposure, neglect, if not with the dignified patience of martyrdom, with the sullen equanimity of indifference.

Temples suppressed.

Palestine itself, and its capital, Jerusalem, was an

---

b Euseb. Vit. Const. iii. 55.   c Ibid. iii. 56.

open province, of which Christianity took entire and almost undisputed possession. Paganism, in the adjacent regions, had built some of its most splendid temples; the later Roman architecture at Gerasa, at Petra, and at Baalbec, appears built on the massive and enormous foundations of the older native structures. But in Palestine Proper it had made no strong settlement. Temples had been raised by Hadrian, in his new city, on the site of Jerusalem. One dedicated to Aphrodite occupied the spot which Christian tradition or later invention asserted to be the sepulchre of Christ.[d] The prohibition issued by Hadrian against the admission of the Jews into the Holy City, doubtless was no longer enforced; but, though not forcibly depressed by public authority, Judaism itself waned, in its own native territory, before the ascendancy of Christianity.

It was in Palestine that the change which had been slowly working into Christianity itself, began to assume a more definite and apparent form. The religion reissued as it were from its cradle, in a character, if foreign to its original simplicity, singularly adapted to achieve and maintain its triumph over the human mind. It no longer confined itself to its purer moral influence; it was no more a simple, spiritual faith, despising all those accessories which captivate the senses, and feed the imagination with new excitement. It no longer disdained the local sanctuary, nor stood independent of those associations with place, which beseemed an universal and spiritual religion. It began to

---

[d] This temple was improbably said to have been built on this spot by Hadrian to insult the Christians; but Hadrian's hostility was against the rebellious Jews, not against the Christians.

have its hero-worship, its mythology; it began to crowd
the mind with images of a secondary degree of sanctity,
but which enthralled and kept in captivity those who
were not ripe for the pure moral conception of the
Deity, and the impersonation of the Godhead in Jesus
Christ. It was, as might not unreasonably be antici-
pated, a female, the Empress Helena, the mother of
Constantine, who gave, as it were, this new colouring to
Christian devotion. In Palestine, indeed, where her
pious activity was chiefly employed, it was the memory
of the Redeemer himself which hallowed the scenes of
his life and death to the imagination of the believer.
Splendid churches arose over the place of his birth at
Bethlehem; that of his burial, near the supposed
Calvary; that of his ascension, on the Mount of Olives.
So far the most spiritual piety could not hesitate to
proceed; to such natural and irresistible claims upon its
veneration no Christian heart could refuse to yield.
The cemeteries of their brethren had, from the commencement of Christianity, exercised a strong influence
over the imagination. They had frequently, in times of
trial, been the only places of religious assemblage.
When hallowed to the feelings by the remains of
friends, of bishops, of martyrs, it was impossible to
approach them without the profoundest reverence; and
the transition from reverence to veneration—to adoration—was too easy and imperceptible to awaken the
jealousy of that exclusive devotion due to God and the
Redeemer. The sanctity of the place where the Redeemer was supposed to have been laid in the sepulchre,
was still more naturally and intimately associated with
the purest sentiments of devotion.

But the next step, the discovery of the true cross, was
more important. It materialised, at once, the spiritual

worship of Christianity. It was reported throughout wondering Christendom, that tradition, or a vision, having revealed the place of the Holy Sepulchre, the fane of Venus had been thrown down by the Imperial command, excavations had been made, the Holy Sepulchre had come to light, and with the Sepulchre three crosses, with the inscription originally written by Pilate in three languages over that of Jesus. As it was doubtful to which of the crosses the tablet with the inscription belonged, a miracle decided to the perplexed believers the claims of the genuine cross.[e] The precious treasure was divided; part, enshrined in a silver case, remained at Jerusalem, from whence pilgrims constantly bore fragments of the still vegetating wood to the West, till enough was accumulated in the different churches to build a ship of war. Part was sent to Constantinople: the nails of the passion of Christ were turned into a bit for the war-horse of the Emperor, or, according to another account, represented the rays of the sun around the head of his statue.

A magnificent church, called at first the Church of the
Churches built in Palestine. Resurrection (Anastasis), afterwards that of the Holy Sepulchre, rose on the sacred spot hallowed by this discovery, in which from that time a large part of the Christian world has addressed its unquestioning orisons. It stood in a large open court, with porticoes on each side, with the usual porch, nave,

---

[e] The excited state of the Christian mind, and the tendency to this materialisation of Christianity, may be estimated by the undoubting credulity with which they entertained the improbable notion that the crosses were buried with our Saviour, not only that on which He suffered, but those of the two thieves also. From the simple account of the burial in the Gospels, how singular a change to that of the discovery of the cross in the ecclesiastical historians! Socrates, i. 17. Sozomen, ii. 1. Theodoret, i. 18.

and choir. The nave was inlaid with precious marbles;
and the roof, overlaid with gold, showered down a flood
of light over the whole building; the roofs of the aisles
were likewise overlaid with gold. At the farther end
arose a dome supported by twelve pillars, in commemo-
ration of the Twelve Apostles; the capitals of these
were silver vases. Within the church was another
court, at the extremity of which stood the Chapel of the
Holy Sepulchre, lavishly adorned with gold and precious
stones, as it were to perpetuate the angelic glory which
streamed forth on the day of the Resurrection.[f]

Another sacred place was purified by the command of
Constantine, and dedicated to Christian worship. Near
Hebron[g] there was the celebrated oak or terebinth tree of
Mamre, which tradition pointed out as the spot where
the angels appeared to Abraham. It is singular that
the Heathen are said to have celebrated religious rites
at this place, and to have worshipped the celestial
visitants of Abraham. It was likewise, as usual in the
East, a celebrated emporium of commerce. The worship may have been like that at the Caaba of Mecca
before the appearance of Mohammed, for the fame of
Abraham seems to have been preserved among the
Syrian and Arabian tribes, as well as the Jews. It is
remarkable that, at a later period, the Jews and Christians are said to have met in amicable devotion, and
offered their common incense and suspended their lights
in the church erected over this spot by the Christian
Emperor.[h]

---

[f] Eusebius, Vit. Constant. iii. 29,
et seq.; this seems to be the sense of
the author.

[g] On Hebron, read Dr. Stanley's
most interesting account of his visit
to the tomb of Abraham with H.R.H.
the Prince of Wales.

[h] Antoninus in Itinerario. See
Heinichen, Note on Euseb. Vit. Const.
iii. 53.

CHAPTER IV.

Trinitarian Controversy.

BUT it was as arbiter of religious differences, as pre-
Trinitarian   siding in their solemn councils, that Constan-
controversy.   tine appeared to the Christians the avowed
and ostensible head of their community. Immediately
after his victory over Licinius, Constantine had found
the East, no less than the West, agitated by the dissensions of his Christian subjects. He had hoped to allay
the flames of the Donatist schism, by the consentient
and impartial authority of the Western Churches. A
more extensive, if as yet less fiercely agitated, contest disturbed the Eastern provinces. Outward peace seemed
to be restored only to give place to intestine dissension. I must reascend the course of Christian History
for several years, in `order to trace in one continuous
narrative the rise and progress of the Trinitarian Controversy. This dissension had broken out soon after
Constantine's subjugation of the East; already, before
the building of Constantinople, it had obtained full
possession of the public mind, and the great Council of
Nicæa, the first real senate of Christendom, had passed
its solemn decree. The Donatist schism was but a local
dissension: it raged, indeed, with fatal and implacable
fury; but it was almost entirely confined to the limits
of a single province. The Trinitarian controversy was
the first dissension which rent asunder the whole body
of the Christians, arrayed in almost every part of the

world two hostile parties in implacable opposition, and,
at a later period, exercised a powerful political influence
on the affairs of the world. How singular an illustration
of the change already wrought in the mind of man by
the introduction of Christianity! Questions which, if
they had arisen in the earlier period of the world,
would have been limited to a priestly caste—if in
Greece, would have been confined to the less frequented
schools of Athens or Alexandria, and might have produced some intellectual excitement among the few who
were conversant with the higher philosophy—now agitated the populace of great cities, occupied the councils
of princes, and, at a later period, determined the fate
of kingdoms and the sovereignty of great part of
Europe.[a] It appears still more extraordinary, since
this controversy related to a purely speculative tenet.
The disputants of either party might possibly have
asserted the superior tendency of each system to enforce
the severity of Christian morals, or to excite the ardour
of Christian piety ; but they appear to have dwelt little,
if at all, on the practical effects of the conflicting
opinions.   In morals, in manners, in habits, in usages,
in Church government, in religious ceremonial, there
was no distinction between the parties which divided
Christendom.   The Gnostic sects inculcated a severer
asceticism, and differed, in many of their usages, from
the general body of the Christians.   The Donatist
factions commenced at least with a question of Church
discipline, and almost grew into a strife for political
ascendancy.   The Arians and Athanasians first divided
the world on a pure question of faith.   From this

---

[a] For instance, when the savage | more refined Arianism of the Visigoths
orthodoxy of the Franks made the | a pretext for hostile invasion.

period we may date the introduction of rigorous articles of belief, which required the submissive assent of the mind to every word and letter of an established creed, and which raised the slightest heresy of opinion into a more fatal offence against God, and a more odious crime in the estimation of man, than the worst moral delinquency or the most flagrant deviation from the spirit of Christianity.

The Trinitarian controversy was the natural, though tardy, growth of the Gnostic opinions; it could scarcely be avoided when the exquisite distinctness and subtlety of the Greek language were applied to religious opinions of an Oriental origin. Even the Greek of the New Testament retained something of the significant and reverential vagueness of Eastern expression. This vagueness, even philosophically speaking, may better convey to the mind those mysterious conceptions of the Deity which are beyond the province of reason than the anatomical precision of philosophic Greek. The first Christians were content to worship, with undefined fervour, the Deity as revealed in the Gospel. They assented to, and repeated with devout adoration, the words of the Sacred Writings, or those which had been made use of from the Apostolic age; but they did not decompose them, or, with nice and scrupulous accuracy, appropriate peculiar terms to each manifestation of the Godhead. It was the great characteristic of the Oriental theologies, as described in a former chapter, to preserve the primal and parental Deity at the greatest possible distance from the material creation. This originated in the elementary tenet of the irreclaimable evil of matter. In the present day, the more rational believer labours under the constant dread, if not of materialising, of humanising too

Origin of the controversy.

much the Great Supreme. A certain degree of indistinctness appears inseparable from that vastness of conception, which arises out of the more extended knowledge of the works of the Creator. A more expanding and comprehensive philosophy increases the distance between the Omnific First Cause and the race of man. All that defines seems to limit and circumscribe the Deity.   Yet in thus reverentially repelling *Constant struggle between the intellectual and devotional conception of the Deity.* the Deity into an unapproachable sphere, and investing him, as it were, in a nature absolutely unimaginable by the mind; in thus secluding him from the degradation of being vulgarised, if the expression may be ventured, by profane familiarity, or circumscribed by the narrowness of the human intellect, God is gradually subtilised and sublimated into a being beyond the reach of devotional feelings, almost superior to adoration. There is in mankind, and in the individual man, on the one hand, an intellectual tendency to refine the Deity into a mental conception; and, on the other, an instinctive counter-tendency to impersonate him into a material, and, when the mind is ruder and less intellectual, a mere human being. Among the causes which have contributed to the successful promulgation of Christianity and the maintenance of its influence over the mind of man, was the singular beauty and felicity with which its theory of the conjunction of the divine and human nature, each preserving its separate attributes, on the one hand, enabled the mind to preserve inviolate the pure conception of the Deity, on the other, to approximate it, as it were, to human interests and sympathies.   But this is done rather by a process of instinctive feeling than by strict logical reasoning. Even here, there is a perpetual strife between the intel-

lect, which guards with jealousy the divine conception
of the Redeemer's nature; and the sentiment, or even
the passion, which so draws down the general notion to
its own capacities, so approximates and assimilates it to
its own ordinary sympathies, as to absorb the Godhead
in the human nature.

The Gnostic systems had universally admitted the
seclusion of the primal Deity from all intercourse with
matter; that intercourse had taken place, through
a derivative and intermediate being, more or less remotely proceeding from the sole fountain of Godhead.
This, however, was not the part of Gnosticism which
was chiefly obnoxious to the general sentiments of the
Christian body.   Their theories about the malignant
nature of the Creator; the identification of the God of
the Jews with this hostile being; the Docetism which
asserted the unreality of the Redeemer—these points,
with their whole system of the origin of the worlds and
of mankind, excited the most vigorous and active resistance.   But when the wilder theories of Gnosticism
began to die away, or to rank themselves under the
hostile standard of Manicheism; when their curious
cosmogonical notions were dismissed, and the greater
part of the Christian world began to agree in the plain
doctrines of the eternal supremacy of God; the birth,
the death, the resurrection of Christ as the Son of
God; the effusion of the Holy Spirit,—questions began
to arise as to the peculiar nature and relation between
the Father, Son, and Holy Ghost.   In all the systems a
binary, in most a triple, modification of the Deity was
admitted.   The Logos, the Divine Word or Reason,
might differ, in the various schemes, in his relation to
the parental Divinity and to the universe; but there
was this distinctive and ineffaceable character, that he

was the Mediator, the connecting link between the unseen and unapproachable world and that of man. This Platonism, if it may be so called, was universal. It differed, indeed, widely in most systems from the original philosophy of the Athenian sage; it had acquired a more Oriental and imaginative cast. Plato's poetry of words had been expanded into the poetry of conceptions. It may be doubted whether Plato himself impersonated the Logos, the Word or Reason, of the Deity; with him it was rather an attribute of the Godhead. In one sense it was the chief of these archetypal ideas, according to which the Creator framed the universe; in another, the principle of life, motion, and harmony which pervaded all things. This Platonism had gradually absorbed all the more intellectual class; it hovered over, as it were, and gathered under its wings all the religions of the world. It had already modified Judaism; it had allied itself with the Syrian and Mithriac worship of the Sun, the visible Mediator, the emblem of the Word; it was part of the general Nature worship; it was attempting to renew Paganism, and was the recognised and leading tenet in the higher Mysteries. Disputes on the nature of Christ were indeed coeval with the promulgation of Christianity. Some of the Jewish converts had never attained to the sublimer notion of his mediatorial character; but this disparaging notion, adverse to the ardent zeal of the rest of the Christian world, had isolated this sect. The imperfect Christianity of the Ebionites had long ago expired in an obscure corner of Palestine. In all the other divisions of Christianity, the Christ had more or less approximated to the office and character of this Being which connected mankind with the Eternal Father.

2 A 2

Alexandria, the fatal and prolific soil of speculative
controversy, where speculative controversy was
most likely to madden into furious and lasting
hostility, gave birth to this new element of disunion in the Christian world. The Trinitarian question,
indeed, had already been agitated within a less extensive
sphere. Noetus, an Asiatic, either of Smyrna or
Ephesus, had dwelt with such exclusive zeal on
the unity of the Godhead, as to absorb, as it were, the
whole Trinity into one undivided and undistinguished
Being. The one supreme and impassible Father united
to himself the man Jesus, whom he had created, by so
intimate a conjunction, that the divine unity was not
destroyed. His adversaries drew the conclusion, that,
according to this blaspheming theory, the Father must
have suffered on the cross, and the ignominious name
of Patripassians adhered to the few followers of this
unprosperous sect.[b]

Sabellianism had excited more attention. Sabellius
was an African of the Cyrenaic province. According to his system it was the same Deity,
under different forms, who existed in the Father, the
Son, and the Holy Ghost. A more modest and unoffending Sabellianism might, perhaps, be imagined in
accordance with modern philosophy. The manifestations of the same Deity, or rather of his attributes,
through which alone the Godhead becomes comprehensible to the human mind, may have been thus successively made in condescension to our weakness of
intellect. It would be the same Deity, assuming, as it

Margin notes: Controversy commences at Alexandria. Noetus. Sabellianism.

[b] I have not thought it necessary to enter into the various shades of Monarchianism, especially in the Church at Rome, on which the Philosophamena has shed new light.

were, an objective form, so as to come within the scope
of the human mind; a real difference, as regards the
conception of man, perfect unity in its subjective existence. This, however, though some of its terms may
appear the same with the Sabellianism of antiquity,
would be the Trinitarianism of a philosophy unknown at
this period. The language of the Sabellians implied, to
the jealous ears of their opponents, that the distinction
between the persons of the Trinity was altogether unreal. While the Sabellian party charged their adversaries with a Heathen Tritheistic worship, they retorted
by accusing Sabellianism of annihilating the separate
existence of the Son and the Holy Ghost. But Sabellianism had not divided Christianity into two irreconcileable parties. Even now, but for the commanding
characters of the champions who espoused each party,
the Trinitarian controversy might have been limited to
a few provinces, and become extinct in some years.
But it arose, not merely under the banners of men
endowed with those abilities which command the multitude; it not merely called into action the energies of
successive disputants, the masters of the intellectual
attainments of the age,—it appeared at a critical period,
when the rewards of success were more splendid, the
penalty upon failure proportionately more severe. The
contest was now not merely for a superiority over a few
scattered and obscure communities, it was agitated on a
vaster theatre, that of the Roman world; the proselytes
whom it disputed were sovereigns; it contested the
supremacy of the human mind, which was now bending
to the yoke of Christianity. It is but judging on the
common principles of human nature to conclude, that
the grandeur of the prize supported the ambition and
inflamed the passions of the contending parties, that

human motives of political power and aggrandisement
mingled with the more spiritual influences of the love of
truth, and zeal for the purity of religion.

The doctrine of the Trinity, that is, the divine nature
Trinitarian-
ism. of the Father, the Son, and the Holy Ghost,
was acknowledged by all. To each of these
distinct and separate beings, both parties ascribed the
attributes of the Godhead, with the exception of self-
existence, which was restricted by the Arians to the
Father. Both admitted the anti-mundane Being of the
Son and the Holy Spirit. But, according to the Arian,
there was a time, before the commencement of the ages,
when the Parent Deity dwelt alone in undeveloped,
undivided unity. At this time, immeasurably, incalculably, inconceivably remote, the majestic solitude
ceased,[c] the divine unity was broken by an act of the
sovereign Will; and the only begotten Son, the image
of the Father, the Vicegerent of all the divine power,
the intermediate Agent in all the long subsequent work
of creation, *began to be.*[d]

Such was the question which led to all the evils of
human strife—hatred, persecution, bloodshed. But, however profoundly humiliating this fact in the history of
mankind, and in the history of Christianity an epoch of
complete revolution from its genuine spirit, it may
fairly be inquired, whether this was not an object more
generous, more unselfish, and at least as wise, as many
of those motives of personal and national advantage and
aggrandisement, or many of those magic words, which,
embraced by two parties with blind and unintelligent
fury, have led to the most disastrous and sanguinary

---

[c] Compare Cyril. Alex. Epist. i.
7 ; Labbe. p. 26.

[d] Compare the letter of Arius, in
Theodoret, lib. i. c. v.

events in the annals of man. It might, indeed, have
been supposed that a profound metaphysical question of
this kind would have been far removed from the passions
of the multitude; but with the multitude, and that multitude often comprehends nearly the whole of society, it
is the passion which seeks the object, not the object
which, of its own exciting influence, inflames the passion.
In fact religion was become the one dominant passion of
the whole Christian world; and everything allied to it,
or rather, in this case, which seemed to concern its very
essence, could no longer be agitated with tranquillity,
or debated with indifference. The Pagan party, miscal-
culating the inherent strength of the Christian system,
saw, no doubt, in these disputes, the seeds of the destruction of Christianity. The contest was brought on the
stage at Alexandria; [e] but there was no Aristophanes,
or rather the serious and unpoetic time could not have
produced an Aristophanes, who might at once show that
he understood, while he broadly ridiculed, the follies of
his adversaries. The days even of a Lucian were past.[f]
Discord, which at times is fatal to a nation or to a sect,
seems at others, by the animating excitement of rivalry,
the stirring collision of hostile energy, to favour the
development of moral strength. The Christian republic,
like Rome when rent asunder by domestic factions,
calmly proceeded in her conquest of the world.

The plain and intelligible principle which united the
opponents of Arius was, no doubt, a vague, and, however
perhaps overstrained, neither ungenerous nor unnatural
jealousy, lest the dignity of the Redeemer, the object of
their grateful adoration, might in some way be lowered

---

[e] Euseb. Vit. Constant. ii. 61;
Socrates, i. 6.

[f] The Philopatris, of whatever age

it may be, is clearly not Lucian's;
and, at most, only slightly touches
these questions.

by the new hypothesis. The divinity of the Saviour seemed inseparably connected with his co-equality with the Father; it was endangered by the slightest concession on this point. It was their argument, that if the Son was not coeval in existence with the Father, he must have been created, and created out of that which was not pre-existent. But a created being must be liable to mutability; and it was asserted in the public address of the Patriarch of Alexandria, that this fatal consequence had been extorted from an unguarded Arian, if not from Arius himself,—that it was *possible* that the Son might have fallen, like the great rebellious angel.[g]

The patriarch of this important see, the metropolis of Egypt, was named Alexander. It was said that Arius, a presbyter of acute powers of reasoning, popular address, and blameless character, had declined that episcopal dignity.[h] The person of Arius[i] was tall and graceful; his countenance calm, pale, and subdued; his manners engaging; his conversation fluent and persuasive. He was well acquainted with human sciences; as a disputant subtle, ingenious, and fertile in resources. His enemies add to this character, which themselves have preserved, that this humble and mortified exterior concealed unmeasured ambition; that his simplicity, frankness, and honesty only veiled his craft

Alexander, Patriarch of Alexandria.

Arius.

---

[g] Epiphan. Hær. 69, tom. i. p. 723-727.

[h] See Philostorgius (the Arian writer). Theodoret, on the other hand, says, that he brought forward his opinions from envy at the promotion of Alexander, i. 2. See the Epistle of Alexander, in Socrat. Hist. Eccl. l. 6.

[i] Arius is said, in his early life, to have been implicated in the sect of the Meletians, which seems to have been rather a party than a sect. They were the followers of Meletius, Bishop of Lycopolis, who had been deposed for having sacrificed during the persecution. Yet this sect or party lasted for more than a century.

and love of intrigue; that he appeared to stand aloof
from all party, merely that he might guide his cabal
with more perfect command, and agitate and govern the
hearts of men.   Alexander was accustomed, whether for
the instruction of the people, or the display of his own
powers, to debate in public these solemn questions on
the nature of the Deity, and the relation of the Son and
the Holy Spirit to the Father.   According to the judgement of Arius, Alexander fell inadvertently into the
heresy of Sabellianism, and was guilty of confounding
in the simple unity of the Godhead the existence of the
Son and of the Holy Ghost.[k]

The intemperate indignation of Alexander at the
objections of Arius, betrayed more of the baffled disputant, or the wounded pride of the dignitary, than the
serenity of the philosopher, or the meekness of the
Christian.   He armed himself ere long in all the terrors
of his office, and promulgated his anathema in terms
full of exaggeration and violence.   " The impious Arius,
the forerunner of Antichrist, had dared to utter his blasphemies against the divine Redeemer."   Arius, expelled
from Alexandria, not indeed before his opinions had
spread through the whole of Egypt and Libya,[m] retired
to the more congenial atmosphere of Syria.[n]   There, his

---

[k] Socrates, i. 5, 6.

[m] The account of Sozomen says,
that Alexander at first vacillated, but
that he afterwards commanded Arius
to adopt his opinions: τὸν Ἄρειον
ὁμοίως φρονεῖν ἐκέλευσε. Sozomen
acknowledges the high character of
many of the Arian bishops; πλεισ-
τους ἀγαθοῦ βίου προσχήματι σεμ-
νοὺς, καὶ πιθανότητι λόγου δεινοὺς,
συλλαμβανομένους τοῖς ἀμφὶ τὸν
Ἄρειον.

[n] It was during his retreat that he
wrote his famous Thalia; the gay and
convivial title of which is singularly
out of keeping with the grave and
serious questions then in agitation.
His adversaries represent this as a
poem full of profane wit, and even of
indecency.   It was written in the
same measure, and to the same air,
with the Sotadic verses, which were
proverbial for their grossness even
among the Greeks.   It is difficult to

vague theory caught the less severely reasoning, and more imaginative minds of the Syrian bishops:° the lingering Orientalism prepared them for this kindred hypothesis. The most learned, the most pious, the most influential, united themselves to his party. The chief of these were the two prelates named Eusebius,—one the ecclesiastical historian, the other, bishop of the important city of Nicomedia. Throughout the East, the controversy was propagated with earnest rapidity. It was not repressed by the attempts of Licinius to interrupt the free intercourse between the Christian communities, and his prohibition of the ecclesiastical synods. The ill-smothered flame burst into tenfold fury on the re-union of the East to the empire of Constantine. The interference of the Emperor was loudly

---

reconcile this account of the Thalia with the subtle and politic character which his enemies attribute to Arius, still less to the protection of such men as Eusebius of Nicomedia, and the other Syrian prelates. Arius, likewise, composed hymns, in accordance with his opinions, to be chanted by sailors, those who worked at the mill, or travellers. Songs of this kind abounded in the Greek poetry: each art and trade had its song;[1] and Arius may have intended no more than to turn this popular practice in favour of Christianity, by substituting sacred for profane songs, which, of course, would be embued with his own opinions. Might not the Thalia have been written in the same vein, and something in the same spirit with which a celebrated modern humorist

and preacher adapted hymns to some of the most popular airs, and declared that the devil ought not to have all the best tunes? The general style of Arius is said to have been soft, effeminate, and popular. The specimen from the Thalia (in Athanas, Or. i. Cont. Ar. c. 5) is very loose and feeble Greek. Yet it is admitted that Arius was an expert dialectician; and no weak orator would have maintained such a contest so long.

° The bishops of Ptolemais, in the Pentapolis, and Theonas of Marmarica, joined his party. The females were inclined to his side. Seven hundred virgins of Alexandria, and of the Mareotic nome, owned him for their spiritual teacher. Compare the letter of Alexander in Theodoret. ch. iv.

---

[1] Ilgen, de Scoliorum Poesi, p. xiii

demanded to allay the strife which distracted the Christendom of the East. The behaviour of Constantine was regulated by the most perfect equanimity, or, more probably, guided by some counsellor of mild and more humane Christianity: his letter of peace was, in its spirit, a model of temper and conciliation.[p] With profound sorrow he had heard that his designs for the unity of the empire, achieved by his victory over Licinius, as well as for the unity of the faith, had been disturbed by this unexpected contest. His impartial rebuke condemned Alexander for unnecessarily agitating such frivolous and unimportant questions, and Arius for not suppressing, in prudent and respectful silence, his objections to the doctrine of the Patriarch. It recommended the judicious reserve of the philosophers, who had never debated such subjects before an ignorant and uneducated audience, and who differed without acrimony on such profound questions. He entreated them, by the unanimous suppression of all feelings of unhallowed animosity, to restore his cheerful days and undisturbed nights. Of the same faith, the same form of worship, they ought to meet in amicable synod, to adore their common God in peaceful harmony, and not fall into discord as to accuracy of expression on these most minute of questions; to enjoy and allow freedom in the sanctuary of their own minds, but to remain united in the common bonds of Christian love.[q]

It is probable that the hand of Hosius, bishop of

Letter of Constantine.

---

[p] See the letter in Euseb. Vit. Constant. ii. 64-72.

[q] Ἃ δ' ὑπὲρ τῶν ἐλαχίστων τούτων ζητήσεων ἐν ἀλλήλοις ἀκριβολογεῖσθε, κἂν μὴ πρὸς μίαν γνώμην συμφέρησθε, μένειν εἴσω λογισμοῦ προσήκει, τῷ τῆς διανοίας ἀπορρήτῳ τηρούμενοι. Euseb. Vit. Constant. ii. 71.

Cordova in Spain, is to be traced in that royal and Christian letter. The influence of Hosius was uniformly exercised in this manner. Wherever the edicts of the government were mild, conciliating, and humane, we find the Bishop of Cordova. It is by no means an improbable conjecture of Tillemont, that he was the Spaniard who afterwards, in the hour of mental agony and remorse, administered to the Emperor the balm of Christian penitence.

Hosius was sent to Egypt, as the imperial Commissioner, to assuage the animosity of the distracted church. But religious strife, in Egypt more particularly, its natural and prolific soil, refused to listen to the admonitions of Christian wisdom or imperial authority. Eusebius compares the fierce conflict of parties—bishops with bishops, people with people—to the collision of the Symplegades.[r] From the mouths of the Nile to the Cataracts, the divided population tumultuously disputed the nature of the divine unity.[s]

A general Council of the heads of the various Christian communities throughout the Roman empire was summoned by the imperial mandate, to establish, on the consentient authority of assembled Christendom, the true doctrine on these contested points, and to allay for ever this propensity to hostile disputation. The same paramount tribunal was to settle definitively another subordinate question, relating to the time of keeping the Easter festival. Many of the Eastern communities shocked their more scrupulous brethren by following the calculations, and observing the same sacred days with the impious

Council of Nice.

Controversy about keeping Easter.

---

[r] Vit. Const. iii 4.
[s] Ἔριδες ἐν ἑκάστῃ πόλει καὶ κώμῃ, καὶ μάχαι περὶ τῶν θείων δογμάτων ἐγίγνοντο. Theodoret. i. 6.

and abhorred Jews ; for the further we advance in the
Christian history, the estrangement of the Christians
from the Jews darkens more and more into absolute
antipathy.

In the month of May or June (the 20th [t]) in the year
325, met the great council of Nicæa. Not half
a century before, the Christian bishops even
in that city had been only marked as the objects of the
most cruel insult and persecution.   They had been
chosen, on account of their eminence in their own communities, as the peculiar victims of the stern policy of
the government.   They had been driven into exile, set
to work in the mines, exposed to every kind of humiliation and suffering, from which some had in mercy been
released by death.   They now assembled, under the
imperial sanction, a religious senate from all parts at
least of the eastern world ; for Italy was represented only
by two presbyters of Rome ; Hosius appeared for Spain,
Gaul, and Britain.   The spectacle was altogether new
to the world.   No wide-ruling sovereign would ever
have thought of summoning a conclave of the sacerdotal
orders of the different religions ; a synod of philosophers
to debate some grave metaphysical or even political
question was equally inconsistent with the ordinary
usages and sentiments of Grecian or Roman society.

The public establishment of post-horses was commanded to afford every facility, and that gratuitously,
for the journey of the assembling bishops.[u] Vehicles or
mules were to be provided, as though the assembly
were an affair of state, at the public charge.   At a
later period, when councils became more frequent, the

A.D. 325.

---

t ·One of these dates rests on the
authority of Socrates, xiii. 26 ; the
other on the Paschal Chronicle, p.

282. Compare Pagi, p. 404.
    u Euseb. Vit. Const. iii. 6 ; Theo-
doret. i. 7.

Heathen historian complains, that the public service was impeded, and the post-horses harassed and exhausted, by the incessant journeying to and fro of the Christian delegates to their councils.[v] They were sumptuously maintained during the sitting at the public charge.[x]

Above three hundred bishops were present, presbyters, deacons, acolyths without number,[y] a considerable body of laity: but it was the presence of the Emperor himself which gave its chief weight and dignity to the assembly. Nothing could so much confirm the Christians in the opinion of their altered position, or declare to the world at large the growing power of Christianity, as this avowed interest taken in their domestic concerns; or so tend to raise the importance attached even to the more remote and speculative doctrines of the new faith, as this unprecedented condescension, so it would seem to the Heathen, on the part of the Emperor. The Council met, probably, in a spacious basilica.[z] Eusebius describes the scene as himself deeply impressed with its solemnity. The assembly sate in profound silence; while the great officers of state and other dignified persons (there was no armed guard) entered the hall, and awaited in proud and trembling expectation the

Marginal notes: Number of bishops present. First meetings of the council.

---

[v] Amm. Marcellinus, xvi. 16. Read in Stanley's Eastern Church the gathering and the names and characters of the assembled bishops, p. 109, et seqq.

[x] Euseb. iii. 9.

[y] There was one bishop from Persia, one from Scythia. Eusebius states the number at 250; that in the text is on the authority of Theodoret, and of the numbers said to have signed the creed.

[z] There is a long note in Heinichen's Eusebius to prove that they did not meet in the palace, but in a church; as though the authority of their proceedings depended upon their place of assembly. It was probably a basilica, or hall of justice; the kind of building usually made over by the government for the purposes of Christian worship; and, in general, the model of the earliest Christian edifices.

appearance of the Emperor of the world in a Christian
council. Constantine at length entered; he was splen-
didly attired; the eyes of the bishops were dazzled by
the gold and precious stones upon his raiment. The
majesty of his person and the modest dignity of his demeanour heightened the effect: the whole assembly
rose to do him honour; he advanced to a low golden
seat prepared for him, and did not take his seat (it is
difficult not to suspect Eusebius of highly colouring the
deference of the Emperor), till a sign of permission had
been given by the bishops.[a] One of the leading prelates
(probably Eusebius the historian) commenced the proceedings with a short address, and a hymn to Almighty
God. Constantine then delivered an exhortation to
unity in the Latin language, which was interpreted
to the Greek bishops. His admonition seems at first to
have produced no great effect. Mutual accusation,
defence, and recrimination, prolonged the debate.[b]
Constantine seems to have been present during the greater part of the sittings, listening with
patience, softening asperities, countenancing those
whose language tended to peace and union, and conversing familiarly, in the best Greek he could command,
with the different prelates. The courtly flattery of the
council might attribute to Constantine himself what was
secretly suggested by the Bishop of Cordova. For
powerful and comprehensive as his mind may have
been, it is incredible that a man so educated, and engaged during the early period of his life with military

Behaviour of
Constantine.

---

[a] Οὐ πρότερον ἢ τοὺς ἐπισκόπους
ἐπινεῦσαι. See also Socrates, i. 8.
In Theodoret (i. 7), this has grown
into his humbly asking permission to
sit down.

[b] Constantine burned the libels
which the bishops had presented
against each other. Many of these
(the ecclesiastical historian intimates)
arose out of private animosities.
Socrates, i. 6.

and civil affairs, could have entered, particularly being imperfectly acquainted with the Greek language, into these discussions on religious metaphysics.

The Council sate for rather more than two months.[c] Towards the close, Constantine, on the occasion of the commencement of the twentieth year of his reign,[d] condescended to invite the bishops to a sumptuous banquet. All attended; and, as they passed through the imperial guard, treated with every mark of respect, they could not but call to mind the total revolution in their circumstances. Eusebius betrays his transport by the acknowledgment that they could scarcely believe that it was a reality, not a vision; to the grosser conception of those who had not purified their minds from the millennial notions, the banquet seemed the actual commencement of the kingdom of Christ.

The Nicene creed was the result of the solemn deliberation of the assembly. It was conceived with some degree of Oriental indefiniteness, harmonised with Grecian subtlety of expression. The vague and somewhat imaginative fulness of its original eastern terms was not too severely limited by the fine precision of its definitions. One fatal word broke the harmony of assent with which it was received by the whole council. Christ was declared Homoousios, of the same *substance* with the Father,[e] and the undeniable, if

Nicene creed.

---

[c] According to some, two months and eleven days, to others, two months and six days.

[d] This seems to reconcile the difficulty started by Heinichen. The 20th year of Constantine's reign began the 8th Cal. Aug. A.D. 325. Eusebius uses the inaccurate word ἐπληροῦτο. Vit. Const. iii. 14.

[e] Athanasius himself allowed that the bishops who deposed Paul of Samosata, were justified in rejecting the word ὁμοούσιον, because they understood it in a material or corporeal sense. But the privilege allowed to those who had died in orthodox reputation was denied to the Arians, and semi-Arians : de Synodis, Athannas. Oper. i. p. 759. It is impossible to read some pages of this trea-

perhaps inevitable, ambiguity of this single term, involved Christianity in centuries of hostility. To one party it implied absolute identity, and was therefore only ill-disguised Sabellianism; to the other it was essential to the co-equal and co-eval dignity of the three persons in the Godhead. To some of the Syrian bishops it implied or countenanced the material notion of the Deity.[r] It was, it is said by one ecclesiastical historian, a battle in the night, in which neither party could see the meaning of the other.[g]

Three hundred and eighteen bishops confirmed this creed by their signatures; five alone still contested the single expression, the Homoousion: Eusebius of Nicomedia, Theognis of Nicæa, Theonas of Marmarica, Maris of Chalcedon, and Eusebius of Cæsarea.

Five recusants.

---

tise without the unpleasant conviction, that Athanasius was determined to make out the Arians to be in the wrong.

[r] Μήτε γὰρ δύνασθαι τὴν αὔλον καὶ νοέραν καὶ ἀσώματον φύσιν, σωμάτικόν τι πάθος ὑφίστασθαι. This is the language of Eusebius.

Φασὶ δὲ ὅμως περὶ τούτου, ὡς ἄρα θέλων ὁ Θεὸς τὴν γεννητὴν κτίσαι φύσιν, ἐπειδὴ ἑώρα μὴ δυναμένην αὐτὴν μετασχεῖν τῆς τοῦ πατρὸς ἀκράτου, καὶ τῆς παρ' αὑτοῦ δημιουργίας, ποιεῖ καὶ κτίζει πρώτως μόνος μόνον ἕνα, καὶ καλεῖ τοῦτον υἱὸν καὶ λόγον. ἵνα τούτου μέσου γενομένου, οὕτως λοιπὸν καὶ τὰ πάντα δι' αὐτοῦ γενέσθαι δυνηθῇ. ταῦτα οὐ μόνον εἰρήκασιν, ἀλλὰ καὶ γράψαι τετολμήκασιν Εὐσέβιός τε, καὶ Ἄρειος καὶ ὁ θύσας Ἀστέριος. Athan. Orat. ii. c. 24. Compare Möhler (a learned and strongly orthodox Roman Catholic writer),

Athanasius der Grösse, b. i. p. 195. Möhler but dimly sees the Gnostic or Oriental origin of this notion, which lies at the bottom of Arianism.

[g] This remarkable sentence does credit to the judgement and impartiality of Socrates: Νυκτομαχίας δὲ οὐδὲν ἀπεῖχε τὰ γιγνομένα, οὐτὲ γάρ ἀλλήλους ἐφαίνοντο νοοῦντες, ἀφ' ὧν ἀλλήλους βλασφημεῖν ὑπελάμβανον· οἱ μὲν γὰρ τοῦ ὁμοουσίου τὴν λέξιν ἐκκλίνοντες τὴν Σαβελλίου καὶ Μοντανοῦ δόξαν εἰσηγεῖσθαι αὐτὴν τοὺς προσδεχομένους ἐνόμιζον· καὶ διὰ τοῦτο βλασφήμους ἐκάλουν, ὡς ἀναιροῦντες τὴν ὕπαρξιν τοῦ υἱοῦ τοῦ Θεοῦ· οἱ δὲ πάλιν τῷ ὁμοουσίῳ προσκείμενοι πολυθείαν εἰσάγειν τοὺς ἑτέρους νομίζοντες, ὡς Ἑλληνισμὸν εἰσαγόντας ἐξετράποντο. C. 23. Add to these, above all, the decisive words of Arius himself, quoted in Latin Christianity, i. 131.

Eusebius of Nicomedia and Theognis were banished.
Eusebius of Cæsarea, after much hesitation, consented
to subscribe; but sent the creed into his diocese with a
comment, explanatory of the sense in which he understood the contested word. His chief care was to guard
against giving the slightest countenance to the material
conception of the Deity. Two only withstood with uncompromising resistance the decree of the council. The
Banishment   solemn anathema of this Christian senate was
of Arius.   pronounced against Arius and his adherents;
they were banished by the civil power; and they were
especially interdicted from disturbing the peace of Alexandria by their presence.[h]

Peace might seem to be restored; the important
question set at rest by the united authority of the
Emperor, and a representative body which might fairly
presume to deliver the sentiments of the whole Christian
world. But the Arians were condemned, not convinced;
discomfited, not subdued.[i] Rather more than two years
elapsed, eventful in the private life of Constantine, but
tranquil in the history of the Christian church. The
imperial assessor in the Christian council had appeared
in the West under a different character, as the murderer
of his son and of his wife. He returned to the East,
determined no more to visit the imperial city of the
West; where, instead of the humble deference with which
all parties courted his approbation, he had been unable

---

[h] In one passage in the De Synodis,
Athanasius accused not only the Arian
but the semi-Arian party, Eusebius
as well as Arius, of something like
Socinianism.

'Ως ἔστιν υἱὸς ὅμοιος πάτρι, ἀλλὰ
διὰ τὴν συμφωνίαν δόγματων καὶ
τῆς διδασκαλίας. (p. 766, Athan.

Oper. 1.)

[i] The writings of Arius and his
followers were condemned to be burned.
If we are to believe Sozomen (which,
I confess, that I am disinclined to do),
the concealment of such heretical
works was made a capital offence!
E. H. Lib. i. c. 21.

to close his ears against the audacious and bitter pasquinade which arraigned his cruelty to his own family.
His return to the East, instead of overawing the contending factions into that unity, which he declared to be
the dearest wish of his heart, by his own sudden change
of conduct, was the signal for the revival of the fiercest
contentions.   The Christian community was Change in the
opinions of
now to pay a heavy penalty for the pride and Constantine.
triumph with which they had hailed the interference of
the Emperor in their religious questions.   The imperial
decisions had been admitted by the dominant party
when on their own side, to add weight to the decree of
the Council.   At least they had applauded the sentence
of banishment pronounced by the civil power against
their antagonists; that authority now assumed a different
tone, and was almost warranted, by their own admission,
in expecting the same prompt obedience.   The power
which had exiled, might restore the heretic to his place
and station.   Court influence, however obtained through
court intrigue, or from the caprice of the ruling sovereign, by this fatal, perhaps inevitable step, became the
arbiter of the most vital questions of Christian faith and
discipline; and thus the first precedent of a
temporal punishment for an ecclesiastical of-   A.D. 326, 336.
fence was a dark prognostic, and an example, of the
difficulties which would arise during the whole history
of Christianity, when the communities, so distinctly two
when they were separate and adverse, became one by the
identification of the Church and the State.   The restoration of a banished man to the privileges of a citizen by
the civil power, seemed to command his restoration to
religious privileges by the ecclesiastical authority.[k]

---

[k] Socr. i. 25, 26 ; Soz. ii. 27.

The Arian party gradually grew into favour. A presbyter of Arian sentiments had obtained complete command over the mind of Constantia, the sister of Constantine. On her dying bed she entreated the Emperor to reconsider the justice of the sentence against that innocent, as she declared, and misrepresented man. Arius could not believe the sudden reverse of fortune; and not till he received a pressing letter from Constantine himself, did he venture to leave his place of exile. A person of still greater importance was at the same time reinstated in the imperial favour.

Eusebius of Nicomedia. Among the adherents of the Arian form, perhaps the most important was Eusebius, Bishop of Nicomedia. A dangerous suspicion that he had been too closely connected with the interests of Licinius during the recent struggle for empire, had alienated the mind of Constantine, and deprived Eusebius of that respectful attention which he might have commanded by his station, ability, and experience. With A.D. 327. Theognis, Bishop of Nicæa, his faithful adherent in opinion and in fortune, he had been sent into exile; it is remarkable that the prelates of these two sees, the most important in that part of Asia, should have concurred in these views. The exiled prelates, in their petition for reinstatement in their dioceses, declared and (notwithstanding the charge of falsehood which their opponents to the present day do not scruple to make, would they have ventured in a public document addressed to Constantine to misstate a fact so notorious?) they solemnly protested that they had not refused their signatures to the Nicene creed, but only to the anathema pronounced against Arius and his followers. "Their obstinacy arose not from want of faith, but from excess of charity." They returned in triumph to their dioceses, and ejected the bishops who had been appointed in their place.   No resistance appears to have been made.

But the Arians were not content with their peaceable re-establishment in their former station.   However they might attempt to harmonise their doctrines with the belief of their adversaries, by their vindictive aggression on the opposite party, they belied their pretensions to moderation and the love of peace.   Eusebius, whom Constantine had before publicly denounced in no measured terms, grew rapidly into favour.   The complete dominion, which from this time he appears to have exercised over the mind of Constantine, confirms the natural suspicion that the opinions of the Emperor were by no means formed by his own independent judgment, but entirely governed by the Christian teacher who might obtain his favour.   Eusebius seems to have succeeded to the influence exercised with so much wisdom and temper by Hosius of Cordova.   He became Bishop of Constantinople, and was the companion of Constantine in his visits to Jerusalem;[m] and the high estimation in which the Emperor held also Eusebius of Cæsarea, according to the statements made, and the documents ostentatiously preserved by that writer in his ecclesiastical history, could not but contribute to the growing ascendancy of Arianism.   They were in possession of some of the most important dioceses in Asia; they were ambitious of establishing their supremacy in Antioch.

The suspicious brevity with which Eusebius glides over the early part of this transaction, which his personal vanity could not allow him to omit, confirms the state-

---

[m] Theodoret. i. 2.

ment of their adversaries, as to the unjustifiable means
employed by the Arians to attain this object.
Eusebius of Nicomedia and Theognis passed
through Antioch on their way to Jerusalem.
On their return, they summoned Eustathius, the
Bishop of Antioch, whose character had hitherto been
blameless, to answer before a hastily assembled council
of bishops, on two distinct charges of immorality and
heresy. The unseemly practice of* bringing forward
women of disreputable character to charge men of high
station in the church with incontinency, formerly employed by the Heathens to calumniate the Christians,
was now adopted by the reckless hostility of Christian
faction. The accusation of a prostitute against Eustathius, of having been the father of her child, is said
afterwards to have been completely disproved. The
heresy with which Eustathius was charged, was that of
Sabellianism, the usual imputation of the Arians against
the Trinitarians of the opposite creed. Two Arian
bishops having occupied the see of Antioch, but for a
very short time, an attempt was made to remove Eusebius of Cæsarea to that diocese, no doubt to overawe by
the high reputation of his talents, or to conciliate the
Eustathian party. Eusebius, with the flattering approbation of the Emperor, declined the dangerous post.
Eustathius was deposed, and banished, by the imperial
edict, to Thrace; but the attachment, at least of a large
part, of the Christian population of Antioch refused to
acknowledge the authority of the tribunal, or the justice
of the sentence. The city was divided into two fierce
and hostile factions—they were on the verge of civil war;
and Antioch, where the Christians had first formed
themselves into a separate community, but for the
vigorous interference of the civil power and the timely

appearance of an imperial commissioner, might have witnessed the first blood shed, at least in the East, in a Christian quarrel.

It is impossible to calculate how far the authority and influence of the Syrian bishops, with the avowed countenance of the Emperor (for Constantius, the son of Constantine, was an adherent of the Arian opinions), might have subdued the zeal of the orthodox party. It is possible that, but for the rise of one inflexible and indomitable antagonist, the question might either have sunk to rest, or the Christian world acquiesced, at least the East, in a vague and mitigated Arianism.

Athanasius had been raised by the discernment of Alexander to a station of confidence and dignity. He had filled the office of secretary to the Alexandrian prelate.   In the Council of Nicæa he had borne a distinguished part, and his zeal and talents designated him at once as the head of the Trinitarian party.   On the death of Alexander, the universal voice of the predominant anti-Arians demanded the elevation of Athanasius.   In vain he attempted to conceal himself, and to escape the dangerous honour.   At thirty years of age, Athanasius was placed on the episcopal throne of the see, which ranked with Antioch, and afterwards with Constantinople, as the most important spiritual charge in the East.[n]

The imperial mandate was issued to receive Arius and his followers within the pale of the Christian communion.[o]   But Constantine found, to his astonishment, that an imperial edict, which would have been obeyed

Athanasius.

A.D. 326.

---

[n] The Arians asserted this election to have been carried by the irregular violence of a few bishops, contrary to the declared suffrages of the majority.

[o] Athanas. Apol. contra Ar. Soz. ii. 22.

in trembling submission from one end of the Roman
empire to the other, even if it had enacted a complete
political revolution, or endangered the property and
privileges of thousands, was received with deliberate and
steady disregard by a single Christian bishop. During
two reigns, Athanasius contested the authority of the
Emperor. He endured persecution, calumny, exile; his
life was frequently endangered in defence of one single
tenet; and that, it may be permitted to say, the most
purely intellectual, and apparently the most remote from
Charges   the ordinary passions of man: he confronted
against
Athanasius. martyrdom, not for the broad and palpable
distinction between Christianity and Heathenism, but
for fine and subtle expressions of the Christian creed.[p]
He began and continued the contest not for the toleration, but for the supremacy, of his own opinions.

Neither party, in truth, could now yield without the
humiliating acknowledgment that all their contest had
been on unimportant and unessential points. The
passions and the interests, as well as the conscience,
were committed in the strife. The severe and uncompromising temper of Athanasius, no doubt, gave some
advantage to his jealous and watchful antagonists.
Criminal charges began to multiply against a prelate
who was thus fallen in the imperial favour.[q] They

---

[p] I am not persuaded, either by
the powerful eloquence of Athanasius
himself, or by his able modern apologist, Möhler, that the opinions, at
least, of the Syrian semi-Arians, were
so utterly irreconcileable with the
orthodoxy of Athanasius, or likely to
produce such fatal consequences to the
general system of Christianity as are
extorted from them by the keen theo-

logical precision of Athanasius.

[q] Theodoret mentions one of these
customary charges of licentiousness,
in which a woman of bad character
accused Athanasius of violating her
chastity. Athanasius was silent; while
one of his friends, with assumed indignation demanded, " Do you accuse
me of this crime?" " Yes," replied
the woman, supposing him to be

were assiduously instilled into the ears of Constantine;
yet the extreme frivolousness of some of these accusations, and the triumphant refutation of the more
material charges, before a tribunal of his enemies,
establish, undeniably, the unblemished virtue of Athanasius.[r] He was charged with taxing the city to provide
linen vestments for the clergy; and with treasonable
correspondence with an enemy of the Emperor. Upon
this accusation he was summoned to Nicomedia, and
acquitted by the Emperor himself. He was charged, as
having authorised the profanation of the holy vessels,
and the sacred books, in a church in the Mareotis, a
part of his diocese. A certain Ischyras had assumed the
office of presbyter, without ordination. Macarius, who
was sent by Athanasius to prohibit his officiating in his
usurped dignity, was accused 'by Ischyras of overthrow-
ing the altar, breaking the cup, and burning the
Scriptures. It is not impossible that the indiscreet
zeal of an inferior may have thought it right to destroy
sacred vessels thus profaned by unhallowed hands. But
from Athanasius himself the charge recoiled without the
least injury. But a darker charge remained behind—
comprehending two crimes, probably in those days

Athanasius, of whose person she was
ignorant, "*you* were the violator of
my chastity." L. i. c. 30.

[r] It is remarkable, how little stress
is laid on the persecutions which
Athanasius is accused of having carried on through the civil authority.
Accusatus præterea est de injuriis,
violentiâ, cæde, atque ipsâ episcoporum
internecione. Quique etiam diebus
sacratissimis paschæ tyrannico more
sæviens, Ducibus atque Comitibus
junctus: quique propter ipsam aliquos

in custodiâ recludebant, aliquos vero
verberibus   flagellisque   vexabant,
cæteros diversis tormentis ad com-
munionem ejus sacrilegam adigebant.
These charges neither seem to have
been pressed nor refuted, as half so
important as the act of sacrilege. See
the protest of the Arian bishops at
Sardica, in Hilarii Oper. Hist. Fragm.
iii. c. 6. See also the accusations of
violence on his return to Alexandria.
Ibid. 8.

looked upon with equal abhorrence—magic and murder.
The enemies of Athanasius produced a human hand said
to be that of Arsenius, a bishop attached to the Meletian
heresy, who had disappeared from Egypt in a suspicious
manner. The hand of the murdered bishop had been
kept by Athanasius for unhallowed purposes of witch-
craft. In vain the emissaries of Athanasius sought for
Arsenius in Egypt, though he was known to be concealed in that country; but the superior and one of the
monks of a monastery were seized, and compelled to
confess that he was still living, and had lain hid in their
sanctuary. Yet the charge was not abandoned: it
impended for more than two years over the head of
Athanasius.

A council, chiefly formed of the enemies of Athanasius, was summoned at Tyre. It was intimated to the
Alexandrian prelate, that, if he refused to appear before
the tribunal, he would be brought by force. Athana-
Synod of sius stood before the tribunal. He was arraigned
Tyre.
A.D. 335. on this charge; the hand was produced. To
the astonishment of the court, Athanasius calmly demanded whether those present were acquainted with
the person of Arsenius? He had been well known to
many. A man was suddenly brought into the court with
his whole person folded in his mantle. Athanasius un-
covered the head of the witness. He was at once recognised as the murdered Arsenius. Still the severed hand
lay before them, and the adversaries of Athanasius
expected to convict him of having mutilated the victim
of his jealousy. Athanasius lifted up the mantle on one
side, and showed the right hand; he lifted up the other,
and showed the left. In a calm tone of sarcasm he
observed, that the Creator had bestowed two hands on
man; it was for his enemies to explain how Arsenius

had possessed a third.[s]   A fortunate accident had
brought Arsenius to Tyre; he had been discovered by
the friends of Athanasius.   Though he denied his name,
he was known by the bishop of Tyre; and this dramatic
scene had been arranged as the most effective means of
exposing the malice of the prelate's enemies.   His discomfited accusers fled in the confusion.

The implacable enemies of Athanasius were constrained to fall back upon the other exploded charge, the
profanation of the sacred vessels by Macarius.   A commission of inquiry had been issued, who conducted
themselves, according to the statement of the friends of
Athanasius, with the utmost violence and partiality.
On their report, the bishop of the important city of
Alexandria was deposed from his dignity.   But Athanasius bowed not beneath the storm.   He appears to have
been a master in what may be called, without disrespect,
theatrical effect.   As the Emperor rode through Athanasius
in Constan-
the city of Constantinople, he was arrested by tinople.
the sudden appearance of a train of ecclesiastics, in the
midst of which was Athanasius.   The offended Emperor, with a look of silent contempt, urged his horse
onward.   "God," said the prelate, with a loud voice,
"shall judge between thee and me, since thou thus
espousest the cause of my calumniators.   I demand only
that my enemies be summoned and my cause heard in
the imperial presence."   The Emperor admitted the
justice of his petition; the accusers of Athanasius were
commanded to appear in Constantinople.   Six of them,
including the two Eusebii, obeyed the mandate.

But a new charge, on a subject skilfully chosen to
awaken the jealousy of the Emperor, counteracted the

---

[s] Theodoret, i. 30,

influence which might have been obtained by the elo-
New accusa- quence or the guiltlessness of Athanasius. It
tions.   is remarkable that an accusation of a very
similar nature should have caused the capital punishment
of the most distinguished among the Heathen philosophic
party, and the exile of the most eminent Christian prelate. Constantinople entirely depended for the supply
of corn upon foreign importation. One-half of Africa,
including Egypt, was assigned to the maintenance of
the new capital, while the Western division alone re-
Death of   mained for Rome. At some period during the
Sopater the
philosopher. later years of Constantine, the adverse winds
detained the Alexandrian fleet, and famine began to
afflict the inhabitants of the city. The populace was in
tumult; the government looked anxiously for means to
allay the dangerous ferment. The Christian party had
seen with jealousy and alarm the influence which a
Heathen philosopher, named Sopater, had obtained over
the mind of Constantine.[t] Sopater was a native of
Apamea, the scholar of Iamblichus. The Emperor took
great delight in his society, and was thus in danger of
being perverted, if not to Heathenism, to that high
Platonic indifferentism, which would leave the two
religions on terms of perfect equality. Sopater was
seen seated on public occasions by the Emperor's side;
and boasted, it was said, that the dissolution of Heathen-

---

[t] Zosimus, ii. 40 ; Sozom. 1-5;
Eunap. in Ædes. p. 24-25 ; edit.
Boissonade. Suidas, voc. Σώπατρος.
If we are to believe Eunapius, the
Christians might reasonably take
alarm at the intimacy of Constantine
with Sopater : ὁ μὲν βασιλεὺς ἑαλώκει
τε ὑπ' αὐτῷ καὶ δημοσίᾳ σύνεδρον
εἶχεν, εἰς τὸν δεξιὸν καθίζων τοπὸν.
ὃ καὶ ακοῦσαι καὶ ἰδεῖν ἄπιστον· οἱ
δὲ παραδυναστεύοντες (the Christians, a remarkable admission of their
influence !) ῥηγνύμενοι τῷ φθόνῳ
πρὸς βασιλείαν ἄρτι φιλοσοφεῖν
μετἀμανθάνουσαν. p. 21.

ism would be arrested by his authority. During the famine the Emperor entered the theatre; instead of the usual acclamations, he was received with a dull and melancholy silence. The enemies of Sopater seized the opportunity of accusing the philosopher of magic: his unlawful arts had bound the winds in the adverse quarter. If the Emperor did not, the populace would readily, believe him to be the cause of all their calamities. He was sacrificed to the popularity of the Emperor; the order for his decapitation was hastily issued, and promptly executed.

In the same spirit which caused the death of the Heathen philosopher, Athanasius was accused of threatening to force the Emperor to his own measures, by stopping the supplies of corn from the port of Alexandria. Constantine listened with jealous credulity to the charge. The danger of leaving the power of starving the capital in the hands of one who might become hostile to the government, touched the pride A.D. 336. of the Emperor in the tenderest point. Atha- Banishment nasius was banished to the remote city of of Athanasius Treves.

But neither the exile of Athanasiûs, nor the unqualified—his enemies of course asserted insincere or hypocritical—acceptance of the Nicene creed by Arius himself, allayed the differences. The presence of Arius in Alexandria had been the cause of new dissensions. He was recalled to Constantinople, where a Arius in Constantinople. council had been held, in which the Arian stantinople. party maintained and abused their predominance. But Alexander, the Bishop of. Constantinople, still firmly resisted the reception of Arius into the orthodox communion. Affairs were hastening to a crisis. The Arians, with the authority of the Emperor on their side, threat-

ened to force their way into the church, and to compel
the admission of their champion. The Catholics, the
weaker party, had recourse to prayer ; the Arians already
raised the voice of triumph. While Alexander was prostrate at the altar, Arius was borne through the wondering
city in a kind of ovation, surrounded by his friends, and
welcomed with loud acclamations by his own party.
As he passed the porphyry column, he was forced to
retire into a house to relieve his natural wants. His
Death of
Arius. return was anxiously expected, but in vain ; he
was found dead, as his antagonists declared,
his bowels had burst out, and relieved the church from
the presence of the obstinate heretic. We cannot wonder
that, at such a period of excitement, the Catholics, in
that well-timed incident, recognised a direct providential
interference in their favour. It was ascribed to the
prevailing prayers of Alexander and his clergy. Under
the specious pretext of a thanksgiving for the deliverance
of the church from the imminent peril of external violence, the Bishop prepared a solemn service. Athanasius, in a public epistle, alludes to the fate of Judas,
which had befallen the traitor to the coequal dignity of
the Son. His hollow charity ill disguises his secret
triumph.[u]

Whatever effect the death of Arius might produce
upon the mind of Constantine, it caused no mitigation
in his unfavourable opinion of Athanasius. He contemptuously rejected the petitions which were sent from
Alexandria to solicit his re-instatement ; he refused to

---

[u] It was a standing argument of
Athanasius, that the death of Arius
was a sufficient refutation of his
heresy.

Εἰς γὰρ τελείαν κατάγνωσιν τῆς

αἱρέσεως τῶν Ἀρειανῶν, αὐτάρκης
ἢ περὶ τοῦ θανάτου Ἀρείου γενο-
μένη παρὰ τοῦ κυρίου κρίσις. Ded.
Epist. ad Monachos, 3. Op. v. i.
344.

recall that " proud, turbulent, obstinate, and intractable,"
prelate.   It was not till he was on his death-bed that
his consent was hardly extorted for this act of mercy,
or rather of justice.

The Baptism of Constantine on his death-bed is one
of those questions which has involved ecclesias- Baptism of
tical historians in inextricable embarrassment. Constantine.
The fact is indisputable, it rests on the united authority
of the Greek and Latin writers.   Though he had so
openly espoused the cause of Christianity—though he
had involved himself so deeply in the interests of the
Christian community, attended on their worship, presided,[x] or at least sanctioned their councils with his
presence, and had been constantly surrounded by the
Christian clergy, the Emperor had still deferred till the
very close of his life his formal reception into the Christian church, the ablution of his sins, the admission to
the privileges and hopes of the Christian, by that indis-
pensable rite of Baptism.[y]   There seems but one plain
solution of this difficulty.   The Emperor constantly
maintained a kind of superiority over the Christian part

---

[x] If we are to believe Eusebius, he
was a preacher of Christianity—a
preacher on some of its most profound
and mysterious doctrines.   I cannot
help suspecting that the Bishop has
transferred some of his own sermons
to the Emperor. V. C. iv. 29. Compare Stanley, p. 233.

[y] Mosheim's observations on the
Christianity of Constantine are characterised by his usual good sense and
judgment.   De rebus Christ. antè
Const. Magnum. p. 965.   I extract
only a few sentences.   "Erat primis
post victum Maxentium annis in animo
ejus cum omnis religionis, tum Christianæ imprimis, parum sana et propius
à Græcorum et Romanorum opinione
remota notio.   Nescius enim salutis
et beneficiorum à Christo humano
generi partorum, Christum Deum esse
putabat, qui cultorum suorum fidem
et diligentiam felicitate hujus vitæ,
rebusque secundis comparare, hostes
vero et contemptores mox pœnis,
malisque omnis generis afficere potuit.
. . . . Ita sensim de vera religionis
Christianæ indole . . . . edoctus stul-
titiam et deformitatem antiquarum
superstitionum clarius perspiciebat, et
Christo uni sincere nomen dabat." p.
977, 978.

of his subjects.   It was still rather the lofty and impartial condescension of a protector, than the spiritual equality of the proselyte.   He still asserted, and in many cases exercised, the privilege of that high indifferentism, which ruled his conduct by his own will or judgement, rather than by the precepts of a severe and definite religion.   He was reluctant, though generally convinced of the truth, and disposed to recognise the superiority of the Christian religion, to commit himself by the irrevocable act of initiation.   He may have been still more unwilling to sever himself entirely from the Heathen majority of his subjects, lest by such a step, in some sudden yet always possible crisis, he might shake their allegiance.   In short, he would not surrender any part of his dignity as Emperor of the world, especially as he might suppose that, even if necessary to his salvation as a Christian, he could command at any time the advantages of baptism.   On the other hand, the Christians, then far more pliant than when their undisputed authority ruled the minds of monarchs with absolute sway, hardly emerged from persecution, struggling for a still contested supremacy, divided among themselves, and each section courting the favour of the Emperor, were glad to obtain an imperial convert on his own terms.   In constant hope that the Emperor himself would take this decisive step, they were too prudent or too cautious to urge it with imperious or unnecessary vehemence.   He was not so entirely their own, but that he might still be estranged by indiscretion or intemperance; he would gradually become more enlightened, and they were content to wait in humble patience till Providence, who had raised up this powerful protector, should render him fully, and exclusively, and openly, their own.

A.D. 337.

If it be difficult to determine the extent to which Constantine proceeded in the establishment of Christianity, it is even more perplexing to estimate how far he exerted the imperial authority in the abolition of Paganism. Conflicting evidence encounters us at every point. Eusebius, in three distinct passages in his 'Life of Constantine,' asserts that he prohibited sacrifice;[z] that he issued two laws to prohibit, both in the city and in the country, the pollutions of the old idolatry, the setting up of statues, divinations, and other unlawful practices; and to command the total abolition of sacrifice;[a] that throughout the Roman empire the "doors of idolatry" were closed to the people and to the army, and every kind of sacrifice was prohibited.[b] Theodoret asserts[c] that Constantine prohibited sacrifice, and, though he did not destroy, shut up all the temples. In a passage of his Panegyric,[d] Eusebius asserts that the Emperor sent two officers into every part of the empire, who forced the priests to surrender up the statues of their gods, which, having been despoiled of their ornaments, were melted or destroyed. These strong assertions of Eusebius are, to a certain extent, confirmed by expressions in the laws of Constantine's successors, especially one of Constans, which

Extent to which Paganism was suppressed.

---

[z] Θύειν ἀπείρητο, ii. 44.

[a] Δύο κατὰ τὸ αὐτὸ ἐπέμποντο νόμοι· ὁ μὲν εἴργων τὰ μυσαρὰ τῆς κατὰ πόλεις καὶ χώρας τὸ παλαιὸν συντελουμένης εἰδωλολατρίας, ὡς μήτε ἐγέρσεις ξοάνων ποιεῖσθαι τολμᾶν, μήτε μαντείαις καὶ ταῖς ἄλλαις περιεργίαις ἐπιχειρεῖν, μήτε μὴν θύειν καθόλου μηδένα. ii. 45.

[b] Καθόλου, δε τοῖς ὑπὸ τῇ Ῥω-

μαίων ἀρχῇ δήμοις τε καὶ στρατιωτικοῖς, πύλαι ἀπεκλείοντο εἰδωλολατρίας, θυσίας τε τρόπος ἀπηγορεύετο πᾶς. iv. 23. διεκωλύετο μὲν θύειν εἰδώλοις. ibid. 25. δήμοις may mean the magistracy, the public ceremonial.

[c] Theodoret, vi. 21. Compare Sozomen, iii. 17; Orosius, vii. 28.

[d] De Laudib. Constant. i. 8.

appeals to an edict of his father Constantine, which prohibited sacrifice.[e]

On the other hand, Eusebius himself inserts, and ascribes to a date posterior to some of these laws, documents, which he professes to have seen in Constantine's own hand, proclaiming the most impartial toleration to the Pagans, and deprecating compulsion in religious matters. "Let all enjoy the same peace; let no one disturb another in his religious worship; let each act as he thinks fit; let those who withhold their obedience from Thee (it is an address to the Deity), have their temples of falsehood if they think right."[f] He exhorts to mutual charity, and declares, "It is a very different thing willingly to submit to trials for the sake of immortal life, and to force others by penalties to embrace one faith."[g] These generous sentiments, if Constantine were issuing edicts to close the temples, and prohibiting the sacred rites of his Pagan subjects, had been the grossest hypocrisy. The laws against the soothsayers spoke, as was before shown, the same tolerant language with regard to the public ceremony of the religion.[h]

---

[e] "Cesset superstitio, sacrificiorum aboleatur insania. Nam quicunque contra legem divi Principis, parentis nostri, et hanc nostræ mansuetudinis jussionem ausus fuerit sacrificia celebrare, competens in eum vindicta, et præsens sententia exseratur." Cod. Theodos. xvi. 10. 2. See likewise the note of Godefroy.

[f] 'Ομοίαν τοῖς πιστεύουσιν οἱ πλανώμενοι χαίροντες λαμβανέτωσαν εἰρήνης τε καὶ ἡσυχίας ἀπόλαυσιν . . . . Μηδεὶς τὸν ἕτερον παρετω· νοχλεί ἕκαστος ὅπερ ἡ ψυχὴ

βούλεται τοῦτο καὶ πραττέτω . . . Οἱ δ' ἑαυτοὺς ἀφέλκοντες, ἐχόντων βουλόμενοι τὰ τῆς ψευδολογίας τεμένη. Vit. Const. ii. 26.

[g] Ἄλλο γάρ ἐστι, τὸν ὑπὲρ ἀθανασίας ἆθλον ἑκουσίως ἐπαναιρεῖσθαι, ἄλλο τὸ μετὰ τιμωρίας ἐπαναγκάζειν. c. 60.

[h] "Qui vero id vobis existimatis conducere, adite aras publicas atque delubra et consuetudinis vestræ celebrate solemnia; nec enim prohibemus præteritæ usurpationis officia libera luce tractari." Cod. Theodos. xvi. 10

Can the victory over Licinius so entirely have changed the policy of Constantine, as to have induced him to prohibit altogether rites, which but a few years before he had sanctioned by his authority?

The Pagan writers, who are not scrupulous in their charges against the memory of Constantine, and dwell with bitter resentment on all his overt acts of hostility to the ancient religion, do not accuse him of these direct encroachments on Paganism. Neither Julian nor Zosimus lay this to his charge. Libanius distinctly asserts that the temples were left open and undisturbed during his reign, and that Paganism remained unchanged.[i]

All historical records strongly confirm the opinion that Paganism was openly professed; its temples restored;[k] its rites celebrated; neither was its priesthood degraded from their immunities, nor the estates belonging to the temples generally alienated; in short, that it was the public religion of a great part of the empire; and still confronted Christianity, if not on equal terms, still with pertinacious resistance, down to the reign of Theodosius, and even that of his sons. Constantine himself, though he neither offered sacrifices, nor consulted the Sibylline books, nor would go up to the temple of the Capitoline Jupiter with the senate and the people,

---

[i] Τῆς κατὰ νόμου δὲ θεραπείας ἐκίνησεν οὐδὲ ἕν. Pro Templis, vol. ii. p. 162.

Libanius adds that Constantius, on a certain change of circumstances, *first* prohibited sacrifice. Compare also Orat. 26. Julian Orat. vii. p. 424.

[k] See, in Gruter, p. 100. n. 6, the inscription on the restoration of the Temple of Concord, during the consulship of Paulinus (A. C. 331, 332), by

the authority of the præfect of the city, and S. P. Q. R. Altars were erected to other Pagan gods. Compare Beugnot, i. 106.

M. Beugnot, in his Destruction du Paganisme en Occident, has collected with great industry the proofs of this fact, from inscriptions, medals, and other of the more minute contemporary memorials.

2 c 2

performed, nevertheless, some of the functions, at least
did not disdain the appellation, of Supreme Pontiff.[1]

Perhaps we may safely adopt the following conclusions.
There were two kinds of sacrifices abolished by Constantine. I. The private sacrifices, connected with unlawful
acts of theurgy and of magic; those midnight offerings
to the powers of darkness, which, in themselves, were
illegal, and led to scenes of unhallowed licence.[m] II.
Those which might be considered the · state sacrifices
offered by the Emperor himself, or by his representatives
in his name, either in the cities or in the army. Though
Constantine advanced many Christians to offices of trust,
and no doubt many who were ambitious of such offices
conformed to the religion of the Emperor, probably most
of the high dignities of the state were held by Pagans.
An edict might be required to induce them to depart
from the customary usage of sacrifice, which with the
Christian officers would quietly fall into desuetude.[n]
But still, the sacrifices made by the priesthood, at the
expense of the sacerdotal establishments, and out of
their own estates—though in some instances these

---

[1] There is a medal extant of Constantine as Supreme Pontiff.

[m] See the laws relating to divination, above, p. 292.

M. la Bastie and M. Beugnot, would
consider the terms τὰ μυσαρὰ τῆς
εἰδωλολατρίας, in the rescript of
Constantine, and the " insana superstitio " of the law of Constans, to
refer exclusively to these nocturnal
and forbidden sacrifices. M. Beugnot
has observed, that Constantine always
uses respectful and courteous language
concerning Paganism. Vetus obser-
vantia, vetus consuetudo; templorum

solemnia; consuetudinis gentilitiæ
solemnitas. The laws of the later
emperors employ very different terms.
Error; dementia; error veterum;
profanus ritus; sacrilegus ritus;
nefarius ritus; superstitio Pagana,
damnabilis, damnata, deterrima, impia;
funestæ superstitionis errores; stolidus
Paganorum error. Cod. Theodos.
t. v. p. 255. Beugnot, tom. i. p. 80.

[n] The prohibition to the δῆμοι and
στρατιωτικοὶ (see quotation above
from Eusebius) refers, I conceive, to
these.

estates were seized by Constantine, and the sacerdotal colleges reduced to poverty—and the *public* sacrifices, offered by the piety of distinguished individuals, would be made as usual. In the capital there can be little doubt that sacrifices were offered, in the name of the senate and people of Rome, till a much later period.

Christianity may now be said to have ascended the imperial throne : with the single exception of Julian, from this period the monarchs of the Roman empire professed the religion of the Gospel. *Legal establishment of Christianity.* This important crisis in the history of Christianity almost forcibly arrests the attention to contemplate the change wrought in Christianity by its advancement into a dominant power in the state ; and the change in the condition of mankind up to this period, attributable to the direct authority or indirect influence of the new religion. By ceasing to exist as a separate *Effects of this on the religion.* community, and by advancing its pretensions to influence the general government of mankind, Christianity, to a certain extent, forfeited its independence. It could not but submit to these laws, framed, as it might seem, with its own concurrent voice. It was no longer a republic, governed exclusively—as far at least as its religious concerns—by its own internal polity. The interference of the civil power in some of its most private affairs, the promulgation of its canons, and even in some cases the election of its bishops, by the state, was the price which it must inevitably pay for its association with the ruling power. The natural satisfaction, the more than pardonable triumph, in seeing the Emperor of the world a suppliant with themselves at the foot of the cross, would blind the Christian world, in general, to these consequences of their more exalted position. The more ardent and unworldly would fondly suppose that a Christian emperor would always be actuated by Christian motives, and that the imperial authority, instead of making aggressions on Christian independence, would rather bow in humble submission to its acknowledged dominion. His main object would be to develope the energies of the new religion in the amplest freedom, and allow them full scope in the subjugation of the world.

The Emperor as little anticipated that he was introducing as an antagonistic power, an inextinguishable principle of liberty, into the administration of human affairs. This liberty was based on deeper foundations than the hereditary freedom of the ancient republics. It appealed to a tribunal higher than any which could exist upon earth. This antagonistic principle of independence, however, at times apparently crushed, and submitting to voluntary slavery, or even lending itself to be the instrument of arbitrary despotism, was inherent in the new religion, and would not cease till it had asserted and, for a considerable period, exercised an authority superior to that of the civil government. Already in Athanasius might be seen the one subject of Constantine who dared to resist his will. From Athanasius, who owned himself a subject, but with inflexible adherence to his own opinions, to Ambrose, who rebuked the great Theodosius, and from Ambrose up to the Pope who set his foot on the neck of the prostrate Emperor, the progress was slow, but natural and certain. In this profound prostration of the human mind and the total extinction of the old sentiments of Roman liberty, in the adumbration of the world by what assumed the pomp and the language of an Asiatic despotism, it is impossible to calculate the latent as well as open effect of this moral resistance. In Constantinople, indeed, and in the East, the clergy never ob-

On the civil power.

tained sufficient power to be formidable to the civil
authority; their feuds too often brought them in a sort
of moral servitude to the foot of the throne; still the
Christian, and the Christian alone, throughout this long
period of human degradation breathed an atmosphere of
moral freedom, which raised him above the general level
of servile debasement.

During the reign of Constantine, Christianity had
made a rapid advance, no doubt in the number How far the
of its proselytes, as well as in its external religion of
the empire.
position. It was not yet the established religion of the
empire. It did not as yet stand forward as the new
religion adapted to the new order of things, as a part of
the great simultaneous change, which gave to the Roman
world a new capital, a new system of government, and,
in some important instances, a new jurisprudence. Yet
having sprung up at once, under the royal favour, to a
perfect equality with the prevailing Heathenism, the
mere manifestation of that favour, where the antagonistic
religion hung so loose upon the minds of men, gave it
much of the power and authority of a dominant faith.
The religion of the Emperor would soon become that of
the court; and, by somewhat slower degrees, that of the
empire. At present, however, as we have seen, little
open aggression took place upon Paganism. The few
temples which were closed were insulated cases, and
condemned as offensive to public morality. In general,
the edifices stood in all their former majesty; for as yet
the ordinary process of dissolution, from neglect or decay,
could have produced little effect. The difference was,
that the Christian churches began to assume a more
stately and imposing form. In the new capital, they
surpassed in grandeur, and probably in decoration, the

Pagan temples which belonged to old Byzantium. The immunities granted to the Christian clergy only placed them on the same level with the Pagan priesthood. The pontifical offices were still held by the distinguished men of the state: the Emperor himself was long the chief pontiff; but the religious office had become a kind of appendage to the temporal dignity. The Christian prelates were constantly admitted, in virtue of their office, to the imperial presence.

On the state of society at large, on its different forms and gradations, little impression had as yet been made by Christianity. The Christians were still a separate people; Christian literature was exclusively religious, and addressed, excepting in its apologies, or its published exhortations against Paganism, to the initiate alone. Its language would be unintelligible to those uninstructed in Christian theology. Yet the general legislation of Constantine, independent of those edicts which concerned the Christian community, bears some evidence of the silent underworking of Christian opinion. The rescript, indeed, for the religious observance of the Sunday, which enjoined the suspension of all public business and private labour, except that of agriculture, was enacted, according to the apparent terms of the decree, for the whole Roman empire. Yet, unless we had direct proof, that the decree set forth the Christian reason for the sanctity of the day, it may be doubted whether the act would not be received by the greater part of the empire, as merely adding one more festival to the Fasti of the empire, as proceeding entirely from the will of the Emperor, or even grounded on his authority as Supreme Pontiff, by which he had the plenary

Effect of legal establishment of Christianity on society.

Laws relating to Sundays.

power of appointing holy-days.[c]   In fact, as we have
before observed, the day of the Sun would be willingly
hallowed by almost all the Pagan world, especially that
part which had admitted any tendency towards the
Oriental theology.

Where the legislation of Constantine was of a humaner
cast, it would be unjust not to admit the influ- Laws tending
to humanity.
ence of Christian opinions, spreading even
beyond the immediate circle of the Christian community, as at least a concurrent cause of the improvement.   In one remarkable instance, there is direct
authority that a certain measure was adopted by the
advice of an influential Christian.   During the period
of anarchy and confusion which preceded the universal
empire of Constantine, the misery had been so great,
particularly in Africa and Italy, that the sale of infants
for slaves, their exposure, and even infanticide, had
become fearfully common.   Constantine issued an edict,
in which he declared that the Emperor should be considered the father of all such children.   It was a cruelty,
irreconcileable with the spirit of the times, to permit
any subjects of the empire to perish of starvation, or to
be reduced to any unworthy action by actual hunger.
Funds were assigned for the food and clothing of such
children as the parents should declare themselves unable
to support, partly on the imperial revenues, partly on
the revenues of the neighbouring cities.   As this measure
did not prevent the sale of children, parents were declared incapable of reclaiming children thus sold, unless
they paid a reasonable price for their enfranchisement.[p]

---

[c] Cod. Theod. l. 2, tit. 8; l. 8,
tit. 8; l. 5, tit. 3.   Cod. Just. iii. 12;
Euseb. Vit. Const. 18, 19, 20; Sozom.
i. 8.

[p] Codex. Theodos. v. vii. l.   On
the exposure of children at this time,
compare Lactantius.   D. I. ii. 20.

Children which had been exposed could not be reclaimed from those who had received them into their families, whether by adoption or as slaves. Whatever may have been the wisdom, the humanity of these ordinances is unquestionable. They are said to have been issued by the advice of Lactantius, to whom had been entrusted the education of Crispus, the son of Constantine.

Child-stealing, for the purpose of selling the children for slaves, was visited with a penalty, which both in its nature and barbarity retained the stamp of the old Roman manners. The criminal was condemned to the amphitheatre, either to be devoured by wild beasts or exhibited as a gladiator. Christianity had not as yet allayed the passion for these savage amusements of the Roman people; yet, in conjunction with the somewhat milder manners of the East, it excluded gladiatorial exhibitions from the new capital. The Grecian amusements of the theatre and of the chariot-race satisfied the populace of Constantinople. Whatever might be the improved condition of the slaves within the Christian community, the tone of legislation preserves the same broad and distinct line of demarcation between the two classes of society. The master, indeed, was deprived of the arbitrary power of life and death. The death of a slave under torture, or any excessive severity of punishment, was punishable as homicide; but if he died under a *moderate* chastisement, the master was not responsible. In the distribution of the royal domains, care was to be taken not to divide the families of the prædial slaves. It is a cruelty, says the law, to separate parents and children, brothers and sisters, husbands and wives.[q] But marriages of free

Concerning slavery.

---

[q] Cod. Theod. l. v. t. 25. On the whole question of the effect of Chris-

tianity on slavery, read the third volume of the excellent work of

women with slaves were punishable with death; the children of such unions were indeed free, but could not inherit their mothers' property. The person of dignity and station, who had children by a marriage contracted with a woman of base condition, could not make a testament in their favour; even purchases made in their names or for their benefit, might be claimed by the legitimate heirs. The base condition comprehended not only slaves but freed women, actresses, tavern-keepers, and their daughters, as well as those of courtezans or gladiators. Slaves who were concerned in the seduction of their masters' children were to be burned alive without distinction of sex. The barbarity of this punishment rather proves the savage manners of the time than the inferior condition of the slave; for the receivers of the royal domains who were convicted of depredation or fraud were condemned to the same penalty.[r]

It can scarcely be doubted that the stricter moral tone of Constantine's legislation more or less remotely emanated from Christianity. The laws against rape and seduction were framed with so much rigour, as probably to make their general execution difficult, if not impracticable.[s] The ravisher had before escaped with impunity: if the injured party did not prosecute him for his crime, she had the right of demanding reparation by marriage. By the law of

Law against rape and abduction.

Wallon, Sur l'Esclavage dans l'Antiquité.

[r] Manumission, which was performed under the sanction of a religious ceremonial in the Heathen temples, might now be performed in the church: the clergy might manumit their slaves, in the presence of the church. Cod. Theod. iv. 7, 1.

This law must have connected Christianity in the general sentiment with the emancipation of slaves. Compare Sozomen, i. 9, who says, that Constantine issued three laws on the subject. The manumission took place publicly at Easter. Greg. Nyss.

[s] Cod. Theod. l. iv. t. 24.

Constantine, the consent of the female made her an accomplice in the crime; she was amenable to the same penalty. What that penalty was is not quite clear, but it seems that the ravisher was exposed to the wild beasts in the amphitheatre. Even where the female had suffered forcible abduction, she had to acquit herself of all suspicion of consent, either from levity of manner, or want of proper vigilance. Those pests of society, the pandars, who abused the confidence of parents, and made a traffic of the virtue of their daughters, were in the same spirit condemned to a punishment so horrible, as, no doubt, more frequently to ensure their impunity: melted lead was to be poured down their throats. Parents who did not prosecute such offences were banished, and their property confiscated. It is not, however, so much the severity of the punishments, indicating a stronger abhorrence of the crime, as the social and moral evils of which it took cognisance, which shows the remoter workings of a sterner moral principle. A religion which requires of its followers a strict, as regards the Christianity of this period, it may be said an ascetic rigour, desires to enforce on the mass of mankind by the power of the law that which it cannot effect by the more legitimate and permanent means of moral influence. In a small community where the law is the echo of the public sentiment, or where it rests on an acknowledged divine authority, it may advance further into the province of morality, and extend its provisions Law against into every relation of society. The Mosaic law, adultery. which, simultaneously with the Christian spirit, began to enter into the legislation of the Christian emperors, in its fearful penalties imposed upon the illicit commerce of the sexes, concurred with the rigorous jealousy of the Asiatic tribes of that region con-

cerning the honour of their women.   But when the laws
of Constantine suddenly classed the crime of adultery
with those of poison and assassination, and declared it a
capital offence, it may be doubted whether any improvement ensued, or was likely to ensue, in the public
morals.   Unless Christianity had already greatly cor-
rected the general licentiousness of the Roman world,
not merely within but without its pale, it may safely be
affirmed that the general and impartial execution of
such a statute was impossible.[t]   The severity Concerning
of the law against the breach of conjugal divorce.
fidelity was accompanied with strong restrictions upon
the facility of divorce.   Three crimes alone, in the husband, justified the wife in demanding a legal separation—homicide, poisoning, or the violation of sepulchres.
This latter crime was, apparently, very frequent, and
looked upon with great abhorrence.[u]   In these cases,
the wife recovered her dowry; if she separated for any
other cause, she forfeited all to a single needle, and was
liable to perpetual banishment.[x]   The husband, in order
to obtain a divorce, must convict his wife of poisoning,
adultery, or keeping notoriously infamous company.   In
all other cases, he restored the whole of the dowry.   If
he married again, the former wife, thus illegally cast off,
might claim his whole property, and even the dowry of

---

[t] It may be admitted, as some
evidence of the inefficiency of this law,
that in the next reign the penalties
were actually aggravated. The criminals were condemned either to be
burned alive, or sewed up in a sack
and cast into the sea.

[u] Codex. Theodos. iii. 16, 1.

[x] The law of Constantine and Constans, which made intermarriage with

a niece a capital crime, is supposed by
Godefroy to have been a local act,
directed against the laxity of Syrian
morals in this respect. Cod. Theod.
iii. 12, 1.   The law issued at Rome,
prohibiting intermarriage with the
sister of a deceased wife, annulled the
marriage, and bastardised the children.
iii. 12, 2.

the second wife. These impediments to the dissolution of the marriage tie, the facility of which experience and reason concur in denouncing as destructive of social virtue and of domestic happiness, with penalties affecting the property rather than the person, were more likely to have a favourable and extensive operation than the sanguinary proscription of adultery. Marriage being a civil contract in the Roman world, the state had full right to regulate the stability and the terms of the compact. In other respects, in which the jurisprudence assumed a higher tone, Christianity, I should conceive, was far more influential through its religious persuasiveness, than by the rigour which it thus impressed upon Against the laws of the empire. That nameless crime, pæderasty. the universal disgrace of Greek and Roman society, was far more effectively repressed by the abhorrence infused into the public sentiment by the pure religion of the Gospel, than by the penalty of death, enacted by statute against the offence. Another law of unquestionable humanity, and, probably, of more extensive operation, prohibited the making of Making of eunuchs. eunuchs. The slave who had suffered this mutilation might at once claim his freedom.[y]

Perhaps the greatest evidence of the secret aggression Laws favourable to celibacy. of Christianity, or rather, in my opinion, of the foreign Asiatic principle which was now completely interwoven with Christianity, was the gradual relaxation of the laws unfavourable to celibacy. The Roman jurisprudence had always proceeded on the principle of encouraging the multiplication of citizens, particularly in the higher orders, which, from various

---

[y] All these laws will be found in the Theodosian Code, under the name of Constantine, at the commencement of each book.

causes, especially the general licentiousness under the later republic and the early empire, were in danger of becoming extinct. The parent of many children was a public benefactor, the unmarried man a useless burden, if not a traitor, to the well-being of the state. The small establishment of the vestal virgins was evidently the remains of an older religion, inconsistent with the general sentiment and manners of Rome.

On this point the encroachment of Christianity was slow and difficult. The only public indication of its influence was the relaxation of the Papia Poppæan law. This statute enforced certain disabilities on those who were unmarried, or without children by their marriage, at the age of twenty-five. The former could only inherit from their nearest relations; the latter obtained only the tenth of any inheritance which might devolve on their wives, the moiety of property devised to them by will. The forfeiture went to the public treasury, and was a considerable source of profit. Constantine attempted to harmonise the two conflicting principles. He removed the disqualifications on celibacy, but he left the statute in force against married persons who were without children. In more manifest deference to Christianity, he extended the privilege hitherto confined to the vestal virgins of making their will, and that before the usual age appointed by the law, to all who had made a religious vow of celibacy.

Even after his death, both religions vied, as it were, for Constantine. He received with impartial favour the honours of both. The first Christian emperor was deified by the Pagans, in a later period he was worshipped as a saint by part of the Christian church. On the same medal appears his title of " God," with the monogram, the sacred symbol of Christianity ; in an-

Burial of Constantine.

other he is seated in the chariot of the Sun, in a car
drawn by four horses, with a hand stretched forth from
the clouds to raise him to Heaven.[z] But to show
respect at once to the Emperor and to the Christian
Apostle, contrary to the rigid usage, which forbade any
burial to take place within the city, Constantine was
interred in the porch of the church dedicated to the
Apostles. Constantius did great honour (in Chrysostom's opinion) to his imperial father, by burying him in
the Fisherman's Porch.[a]

During the reign of Constantine, Christianity con-
Conversion tinued to advance beyond the borders of the
of Æthiopia. Roman empire, and, in some degree, to indem-
nify herself for the losses which she sustained in the
kingdom of Persia. The Ethiopians appear to have
attained some degree of civilisation ; a considerable part
of the Arabian commerce was kept up with the other
side of the Red Sea, through the port of Adulis ; and
Greek letters appear, from inscriptions recently discovered,[b] to have made considerable progress among this
barbarous people. The Romans called this country,
with that of the Homerites on the other side of the Arabian gulph, by the vague name of the nearer India.
Travellers were by no means uncommon in these times,
whether for purposes of trade, or, following the tradi-
tional history of the ancient sages, from the more disin-

---

[z] Inter Divos meruit referri ;
Eutrop. x. 8 ; Eckhel. doct. numm.
viii. 92, 93 ; Bolland, 21st Maij.
Compare Le Beau, Hist. du Bas Empire,
i. p. 388. Beugnot, i. 109.

There exists a calendar in which
the festivals of the new God are indicated. Acad. des Inscrip. xv. 106.

[a] Chrysost. Hom. 60, in 2 Cor.

[b] That published by Mr. Salt, from
the ruins of Axum, had already appeared in the work of Cosmas Indico-
pleustes, edited by Montfaucon ;
Niebuhr published another, discovered
by Gau, in Nubia, relating to Silco,
king of that country.

terested desire of knowledge. Metrodorus, a philosopher, had extended his travels throughout this region,[c] and, on his return, the account of his adventures induced another person of the same class, Meropius of Tyre, to visit the same regions. Meropius was accompanied by two youths, Edesius and Frumentius. Meropius, with most of his followers, fell in a massacre, arising out of some sudden interruption of the peace between the Ethiopians and the Romans. Edesius and Frumentius were spared on account of their youth. They were taken into the service of the King, and gradually rose, till one became the royal cup-bearer; the other, the adminis-trator of the royal finances. The King died soon after they had been elevated to these high distinctions, and bequeathed their liberty to the strangers. The queen

---

[c] The same Metrodorus afterwards made a journey into further India; his object was to visit the Brahmins, to examine their religious tenets and practices. Metrodorus instructed the Indians in the construction of water-mills and baths. In their gratitude, they opened to him the inmost sanc-tuary of their temples. But the virtue of the philosopher Metrodorus, was not proof against the gorgeous trea-sures which dazzled his eyes; he stole a great quantity of pearls, and other jewels; others, he said that he had received as a present to Constantine from the King of India. He appeared in Constantinople. The Emperor re-ceived, with the highest satisfaction, those magnificent gifts which Metro-dorus presented in his own name. But Metrodorus complained that his offerings would have been far more sumptuous if he had not been attacked on his way through Persia, contrary to the spirit of the existing peace between the empires, and plundered of great part of his treasures. Constan-tine, it is said, wrote an indignant remonstrance to the King of Persia. This story is curious, as it shows the connection kept up by traders and travellers with the further East, which accounts for the allusions to Indian tenets and usages in the Christian, as well as the Pagan, writers of the time. It rests on the late authority of Cedrenus (t. i. p. 295), but is confirmed by a passage of Ammianus Marcellinus, who, however, places it in the reign of Constantius. Sed Constantium ardores Parthicos suc-cendisse, cum Metrodori mendaciis avidius acquiescit, lxxv. c. 4. Com-pare St. Martin's additions to Le Beau, i. 343.

entreated them to continue their valuable services till her son should attain to full age. The Romans complied with her request, and the supreme government of the kingdom of Ethiopia was administered by these two Romans, but the chief post was occupied by Frumentius. Of the causes which disposed the mind of Frumentius towards Christianity we know nothing; he is represented as seized with an eager desire of becoming acquainted with its tenets, and anxiously inquiring whether any Christians existed in the country, or could be found among the Roman travellers who visited it.[d] It is more probable, since there were so many Jews, both on the Arabian and the African side of the gulf, that some earlier knowledge of Christianity had spread into these regions. But it was embraced with ardour by Frumentius; he built a church, and converted many of the people. When the young king came of age, notwithstanding the remonstrances of the prince and his mother, Frumentius and his companion returned to their native country. Frumentius passed through Alexandria, and having communicated to Athanasius the happy beginnings of the Gospel in that wild region, the influence of that commanding prelate induced him to accept the mission of the Apostle of India. He was consecrated Bishop of Axum by the Alexandrian prelate, and that see was always considered to owe allegiance to the patriarchate of Alexandria. The preaching of Frumentius was said to have been eminently successful, not merely among the Ethiopians, but also among the neighbouring tribes of Nubians and Blemmyes. His

---

[d] Sozomen, in his ignorance, has ecourse to visions, or direct divine ınspiration. Θείαις ἴσως προτραπεὶς ἐπιφανείαις, ἢ καὶ αὐτομάτως τοῦ Θεοῦ κινοῦντος.

name is still reverenced as the first of the Ethiopian pontiffs. But probably in no country did Christianity so soon degenerate into a mere form of doctrine; the wild inhabitants of these regions sank downward rather than ascended in the scale of civilisation; and the fruits of Christianity, humanity, and knowledge, were stifled amid the conflicts of savage tribes, by ferocious manners, and less frequent intercourse with more cultivated nations.[e]

The conversion of the Iberians[f] was the work of a holy virgin. Nino was among the Armenian maidens who fled from the persecutions of the Persians, and found refuge among the warlike nation of Iberia, the modern Georgia. Her seclusion, her fasting, and constant prayers, excited the wonder of these fierce warriors. Two cures which she is said to have wrought, one on the wife of the king, still further directed the attention of the people to the marvellous stranger. The grateful queen became a convert to Christianity. Mihran, the king, still wavered between the awe of his ancient deities, the fear of his subjects, and his inclination to the new and wonder-working faith. One day when he was hunting in a thick and intricate wood, he was enveloped in a sudden and impenetrable mist. Alone, separated from his companions, his awe-struck mind thought of the Christians' God; he determined to embrace the Christian faith. On a sudden the mist cleared off, the light shone gloriously down, and in this natural image the king beheld the confirmation of the light of truth spread abroad within his soul. After much oppo-

Of the Iberians.

---

[e] Compare Stanley, Eastern Church, 12, 14, and in other passages.
[f] Socrates, i. 20   Sozomen, ii. c. 7;   Rufin. x. 10; Theodoret, i. 24; Moses Choren, Lib. ii. c. 83; Klaproth, Travels in Georgia.

sition, the temple of the great god Aramazd (the Ormuzd
of the Persian system) was levelled with the earth.   A
cross was erected upon its ruins by the triumphant Nino,
which was long worshipped as the palladium of the kingdom.[g]   Wonders attended on the construction of the
first Christian church.   An obstinate pillar refused to
rise, and defied the utmost mechanical skill of the
people to force it from its oblique and pendant position.
The holy virgin passed the night in prayer.   On the
morning the pillar rose majestically of its own accord,
and stood upright upon its pedestal.   The wondering
people burst into acclamations of praise to the Christians' God, and generally embraced the faith.   The king
of Iberia entered into an alliance with Constantine,
who sent him valuable presents, and a Christian bishop.
Eustathius: it is said, the deposed patriarch of Antioch, undertook this mission by the command of the
Emperor; and Iberia was thus secured to the Christian
faith.

[g] In 1801 this cross, or that which
perpetual tradition accounted as the
identical cross, was removed to Peters-
burg by Prince Bagration. It was
restored, to the great joy of the nation,
by order of the Emperor Alexander.

CHAPTER V.

Christianity under the sons of Constantine.

IF Christianity was making such rapid progress in the conquest of the world, the world was making fearful reprisals on Christianity. By enlisting new passions and interests in its cause, religion surrendered itself to an inseparable fellowship with those passions and interests. The more it mingles with the tide of human affairs, the more turbid becomes the stream of Christian history. In the intoxication of power, the Christian, like ordinary men, forgot his original character; and the religion of Jesus, instead of diffusing peace and happiness through society, might, to the superficial observer of human affairs, seem introduced only as a new element of discord and misery into the society of man.

The Christian emperor dies; he is succeeded by his sons, educated in the faith of the Gospel. The first act of the new reign is the murder of one of the brothers, and of the nephews of the deceased sovereign, who were guilty of being named in the will of Constantine as joint heirs to the empire. This act, indeed, was that of a ferocious soldiery, though the memory of Constantius is not free from the suspicion, at least of connivance in these bloody deeds. Christianity appears only in a favourable light as interposing between the assassins and their victim. Marcus, Bishop of Arethusa, saved Julian from his enemies: the future apostate was con-

cealed under the altar of the church.   Yet, on the
accession of the sons of Constantine, to the causes of
fraternal animosity usual on the division of a kingdom
Religious
differences
of the two
surviving
sons. between several brothers, was added that of
religious hostility.   The two Emperors (for
they were speedily reduced to two) placed
themselves at the head of the two contending parties in
Christianity.   The weak and voluptuous Constans adhered with inflexible firmness to the cause of Athanasius; the no less weak and tyrannical Constantius, to
that of Arianism.   The East was arrayed against the
West.   At Rome, at Alexandria, at Sardica, and, afterwards, at Arles and Milan, Athanasius was triumphantly
acquitted; at Antioch, at Philippopolis, and finally at
Rimini, he was condemned with almost equal unanimity.
Even within the church itself, the distribution of the
superior dignities became an object of fatal ambition and
strife.   The streets of Alexandria and of Constantinople
were deluged with blood by the partisans of rival
bishops.   In the latter, an officer of high distinction,
sent by the Emperor to quell the tumult, was slain, and
his body treated with the utmost indignity by the
infuriated populace.

To dissemble or to disguise these melancholy facts, is
alike inconsistent with Christian truth and wisdom.   In
some degree they are accounted for by the proverbial
reproach against history, that it is the record of human
folly and crime ; and history, when the world became
impregnated with Christianity, did not at once assume a
higher office.   In fact, it extends its view only over the
surface of society, below which, in general, lie human
virtue and happiness.   This would be especially the case
with regard to Christianity, whether it withdrew from
the sight of man, according to the monastic interpreta-

tion of its precepts, into solitary communion with the
Deity; or, in its more genuine spirit, was content with
exercising its humanising influence in the more remote
and obscure quarters of the general social system.

Even the annals of the Church take little notice of
those cities where the Christian episcopate passed calmly
down through a succession of pious and beneficent prelates, who lived and died in the undisturbed attachment
and veneration of their Christian disciples, and respected
by the hostile Pagans; men whose noiseless course of
beneficence was constantly diminishing the mass of
human misery, and improving the social, the moral, as
well as the religious condition of mankind.   But an
election contested with violence, or a feud which divided
a city into hostile parties, arrested the general attention,
and was perpetuated in the records, at first of the
Church, afterwards of the Empire.

But, in fact, the theological opinions of Christianity
naturally made more rapid progress than its
moral influence. The former had only to over-
power the resistance of a religion which had
already lost its hold upon the mind, or a philosophy too
speculative for ordinary understandings and too unsatisfactory for the more curious and enquiring; they had only
to enter, as it were, into a vacant place in the mind of
man.   But the moral influence had to contest, not only
with the natural dispositions of man, but with the barbarism and depraved manners of ages. While, then,
the religion of the world underwent a total change;
while the Church rose on the ruins of the temple, and
the pontifical establishment of Paganism became gradually extinct, or suffered violent suppression; the moral
revolution was far more slow and far less complete.
With a large portion of mankind, it must be admitted

Moral more slow than religious revolution.

that the religion itself was Paganism under another
form and with different appellations; with another
part, it was the religion passively received without any
change in the moral sentiments or habits; with a third,
and, perhaps, the more considerable part, there was a
transfer of the passions and the intellectual activity to a
new cause.[a] They were completely identified with
Christianity, and to a certain degree actuated by its
principles, but they did not apprehend the beautiful
harmony which subsists between its doctrines and its
moral perfection. Its dogmatic purity was the sole
engrossing subject; the unity of doctrine superseded
and obscured all other considerations, even of that
sublimer unity of principles and effects, of the loftiest
views of the divine nature with the purest conceptions
of human virtue. Faith not only overpowered, but dis-
carded from her fellowship, Love and Peace. Everywhere there was exaggeration of one of the constituent
elements of Christianity; that exaggeration which is
the inevitable consequence of a strong impulse upon the
human mind. Wherever men feel strongly, they act
violently. The more speculative Christians, therefore,
who were more inclined, in the deep and somewhat
selfish solicitude for their own salvation, to isolate themselves from the infected mass of mankind, pressed into
the extreme of asceticism; the more practical, who
were earnest in the desire of disseminating the blessings
of religion throughout society, scrupled little to press
into their service whatever might advance their cause.

---

[a] "If," said the dying Bishop of
Constantinople, "you would have for
my successor a man who would edify
you by the example of his life, and
improve you by the purity of his precepts, choose Paul; if a man versed
in the affairs of the world, and able
to maintain the interests of the religion, your suffrages must be given to
Macedonius."   Socr. E. C. ii. 6.

With both extremes, the dogmatical part of the religion predominated. The monkish believer imposed the same severity upon the aberrations of the mind as upon the appetites of the body; and, in general, those who are severe to themselves, are both disposed, and think themselves entitled, to enforce the same severity on others. The other, as his sphere became more extensive, was satisfied with an adhesion to the Christian creed, instead of that total change of life demanded of the early Christian, and watched over with such jealous vigilance by the mutual superintendence of a small society. The creed, thus become the sole test, was enforced with all the passion of intense zeal, and guarded with the most subtle and scrupulous jealousy. In proportion to the admitted importance of the creed, men became more sternly and exclusively wedded to their opinions. Thus an antagonistic principle of exclusiveness co-existed with the most comprehensive ambition. While they swept in converts indiscriminately from the palace and the public street; while the Emperor and the lowest of the populace were alike admitted on little more than the open profession of allegiance, they were satisfied if the allegiance in this respect was blind and complete. Hence a far larger admixture of human passions and of the common vulgar incentives of action was infused into the expanding Christian body. Men became Christians, orthodox Christians, with little sacrifice of that which Christianity aimed chiefly to extirpate. Yet, after all, this imperfect view of Christianity had probably some effect in concentrating the Christian community, and holding it together by a new and more indissoluble bond. The world divided into two parties. Though the shades of Arianism, perhaps, if strictly decomposed, of Trinitarianism, were countless as the varying powers of conception or expression in man, yet they were soon consolidated into two compact masses. The semi-Arians, who approximated so closely to the Nicene creed, were forced back into the main body. Their fine distinctions were not seized by their adversaries, or by the general understanding of the Christians. The bold and decisive definitiveness of the Athanasian doctrine admitted less discretion; and no doubt, though political vicissitudes had some influence on the final establishment of their doctrines, the more illiterate and less imaginative West was predisposed to the Athanasian opinions by its natural repugnance to the more vague and dubious theory. All, however, were enrolled under one or the other standard, and the party which triumphed, eventually would rule the whole Christian world.

Even the feuds of Christianity at this period, though with the few more dispassionate and reasoning of the Pagans they might retard its progress, in some respects contributed to its advancement; they assisted in breaking up that torpid stagnation which brooded over the general mind. It gave a new object of excitement to the popular feeling. The ferocious and ignorant populace of the large cities, which found a new aliment in Christian faction for their mutinous and sanguinary outbursts of turbulence, had almost been better left to sleep on in the passive and undestructive quiet of Pagan indifference. They were dangerous allies, more than dangerous—fatal to the purity of the Gospel.

Athanasius stands out as the prominent character of the period in the history, not merely of Christianity, but of the world. That history is one long controversy, the life of Athanasius one unwearied

Athanasius.

and incessant strife.[b] It is neither the serene course of a being elevated by his religion above the cares and tumults of ordinary life, nor the restless activity of one perpetuallv employed in a conflict with the ignorance, vice, and misery of an unconverted people. Yet even now (so completely has this polemic spirit become incorporated with Christianity) the memory of Athanasius is regarded by many wise and good men with reverence, which, in Catholic countries, is actual adoration, in Protestant, approaches towards it.[c] It is impossible, indeed, not to admire the force of intellect which he centered on this minute point of theology, his intrepidity, his constancy; but had he not the power to allay the feud which his inexorable spirit tended to keep alive? Was the term Consubstantialism absolutely essential to Christianity? If a somewhat wider creed had been accepted, would not the truth at least as soon and as generally have prevailed? Could not the commanding or persuasive voice of Christianity have awed or charmed the troubled waters to peace?

But Athanasius, in exile, would consent to no peace which did not prostrate his antagonists before his feet. He had obtained complete command over the minds of the western Emperors. The demand for his restoration to his see was not an appeal to the justice, or to the fraternal affection of Constantius; it was a question of peace or war. Constantius submitted; he received the

---

[b] Life of Athanasius prefixed to his Works. Tillemont, Vie d'Athanase.

[c] Compare Möhler, Athanasius der Grosse und seine zeit (Maintz, 1827), and Newman's Arians. The former is the work of a very powerful Roman Catholic writer, labouring to show that all the vital principles of Christianity were involved in this controversy; and stating *one side* of the question with consummate ability. It is the panegyric of a dutiful son on him whom he calls the father of church theology, p. 304.

prelate, on his return, with courtesy, or rather with favour and distinction. Athanasius now entered Alex-

A.D. 338.
Restoration
of Athanasius
to Alexan-
dria.
A.D. 340. andria at the head of a triumphal procession; the bishops of his party resumed their sees; all Egypt returned to its obedience; but the more inflexible Syria still waged the war with unallayed activity. A council was held at Tyre, in which new charges were framed against the Alexandrian prelate :—the usurpation of his see in defiance of his condemnation by a council (the imperial power seems to have been treated with no great respect,—for a prelate, it was asserted, deposed by a council, could only be restored by the same authority); violence and bloodshed during his re-occupation of the see; and malversation of sums of money intended for the poor, but appropriated to his own use. A rival council at Alexandria at once acquitted Athanasius on all these points; asserted his right to the see; appealed to and avouched the universal rejoicings at his restoration, and his rigid administration of the funds entrusted to his care.[d]

A more august assembly of Christian prelates met in

A.D. 341.
Council at
Antioch. the presence of the Emperor at Antioch. Ninety bishops celebrated the consecration of a splendid edifice, called the Church of Gold. The council then entered on the affairs of the church. A creed was framed satisfactory to all, except that it seemed carefully to exclude the term consubstantial or Homoousion. The council ratified the decrees of that of Tyre, with regard to Athanasius. It is asserted on his part that the majority had withdrawn to their dioceses before the introduction of this question, and that a factious

---

[d] Compare throughout the ecclesiastical historians, Theodoret, Socrates, and Sozomen.

minority of forty prelates assumed and abused the authority of the council. They proceeded to nominate a new
bishop of Alexandria. Pistus, who had before been
appointed to the see, was passed over in silence, probably as too inactive or unambitious for their purpose.
Gregory, a native of the wilder region of Cappadocia,
but educated under Athanasius himself in the more
polished schools of Alexandria, was invested with this
important dignity. Alexandria, peacefully reposing, it
is said, under the parental episcopate of Athanasius,
was suddenly startled by the appearance of an edict,
signed by the imperial prefect, announcing the degradation of Athanasius, and the appointment of Gregory.
Scenes of savage conflict ensued; the churches were
taken as it were by storm; the priests of the Athanasian party were treated with the utmost indignity;
virgins scourged; every atrocity perpetrated by unbridled multitudes, embittered by every shade of religious faction. The Alexandrian populace were always
ripe for tumult and bloodshed. The Pagans and the
Jews mingled in the fray, and seized the opportunity,
no doubt, of shewing their impartial animosity to both
parties; though the Arians (and, as the original causes
of the tumult, not without justice) were loaded with the
unpopularity of this odious alliance. They arrayed
themselves on the side of the soldiery appointed to
execute the decree of the prefect; and the Arian
bishop is charged, not with much probability, with
abandoning the churches to their pillage.

Athanasius fled; a second time an exile, he took refuge
in the West. He appeared again at Rome, in   Athanasius
the dominions and under the protection of an   flies to Rome.
orthodox Emperor; for Constans, who, after the death
of Constantine, the first protector of Athanasius, had

obtained the larger part of the empire belonging to his murdered brother, was no less decided in his support of the Nicene opinions. The two great Western prelates, Hosius of Cordova, eminent from his age and character, and Julius, bishop of Rome; from the dignity of his see, openly espoused his cause. Wherever Athanasius resided,—at Alexandria, in Gaul, in Rome,—in general the devoted clergy, and even the people, adhered with unshaken fidelity to his tenets. Such was the commanding dignity of his character, such his power of profoundly stamping his opinions on the public mind.

The Arian party, independent of their speculative opinions, cannot be absolved from the unchristian heresy of cruelty and revenge. However darkly coloured, we cannot reject the general testimony to their acts of violence, wherever they attempted to regain Usurpation their authority. Gregory is said to have attempted of Gregory. to compel bishops, priests, monks, and holy virgins, to Christian communion with a prelate thus forced upon them, by every kind of insult and outrage; by scourging and beating with clubs: those were fortunate who escaped with exile.[e] But if Alexandria was disturbed by the hostile excesses of the Arians, in Constantinople itself the conflicting religious parties gave rise to the first of those popular tumults which so frequently, in later times, distracted and disgraced the city. Eusebius, formerly Bishop of Nicomedia, the main support of the Arian party, A.D. 338. had risen to the episcopacy of the imperial city. His enemies reproached the worldly ambition which deserted an humbler for a more eminent see;

---

e Athanas. Oper., p. 112, 149, 350, 352, and the ecclesiastical historians in loc.

but they were not less inclined to contest this important post with the utmost activity. At his death the Athanasian party revived the claims of Paul, whom they asserted to have been canonically elected and unjustly deposed from the see; the Arians supported Macedonius. The dispute spread from the church into the streets, from the clergy to the populace; blood was shed; the whole city was in arms on one part or the other.

Bloody quarrel at Constantinople. A.D. 342.

The Emperor was at Antioch; he commanded Hermogenes, who was appointed to the command of the cavalry in Thrace, to pass through Constantinople, and expel the intruder Paul. Hermogenes, at the head of his soldiery, advanced to force Paul from the church. The populace rose; the soldiers were repelled; the general took refuge in a house, which was instantly set on fire; the mangled body of Hermogenes was dragged through the streets, and at length cast into the sea. Constantius heard this extraordinary intelligence at Antioch. The contempt of the imperial mandate; the murder of an imperial officer in the contested nomination of a bishop, were as yet so new in the annals of the world, as to fill him with equal astonishment and indignation. He mounted his horse, though it was winter and the mountain-passes were dangerous and difficult with snow; he hastened with the utmost speed to Constantinople. But the deep humiliation of the senate and the heads of the people, who prostrated themselves at his feet, averted his resentment: the people were punished by a diminution of the usual largess of corn. Paul was expelled; but, as though some blame adhered to both the conflicting parties, the election of Macedonius was not confirmed, although he was allowed to exercise the episcopal functions. Paul

retired, first to Thessalonica, subsequently to the court
of Constans.

The remoter consequences of the Athanasian controversy began to develope themselves at this
early period. The Christianity of the East
and the West gradually assumed a divergent
and independent character. Though, during a short
time, the Arianism of the Ostrogothic conquerors gave
a temporary predominance in Italy to that creed, the
West in general submitted, in unenquiring acquiescence,
to the Trinitarianism of Athanasius. In the East, on
the other hand, though the doctrines of Athanasius
eventually obtained the superiority, the controversy
gave birth to a long and unexhausted line of subordinate disputes. The East retained its mingled character
of Oriental speculativeness and Greek subtlety. It
could not abstain from investigating and analysing the
divine nature, and the relations of Christ and the Holy
Ghost to the Supreme Being. Macedonianism, Nes-
torianism, Eutychianism, with the fatal disputes relating to the procession of the Holy Ghost during
almost the last hours of the Byzantine empire, may be
considered the lineal descendants of this prolific controversy. The opposition between the East and West of
itself tended to increase the authority of that prelate,
who assumed his acknowledged station as the head and
representative of the Western churches. The commanding and popular part taken by the Bishop of
Rome, in favour of Athanasius and his doctrines, enabled him to stand forth in undisputed superiority, as at
once the chief of the Western episcopate and the
champion of orthodoxy. The age of Hosius,
and his residence in a remote province, withdrew the only competitor for this superiority. Athana-

sius took up his residence at Rome, and, under the protection of the Roman prelate, defied his adversaries to a new contest.   Julius summoned the accusers $_{\text{Julius,}}$ of Athanasius to plead the cause before a $_{\text{Bishop of Rome.}}$ council in Rome.[f]   The Eastern prelates altogether disclaimed his jurisdiction, and rejected his pretensions to rejudge the cause of a bishop already condemned by the council of Tyre.   The answer of Julius is directed rather to the justification of Athanasius than to the assertion of his own authority.   The synod of Rome solemnly acquitted Athanasius, Paul, and all their $_{\text{Synod at}}$ adherents.   The Western Emperor joined in $_{\text{Rome.}}$ the sentiments of his clergy.   A second council at Milan, in the presence of Constans, confirmed $_{\text{A.D. 343.}}$ the decree of Rome.   Constans proposed to $_{\text{At Milan.}}$ his brother to convoke a general council of both empires.   A neutral or border ground was chosen for this decisive conflict.   At Sardica met one hundred $_{\text{Council of}}$ prelates from the West, from the East only $_{\text{A.D. 345-6.}}^{\text{Sardica.}}$ seventy-five.[g]   Notwithstanding his age and infirmities, Hosius travelled from the extremity of the empire: he at once took the lead in the assembly ; and it is remarkable that the Bishop of Rome, so zealous in the cause of Athanasius, alleged an excuse for his absence, which may warrant the suspicion that he was unwilling to be obscured in this important scene by the superior

---

[f] Julius is far from asserting any individual authority, or pontifical supremacy.   "Why do you alone write ? "   "Because I represent the *opinions* of the bishops of Italy."   Epist. Julian. Athanas. Op. 1. 146.

The ecclesiastical historians, however, in the next century, assert that Rome claimed a right of adjudica-tion.   Γνωρίζουσιν οὖν τῷ ἐπισκόπῳ Ῥώμης Ἰουλίῳ τὰ καθ' ἑαυτούς· ὁ δὲ ἅτε προνόμεα τῆς ἐν Ῥώμῃ ἐκκλησίας ἐχούσης.   Socr. E. H. ii. 15.   Οἷα δὲ τῶν πάντων κηδεμονίας αὐτῷ προσηκούσης διὰ τὴν ἀξίαν τοῦ θρόνου.   Soz. E. H. iii. 8.

[g] By some accounts there were 100 Western bishops : 73 Eastern.

authority of Hosius. Five of the Western prelates, among whom were Ursacius of Singidunum and Valens of Mursa, embraced the Arian cause: the Arians complained of the defection of two bishops from their body, who betrayed their secret counsels to their adversaries.[h] In all these councils, it appears not to have occurred, that, religion being a matter of faith, the suffrages of the majority could not possibly impose a creed upon a conscientious minority. The question had been too often agitated to expect that it could be placed in a new light.

On matters of fact, the suffrages of the more numerous party might have weight, in the personal condemnation, for instance, or the acquittal of Athanasius; but as these suffrages could not convince the understanding of those who voted on the other side, the theological decisions must of necessity be rejected, unless the minority would submit likewise to the humiliating confession of insincerity, ignorance, or precipitancy in judgment.[i] The Arian minority did not await this issue; having vainly attempted to impede the progress of the council, by refusing to sanction the presence of persons excommunicated, they seceded to Philippopolis in Thrace. In these two cities

Rival council at Philippopolis.

sate the rival councils, each asserting itself the genuine representative of Christendom, issuing decrees, and anathematising their adversaries. The Arians are accused of maintaining their influence, even in the East, by acts of great cruelty. In Adrianople,

---

[h] Concilia Labbe, vol. iii. Athanas. contr. Arian. &c.

[i] The Oriental bishops protested against the assumption of supremacy by the Western. "Novam legem introducere putaverunt, ut Orientales Episcopi ab Occidentalibus judicarentur." Apud Hilar. Fragm. iii.

in Alexandria, they enforced submission to their tenets by the scourge, and by heavy penalties.[k]

The Western Council at Milan accepted and ratified the decrees of the council of Sardica, absolving Athanasius of all criminality, and receiving his doctrines as the genuine and exclusive truths of the Gospel. On a sudden, affairs took a new turn; Constantius threw himself, as it were, at the feet of Athanasius, and in three successive letters entreated him to resume his episcopal throne. The Emperor and the prelate (who had delayed at first to obey, either from fear or from pride, the flattering invitation), met at Antioch with mutual expressions of respect and cordiality.[m] Constantius ordered all the accusations against Athanasius to be erased from the registers of the city. He commended the prelate to the people of Alexandria in terms of courtly flattery, which harshly contrast with his former, as well as with his subsequent, conduct to Athanasius. The Arian bishop, Gregory, was dead, and Athanasius, amid the universal joy, re-entered the city. The bishops crowded from all parts to salute and congratulate the prelate who had thus triumphed over the malice even of imperial enemies. Incense curled up in all the streets; the city was brilliantly illuminated. It was an ovation by the admirers of Athanasius; it is said to have been a Christian ovation; alms were lavished on the poor; every house resounded with prayer and thanksgiving as if it were a church;

Reconciliation of Constantius with Athanasius. *A.D. 349.*

---

[k] The cause of Marcellus of Ancyra, whom the Eusebian party accused of Sabellianism, was throughout connected with that of Athanasius.

[m] The Emperor proposed to Athanasius to leave one church to the Arians at Alexandria; Athanasius dexterously eluded the request, by very fairly demanding that one church in Antioch, where the Arians predominated, should be set apart for those of his communion.

the triumph of Athanasius was completed by the re-
cantation of Ursacius and Valens, two of his most
powerful antagonists.[n]

This sudden change in the policy of Constantius is
scarcely explicable upon the alleged motives.

A.D. 349.   It is ascribed to the detection of an infamous
conspiracy against one of the Western bishops, deputed
on a mission to Constantius.   The aged prelate was
charged with incontinence, but the accusation recoiled
on its inventors.   A man of infamous character, Onager
the wild ass, the chief conductor of the plot, on being
detected, avowed himself the agent of Stephen, the
Arian bishop of Antioch.   Stephen was ignominiously
deposed from his see.   Yet this single fact would
scarcely have at once estranged the mind of Constantius from the interests of the Arian party; his subsequent conduct when, as Emperor of the whole world,
he could again dare to display his deep-rooted hostility
to Athanasius, induces the suspicion of political reasons.
Constantius was about to be embarrassed with the Persian war; at this dangerous crisis, the admoni-
Persian war.   tions of his brother, not unmingled with warlike menace, might enforce the expediency at least of a
temporary reconciliation with Athanasius.   After that
reconciliation and the triumph of Athanasius, the political troubles of three years suspended the religious
strife.   The war of Persia brought some fame to the
arms of Constantius; and in the more honourable cha-
Death of   racter, not of the antagonist, but the avenger
Constans.   of his murdered brother, the surviving son of
Constantine again united the East and West under his
sole dominion.   Magnentius, who had usurped the

---

[n] Greg. Nazian. Enc. Athanas.   Athanas. Hist. Arian.

Western Empire and mounted the throne over the bloody corpse of the murdered Constans, fell before the avenging arm of Constantius.

The battle of Mursa, if we are to credit a writer somewhat more recent, was no less fatal to the interests of Athanasius than to the arms of Magnen- War with tius.[o] Ursacius and Valens, after their re- Magnentius.
A.D. 351. cantation, had relapsed to Arianism. Valens was the Bishop of Mursa, and in the immediate neighbourhood of that town was fought the decisive battle. Constantius retired with Valens into the principal church, to assist with his prayers-rather than with his directions or personal prowess, the success of his army. Battle of The agony of his mind may be conceived, Mursa. during the long suspense of a conflict on which the sovereignty of the world depended, and in which the conquerors lost more men than the vanquished.[p] Valens stood or knelt by his side; on a sudden, when the Emperor was wrought to the highest state of agitation, Valens proclaimed the tidings of his complete victory ; intelligence communicated to the prelate by an angel from heaven. Whether Valens had anticipated the event by a bold fiction, or arranged some plan for obtaining rapid information, he appeared from that time to the Emperor as a man especially favoured by Heaven, a prophet, and one of good omen. With Valens Arianism reassumed its authority over the vacillating mind of Constantius.

But either the fears of the Emperor or the caution of the Arian party, delayed yet for three or four years

---

[o] Sulpicius Severus, ii. c. 54.

[p] Magnentius is said by Zonoras, to have sacrificed a girl, to propitiate the gods on this momentous occasion. Lib. xiii. t. ii. p. 16, 17.

to execute their revenge on Athanasius. They began
A.D. 351. with a less illustrious victim. Philip, the
to 355. prefect of the East, received instructions to
expel Paul, and to replace Macedonius on the episcopal
throne of Constantinople. Philip remembered the fate
of Hermogenes; he secured himself in the thermæ of
Zeuxippus, and summoned the prelate to his presence.
He then communicated his instructions, and frightened
or persuaded the aged Paul to consent to be secretly
Paul deposed from the transported in a boat over the Bosphorus. In
bishopric of Constantino- the morning, Philip appeared in his car, with
ple. Macedo- Macedonius by his side in the pontifical attire;
nius rein-stated. he drove directly to the church, but the soldiers were obliged to hew their way through the dense
and resisting crowd to the altar. Macedonius passed
over the murdered bodies (three thousand are said to
have fallen) to the throne of the Christian prelate.
Paul was carried in chains first to Emesa, afterwards to
a wild town in the deserts about Mount Taurus. He
had disappeared from the sight of his followers, and it
is certain that he died in those remote regions. The
Arians gave out that he died a natural death. It was
the general belief of the Athanasians that his death
was hastened, and even that he had been strangled by
the hands of the prefect Philip.[g]

But before the decisive blow was struck against
Athanasius, Constantius endeavoured to subdue the
West to the Arian opinions. The Emperor, released
from the dangers of war, occupied his triumphant leisure
in Christian controversy. He seemed determined to
establish his sole dominion over the religion as well as

---

q Athenas. Oper. i. 322, 348. Socrat. E. H. ii. 26.

the civil obedience of his subjects.   The Western
bishops firmly opposed the conqueror of Mag- Councils of
nentius.   At the councils, first of Arles and Arles and
Milan.
afterwards of Milan, they refused to subscribe A.D. 353, 355.
the condemnation of Athanasius, or to communicate with
the Arians.   Liberius, the new Bishop of Rome, Persecution
refused the timid and disingenuous compro- of Liberius,
Bishop of
mise to which his representative at Arles, Vin- Rome.
cent, deacon of Rome, had agreed—assent to the condemnation of Athanasius, if, at the same time, a decisive
anathema should be issued against the tenets of Arius.
At Milan, the bishops boldly asserted the independence
of the church upon the empire.   The Athanasian party
forgot, or chose not to remember, that they had unani-
mously applauded the interference of Constantine,
when, after the Nicene council, he drove the Arian
bishops into exile.   Thus it has always been: the sect
or party which has the civil power in its favour is
embarrassed with no doubts as to the legality of its
interference; when hostile, it resists as an unwarrant-
able aggression on its own freedom, that which it has
not scrupled to employ against its adversaries.

The new charges against Athanasius were of very
different degrees of magnitude and probability. New charges
against
He was accused of exciting the hostility of Athanasius.
Constans against his brother.   The fact that Constans
had threatened to reinstate the exiled prelate by force
of arms might give weight to this charge ; but the subsequent reconciliation, the gracious reception of Athanasius by the Emperor, the public edicts in his favour,
had, in all justice, cancelled the guilt, if there were
really guilt, in this undue influence over the mind of
Constans.   He was accused of treasonable correspondence
with the usurper Magnentius.   Athanasius repelled this

charge with natural indignation. He must have been a
monster of ingratitude, worthy a thousand deaths, if he
had leagued with the murderer of his benefactor, Constans.
He defied his enemies to the production of any letters;
he demanded the severest investigation, the strictest
examination, of his own secretaries or those of Magnentius. The descent is rapid from these serious charges
to that of having officiated in a new and splendid
church, the Cæsarean, without the permission of the
Emperor; and the exercising a paramount and almost
monarchical authority over the churches along the
whole course of the Nile, even beyond his legitimate
jurisdiction. The first was strangely construed into an
intentional disrespect to the Emperor; the latter might
fairly be attributed to the zeal of Athanasius for the
extension of Christianity. Some of these points might
appear beyond the jurisdiction of an ecclesiastical tribunal; and in the council of Milan there seems to
have been an inclination to separate the cause of
Athanasius from that of his doctrine. As at Arles,
some proposed to abandon the person of Athanasius to
the will of the Emperor, if a general condemnation
should be passed against the tenets of Arius.

Three hundred ecclesiastics formed the council of
Milan. Few of these were from the East. The
Bishop of Rome did not appear in person to
lead the orthodox party. His chief representative was
Lucifer of Cagliari, a man of ability, but of violent
temper and unguarded language. The Arian faction
was headed by Ursacius and Valens, the old adversaries
of Athanasius, and by the Emperor himself. Constantius, that the proceedings might take place more immediately under his own superintendence, adjourned the
assembly from the church to the palace. This un-

Council of Milan.

seemly intrusion of a layman in the deliberations of the
clergy, unfortunately, was not without precedent. Those
who had proudly hailed the entrance of Constantine
into the synod of Nicæa could not, consistently, deprecate the presence of his son at Milan.

The controversy became a personal question between
the Emperor and his refractory subject. The
Emperor descended into the arena, and min-   A.D. 355.
gled in all the fury of the conflict. Constantius was
not content with assuming the supreme place as Emperor, or interfering in the especial province of the
bishops—the theological question—he laid claim to
direct inspiration. He was commissioned by a vision
from Heaven to restore peace to the afflicted church.
The scheme of doctrine which he proposed was asserted
by the Western bishops to be strongly tainted with
Arianism. The prudence of the Athanasian party was
not equal to their firmness and courage. The obsequious and almost adoring court of the Emperor must
have stood aghast at the audacity of the ecclesiastical
synod. Their language was that of vehement invective,
rather than dignified dissent or calm remonstrance.
Constantius, concealed behind a curtain, listened to the
debate; he heard his own name coupled with that of
heretic, of Antichrist. His indignation now knew no
bounds. He proclaimed himself the champion of the
Arian doctrines, and the accuser of Athanasius. Yet
flatteries, persuasions, bribes, menaces, penalties, exiles,
were necessary to extort the assent of the resolute
assembly. Then they became conscious of the impro-
priety of a lay Emperor's intrusion into the debates of
an ecclesiastical synod. They demanded a free council,
in which the Emperor should neither preside in person
nor by his commissary. They lifted up their hands,

and entreated the angry Constantius not to mingle up the affairs of the state and the church.[r] Three prelates, Lucifer of Cagliari, Eusebius of Vercellæ, Dionysius of Milan, were sent into banishment, to places remote from each other, and the most inhospitable regions of the empire. Liberius, the Roman pontiff, rejected with disdain the presents of the Emperor; he resisted with equal firmness his persuasions and his acts of violence.

Though his palace in Rome was carefully closed and garrisoned by some of his faithful flock, Liberius was seized at length, and carried to Milan. He withstood, somewhat contemptuously, the personal entreaties and arguments of the Emperor.[s] He rejected with disdain the imperial offers of money for his journey, and told the Emperor to keep it to pay his army. The same offer was made by Eusebius the eunuch:—" Does a sacrilegious robber like thee think to give alms to me, as to a mendicant ? " The Bishop of Rome was exiled to Berbea, a city of Thrace. An Arian prelate, Felix, was forced upon the unwilling city.

Fall of Liberius.

But two years of exile broke the spirit of Liberius. He began to listen to the advice of the Arian bishop of Berbea; the solitude, the cold climate, and the discomforts of this uncongenial region, had more effect than the presents or the menaces of the Emperor. Pope Liberius signed the Arian formulary of Sirmium; he assented to the condemnation of Athanasius. The fall of the aged Hosius increased the triumph of the Arians. Some of the Catholic writers reproach with undue bitterness the weakness of an old

Fall of Hosius.

---

[r] Μηδὲ ἀναμίσγειν τὴν Ῥωμαϊκην τῇ τῆς ἐκκλησίας διατάγῃ. Athanas. | ad Mon. c. 34, 36. Compare c. 52. | [s] Theodoret, iv. 16.

man, whose nearer approach to the grave, they assert, ought to have confirmed him in his inalienable fidelity to Christ. But even Christianity has no power over that mental imbecility which accompanies the decay of physical strength; and this act of feebleness ought not, for an instant, to be set against the unblemished virtue of a whole life.

Constantius, on his visit to Rome, was astonished by an address, presented by some of the principal females of the city in their most splendid attire, to entreat the restoration of Liberius. The Emperor offered to re-admit Liberius to a co-ordinate authority with the Arian bishop, Felix. The females rejected with indignant disdain this dishonourable compromise; and when Constantius commanded a similar proposition to be publicly read in the circus at the time of games, he was answered by a general shout, "One God, one Christ, one bishop." *Reception of Constantius at Rome.*

Had then the Christians, if this story be true, already overcome their aversion to the public games? or are we to suppose that the whole populace of Rome took an interest in the appointment of the Christian pontiff?

Athanasius awaited in tranquil dignity the bursting storm. He had eluded the imperial summons to appear at Milan, upon the plea that it was ambiguous and obscure. Constantius, either from some lingering remorse, from reluctance to have his new condemnatory ordinances confronted with his favourable, and almost adulatory, testimonies to the innocence of Athanasius, or from fear lest a religious insurrection in Alexandria and Egypt should embarrass the government, and cut off the supplies of corn from the Eastern capital, refused to issue any written order for the deposal and expulsion of Athanasius. He chose, *Orders to remove Athanasius.*

apparently, to retain the power, if convenient, of disowning his emissaries. Two secretaries were despatched with a verbal message, commanding the prelate's abdication. Athanasius treated the imperial officers with the utmost courtesy; but respectfully demanded their written instructions. A kind of suspension of hostilities seems to have been agreed upon, till further instructions could be obtained from the Emperor. But in the mean time, Syrianus, the duke of the province, was drawing the troops from all parts of Libya and Egypt to invest and occupy the city. A force of 5000 men was thought necessary to depose a peaceable Christian Bishop. The great events in the life of Athanasius, as we have already seen on two occasions, seem, either designedly or of themselves, to take a highly dramatic form. It was midnight, and the archbishop, surrounded by the more devout of his flock, was performing the solemn ceremony, previous to the sacramental service of the next day, in the church of St. Theonas. Suddenly the sound of trumpets, the trampling of steeds, Tumult in the clash of arms, the bursting the bolts of the church of the doors, interrupted the silent devotions of Alexandria. the assembly. The archbishop on his throne, in the depth of the choir, on which fell the dim light of the lamps, beheld the gleaming arms of the soldiery, as they burst into the nave of the church. The archbishop, as the ominous sounds grew louder, commanded the chanting of the 135th (136th) Psalm. The choristers' voices swelled into the solemn strain :—" Oh, give thanks unto the Lord, for he is gracious;" the people took up the burthen, "For his mercy endureth for ever!" The clear, full voices of the congregation rose over the wild tumult, now without, and now within, the church.

A discharge of arrows commenced the conflict; and Athanasius calmly exhorted his people to continue their only defensive measures, their prayers to their Almighty Protector.   Syrianus at the same time ordered the soldiers to advance.   The cries of the wounded; the groans of those who were trampled down in attempting to force their way out through the soldiery; the shouts of the assailants, mingled in wild and melancholy uproar.   But before the soldiers had reached the end of the sanctuary, the pious disobedience of his clergy and of a body of monks, hurried the archbishop by some secret passage out of the tumult.   His escape appeared little less than miraculous to his faithful followers.   The riches of the altar, the sacred ornaments of the church, and even the consecrated virgins, were abandoned to the licence of an exasperated soldiery.   The Catholics in vain drew up an address to the Emperor, appealing to his justice against this sacrilegious outrage; they suspended the arms of the soldiery, which had been left on the floor of the church, as a reproachful memorial of the violence. Constantius confirmed the acts of his officers.[t]

The Arians were prepared to replace the deposed prelate; their choice fell on another Cappa-   George of docian more savage and unprincipled than the   Cappadocia. former one.   Constantius commended George of Cappadocia to the people of Alexandria, as a prelate above praise, the wisest of teachers, the fittest guide to the kingdom of heaven.   His adversaries paint him in the blackest colours; the son of a fuller, he had been in turns a parasite, a receiver of taxes, a bankrupt.   Ignorant of letters, savage in manners, he was taken up,

---

[t] Athanas. Apol. de Fugâ, vol. i. | 395; ad Const. 307, 310. Tillemont,
p. 334; ad Monachos, 373, 378, 393, | Vie d'Athanase.

while leading a vagabond life, by the Arian prelate of
Antioch, and made a priest before he was a Christian.
He employed the collections gathered for the poor in
bribing the eunuchs of the palace. But he possessed,
no doubt, great worldly ability; he was without fear and
without remorse. He entered Alexandria environed by
the troops of Syrianus. His presence let loose the rabid
violence of party; the Arians exacted ample vengeance
for their long period of depression; houses were plundered; monasteries burned; tombs broken open, to
search for concealed Athanasians, or for the prelate
himself, who still eluded their pursuit; bishops were
insulted; virgins scourged; the soldiery encouraged to
break up every meeting of the Catholics by violence,
and even by inhuman tortures. The Duke Sebastian,
at the head of 3000 troops, charged a meeting of the
Athanasian Christians. No barbarity was too revolting;
they are said to have employed instruments of torture
to compel them to Christian unity with the Arians;
females were scourged with the prickly branches of the
palm-tree. The Pagans readily transferred their allegiance, so far as allegiance was demanded; while the
savage and ignorant among them rejoiced in the occasion for plunder and cruelty. Others hailed these feuds,
and almost anticipated the triumphant restoration of
their own religion. Men, they thought, must grow
weary and disgusted with a religion productive of so
much crime, bloodshed, and misery. Echoing back the
language of the Athanasians, they shouted out—" Long
life to the Emperor Constantius, and the Arians who
have abjured Christianity." And Christianity they seem
to have abjured, though not in the sense intended by
their adversaries. They had abjured all Christian
humanity, holiness, and peace.

The avarice of George was equal to his cruelty. Exactions were necessary to maintain his interest with the eunuchs, to whom he owed his promotion. The prelate of Alexandria forced himself into the secular affairs of the city. He endeavoured to secure a monopoly of the nitron produced in the lake Mareotis, of the salt-works, and of the papyrus. He became a manufacturer of those painted coffins which were still in use among the Egyptians. Once he was expelled by a sudden insurrection of the people, who surrounded the church, in which he was officiating, and threatened to tear him in pieces. He took refuge in the court, which was then at Sirmium, and a few months beheld him reinstated by the command of his faithful patron the Emperor.[u] A reinstated tyrant is, in general, the most cruel oppressor; and, unless party violence has blackened the character of George of Cappadocia beyond even its ordinary injustice, the addition of revenge, and the haughty sense of impunity, derived from the imperial protection, to the evil passions already developed in his soul, rendered him a still more intolerable scourge to the devoted city.

Everywhere the Athanasian bishops were expelled from their sees; they were driven into banishment. The desert was constantly sounding with the hymns of these pious and venerable exiles, as they passed along, loaded with chains, to the remote and savage place of their destination; many of them bearing the scars, and wounds, and mutilations, which had been inflicted upon them by their barbarous persecutors, to enforce their compliance with the Arian doctrines.

Athanasius, after many strange adventures; having

---

[u] He was at Sirmium, May, 359; restored in October.

been concealed in a dry cistern, and in the chamber
Escape and
retreat of
Athanasius. of a beautiful woman, who attended him with
the most officious devotion (his awful character
was not even tinged with the breath of suspicion), found
A.D. 356. refuge at length among the monks of the
desert. Egypt is bordered on all sides by
wastes of sand, or by barren rocks, broken into caves
and intricate passes ; and all these solitudes were now
peopled by the fanatic followers of the hermit Antony.
They were all devoted to the opinions and attached to
the person of Athanasius. The austerities of the prelate
extorted their admiration : as he had been the great
example of a dignified, active, and zealous bishop, so
was he now of an ascetic and mortified solitary. The
most inured to self-inflicted tortures of mind and body
found themselves equalled, if not outdone, in their fasts
and austerities by the lofty Patriarch of Alexandria.
Among these devoted adherents, his security was complete : their passionate reverence admitted not the fear
of treachery. The more active and inquisitive the
search of his enemies, he had only to plunge deeper
into the inaccessible and inscrutable desert. From this
solitude Athanasius himself is supposed sometimes to
have issued forth, and, passing the seas, to have traversed even parts of the West, animating his followers,
and confirming the faith of his whole widely-dissemi-
nated party. His own language implies his personal,
though secret presence at the councils of Seleucia and
Rimini.[x]

From the desert, unquestionably, came forth many
of those writings which must have astonished the
Heathen world by their unprecedented boldness. For

---

[x] Athanas. Oper. vol. i. p. 869. Compare Tillemont, Vie d'Athanase.

the first time since the foundation of the empire, the
Government was more or less publicly assailed in addresses, which arraigned its measures as unjust and as
transgressing its legitimate authority, and which did not
spare the person of the reigning Emperor. In the West,
as well as in the East, Constantius was assailed with
equal freedom of invective. The book of Hilary of
Hilary of Poictiers against Constantius is said Poictiers.
not to have been made public till after the death of the
Emperor; but it was most likely circulated among the
Catholics of the West; and the author exposed himself
to the activity of hostile informers, and the indiscretion
of fanatical friends. The Emperor, in that book, is declared to be Antichrist, a tyrant, not only in secular, but
likewise in religious affairs; the sole object of his reign
was to make a free gift to the devil of the whole world,
for which Christ had suffered.[y] Lucifer of Cagliari,

---

[y] " Nihil prorsus aliud egit, quam
ut orbem terrarum, pro quo Christus
passus est, diabolo condonaret." Adv.
Constant. c. 15. Hilary's highest
indignation is excited by the gentle
and insidious manner with which he
confesses that Constantius endeavoured
to compass his unholy end. He would
not honour them with the dignity of
martyrs, but he used the prevailing
persuasion of bribes, flatteries, and
honours—" Non dorsa cædit, sed ven-
trem palpat ; non trudit carcere ad
libertatem, sed intra palatium honorat
ad servitutem ; non latera vexat, sed
cor occupat . . . . non contendit ne
vincatur, sed adulatur ut dominetur."
There are several other remarkable
passages in this tract. Constantius
wished to confine the creed to the
language of Scripture. This was rejected, as infringing on the authority
of the bishops, and the forms of Apostolic preaching. " Nolo, inquit, verba
quæ non scripta sunt dici. Hoc tandem
rogo, quis episcopis jubeat et quis apos-
tolicæ prædicationis vetet formam ? "
c. 16. Among the sentences ascribed
to the Arians, which so much shocked
the Western bishops, there is one which
is evidently the argument of a strong
anti-materialist asserting the sole
existence of the Father, and that the
terms of son and generation, &c., are
not to be received in a literal sense.
" Erat Deus quod est. Pater non erat,
quia neque ei filius ; nam si filius,
necesse est ut et fœmina sit," &c. One
phrase has a singularly Oriental, I
would say, Indian cast. " How much
soever the Son expands himself towards
the knowledge of the Father, so much

whose violent temper afterwards distracted the Western
church with a schism, is now therefore repudiated by the common consent of all parties.
But Athanasius speaks in ardent admiration of the intemperate writings of this passionate man, and once
describes him as inflamed by the spirit of God. Lucifer,
in his banishment, sent five books full of the most viru-
lent invective to the Emperor. Constantius—it was the
brighter side of his religious character—received these
addresses with almost contemptuous equanimity. He
sent a message to Lucifer, to demand if he was the
author of these works. Lucifer replied not merely by
an intrepid acknowledgment of his former writings, but
by a sixth, in still more unrestrained and exaggerated
language. Constantius was satisfied with banishing him
to the Thebaid. Athanasius himself, who in his public
vindication addressed to Constantius, maintained the
highest respect for the imperial dignity, in his Epistle
to the Solitaries gives free vent and expression to his
vehement and contemptuous sentiments. His recluse
friends are cautioned, indeed, not to disclose the dangerous document, in which the tyrants of the Old
Testament, Pharaoh, Ahab, Belshazzar, are contrasted,

---

the Father super-expands himself, lest
he should be known by the Son."
"Quantum enim Filius se extendit
cognoscere Patrem, tantum Pater
superextendit se, ne cognitus Filio
sit." c. 13. The parties, at least in
the West, were speaking two totally
distinct languages. It would be unjust
to Hilary not to acknowledge the
beautiful and Christian sentiments
scattered through his two former
addresses to Constantius, which are
firm, but respectful; and if rigidly,

yet sincerely, dogmatic. His plea for
toleration, if not very consistently
maintained, is expressed with great
force and simplicity. "Deus cogni-
tionem sui docuit potius quam exegit.
. . . Deus universitatis est Dominus;
non requirit coactam confessionem.
Nostrâ potius non suâ causâ vene-
randus est . . . . simplicitate quæ-
rendus est, confessione discendus est,
charitate amandus est, timore vene-
randus est, voluntatis probitate reti-
nendus est." Lib. i. c. 6.

to his disadvantage, with the base, the cruel, the hypocritical Constantius.   It is curious to observe this new element of freedom, however at present working in a concealed, irregular, and, perhaps, still guarded manner, mingling itself with, and partially up-heaving, the general prostration of the human mind.   The Christian, or, in some respects, it might be more justly said, the hierarchical principle, was entering into the constitution of human society, as an antagonistic power to that of the civil sovereign.   The Christian community was no longer a separate republic, governed within by its own laws, yet submitting, in all but its religious observances, to the general ordinances.   By the establishment of Christianity under Constantine, and the gradual reunion of two sections of mankind into one civil society, those two powers, that of the Church and the State, became coordinate authorities, which, if any difference should arise between the heads of the respective supremacies,—if the Emperor and the dominant party in Christendom should take opposite sides, led to inevitable collision.   This crisis had already arrived.   An Arian emperor was virtually excluded from a community in which the Athanasian doctrines prevailed.   The son of Constantine belonged to an excommunicated class, to whom the dominant party refused the name of Christians.   Thus these two despotisms, both founded on opinion (for obedience to the imperial authority was rooted in the universal sentiment), instead of gently counteracting and mitigating each other, came at once into direct and angry conflict.   The Emperor might with justice begin to suspect that, instead of securing a peaceful and submissive ally, he had raised up a rival or a master ; for the son of Constantine was thus in his turn disdainfully ejected from the society which his father had incor-

2 F 2

porated with the empire.   It may be doubted how far
the violences and barbarities ascribed by the Catholics
to their Arian foes may be attributed to the indignation
of the civil power at this new and determined resistance.
Though Constantius might himself feel or affect a compassionate disdain at these unusual attacks on his person
and dignity, the general feeling of the Heathen population, and of many among the local governors, might
resist this contumacious contempt of the supreme authority.   It is difficult otherwise to account for the
general tumults excited by these disputes in Alexandria,
in Constantinople, and in Rome, where at least a very
considerable part of the population had no concern in
the religious quarrel.   The old animosity against Christianity would array itself under the banners of one of
the conflicting parties, or take up the cause of the
insulted sovereignty of the Emperor.   The Athanasians
constantly assert that the Arians courted, or at least
did not decline, the invidious alliance of the Pagans.

But in truth, in the horrible cruelties perpetrated
Mutual
accusations
of cruelty.
during these unhappy divisions, it was the
same savage ferocity of manners, which half a
century before had raged against the Christian church,
which now apparently raged in its cause.[z]   The abstruse

---

[z] See the depositions of the bishops
assembled at Sardica, of the violence
which they had themselves endured at
the hands of the Arians.   "Alii autem
gladiorum signa, plagas et cicatrices
estendebant.   Alii se fame ab ipsis
excruciatos querebantur.   Et hæc non
ignobiles testificabantur viri, sed de
ecclesiis omnibus electi propter quas
huc convenerunt, res gestas edocebant,
milites armatos, populos cum fustibus,
judicum minas, falsarum literarum

suppositiones. . . . Ad hæc virginum
nudationes, incendia ecclesiarum, car-
ceres adversos ministros Dei." Hilar.
Fragm. Op. Hist. ii. c. 4.
The Arians retort the same accusations of violence, cruelty, and persecution, against Athanasius.   They say—
" Per vim, per cædem, per bellum, Alex-
andrinorum ecclesias deprædatus ;" and
this, "per pugnas et cædes gentilium."
Decretum Synodi Orientalium Episcoporum apud Sardicam, apud S. Hilarium.

tenets of the Christian theology became the ill-understood, perhaps unintelligible, watchwords of violent and disorderly men. The rabble of Alexandria and other cities availed themselves of the commotion to give loose to their suppressed passion for the excitement of plunder and bloodshed. How far the doctrines of Christianity had worked down into the populace of the great cities cannot be ascertained, or even conjectured; its spirit had not in the least mitigated their ferocity and inhumanity. If Christianity is accused as the immediate exciting cause of these disastrous scenes, the predisposing principle was in that uncivilised nature of man, which not merely was unallayed by the gentle and humanising tenets of the Gospel, but, as it has perpetually done, pressed the Gospel itself, as it were, into its own unhallowed service.

The severe exclusiveness of dogmatic theology attained its height in this controversy. Hitherto, the Catholic and heretical doctrines had receded from each other at the first outset, and drawn off to opposite and irreconcileable extremes. The heretics had wandered away into the boundless regions of speculation; they had differed on some of the most important elementary principles of belief; they had rarely admitted any common basis for argument. Here the contending par-

---

"Immensa autem contluxerat ad Sardicam multitudo sceleratorum omnium et perditorum, adventantium de Constantinopoli, de Alexandriâ, qui rei homicidiorum, rei sanguinis, rei cædis, rei latrociniorum, rei prædarum, rei spoliorum, nefandorumque omnium sacrilegiorum et criminum rei; qui altaria confregerunt, ecclesias incenderunt, domosque privatorum compilaverunt; profanatores mysteriorum, proditoresque sacramentorum Christi; que impiam sceleratamque hæreticorum doctrinam contra ecclesiæ fidem asserentes, sapientissimos presbyteros Dei, diaconos, sacerdotes, atrociter demactaverunt." Ibid. 19. And this protest, full of these tremendous charges, was signed by the eighty seceding Eastern bishops.

ties set out from nearly the same principles, admitted
the same authority, and seemed, whatever their secret
bias or inclination, to differ only on the import of one
word. Their opinions appeared to be constantly approximating, yet found it impossible to unite. The
Athanasians taunted the Arians with the infinite variations in their belief: Athanasius recounts no less than
eleven creeds. But the Arians might have pleaded
their anxiety to reconcile themselves to the church, their
earnest solicitude to make every advance towards a
reunion, provided they might be excused the adoption
of the one obnoxious word, the Homoousion, or Consubstantialism. But the inflexible orthodoxy of Athanasius will admit no compromise ; nothing less than
complete unity, not merely of expression, but of mental
conception, will satisfy the rigour of the ecclesiastical
dictator, who will permit no single letter, and, as far as
he can detect it, no shadow of thought, to depart from
his peremptory creed. He denounces his adversaries,
for the least deviation, as enemies of Christ; he presses
them with consequences drawn from their opinions;
and, instead of spreading wide the gates of Christianity,
he seems to unbar them with jealous reluctance, and to
admit no one without the most cool and inquisitorial
scrutiny into the most secret arcana of his belief.

In the writings of Athanasius is embodied the perfection of polemic divinity. His style, indeed,
has no splendour, no softness, nothing to kindle
the imagination, or melt the heart. Acute, even to
subtlety, he is too earnest to degenerate into scholastic
trifling. It is stern logic, addressed to the reason of
those who admitted the authority of Christianity. There
is no dispassionate examination, no candid philosophic
inquiry, no calm statement of his adversaries' case, no

Athanasius as a writer.

liberal acknowledgment of the infinite difficulties of the subject, scarcely any consciousness of the total insufficiency of human language to trace the question to its depths; all is peremptory, dictatorial, imperious; the severe conviction of the truth of his own opinions, and the inference that none but culpable motives, either of pride, or strife, or ignorance, can blind his adversaries to their cogent and irrefragable certainty. Athanasius walks on the narrow and perilous edge of orthodoxy with a firmness and confidence which it is impossible not to admire. It cannot be doubted that he was deeply, intimately, persuaded that the vital power and energy, the truth, the consolatory force of Christianity, entirely depended on the unquestionable elevation of the Saviour to the most absolute equality with the Parent Godhead. The ingenuity with which he follows out his own views of the consequences of their errors is wonderfully acute; but the thought constantly occurs, whether a milder and more conciliating tone would not have healed the wounds of afflicted Christianity; whether his lofty spirit is not conscious that his native element is that of strife rather than of peace.[a]

Though nothing can contrast more strongly with the expansive and liberal spirit of primitive Christianity than the repellent tone of this exclusive theology, yet this remarkable phasis of Christianity seems to have been necessary, and doubtless not without advantage to the permanence of the religion. With the civilisation of mankind, Christianity was about to pass through the ordeal of those dark ages which followed the irruption of the barbarians. During this period, Christianity was

---

[a] At a later period, Athanasius seems to have been less rigidly exclu- sive against the Semi-Arians. Compare Möhler, ii. p. 230.

to subsist as the conservative principle of social order and the sacred charities of life, the sole, if not always faithful, guardian of ancient knowledge, of letters, and of arts. But in order to preserve its own existence, it assumed, of necessity, another form. It must have a splendid and imposing ritual to command the barbarous minds of its new proselytes, and one which might be performed by an illiterate priesthood; for the mass of the priesthood could not but be involved in the general darkness of the times. It must likewise have brief and definite formularies of doctrine. As the original languages, and even the Latin, fell into disuse, and before the modern languages of Europe were sufficiently formed to admit of translations, the sacred writings receded from general use; they became the depositaries of Christian doctrine, totally inaccessible to the laity, and almost as much so to the lower clergy. Creeds Necessity of creeds during the succeeding centuries. therefore became of essential importance to compress the leading points of Christian doctrine into a small compass. And as the barbarous and ignorant mind cannot endure the vague and the indefinite, so it was essential that the main points of doctrine should be fixed and cast into plain and emphatic propositions. The theological language was firmly established before the violent breaking up of society; and no more was required of the barbarian convert than to accept with unenquiring submission the established formulary of the faith, and gaze in awe-struck veneration at the solemn ceremonial.

The Athanasian controversy powerfully contributed to establish the supremacy of the Roman pontiff. It became almost a contest between Eastern and Western Christendom; at least the West was neither divided like the East, nor submitted with the same comparatively willing obedience

Influence of Athanasian controversy on the growth of the papal power.

to the domination of Arianism under the imperial authority. It was necessary that some one great prelate should take the lead in this internecine strife. The only Western bishop whom his character would designate as this leader was Hosius, the Bishop of Cordova. But age had now disqualified this good man, whose moderation, abilities, and probably important services to Christianity in the conversion of Constantine, had recommended him to the common acceptance of the Christian world, as president of the council of Nicæa. Where this acknowledged superiority of character and talent was wanting, the dignity of the see would command the general respect; and what see could compete, at least, in the West, with Rome? Antioch, Alexandria, or Constantinople, could alone rival, in pretensions to Christian supremacy, the old metropolis of the empire: and those sees were either fiercely contested, or occupied by Arian prelates. Athanasius himself, by his residence, at two separate periods, at Rome, submitted as it were his cause to the Roman pontiff. Rome became the centre of the ecclesiastical affairs of the West; and, since the Trinitarian opinions eventually triumphed through the whole of Christendom, the firmness and resolution with which the Roman pontiffs, notwithstanding the temporary fall of Liberius, adhered to the orthodox faith; their uncompromising attachment to Athanasius, who, by degrees, was sanctified and canonised in the memory of Christendom, might be one groundwork for that belief in their infallibility, which, however it would have been repudiated by Cyprian, and never completely prevailed in the East, became throughout the West the inalienable spiritual heirloom of the Roman pontiffs. Christian history will hereafter show how powerfully this monarchical principle, if not established, yet greatly strengthened, by these consequences

of the Athanasian controversy, tended to consolidate and
so to maintain, in still expanding influence, the Christianity of Europe.[b]

This conflict continued with unabated vigour till the
Superiority close of the reign of Constantius. Arianism
of Arianism. gradually assumed the ascendant, through the
violence and the arts of the Emperor; all the more distinguished of the orthodox bishops were in exile, or, at
least, in disgrace. Though the personal influence of
Athanasius was still felt throughout Christendom, his
obscure place of concealment was probably unknown to
the greater part of his own adherents. The aged Hosius
had died in his apostasy. Hilary of Poictiers, the
Bishop of Milan, and the violent Lucifer of Cagliari,
were in exile; and, though Constantius had consented to
the return of Liberius to his see, he had returned with
the disgrace of having consented to sign the new formulary framed at Sirmium, where the term, Consubstantial,
if not rejected, was, at least, suppressed. Yet the popularity of Liberius was undiminished, and the whole city
indignantly rejected the insidious proposition of Constantius, that Liberius and his rival Felix should rule
the see with conjoint authority. The parties had already

---

[b] The orthodox Synod of Sardica
admits the superior dignity of the
successors of St. Peter. "Hoc enim
optimum et valde congruentissimum
esse videbitur, si ad caput, id est, ad
Petri Apostoli sedem, de singulis
quibusque provinciis Domini referant
sacerdotes." Epist. Syn. Sard. apud
Hilarium, Fragm. Oper. Hist. ii. c. 9.
It was disclaimed with equal distinctness by the seceding Arians. "Novam
legem introducere putaverunt, ut
Orientales Episcopi ab Occidentalibus
judicarentur." Fragm. iii. c. 12. In
a subsequent clause, they condemn
Julius, Bishop of Rome, by name.
It is difficult to calculate the effect
which would commonly be produced
on men's minds by their involving in
one common cause the two tenets,
which, in fact, bore no relation to
each other,—the orthodox belief in
the Trinity, and the supremacy of the
Bishop of Rome. Sozomen, iv. 11,
13; Theodoret, ii. 17; Philostorgius,
iv. 3.

come to blows, and even to bloodshed, when Felix, who it was admitted, had never swerved from the creed of Nicæa, and whose sole offence was entering into communion with the Arians, either from moderation, or conscious of the inferiority of his party, withdrew to a neighbouring city, where he soon closed his days, and relieved the Christians of Rome from the apprehension of a rival pontiff.   The unbending resistance of the Athanasians was no doubt confirmed,-not merely by the variations in the Arian creed, but by the new opinions which they considered its legitimate offspring, and which appeared to justify their worst apprehensions of its inevitable consequences.

Aetius formed a new sect, which not merely denied the consubstantiality, but the similitude of the Son to the Father.   He was not only not of the same, but of a totally different, nature.   Aetius, according to the account of his adversaries, was a bold and unprincipled adventurer;[c] and the career of a person of this class is exemplified in his life.   The son of a soldier, at one time condemned to death and to the confiscation of his property, Aetius became a humble artisan, first as a worker in copper, afterwards in gold. His dishonest practices obliged him to give up trade, but not before he had acquired some property.   He attached himself to Paulinus, Bishop of Antioch; was expelled from the city by his successor; studied gram-

Heresy of Aetius.

---

[c] Socrates, ii. 35.   Sozomen, iii. 15, iv. 12.   Philostorg. iii. 15, 17. Suidas, voc. Aετιος.   Epiphan. Hæres. 76.   Gregor. Nyss. contra Eunom.

The most curious part in the History of Aetius is his attachment to the Aristotelian philosophy.   With him appears to have begun the long strife between Aristotelianism and Platonism in the church.   Aetius, to prove his unimaginative doctrines, employed the severe and prosaic categories of Aristotle, repudiating the prevailing Platonic mode of argument used by Origen and Clement of Alexandria.   Socrates, ii. c. 35.

mar at Anazarba; was encouraged by the Arian bishop
of that see, named Athanasius; returned to Antioch;
was ordained deacon; and again expelled the city.
Discomfited in a public disputation with a Gnostic, he
retired to Alexandria, where, being exercised in the art
of rhetoric, he revenged himself on a Manichean, who
died of shame.   He then became a public itinerant
teacher, practising, at the same time, his lucrative art of
a goldsmith.   The Arians rejected Aetius with no less
earnest indignation than the orthodox, but they could
not escape being implicated, as it were, in his unpopularity; and the odious Anomeans, those who denied the
similitude of the Son to the Father, brought new discredit even on the more temperate partisans of the
Arian creed.   Another heresiarch, of a higher rank,
still further brought disrepute on the Arian party.
Of Macedo-   Macedonius, the Bishop of Constantinople, to
nius.   the Arian tenet of the inequality of the Son to
the Father, added the total denial of the divinity of the
Holy Ghost.

Council still followed council.   Though we may not
concur with the Arian bishops in ascribing to their
adversaries the whole blame of this perpetual tumult
and confusion in the Christian world, caused by these
incessant assemblages of the clergy, there must have
been much melancholy truth in their statement.   "The
East and the West are in a perpetual state of restless-
ness and disturbance.   Deserting our spiritual charges;
abandoning the people of God; neglecting the preaching of the Gospel; we are hurried about from place to
place, sometimes to great distances, some of us infirm
with age, with feeble constitutions or ill health, and are
sometimes obliged to leave our sick brethren on the
road.   The whole administration of the empire, of the

Emperor himself, the tribunes, and the commanders, at this fearful crisis of the state, are solely occupied with the lives and the condition of the bishops. The people are by no means unconcerned. The whole brotherhood watches in anxious suspense the event of these troubles; the establishment of post-horses is worn out by our journeyings; and all on account of a few wretches, who, if they had the least remaining sense of religion, would say with the Prophet Jonah, ' Take us up and cast us into the sea; so shall the sea be calm unto you; for we know that it is on our account that this great tempest is upon you.' " [d]

The synod at Sirmium had no effect in reconciling the differences, or affirming the superiority of either party. A double council was appointed, of the Eastern prelates at Seleucia, of the Western at Rimini. The Arianism of Constantius himself had by this time degenerated still farther from the creed of Nicæa. Eudoxus, who had espoused the Anomean doctrines of Aetius, ruled his untractable but passive mind. The council of Rimini consisted of at least 400 bishops, of whom not above eighty were Arians. Their resolutions were firm and peremptory. They repudiated the Arian doctrines; they expressed their rigid adherence to the formulary of Nicæa. Ten bishops, however, of each party, were deputed to communicate their decrees to Constantius. The ten Arians were received with the utmost respect, their rivals with every kind of slight and neglect. Insensibly the Athanasians were admitted to more intimate intercourse; the flatteries, perhaps the bribes, of the Emperor prevailed; they returned, having signed a formulary directly opposed to

Council of Rimini.

---

[d] Hilar. Oper. Hist. Fragm. xi. c. 25.

their instructions. Their reception at first was unpro-
mising; but by degrees the council, from which its
firmest and most resolute members had gradually departed, and in which many poor and aged bishops still
retained their seats, wearied, perplexed, worn out by the
expense and discomfort of a long residence in a foreign
city, consented to sign a creed in which the contested
word, the homoousion, was carefully suppressed.[e] Arianism was thus deliberately adopted by a council, of which
the authority was undisputed. The world, says Jerome,
groaned to find itself Arian. But, on their return to
their dioceses, the indignant prelates everywhere protested against the fraud and violence which had been
practised against them. New persecutions followed:
Gaudentius, Bishop of Rimini, lost his life.

The triumph of Arianism was far easier among the
hundred and sixty bishops assembled at Seleucia. But
it was more fatal to their cause: the Arians, and Semi-
Arians, and Anomeans, mingled in tumultuous strife,
and hurled mutual anathemas against each other.

The new council met at Constantinople. By some
strange political or religious vicissitude, the party of the
Anomeans triumphed, while Aetius, its author, was sent
into banishment.[f] Macedonius was deposed; Eudoxus

---

[e] It is curious enough, that the
Latin language did not furnish terms
to express this fine distinction. Some
Western prelates, many of whom
probably did not understand a word
of Greek, proposed, " jam usiæ et
homoousii nomina recedant quæ in
divinis Scripturis de Deo, et Dei
Filio, non inveniuntur scripta." Apud
Hilarium, Oper. Hist. Fragm. ix.

[f] Aetius and Eunomius seem to

have been the heroes of the historian
Philostorgius, fragments of whose
history have been preserved by the
pious hostility of Photius. This dimi-
nishes our regret for the loss of the
original work, which would be less
curious than a genuine Arian history.
Philostorgius seems to object to the
anti-materialist view of the Deity
maintained by the Semi-Arian Eusebius, and, according to him, by Arius

of Antioch was translated to the imperial see; and the
solemn dedication of the church of St. Sophia was celebrated by a prelate who denied the similitude of nature
between the Father and the Son. The whole Christian
world was in confusion; these fatal feuds penetrated
almost as far as the Gospel itself had reached. The
Emperor, whose alternately partial vehemence and subtlety had inflamed rather than allayed the tumult, found
his authority set at nought; a deep, stern, and ineradic-
able resistance opposed the imperial decrees. A large
portion of the empire proclaimed aloud that there were
limits to the imperial despotism; that there was a
higher allegiance, which superseded that due to the
civil authority; that in affairs of religion they would
not submit to the appointment of superiors who did not
profess their views of Christian orthodoxy.[g] The Emperor himself, by mingling with almost fanatical passion
and zeal in these controversies, at once lowered himself
to the level of his subjects, and justified the importance
which they attached to these questions. If Constantius
had firmly, calmly, and consistently, enforced mutual
toleration,—if he had set the example of Christian
moderation and temper; if he had set his face solely
against the stern refusal of Athanasius and his party to
admit the Arians into communion,—he might, perhaps,
have retained some influence over the contending parties. But he was not content without enforcing the
dominance of the Arian party; he dignified Athanasius

---

himself. He reproaches Eusebius with
asserting the Deity to be incomprehensible and inconceivable: ἄγνωστος
καὶ ἀκατάληπτος.   Lib. i. 2, 3.

    [g] Hilary quotes the sentence of St.

Paul, "Ubi fides est, ibi et libertas
est;" in allusion to the Emperor's
assuming the cognisance over religious
questions. Oper. Hist. Fragm. i. c. 5.

with the hatred of a personal enemy, almost of a rival; and his subjects, by his own apparent admission that these were questions of spiritual life and death, were compelled to postpone his decrees to those of God; to obey their bishops, who held the keys of heaven and hell, rather than Cæsar, who could only afflict them with civil disabilities, or penalties in this life.

CHAPTER VI.

Julian.

AMIDST all this intestine strife within the pale of Christianity, and this conflict between the civil and religious authorities concerning their respective limits, Paganism made a desperate effort to regain its lost supremacy. Julian has, perhaps, been somewhat unfairly branded with the ill-sounding name of Apostate. His Christianity was but the compulsory obedience of youth to the distasteful lessons of education, enforced by the hateful authority of a tyrannical relative. As early as the maturity of his reason,—at least as soon as he dared to reveal his secret sentiments,—he avowed his preference for the ancient Paganism.

The most astonishing part of Julian's history is the development and partial fulfilment of all his vast designs during a reign of less than two years. His own age wondered at the rapidity with which the young Emperor accomplished his military, civil, and religious schemes.[a] During his separate and subordinate command as Cæsar, his time was fully occupied with his splendid campaigns upon the Rhine.[b] Julian was the vindicator of the old majesty of the empire; he threw

---

[a] "Dicet aliquis : quomodo tam multa tam brevi tempore. Et rectè. Sed Imperator noster addit ad tempus quod otio suo detrahit. . . . . Itaque grandævum jam imperium videbitur his, qui non ratione dierúm et mensium. sed operum multitudine et effectarum rerum modo Juliani tempora metientur." Mamertini Grat. Actio. c. xiv.

[b] Six years, from 355 to 361.

back with a bold and successful effort the inroad of barbarism, which already threatened to overwhelm the
Roman civilisation of Gaul.   During the two unfinished
Short reign
of Julian.
A.D. 361-363. years of his sole government, Julian had reunited the whole Roman empire under his
single sceptre ; he had reformed the army, the court,
the tribunals of justice ; he had promulgated many
useful laws, which maintained their place in the jurisprudence of the empire ; he had established peace on
all the frontiers ; he had organised a large and well-
disciplined force to chastise the Persians for their
aggressions on the eastern border ; and, by a formidable
diversion within their own territories, to secure the
Euphratic provinces against the most dangerous rival of
the Roman power.   During all these engrossing cares of
empire, he devoted himself with the zeal and activity of
a mere philosopher and man of letters to those more
tranquil pursuits.   The conqueror of the Franks and
the antagonist of Sapor delivered lectures in the schools,
and published works, which, whatever may be thought
of their depth and truth, display no mean powers of
composition : as a writer, Julian will compete with most
of his age.   Besides all this, his vast and restless spirit
contemplated, and had already commenced, nothing less
than a total change in the religion of the empire; not
merely the restoration of Paganism to the legal supremacy which it possessed before the reign of Constantine, and the degradation of Christianity into a
private sect ; but the actual extirpation of the new religion from the minds of men by the reviving energies of
a philosophic, and at the same time profoundly religious,
Paganism.

The genius of ancient Rome and of ancient Greece
might appear to revive in amicable union in the soul

of Julian. He displayed the unmeasured military ambition, which turned the defensive war into Character of
a war of aggression on all the imperilled Julian.
frontiers; the broad and vigorous legislation; the unity
of administration; the severer tone of manners, which
belonged to the better days of Rome; so too the fine
cultivation; the perspicuous philosophy; the lofty conceptions of moral greatness and purity, which distinguished the old Athenian. If in the former (the Roman
military enterprise), he met eventually with the fate of
Crassus or of Varus, rather than the glorious successes
of Germanicus or Trajan, the times were more in fault
than the general: if in the latter (the Grecian elevation and elegance of mind), Julian more resembled at
times the affectation of the Sophist and the coarseness
of the Cynic, than the lofty views and exquisite harmony of Plato or the practical wisdom of Socrates, the
effete and exhausted state of Grecian letters and philosophy must likewise be taken into the account.

In the uncompleted two years of his sole empire,[c]
Julian had advanced so far in the restoration of the
internal vigour and unity of administration, that it is
doubtful how much further, but for the fatal Persian
campaign, he might have fulfilled the visions of his
noble ambition. He might have averted, at least for
a time, the terrible calamities which burst upon the
Roman world during the reign of Valentinian and
Valens. But difficult and desperate as the enterprise
might appear, the re-organisation of a decaying empire
was less impracticable than the restoration of an all but
extinguished religion. A religion may awaken from

---

[c] One year, eight months, and twenty-three days. La Bleterre, Vie de
Julien, p. 494.

indifference, and resume its dominion over the minds of men; but not if supplanted by a new form of faith which has identified itself with the opinions and sentiments of the general mind. It can never dethrone a successful invader, who has been recognised as a lawful sovereign. And Christianity (could the clear and sagacious mind of Julian be blind to this essential difference?) had occupied the whole soul of man with a fulness and confidence which belonged, and could belong, to no former religion. It had intimately blended together the highest truths of philosophy with the purest morality; the loftiest speculation with the most practical spirit. The vague theory of another life, timidly and dimly announced by the later Paganism, could ill compete with the deep and intense conviction, now rooted in the hearts of a large part of mankind by Christianity; the source in some of harrowing fears, in others of the noblest hopes.

Julian united in his own mind, and attempted to work Religion of into his new religion, the two incongruous cha-Julian. racters of a zealot for the older superstitions and for the more modern philosophy of Greece. He had fused together, in that which appeared to him an harmonious system, Homer and Plato. He thought that the whole ritual of sacrifice would combine with that allegoric interpretation of the ancient mythology, which undeified the greater part of the Heathen Pantheon. All that Paganism had borrowed from Christianity, it had rendered comparatively cold and powerless. The one Supreme Deity was a name and an abstract conception, a metaphysical being. The visible representative of the Deity, the Sun, which was in general an essential part of the new system, was, after all, foreign and Oriental; it belonged to the genuine mythology

neither of Greece nor Rome. The Theurgy, or awful
and sublime communion of the mind with the spiritual
world, was either too fine and fanciful for the vulgar
belief, or associated, in the dim confusion of the popular
conception, with that magic, against which the laws of
Rome had protested with such stern solemnity; and
which, therefore, however eagerly pursued and reverenced with involuntary awe, was always associated with
impressions of its unlawfulness and guilt. Christianity,
on the other hand, had completely incorporated with
itself all that it had admitted from Paganism, or which,
if we may so speak, constituted the Pagan part of Christianity. The Heathen Theurgy, even in its purest form,
its dreamy intercourse with the intermediate race of
dæmons, was poor and ineffective, compared with the
diabolic and angelic agency, which became more and
more mingled up with Christianity. Where these subordinate dæmons were considered by the more philosophic Pagan to have been the older deities of the
popular faith, it was rather a degradation of the ancient
worship; where this was not the case, this fine percep-
tion of the spiritual world was the secret of the initiate
few, rather than the all-pervading superstition of the
many. The Christian dæmonology, on the other hand,
which began to be heightened and multiplied by the
fantastic imagination of the monks, brooding in their
solitudes, seemed at least to grow naturally out of the religious system. The gradually darkening into superstition
was altogether imperceptible and harmonised entirely
with the general feelings of the time. Christianity was
a living plant, which imparted its vitality to the foreign
suckers grafted upon it; the dead and sapless trunk of
Paganism withered even the living boughs which were
blended with it, by its own inevitable decay.

On the other hand, Christianity at no period could
Unfavour-   appear in a less amiable and attractive light
able state of
Christianity.   to a mind preindisposed to its reception.   It
was in a state of universal fierce and implacable discord : the chief cities of the empire had run with blood
shed in religious quarrels.   The sole object of the conflicting parties seemed to be to confine to themselves
the temporal and spiritual blessings of the faith; to
exclude as many as they might from that eternal life,
and to anathematise to that eternal death, which were
revealed by the Gospel, and placed, according to the
general belief, under the special authority of the clergy.
Society seemed to be split up into irreconcileable parties; to the animosities of Pagan and Christian, were
now added those of Christian and Christian.   Christianity had passed through its earlier period of noble
moral enthusiasm ; of the energy with which it addressed
its first proclamation of its doctrines to man ; of the
dignity with which it stood aloof from the intrigues and
vices of the world ; and of its admirable constancy under
persecution.   It had not fully attained its second state
as a religion generally established in the minds of men,
by a dominant hierarchy of unquestioned authority.
Its great truths had no longer the striking charm of
novelty ; nor were they yet universally and profoundly
implanted in the general mind by hereditary transmission or early education, and ratified by the unquestioning sanction of ages.

The youthful education of Julian had been, it might
almost appear, studiously and skilfully conducted, so as
to show the brighter side of Paganism, the darker of
Christianity.   His infant years had been clouded by the
murder of his father.   How far his mind might retain
any impression of that awful event, or remembrance of

the place of his refuge, the Christian church, or of the saviour of his life, the virtuous Bishop of Arethûsa, it is of course impossible to conjecture. But Julian's first instructor was a man who, born a Scythian, and educated in Greece,[d] united the severe morality of his ruder ancestors with the elegance of Grecian accomplishments. He enforced upon his young pupil the strictest modesty, contempt for the licentious or frivolous pleasures of youth, for the theatre and the bath. At the same time, while he delighted his mind with the poetry of Homer, his graver studies were the Greek and Latin languages, the elements of the philosophy of Greece, and music, that original and attractive element of Grecian education.[e] At the age of about fourteen or fifteen, Julian was shut up, with his brother Gallus, in Macellæ, a fortress in Asia Minor, and committed in this sort of honourable prison to the rigid superintendence of ecclesiastics. By his Christian instructors, the Education of young and ardent Julian was bound down to a Julian. course of the strictest observances, the midnight vigil, the fast, the long and weary prayer, and visits to the tombs of martyrs, rather than a wise and rational initiation in the genuine principles of the Gospel; or a judicious familiarity with the originality, the beauty, and the depth of the Christian morals and Christian religion. He was taught the virtue of implicit submission to his ecclesiastical superiors; the munificence of conferring gifts upon the churches; with his brother Gallus he was permitted, or rather incited, to build a chapel over the tomb of St. Mammas.[f] For six years, he

[d] His name was Mardonius. Julian. ad Athen. et Misopogon. Socrat. E. H. iii. 1. Amm. Marc. xxii. 12.

[e] See the high character of this man

in the Misopogon, p. 351.

[f] Julian is said even thus early to have betrayed his secret inclinations; in his declamations he took delight in

bitterly asserts, he was deprived of every kind of useful instruction.[g] Julian and his brother, it is even said, were ordained readers, and officiated in public in that character. But the passages of the sacred writings, with which he might thus have become acquainted, were imposed as lessons; and in the mind of Julian, Christianity, thus taught and enforced, was inseparably connected with the irksome and distasteful feelings of confinement and degradation. No youths of his own rank, or of ingenuous birth, were permitted to visit his prison; he was reduced, as he indignantly declares, to the debasing society of slaves.

At the age of twenty, Julian was permitted to reside in Constantinople, afterwards at Nicomedia. The jealousy of Constantius in Constantinople was excited by the popular demeanour, sober manners, and the reputation for abilities, which directed all eyes towards his youthful nephew. He dismissed Julian to the more dangerous and fatal residence in Nicomedia, in the neighbourhood of the most celebrated and most attractive of the Pagan party. The most faithful adherents of Paganism were that class with which the tastes and inclinations of Julian brought him into close intimacy, the sophists, the men of letters, the rhetoricians, the poets, the philosophers. He was forbidden, indeed, perhaps by the jealousy of his appointed instructor Ecebolus, who at this time conformed to the religion of the court, to hear the dangerous lectures of Libanius,

---

defending the cause of Paganism against Christianity. A prophetic miracle foreboded his future course. While this church rose expeditiously under the labour of Gallus, the obstinate stones would not obey that of Julian; an invisible hand disturbed the foundations, and threw down all his work. Gregory Nazianzen declares that he had heard this from eye-witnesses; Sozomen, from those who had heard it from eye-witnesses. Gregor. Or. iii. p. 59, 61. Sozomen, v. 2.

[g] Πάντος μαθήματος σπουδαίου.

equally celebrated for his eloquence and his ardent attachment to the old religion. But Julian Intercourse with the philosophers. obtained his writings, which he devoured with all the delight of a stolen enjoyment.[h] Julian formed an intimate acquaintance with the heads of the philosophic school, with Ædesius, his pupils Eusebius and Chrysanthius, and at last with the famous Maximus. These men are accused of practising the most subtle and insidious arts upon the character of their ardent and youthful votary. His grave and meditative mind imbibed with eager delight the solemn mysticism of their tenets, which were impressed more deeply by significant and awful ceremonies. A magician at Nicomedia first excited his curiosity, and tempted him to enter on these exciting courses. At Pergamus he visited the aged Ædesius; and the manner in which these philosophers passed Julian onward from one to another, as if through successive stages of initiation in their mysterious doctrines, bears the appearance of a deliberate scheme to work him up to their purposes. The aged Ædesius addressed him as the favoured child of wisdom; declined the important charge of his instruction, but commended him to his pupils, Eusebius and Chrysanthius, who could unlock the inexhaustible source of light and wisdom. " If you should attain the supreme felicity of being initiated in their mysteries, you will blush to have been born a man, you will no longer endure the name." The pupils of Ædesius fed the greedy mind of the proselyte with all their stores of wisdom, and then skilfully unfolded the greater fame of Maximus. Eusebius professed to despise the vulgar arts of wonder-working, at least in comparison with the purification of the soul; but

---

[h] Liban. Orat. Par. t. i. p. 526.

he described the power of Maximus in terms to which
Julian could not listen without awe and wonder. Maximus had led them into the temple of Hecate; he had
burned a few grains of incense, he had murmured a
hymn, and the statue of the goddess was seen to smile.
They were awe-struck, but Maximus had declared that
this was nothing. The lamps throughout the temple
shall immediately burst into light: as he spoke, they
had kindled and blazed up. "But of these mystical
wonder-workers, we think lightly," proceeded the skilful
speaker, "do thou, like us, think only of the internal
purification of the reason." "Keep to your book,"
broke out the impatient youth, "this is the man I
seek."[i] Julian hastened to Ephesus. The person and
demeanour of Maximus were well suited to keep up the
illusion. He was a venerable man, with a long white
beard, with keen eyes, great activity, soft and persuasive voice, rapid and fluent eloquence. By Maximus,
who summoned Chrysanthius to him, Julian was brought
into direct communion with the invisible world. The
faithful and officious Genii from this time watched over
Julian in peace and war; they conversed with him in
his slumbers, they warned him of dangers, they conducted his military operations. Thus far we proceed on
the authority of Pagan writers; the scene of his solemn
initiation rests on the more doubtful testimony of Christian historians,[k] which, as they were little likely to be
admitted into the secrets of these dark and hidden rites,
is to be received with grave suspicion; more especially
as they do not scruple to embellish these rites with
Christian miracle. Julian was led first into a temple,

---

[i] Eunapius, in Vit. Ædesii et
Maximi.

[k] Greg. Naz. Orat. iii. 71. Theodoret. iii. 3.

then into a subterranean crypt, in almost total darkness.
The evocations were made ; wild and terrible sounds
were heard ; spectres of fire jibbered around. Julian, in
his sudden terror, made the sign of the cross. All disappeared, all was silent. Twice this took place, and
Julian could not but express to Maximus his astonishment at the power of this sign.   " The gods," returned
the dexterous philosopher, " will have no communion
with so profane a worshipper." From this time, it is
said, on better authority,[m] Julian burst, like a lion in
his wrath, the slender ties which bound him to Christianity. But he was still constrained to dissemble his
secret apostasy. His enemies declared that he redoubled
his outward zeal for Christianity, and even shaved his
head in conformity with the monastic practice.   His
brother Gallus had some suspicion of his secret views,
and sent the Arian bishop Aetius to confirm him in the
faith.

How far Julian, in this time of danger, stooped to
disguise his real sentiments, it were rash to Conduct of
decide. But it would by no means commend to Julian.
Christianity to the respect and attachment of Julian,
that it was the religion of his imperial relative.   Popular rumour did not acquit Constantius of the murder of
Julian's father ; and Julian himself afterwards publicly
avowed his belief in this crime.[n] He had probably
owed his own escape to his infant age and to the activity
of his friends.   Up to this time, his life had been the
precarious and permissive boon of a jealous tyrant, who
had inflicted on him every kind of degrading restraint.
His place of education had been a prison, and his subsequent liberty was watched with suspicious vigilance.

[m] Libanius.
[n] Ad Senatum Populumque Atheniensem.   Julian Oper. p. 270.

The personal religion of Constantius; his embarking
with alternate violence and subtlety in theological dis-
putations; his vacillation between timid submission to
priestly authority and angry persecution, were not likely
to make a favourable impression on a wavering mind.
The Pagans themselves, if we may take the best historian of the time as the representative of their opinions,[o]
considered that Constantius dishonoured the Christian
religion by mingling up its perspicuous simplicity with
anile superstition. If there was little genuine Christianity in the theological discussions of Constantius,
there had been less of its beautiful practical spirit in his
conduct to Julian. It had allayed no jealousy, mitigated no hatred; it had not restrained his temper from
overbearing tyranny, nor kept his hands clean from
blood. And now, the death of his brother Gallus, to
whom he seems to have cherished warm attachment,
was a new evidence of the capricious and unhumanised
tyranny of Constantius, a fearful omen of the uncer-
tainty of his own life under such a despotism. He had
beheld the advancement and the fate of his brother;
and his future destiny presented the alternative either
of ignominious obscurity or fatal distinction. His life
was spared only through the casual interference of the
humane and enlightened Empress; and her influence
gained but a slow and difficult triumph over the malignant eunuchs, who ruled the mind of Constantius. But
he had been exposed to the ignominy of arrest and
imprisonment, and a fearful suspense of seven weary
months.[p] His motions, his words, were watched; his
very heart scrutinised; he was obliged to suppress the

---

[o] Ammianus Marcellinus.

[p] Ἐμὲ δὲ ἀφῆκε μόγις, ἑπτὰ

μηνῶν ὅλων ἐλκύσας τῇδε κᾳκεῖσε.
Ad. S. P. Ath. p. 272.

natural emotions of grief for the death of his brother;
to impose silence on his fluent eloquence, and `act the
hypocrite to nature as well as to religion.

His retreat was Athens, of all cities in the empire
that, probably, in which Paganism still main- Julian at
tained the highest ascendancy, and appeared Athens.
in the most seductive form.   The political religion of
Rome had its stronghold in the capital; that of Greece,
in the centre of intellectual culture and of the fine arts.
Athens might still be considered the university of the
empire; from all quarters, particularly of the East,
young men of talent and promise crowded to complete
their studies in those arts of grammar, rhetoric, philosophy; which, however, by no means disdained by the
Christians, might still be considered as more strictly
attached to the Pagan interest.

Among the Christian students who at this time paid
the homage of their residence to this great centre of
intellectual culture, were Basil and Gregory of Nazian-
zum.   The latter, in the orations with which in later
times he condemned the memory of Julian, has drawn,
with a coarse and unfriendly hand, the picture of his
person and manners.   His manners did injustice to the
natural beauties of his person, and betrayed his restless,
inquisitive, and somewhat incoherent, character.   The
Christian (we must remember, indeed, that these predictions were published subsequent to their fulfilment,
and that, by their own account, Julian had already
betrayed, in Asia Minor, his secret propensities) already
discerned in the unquiet and unsubmissive spirit, the
future apostate.   But the general impression which
Julian made was far more favourable.   His quickness,
his accomplishments, the variety and extent of his
information; his gentleness, his eloquence, and even his

modesty, gained universal admiration, and strengthened the interest excited by his forlorn and perilous position.

Of all existing Pagan rites, those which still main- Julian initiated at Eleusis. tained the greatest respect, and would impress a mind like Julian's with the profoundest veneration, were the Eleusinian mysteries. They united the sanctity of almost immemorial age with some similitude to the Platonic Paganism of the day, at least sufficient for the ardent votaries of the latter to claim their alliance. The Hierophant of Eleusis was admitted to be the most potent theurgist in the world.[q] Julian honoured him, or was honoured by his intimacy; and the initiation in the Mystery of those, emphatically called the Goddesses, with all its appalling dramatic machinery, and its high speculative and imaginative doctrines, the impenetrable, the ineffable tenets of the sanctuary, consummated the work of Julian's conversion.

The elevation of Julian to the rank of Cæsar was at Elevation of Julian to the rank of Cæsar. length extorted from the necessities, rather than freely bestowed by the love, of the Emperor. Nor did the jealous hostility of Constantius cease with this apparent reconciliation. Constantius, with cold suspicion, thwarted all his measures, crippled his resources, and appropriated to himself, with unblushing injustice, the fame of his victories.[r] Julian's assump-

---

q Compare (in Eunap. Vit. Ædes. p. 52, edit. Boissonade) the prophecy of the dissolution of Paganism ascribed to this pontiff; a prediction which may do credit to the sagacity, or evince the apprehensions of the seer, but will by no means claim the honour of divine foreknowledge.

r Ammianus, l. xv. 8, et seqq. Socrates, iii. 1. Sozomen, v. n. La Bleterie, Vie de Julien, 89 et seqq.

The campaigns of Julian, in La Bleterie, lib. ii. Gibbon, iv. pp. 1, 4.

The well-known passage in Ammianus shows the real sentiments of the court towards Julian. "In odium venit cum victoriis suis capella non homo; ut hirsutum Julianum carpentes appellantesque loquacem talpam, et purpuratam simiam, et litterionem Græcum." Amm. Marc. xvii. 11.

tion of the purple, whether forced upon him by the
ungovernable attachment of his soldiery, or prepared by
his own subtle ambition, was justified, and perhaps compelled, by the base ingratitude of Constantius; and by
his manifest, if not avowed, resolution of preparing the
ruin of Julian, by removing his best troops to the East.[s]

The timely death of Constantius alone prevented the
deadly warfare in which the last of the race of Death of
Constantine were about to contest the empire. Constantius.
The dying bequest of that empire to Julian, said to have
been made by the penitent Constantius, could not efface
the recollection of those long years of degradation, of
jealousy, of avowed or secret hostility; still less could it
allay the dislike or contempt of Julian for his weak and
insolent predecessor, who, governed by eunuchs, wasted
the precious time which ought to have been devoted to
the cares of the empire, in idle theological discussions,
or quarrels with contending ecclesiastics. The part in
the character of the deceased Emperor least likely to
find favour in the sight of his successor Julian was his
religion. The unchristian Christianity of Constantius
must bear some part of the guilt of Julian's apostasy.

Up to the time of his revolt against Constantius,
Julian had respected the dominant Chris- Conduct of
tianity. The religious acts of his early youth, Julian.
performed in obedience to, or under the influence of his
instructors ; or his submissive conformity, when his
watchful enemies were eager for his life, ought hardly
to convict him of deliberate hypocrisy. In Gaul, still
under the strictest suspicion, and engaged in almost
incessant warfare, he would have few opportunities to
betray his secret sentiments. But Jupiter was con-

---

[s] Amm. Marc. xx. &c. Zosimus, iii. Liban. Or. x. Jul. ad S. P. Q. A.

sulted in his private chamber, and sanctioned his assumption of the imperial purple.[t]   And no sooner had he marched into Illyria, an independent Emperor at the head of his own army, than he threw aside all concealment, and proclaimed himself a worshipper of the ancient gods of Paganism.   The auspices were taken; and the act of divination was not the less held in honour, because the fortunate soothsayer announced the death of Constantius.   The army followed the example of their victorious general.   At his command, the neglected temples resumed their ceremonies; he adorned them with offerings; he set the example of costly sacrifices.[u] The Athenians in particular obeyed with alacrity the commands of the new Emperor; the honours of the priesthood became again a worthy object of contest; two distinguished females claimed the honour of representing the genuine Eumolpidæ, and of officiating in the Parthenon.   Julian, already anxious to infuse as much of the real Christian spirit, as he could, into reviving Paganism, exhorted the contending parties to peace and unity, as the most acceptable sacrifice to the gods.

The death of Constantius left the whole Roman world open to the civil and religious schemes which lay, floating and unshaped, before the imagination of Julian. The civil reforms were executed with necessary severity; but in some instances, with more than necessary cruelty. The elevation of Paganism into a rational and effective faith, and the depression, and even the eventual extinction of Christianity, were the manifest objects of Julian's religious policy.   Julian's religion was the eclectic Pa-

---

[t] Amm. xxi. 1.

[u] The Western army was more easily practised upon than the Eastern soldiers at a subsequent period.   Θρη- | σκεύομεν τοὺς Θεοὺς ἀναφανδὸν καὶ τὸ πλῆθος τοῦ συγκατελθόντος μοι στρατοπέδου θεοσεβές ἐστιν.   Epist. xxxviii.

ganism of the new Platonic philosophy. The chief
speculative tenet was Oriental rather than Greek or
Roman. The one immaterial inconceivable Father
dwelt alone; though his majesty was held in reverence,
the direct and material object of worship was the great
Sun,[x] the living and animated, and propitious and
beneficent image of the immaterial Father.[y] Below this
primal Deity and his glorious image, there was room for
the whole Pantheon of subordinate deities, of whom, in
like manner, the stars were the material representatives; but who possessed invisible powers, and manifested themselves in various ways, in dreams and visions,
through prodigies and oracles, the flights of birds, and
the signs in the sacrificial victims.[z] This vague and
comprehensive Paganism might include under its dominion all classes and nations which adhered to the
Heathen worship; the Oriental, the Greek, the Roman,
even, perhaps, the Northern barbarian, would not refuse
to admit the simplicity of the primal article of the
creed, spreading out as it did below into the boundless
latitude of Polytheism. The immortality of the soul
appears to follow as an inference from some of Julian's
Platonic doctrines;[a] but it is remarkable how rarely it
is put forward as an important point of difference in his

---

[x] Τὸν μέγαν Ἥλιον, τὸ ζῶν ἄγαλ-
μα καὶ ἔμψυχον, καὶ εὐνοῦν καὶ
ἀγαθοεργὸν, τοῦ νοητοῦ πάτρος.

[y] Compare Julian. apud Cyril., lib.
ii. p. 65.

[z] Julian asserts the various offices
of the subordinate deities, apud Cyril.,
lib. vii. p. 235.

One of the most remarkable illustrations of this wide-spread worship
of the sun is to be found in the address
of Julius Firmicus Maternus to the

Emperors Constantius and Constans.
He introduces the sun as remonstrating
against the dishonourable honours thus
heaped upon him, and protests against
being responsible for the acts, or involved in the fate, of Liber, Attys, or
Osiris. " Nolo ut errori vestro nomen
meum fomenta suppeditet. . . . Quic-
quid sum simpliciter Deo pareo, nec
aliud volo de me intelligatis, nisi quod
videtis." c. 8.

[a] Lib. ii. 58.

religious writings; while, in his private correspondence,
he falls back to the dubious and hesitating language of
the ancient Heathens: "I am not one of those who dis-
believe the immortality of the soul; but the gods alone
can know; man can only conjecture that secret:"[b] but
his best consolation on the loss of friends was the saying of the Grecian philosopher to Darius, that if he
would find three persons who had not suffered the like
calamities, he would restore the king's beautiful wife to
life.[c] Julian's dying language, however, though still
vague and allied to the old Pantheistic system, sounds
more like serene confidence in some future state of
being.

The first care of Julian was to restore the outward
form of Paganism to its former splendour, and
to infuse the vigour of reviving youth into the
antiquated system. The temples were everywhere to
resume their ancient magnificence; the municipalities
were charged with the expense of these costly renova-
tions. Where they had been destroyed by the zeal of
the Christians, large fines were levied on the Churches,
and became, as will hereafter appear, a pretext for
grinding exaction, and sometimes cruel persecution. It
assessed on the whole community the penalty, merited,
perhaps, only by the rashness of a few zealots; it revived
outrages almost forgotten, and injuries perpetrated, perhaps, with the sanction, unquestionably with the connivance, of the former government. In many instances,
it may have revenged, on the innocent and peaceful, the

Restoration of Paganism.

---

[b] Οὐ γὰρ δὴ καὶ ἡμεῖς ἐσμεν τῶν
πεπεισμένων τὰς ψυχὰς ἤτοι προ-
απόλλυσθαι τῶν σωμάτων ἢ συνα-
πόλλυσθαι. . . . . Ὡς τοῖς μὲν αν-
θρώποις ἁρμόζει περὶ τοιούτων εἰκά-
ζειν, ἐπίστασθαι δὲ αὐτὰ τοὺς θεοὺς
ἀνάγκη. Epist. lxiii. p. 452.
[c] Epistle to Amerius on the loss of
his wife. Ep. xxxvii. p. 412.

crimes of the avaricious and irreligious; who either plundered under the mask of Christian zeal, or seized the opportunity, when the zeal of others might secure their impunity. That which takes place in all religious revolutions, had occurred to a considerable extent: the powerful had seized the opportunity of plundering the weaker party for their own advantage. The eunuchs and favourites of the court had fattened on the spoil of the temples.[d] If these men had been forced to regorge their ill-gotten gains, justice might have approved the measure; but their crimes were unfairly visited on the whole Christian body. The extent to which the ruin and spoliation of the temples had been carried in the East, may be estimated from the tragic lamentations of Libanius. The soul of Julian, according to the orator, burned for empire, in order to restore the ancient order of things.

In some respects, the success of Julian answered the high-wrought expectations of his partisans. His panegyrist indulges in this lofty language. "Thou, then, I say, O mightiest Emperor, hast restored to the republic the expelled and banished virtues; thou hast rekindled the study of letters; thou hast not only delivered from her trial Philosophy, suspected heretofore and deprived of her honours, and even arraigned as a criminal, but hast clothed her in purple, crowned her with jewels, and seated her on the imperial throne. We may now look on the heavens, and contemplate the stars with fearless gaze, who, a short time ago, like the beasts of the field,

---

[d] " Pasti templorum spoliis," is the strong expression of Ammianus. Libanius says, that some persons had built themselves houses from the materials of the temples. Χρήματα δὲ ἐτέλουν οἱ τοῖς τῶν ἱερῶν λίθοις σφίσιν αὐτοῖς οἰκίας ἐγείροντες. Orat. Parent. p. 504.

fixed our downward and grovelling vision on the earth."[e]
"First of all," says Libanius, "he re-established the
exiled religion, building, restoring, embellishing the
temples.   Everywhere were altars and fires, and the
blood and fat of sacrifice, and smoke, and sacred rites,
and diviners, fearlessly performing their functions.   And
on the tops of mountains were pipings and processions,
and the sacrificial ox, which was at once an offering to
the gods and a banquet to men."[f]   The private temple
in the palace of Julian, in which he worshipped daily,
was sacred to the Sun ; but he founded altars to all the
gods.   He looked with especial favour on those cities
which had retained their temples; with abhorrence on
those which had suffered them to be destroyed, or to fall
to ruin.[g]

Julian so entirely misapprehended Christianity, as to
attribute its success and influence to its external organisation, rather than to its internal authority over the
soul of man.   He thought that the religion grew out of
the sacerdotal power, not that the sacerdotal power was
but the vigorous development of the religion.   He fondly
supposed that the imperial edict, and the authority of
the government, could supply the place of profound religious sentiment ; and transform the whole Pagan priesthood, whether attached to the dissolute worship of the
East, the elegant ceremonial of Greece, or the graver
ritual of Rome, into a serious, highly moral, and blameless hierarchy.   The Emperor was to be at once the
supreme head, and the model of this new sacerdotal
order.   The sagacious mind of Julian might have per-

---

[e] Mam. Grat. Act. c. xxiii. This
clause refers, no doubt, to astrology
and divination.
[f] See v. l. p. 529, one among many

passages ; likewise, the Oratio pro
Templis, and the Monodia.
[g] Orat. Parent. p. 564.

ceived the dangerous power, growing up in the Christian episcopate, which had already encroached upon the imperial authority, and began to divide the allegiance of the world. His political apprehensions may have concurred with his religious animosities, in not merely endeavouring to check the increase of this power, but in desiring to concentrate again in the imperial person both branches of authority. The supreme pontificate of Paganism had indeed passed quietly down with the rest of the imperial titles and functions. But the interference of the Christian emperors in ecclesiastical affairs had been met with resistance, obeyed only with sullen reluctance, or but in deference to the strong arm of power. The doubtful issue of the conflict between the Emperor and his religious antagonist might awaken reasonable alarm for the majesty of the empire. If, on the other hand, Julian should succeed in reorganising the Pagan priesthood in efficiency, respect, and that moral superiority which now belonged to the Christian ecclesiastical system, the supreme pontificate, instead of being a mere appellation or an appendage to the imperial title, would be an office of unlimited influence and authority.[h] The Emperor would be the undisputed and unrivalled head of the religion of the empire; the whole sacerdotal order would be at his command : Paganism, instead of being, as heretofore, a confederacy of different religions, an aggregate of local systems of worship, each under its own tutelar deity, would become a well-regulated monarchy, with its

Julian's new priesthood.

---

[h] See the curious fragment of the sixty-second epistle, p. 450, in which Julian asserts his supremacy not merely as Pontifex Maximus, but as holding a high rank among the worshippers of Cybele. Ἐγὼ τοίνυν ἐπειδήπερ εἰμὶ κατὰ μὲν τὰ πάτρια μέγας Ἀρχιερεύς, ἔλαχον δὲ νῦν καὶ τοῦ Διδυμαίου προφητεύειν.

provincial, civic, and village priesthoods, acknowledging.
the supremacy, and obeying the impulse, of the high
imperial functionary. Julian admitted the distinction
between the priesthood and the laity.[i] In every province
a supreme pontiff was to be appointed, charged with a
superintendence over the conduct of the inferior priesthood, and armed with authority to suspend or to depose
those who should be guilty of any indecent irregularity.
The whole priesthood were to be sober, chaste, temperate in all things. They were to abstain, not merely
from loose society ; but, in a spirit diametrically opposite
to the old religion, were rarely to be seen at public festivals, never where women mingled in them.[k] In
private houses, they were only to be present at the
moderate banquets of the virtuous ; they were never to
be seen drinking in taverns, or exercising any base or
sordid trade. The priesthood were to stand aloof from
society, and only mingle with it to infuse their own
grave decency and unimpeachable moral tone. The
theatre, that second temple, as it might be called, of
the older religion, was sternly proscribed ; so entirely
was it considered sunk from its high religious character,
so incapable of being restored to its old moral influence.
They were to avoid all books, poetry, or tales, which
might inflame their passions ; to abstain altogether
from those philosophical writings which subverted the
foundations of religious belief, those of the Pyrrhonists
and Epicureans, which Julian asserts had happily fallen
into complete neglect, and had almost become obsolete.
They were to be diligent and liberal in almsgiving, and
to exercise hospitality on the most generous scale. The

---

i ’Επεὶ σοὶ πού μέτεστιν ἐμπείριας | μὲν ἱερεύς, τί δὲ ἰδιώτης. Fragm.
(ὅλως) τῶν δικαίων, ὅς οὐκ οἶσθα τί | Epist. lxii.   k See Epist. xlix.

Jews had no beggars; the Christians maintained, indiscriminately, all applicants to their charity; it was a disgrace to the Pagans to be inattentive to such duties; and the authority of Homer is alleged to show the prodigal hospitality of the older Greeks. They were to establish houses of reception for strangers in His every city, and thus to rival or surpass the charitable institutions generosity of the Christians. Supplies of corn from the public granaries were assigned for these purposes, and placed at the disposal of the priests, partly for the maintenance of their attendants, partly for these pious uses. They were to pay great regard to the burial of the dead, a subject on which Grecian feeling had always been peculiarly sensitive, particularly of strangers. The benevolent institutions of Christianity were to imitated be imitated and associated to Paganism. A from Christianity. tax was to be levied in every province for the maintenance of the poor, and distributed by the priesthood. Hospitals for the sick and for indigent strangers of every creed were to be formed in convenient places. The Christians, not without justice, called the Emperor " the ape of Christianity."   Of all homage to the Gospel, this was the most impressive and sincere; and we are astonished at the blindness of Julian in not perceiving that these changes, which thus enforced his admiration, were the genuine and permanent results of the religion; but the disputes, and strifes, and persecutions, the accidental and temporary effects of human passions awakened by this new and violent impulse on the human mind.

Something like an universal ritual formed part of the design of Julian. Three times a day prayer was to be publicly offered in the temples. The Ritual. powerful aid of music, so essential a part of the older and better Grecian instruction, and of which the influence is so elevating to the soul,[m] was called in to impress the minds of the worshippers. Each temple was to have its organised band of choristers. A regular system of alternate chanting was introduced. It would be curious, if it were possible, to ascertain whether the Grecian temples received back their own music and their alternately responding chorus from the Christian churches.

Julian would invest the Pagan priesthood in that respect, or rather that commanding majesty, with which the profound reverence of the Christian world arrayed their hierarchy. Solemn silence was to reign in the temples. All persons in authority were to leave their guards at the door when they entered the hallowed precincts. The Emperor himself forbade the usual acclamations on his entrance into the presence of the Gods. Directly he touched the sacred threshold, he became a private man.

Respect for temples.

It is said that he meditated a complete course of religious instruction. Schoolmasters, catechists, preachers, were to teach,—are we to suppose the Platonic philosophy?—as part of the religion. A penitential form was to be drawn up for the readmission of transgressors into the fold. Instead of throwing open the temples to the free and promiscuous reception of apostatising Christians, the value of the privilege was to be enhanced by the difficulty of attaining it.[n] They were to be slowly admitted to the distinction of rational believers in the gods. The dii averruncatores (atoning deities) were to be propitiated; the believers were to pass through different degrees of initiation. Prayers, expia-

Religious instruction.

---

[m] On Music. See Epist. lvi.　　　[n] See Epist. lii.

tions, lustrations, severe trials, could alone purify their bodies and their minds, and make them worthy participants in the Pagan mysteries.

Animal sacrifices.

But Julian was not content with this moral regeneration of Paganism; he attempted to bring back the public mind to all the sanguinary ritual of sacrifice, to which the general sentiment had been gradually growing unfamiliar and repugnant. The time was passed when men could consider the favour of the gods propitiated according to the number of slaughtered beasts. The philosophers must have smiled in secret at the superstition of the philosophic Emperor. Julian himself washed off his Christian baptism by the new Oriental rite of aspersion by blood, the Taurobolia or Kriobolia of the Mithriac mysteries;[o] he was regenerated anew to Paganism.[p] This indeed was a secret ceremony; but Julian was perpetually seen, himself wielding the sacrificial knife, and exploring with his own hands the reeking entrails of the victims, to learn the secrets of futurity. The enormous expenditure lavished on the sacrifices, the hecatombs of cattle, the choice birds from all quarters, drained the revenue.[q] The Western soldiers, especially the intemperate Gauls, indulged in the feasts on the victims to such excess, and mingled them with such copious libations of wine, as to be carried to their tents amid the groans and mockeries

---

[o] Gregor. Naz. iii. p. 70.

[p] The person initiated descend into a pit or trench; and through a kind of sieve, or stone pierced with holes, the blood of the bull or the ram was poured over his whole person.

[q] Julian acknowledges the reluctance to sacrifice in many parts. "Show me," he says, to the philosopher Aristomenes, "a genuine Greek in Cappadocia." Τέως γὰρ τοὺς μὲν οὐ βουλομένους, ὀλίγους δὲ τινας ἐθέλοντας μὲν, οὐκ εἰδότας δὲ θύειν, ὁρῶ. Epist. iv. p. 375.

of the more sober.[r] The gifts to diviners, soothsayers, and impostors of all classes, offended equally the more wise and rational. In the public, as well as private, conduct of Julian, there was a Heathen Pharisaism, an attention to minute and trifling observances, which could not but excite contempt even in the more enlightened of his own party. Every morning and evening he offered sacrifice to the sun; he rose at night to offer the same homage to the moon and stars. Every day brought the rite of some other god. Julian was constantly seen prostrate before the image of the deity, busying himself about the ceremony, performing the menial offices of cleansing the wood, and kindling the fire with his own breath, till the victim was ready for the imperial hands. The sacrifices were so frequent that had he returned victorious over the Parthians, it was said, there would have been a dearth of cattle.[s]

---

[r] I do not believe the story of human sacrifices in Alexandria and Athens, Socrat. E. H. iii. 13.

[s] "Innumeros sine parsimoniâ mactans; ut crederetur, si revertisset de Parthis," boves jam defecturos. Amm. Marc. xxv. 4.

END OF VOL. II.